FRO

CW01278766

COMPREHENS

HAWAII '92

by Faye Hammel

3bd & Artic — MAPS.

PRENTICE HALL TRAVEL

NEW YORK • LONDON • TORONTO • SYDNEY • TOKYO • SINGAPORE

FROMMER BOOKS

Published by Prentice Hall General Reference
A division of Simon & Schuster Inc.
15 Columbus Circle
New York, NY 10023

ISBN 0-13-334889-X
ISSN 0899-2894

Manufactured in the United States of America

CONTENTS

MAPS

A Disclaimer

Although every effort was made to ensure the accuracy of the prices and travel information appearing in this book, readers are advised that prices fluctuate in the course of time and travel information changes under the impact of the varied and volatile factors that affect the travel industry. The author and publisher cannot be held responsible for the experiences of the reader while traveling. Readers are invited to write the publisher with ideas, comments, and suggestions for future editions.

Safety Advisory

Whenever you're traveling in an unfamiliar city or country, stay alert. Be aware of your immediate surroundings. Wear a moneybelt and keep a close eye on your possessions. Be particularly careful with cameras, purses, and wallets, all favorite targets of thieves and pickpockets.

INTRODUCING HAWAII

1. SOME ELEMENTARY HAWAIIAN GEOGRAPHY
2. WHAT HAWAII IS LIKE
3. THE HAWAIIANS—A BRIEF HISTORY

To get the most for one's travel dollar in thriving, prosperous (and inflationary) Hawaii, the tourist today must be more *akamai* (smart) than ever before.

For Hawaii is no longer the remote, end-of-the-rainbow place it once was. Waikiki once knew only the sound of the surf. Today it bustles with thousands of tourists a year, scores of hotels, literally hundreds of eating spots, and a wealth of sightseeing, entertainment, and sports activities. It is the most popular vacation spot in these United States.

Hawaii has something for everybody. It has luxurious $2,000-a-day suites with broad lanais (balconies) and views of the Pacific, and plain $50-a-day-rooms with views of somebody else's kitchen. It has $45 luaus and $5 bowls of Japanese noodle soup. It has some of the most breathtaking vistas in the world, some of the most exciting cultural activity, and some of the most splendid stretches of sand and surf anywhere. And it has, like any other center of such attraction, its tourist traps.

That's where this book comes in. It takes know-how to get the best accommodations for the price, no matter what the price; to find the most delectable and adventurous food for the money, the most authentic Polynesian entertainment, the most thrilling Hawaiian sights. It takes know-how, too, to make every day count in Paradise. And what we intend to do in these pages is to give you that know-how, to let you in on the inside tips that separate the *kamaainas* (old-timers) from the *malihinis* (newcomers). We'll show you the best way to enjoy the major sights and take you, too, off the beaten path to surprising places that most tourists never hear of. We'll show you the best way to escape to this best of all escape places. In short, we'll tell you how to get such good value for your dollar in Hawaii that you'll have enough money left over to come back again next year. And the year after that. For Hawaii is one of those places that, once experienced, has a way of getting in the blood.

1. Some Elementary Hawaiian Geography

The Hawaiian Islands were spewed forth from the bottom of the Pacific in great volcanic explosions that occurred many thousands of years ago. The entire archipelago includes some 122 islands, most of them merely tiny mountain peaks of a submarine mountain range that stretches for 1,600 miles. The eight largest islands make up the Hawaii we know. Oahu, Maui, Hawaii, and Kauai are the most popular, with tiny Molokai gaining fame as a retreat for those who really want to get away from it all. Lanai, once a plantation island almost totally owned by the Dole Pineapple Company, is abandoning pineapples and going into the tourist industry with the opening of two major luxury resorts. Kahoolawe is a target range for American planes and ships; and Niihau, where the old Hawaiian way of life is still maintained, is kept *kapu* (taboo) to all but those invited by its owners, the Robinson family.

Contrary to popular belief, the Hawaiian Islands are not in the South Pacific; they are much closer to the U.S. mainland, 2,500 miles away, and lie in the northern Pacific Ocean at a latitude about even with the southern part of the United States. With increasing technological advances, a journey from the West Coast to Hawaii takes only about five hours by plane and four days by ship.

2. What Hawaii Is Like

Hawaii is at once like everything you dreamed it would be and totally unlike anything you imagined. It is both a tropical paradise and a cosmopolitan boomtown, a place where the old island gods still hold sway and where speculators and builders and real estate developers have been riding high. It is one of the most fascinating paradoxes of old and new, of beauty and razzle-dazzle, of serenity and show business anywhere. It is an island world that went from the Stone Age to monarchy to statehood in less than 200 years. It is a place where Japanese and Chinese and Polynesians and Americans and Filipinos and Koreans, merchants and missionaries, whalers and working people from all over came together to form a new world. And where, despite everything, the old Hawaiian gentleness, the warmth and hospitality that have come to be known worldwide as *aloha,* still pervades all. This is what makes Hawaii someplace special: No matter how many new hotels and condominium apartment buildings rise above the Waikiki skyline, it will never be as cold and commercial as, say, Miami Beach. The spirit of the Hawaiians still holds forth.

3. The Hawaiians—A Brief History

To know the Hawaiians of today, it helps immeasurably to know a little bit about the Hawaiians of the past. The very earliest

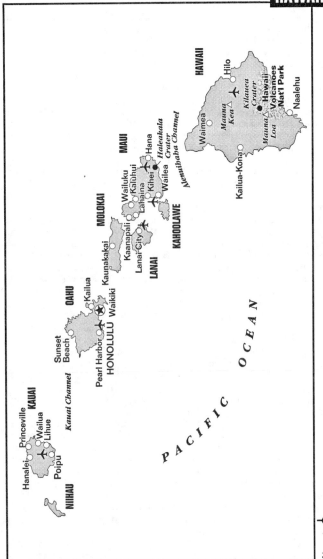

HAWAII

50 km
31 mi

HAWAII
Hilo
Kilauea Crater
Mauna Kea △
Mauna Loa
Hawaii Volcanoes Nat'l Park
Naalehu
Waimea
Kailua-Kona

MAUI
Hana
Haleakala Crater
Wailuku
Kahului
Lahaina
Kihei
Wailea
Alenuihaha Channel

MOLOKAI
Kaunakakai
Kaanapali
Lanai City
LANAI
KAHOOLAWE

OAHU
Kailua
Sunset Beach
Pearl Harbor
HONOLULU
Waikiki

Kauai Channel

KAUAI
Princeville
Hanalei
Wailua
Lihue
Poipu

NIIHAU

PACIFIC OCEAN

Airport ✈

settlers to these volcanic islands arrived from various parts of Polynesia, probably Tahiti and Bora Bora, about A.D. 750. Guiding
themselves by a primitive and probably intuitive navigational science, they crossed thousands of miles of ocean in pairs of large
double-hulled canoes, connected by long bamboo poles that sup-

ported a tiny hut between the hulls. They brought with them their animals and plants, introducing such foods as the sweet potato into a climate that had never yet supported it.

They settled primarily on the largest islands of the Hawaiian archipelago—Hawaii, Kauai, Maui, Molokai, and Oahu. The islands were fragmented into little kingdoms, each ruled by its own chief, with its own *kapus* and particular customs. Power belonged to the strongest, and the bloody overthrow of leaders was quite common. But life was stable, and very probably even comfortable. None of the settlers ever made any attempt to return to the tribes from which they had come. In the warmth of the sun, these Stone Age people, living primitive lives, worshipping their own gods, and keeping the old ways of life, remained undisturbed and untouched by outsiders until the 18th century.

In 1777 Capt. James Cook, who was really looking for the Northwest Passage, stumbled on the island of Kauai. The natives, who had long believed that their great god Lono would one day return to them, mistook Cook and his crew for the god and a full entourage of lesser deities. At first he received a god's reception, but soon fighting broke out between the natives and the sailors, and eight months later, on another voyage, Cook was clubbed to death by natives and drowned off the Kona shore of the island of Hawaii. But from that time on, the Sandwich Islands, as he had named them in honor of the Earl of Sandwich when he claimed them for Great Britain, became part of the modern world. By 1790 King Kamehameha the Great, operating from his home island of Hawaii, conquered the other islands in the chain in a series of bloody forays (except for Kauai, which surrendered) and united them under his rule. Hawaii was already one nation when the first emissaries from the Western world—merchants, fur traders, whaling men—started their invasion of the islands.

In 1820 a band of New England missionaries arrived in Hawaii, determined to save the heathen islanders from the devil. They brought piety, industry, and Christianity to the natives; their coming speeded the end of the old Hawaiian life. (Their story is eloquently told in James Michener's *Hawaii,* in both the novel and the film.) They smashed the idols and continued the destruction of the rigid *kapus* (already weakened by the king prior to their arrival), taught the people to read and write, and "civilized" the natives. And although they undoubtedly did an enormous amount of good, many of the natives here have never forgiven them, as the island saying goes, for doing so well. Some of the missionaries' children turned into businesspeople, bought up the land, and started industries; it is their descendants who are still among the ruling forces of Hawaii's great corporate empires.

The native Hawaiians never really adjusted to the *haole*'s (white man's) world, refused to work his plantations, and died from his diseases in horrendous epidemics. Today, just a few thousand pureblooded Hawaiians remain. The rest have disappeared or become intermingled with the other races—mostly Japanese and Chinese—that came to do the white man's work.

The Asians began to arrive around the 1850s, when the whaling trade was dropping off and the sugar plantations were becoming big business. The Chinese came first to work the plantations, then the Japanese, last the Filipinos. The Hawaiian melting pot began to simmer.

Meanwhile, the reign of Kamehameha II had been short. He and his queen died of measles in London in 1824. Kamehameha III reigned for 30 years, during which time the independence of the islands was declared from Britain. An English-language newspaper was started and a public school opened at that time, both in the islands' capital, Lahaina, on the island of Maui. But the capital remained there only until 1845, when the king and his court moved to Honolulu. Commerce was picking up in the Honolulu harbors, and in 1850 that city was declared the capital of the 19th-century kingdom.

The line of the Kamehameha descent ended after Kamehameha IV and V had passed out of the picture, by 1872. William Lunalilo was elected successor by the legislature, but he died within a year; David Kalakaua succeeded him. Queen Emma, the widow of Kamehameha IV, appeared to have a rightful claim to the throne, and it was to this end that many riots were staged. American and British marines were called in.

In the latter part of the 19th century, industry continued to boom, with sugar the leading crop and coffee a close second. (Rice, now of small importance in the state, was once the number-two crop.) Finally, in 1875, the Hawaiian sugar planters worked out a reciprocal agreement with the U.S. government by which Hawaiian sugar companies were assured an American market and the Americans were given the freedom to use Pearl Harbor as a coaling station. The American age was arising in Hawaii; the annexation of the Republic of Hawaii took place in 1898, but statehood would not be achieved until more than half a century later, in 1959.

King Kalakaua, "The Merry Monarch," was followed by Queen Liliuokalani, the last reigning monarch of the islands. When her plans for a new constitution were violently opposed, she was removed from office in the bloodless uprising of 1893 and replaced by Sanford B. Dole, a *haole* representing American commercial interests. It was while she was under house arrest that she wrote the poignant "Aloha Oe," now a song of good-bye to those leaving the islands. But it was also a lament, a farewell to the days of the past when kings and queens, and even an occasional god, walked the earth.

The 20th-century history of Hawaii began with the booming of the pineapple industry. The U.S. armed forces moved into the area and made Hawaii an independent army department in 1913. Although Hawaii was not directly involved in World War I, many islanders had volunteered for the French and German armies before the U.S. entered the conflict. The depression of the 1930s blew through the islands with the relative calm of a trade wind, compared with the hurricanelike devastation on the mainland. Big business was not yet too big, industry not yet well developed.

But Hawaii felt the impact of World War II more than any American state. Because the U.S. had developed the harbors and military installations on the islands so greatly, they were a prime target area for the enemy. After the dreadful bombing attack of December 7, 1941, Hawaii entered a period of martial law. Liquor consumption was regulated, curfews were imposed, and blackouts were common. Fortunately, the islands' Japanese population was not herded off into concentration camps as it was in California. In fact, a group of nisei volunteers became one of the great heroic regiments of the U.S. Army fighting in southern Europe. The 442nd Regimental Combat Team has been called "probably the most decorated unit in United States military history," and one of its members, Daniel K. Inouye, is the senator of Watergate fame. This participation in the war did a great deal to break down race lines in Hawaii. Today, the Japanese are the largest single ethnic group, and one of the most powerful, in the state.

After the war, increasing lines of transportation developed between the American mainland and Hawaii. Tourism became a major industry and the already existing industries grew at phenomenal rates. Years of labor disputes in the 1940s, spearheaded by the militant ILGWU, raised the standard of living for the Hawaiian working man to an all-time high. Finally, in 1959, after a 30-year struggle for statehood that began with Hawaii's first representative to Congress, Prince Jonah Kuhio Kalanianaole, delegate John A. Burns (later Hawaii's governor) affected passage of the bill that made Hawaii the 50th American state. Dancing in the streets celebrated a goal long promised and arduously won.

Since statehood, Hawaii has blossomed and boomed and burst forth into a new era. Now largely Democratic in politics, with a mostly Japanese legislature, it is liberal in its outlook, proud of its ability to blend the races, to let the newcomer "do his own thing." Garment industries, steel mills, and cement factories are growing. Agriculture uses the most advanced techniques, and pineapple and sugar are still big business. So are tourism and the military. Technology has moved in and made Hawaii the mid-Pacific outpost in America's space efforts and oceanography research. The University of Hawaii and the East-West Center for Cultural and Technical Interchange have raised the level of education in the state remarkably, bringing in scholars from all over the world. Population is up to 1.15 million; more than a hundred thousand tourists are expected annually. Despite economic uncertainty here as everywhere, it looks as if Hawaii is still on the way up.

GETTING TO KNOW HONOLULU

1. TRANSPORTATION WITHIN THE CITY
2. ISLAND GEOGRAPHY
3. THE WEATHER & WHEN TO VISIT
4. A MATTER OF LANGUAGE

You're off the plane and standing in the Hawaiian sunshine. If you're lucky, some doting friend—maybe even the representative of your hotel—has greeted you with an aloha kiss and draped a fragrant lei around your neck. If not, don't worry; there are lei stands all over the islands and you'll have worn dozens by the time you're ready to go home.

Your biggest problem, right now, is getting from the airport to Waikiki, where you'll most likely be staying, a distance of about 10 miles. If you're reserved a car in advance, it's easy; just pick it up and you're on your way. Or you could grab a taxi (they're always waiting at the airport). The tab to Waikiki will run you about $20. It makes more sense for the individual traveler to catch one of the limousine services right into Waikiki. These cost about $5 and will take you right to your Waikiki hotel.

Although we are great believers in the MTL, the local bus system, "TheBUS" (as it is called) is not ideal for baggage-laden tourists. Buses do operate from the terminal into Waikiki, but they have no provisions for your luggage. If, however, you can contain all your belongings in your lap, the price is certainly right—60¢ a ride. And you'll get a head start at meeting the local population.

1. Transportation Within the City

BUSES
Once settled at your hotel, however, you should definitely learn how to use TheBUS. They run all over town and maintain fre-

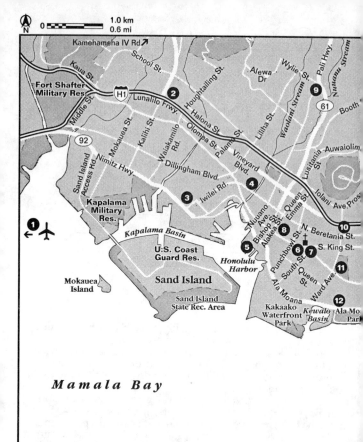

Ala Moana Park 	Foster Botanic Garden
Ala Moana Shopping Center	Hawaii Maritime Museum
Bishop Museum	Hawaii Visitor's Bureau
Diamond Head State Monument	Honolulu Academy of Arts
Dole Cannery Square	Honolulu International Airport
Fisherman's Wharf	Iolani Palace

quent schedules between Waikiki and downtown Honolulu. If you need assistance, call TheBUS information department at 531-1611. The fare, again, is 60¢; have exact change ready. If you want a free transfer to a connecting bus, ask for it as you board. Senior citizens can get free passes; apply at the MTL office, 811 Middle St. (tel. 848-4444). Students aged 6 through high school are charged 25¢.

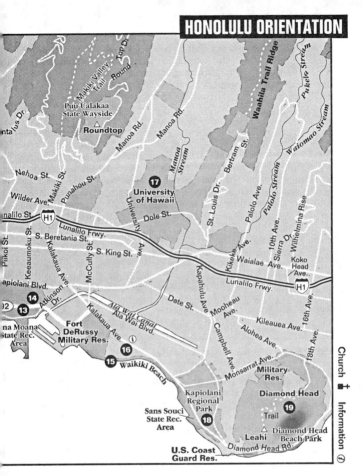

Kapiolani Park **18**

Kawaiaihao Church **6**

Mission Houses Museum **7**

Neal S. Blaisdell Center **11**

Royal Mausoleum State
  Monument **9**

University of Hawaii **17**

Waikiki Beach **15**

TAXIS

They cruise the main streets of Waikiki, so you should have no trouble picking up a cab. Or, you can ask your hotel desk to get one for you, or phone for one yourself (see the yellow pages of the Honolulu phone book for listings). They are quite expensive, but could be cheaper than renting a car if you only have to do minor traveling.

CAR RENTALS

At some time or other during your Hawaiian stay you'll probably want to get behind the wheel of a car, maybe to tour around the
island of Oahu, or for a sightseeing excursion over on the windward
side. The car-rental business is one of the most competitive in the
state. The best idea is to check out the companies on the scene, since
prices change so quickly; the tourist newspapers will give you the
leads. If, however, you know in advance that you're going to do a
great deal of driving (and especially if you're going to the neighbor
islands, where your own set of wheels is a must), you should reserve
your car in advance from one of the reputable island companies. All
of them offer "flat rates," which means that mileage is included:
they usually turn out to be less than the regular rates plus mileage for
extensive driving. **Dollar Rent-A-Car** of Hawaii (tel. toll free 800/
367-7398), **Alamo Rent-A-Car** (tel. toll free 800/327-9633), **Avis
Rent-A-Car** (tel. toll free 800/331-1212), **Budget Rent-A-Car**
(tel. toll free 800/527-7000), and **National Car Rental of Hawaii**
(tel. toll free 800/227-7368) are all reputable firms to do business
with. Depending on the car, the company, and whatever special
deals are available at the time you're there (be sure to inquire about
"all-island" specials), expect to pay from $20 to $40 daily for your
car. Many hotels, especially those belonging to the Outrigger chain,
have room-and-car packages that offer considerable savings; inquire
when you book hotel reservations.

2. Island Geography

Now that you're navigating around the city, either on foot or
by bus or car, you should know something about where you are.
Honolulu is, of course, the state capital, and it's the only major city
on the island of Oahu. But before we get you oriented, we have to
tell you that people here have no use for such terms as "north" or
"south" or "east" or "west"—not even "uptown" or "downtown"
are much help. For the Hawaiian Islands sit in a kind of slantwise
position on the map, and the only reference points that are used are
either place names or directional signals meaning "toward the
mountains" or "toward the sea."

Here's how it works. Let's suppose that you are standing on
Waikiki Beach, looking at Diamond Head crater; this means you are
facing in a Diamond Head direction. You are, of course, at the beach
area, but just a few miles away from this Pacific Riviera the water is
deep enough for oceangoing vessels to dock in Honolulu harbor,
which fronts on the downtown business district. (It was, in fact, that
harbor's depth that made Honolulu a logical center for international commerce.) The downtown area is in an Ewa (eh-vah) direction,
toward the village of Ewa, from Waikiki, and farther out in this section of the island, low plains of rich, red volcanic earth give birth to
tons upon tons of sugar and pineapple. Anything toward the ocean
is *makai*. Over to your left from the beach area, in a *mauka* direction,
are the striking Koolau Mountains, which form the dramatic backdrop for the city. On the other side of the Koolaus is Windward

Oahu, miles of verdant countryside bordering on the water's edge. This is fast being transformed into suburbs, the bedrooms of Honolulu from which commuters speed into the city's offices every day via tunnels bored through the mountains.

3. The Weather & When to Visit

Hawaii is one of those rare, blessed places on earth where the weather is always—well, almost always—wonderful. Any time of the year that you can get here is the right time to come. Most people come during the summer months of June, July, and August (mostly mainland families and young people); or during the dead of the winter (the Christmas to Easter "high season," when prices go up), when the crowd is older and as much Canadian as it is American. Winter here feels like spring somewhere else. An average temperature throughout the state would probably settle at about the 74°F mark; in the summer it's usually in the 80s. Leave your warm coats at home; bring a sweater or light topper for some mountain areas at night; pack a light raincoat too, just in case.

During the summer, a Hawaiian "rain" will probably be a 10-minute light shower during which nobody bothers going inside. During the winter months, there may be an occasional thunder-and-lightning storm, and sometimes it rains for several days in a row; the weather can be cool and cloudy. Some winters it hardly rains at all. The varying amounts of rainfall can be explained in terms of northeasterly winds bringing rain clouds that are subsequently blocked by the main mountain range on the northern side of each island. Each island, therefore, has its windward side (where the rain falls) and leeward side (to which the storm clouds seldom get). Most tourist centers are, naturally, leeward. If you don't like the weather where you are, you can usually drive somewhere where it's better fairly quickly. The gentle trade winds keep the weather on a pretty even keel.

AVERAGE MONTHLY TEMPERATURES IN HAWAII

Month	Temp	Month	Temp
January	72.2	July	77.7
February	71.9	August	78.4
March	72.2	September	78.3
April	73.2	October	77.4
May	74.9	November	75.4
June	76.8	December	73.3

4. A Matter of Language

You don't have to go to Berlitz before you go to Hawaii. English is the one language spoken everywhere in the state, although many first- and second-generation immigrants still use their native languages at home, and the Chinese and Japanese communities even have their own daily newspapers. But some of the old Hawaiian words have become charmingly intertwined into the language, and it's fun to know and use them. So that you'll know your *kanes* (men) from *wahines* (women) and your *kamaainas* (old-timers) from *malihinis* (newcomers), here are some tips.

Remember, first, that Hawaiian is a very simple language, much simpler than English. It contains only the five vowels plus these seven consonants: *h, k, l, m, n, p, w*. Vowels are sounded as they are in Spanish; consonants, as they are in English. The written language was the work of the missionaries who wrote down the native oral language. Mary became *Malia,* John became *Keone,* Britain turned into *Beretania.* Remember that every syllable ends in a vowel, and that you pronounce every syllable, and it all becomes quite simple. You always put the accent on the next-to-the-last syllable. For example, *kamaaina* is pronounced kah-mah-*eye*-nah, *wahine* is wah-*hee*-nay. Don't worry too much about the details, though.

Everyone will think you're pretty *akamai* (smart) if you know that a *haole* is a white person (Caucasian), a *hapa-haole* is half-white, *kau kau* is food, a *keiki* a child, a *luau* a feast, a *hukilau* a fishing festival. *Pupus* means hors d'oeuvres (they're usually served free with cocktails during happy hours), a *punee* is a couch, and *lomi-lomi* means massage (lomi-lomi salmon is literally "massaged"). If you want something done fast, it's *wiki-wiki,* and when something is finished, it's *pau.* The *alii* were royalty, the nobility of old Hawaii, and breaking their *kapus* (taboos) could get a person into plenty of *pilikia* (trouble). You'll most likely have a hotel room with a *lanai* (a porch). A pregnant woman is *hapai.* Everyone, of course, knows that a *lei* is a garland of flowers, a *muumuu* a long, loose-flowing Mother Hubbard–type dress (actually, the nightgowns of the missionary ladies—the only clothes that would fit the ample frames of the old Hawaiians). *Kokua* means cooperation or "take care" (you'll often see road signs saying *kokua*) and *mahalo* is the island way of saying thank you. And once you've been in Hawaii for a couple of days you'll have no need of definitions of *aloha.* The warmest greeting you can give in the islands: *aloha nui loa.*

HONOLULU ACCOMMODATIONS

Somewhere in Honolulu there is a hotel that is exactly right for you—whether *you* are a budget-conscious family counting pennies or a retired millionaire clipping coupons or, like most of us, the average tourist who wants a good time and a good deal. The Honolulu hotel scene covers an incredible variety of accommodations, everything from bohemian haunts as rundown as you'd expect, to hotels where the bedrooms are as big as ballrooms and where presidents, movie stars, Arabian princes, and Greek shipowners feel right at home. And the price range is just enormous. You can rent an oceanfront suite for $2,000 a night at one of the seaside palaces, or a cute little kitchenette apartment a few blocks from the beach for about $60.

What we have attempted to do in this chapter is to pick out what we consider the best accommodations in whatever price category you choose. If you can spring for anywhere from $185 and way up for a double for a night, make your selection from the first category, "Super Deluxe." If you'd prefer to spend $135 plus, stick to the second category, "Deluxe." And if a price tag beginning around $90 suits you better, consult our third category, "Moderately Priced." If you're watching those dollars, turn to the fourth category, "Budget." Here we've described some clean, comfortable, and sometimes surprisingly lovely accommodations where the nightly tab is under $80—sometimes way under—double. Please note that these categories are more general than specific, since there is such a wide variety of rates in each hotel, and that winter rates are usually much higher than summer (see below).

You'll notice that most of our hotel recommendations are in

Waikiki, rather than in downtown Honolulu or other parts of the island of Oahu. Waikiki and the areas near it are certainly the best places for typical visitors, who want to stay close to the turquoise waters and sparkling sands that have lured them perhaps thousands of miles from home. And Waikiki is ideal because it's so small. Bounded on one side by the Pacific, on the other by the Koolau Mountains, it's compact enough so that everything important is within walking distance, or just a short drive or bus ride away.

To help you get your bearings geographically, you should know that there are three major arteries in Waikiki, all of which run parallel to one another. Fronting on the beach is **Kalakaua Avenue,** Waikiki's main street and its choicest location, full of big hotels, shops, restaurants, and thousands of tourists. About three short blocks *mauka* (toward the mountains) is **Kuhio Avenue,** a bit quieter (but just a bit) and less crowded. And a few more blocks *mauka* of that is the **Ala Wai Boulevard,** next to a peaceful waterway close to the mountains, created back in 1920 when a brilliant entrepreneur got the idea of draining the swampland that was Waikiki. It is adjacent to the public and inexpensive Ala Wai Golf Course, and joggers love it.

As you read the hotel descriptions below (and remember there are many other good hotels in Waikiki; these are simply our choices), you'll become aware that, regardless of price structure, there are two general categories of hotel in Hawaii: the big, lively, resort-type hotels that are ideal for active singles and unencumbered couples; and the usually smaller, apartment-type hotels that are better suited for families with children or for anyone who wants to stay in the islands more than the usual week or two. These smaller apartment hotels (most of which are condos) all have a money-saving (and child-pleasing) advantage—a kitchenette, perfect for making breakfast coffee, storing Junior's chocolate milk, and fixing a quick snack when you don't want to eat out. (Most of the large hotels do not have kitchenettes, but some will furnish you with small refrigerators if you request them.) By and large, the condo hotels are on the side streets that run between the three major thoroughfares, and on the Ala Wai Boulevard. Remember, all the hotels are within easy walking or busing distance of one another, and all are near the important attractions of Waikiki. In general, prices are higher the closer you get to the beach; rooms get bigger and tariffs lower as you head toward the Ala Wai.

1. Hotel Know-How

RATES

You should know that most hotels have different rates for high season (usually mid-December to April 1) and low season (the rest of the year). High-season rates add at least $10 to $20 to your bill per day. During slack periods, rates may come down considerably, especially in the smaller establishments. And many hotels offer special considerations for weekly and monthly stays.

Please note that Hawaii's hotel tax is now a whopping 9.43%! Also note that we cannot be responsible for any change in the rates quoted here. The prices listed are those supplied by the hotels as we go to press in the middle of 1991. Even though prices may rise in these inflationary times, we feel these hotels will still offer the best value for the money. Credit card information is listed at the end of each listing.

PRIVATE BATHS & CLEANING SERVICE

Every hotel described below offers private baths; cleaning service can vary from daily or every other day to weekly or none. Always check with condominiums to see how often cleaning service is provided.

AIR CONDITIONING

Most of the newer hotels offer air-conditioned units; where this is not so, trade winds, ceiling fans, and cross ventilation will usually offer enough comfort. If you suffer a lot from the heat, though, you may find an air conditioner important, especially in the warm summer months, July through September. Also remember that it's easy and inexpensive to rent a fan if you need one.

RESERVATIONS

It is always advisable to reserve a hotel room in advance. This way, you can be sure of getting the type of accommodation you prefer at the rate you want to pay. Even without reservations, you will probably find a room in Waikiki; there are usually more hotel rooms than there are guests, unless a big convention is in town. A few weeks' notice is usually adequate, but remember that the more popular the hotel, the more essential it is to reserve well in advance— perhaps even several months. And reservations are particularly important in the high season, from December through Easter and, again, from June until Labor Day. Some very popular hotels request that one reserve at least *a year in advance* for the Christmas–New Year's holidays. The general rule is this: As soon as you know you're going to Hawaii, start making reservations.

BABY-SITTERS

The desk clerks at any hotel can put you in touch with qualified people who will look after Junior while you're out seeing the town.

---

2. Super-Deluxe Hotels: Beginning Around $185

About a 15-minute ride from the razzle-dazzle of Waikiki, in the beautiful Kahala residential area, the **Kahala Hilton,** 5000 Kahala Ave., Honolulu, HI 96816 (tel. 808/734-2211; fax 808/

Telephone Area Code
   The **telephone area code** for all phones in the state of Hawaii is 808.

737-2478; reservations toll free 800/367-2525), is a rare combination of island tranquility and jet-set sophistication, a place where the warmth and graciousness of the staff perfectly match the charm and serenity of the surroundings. So conducive, in fact, is the Kahala to relaxation that about one-third of the guests are repeat visitors who never leave the grounds. We don't blame them.

One could, in fact, spend days here just celebrity-watching. Was that really Michael Jackson, or Tina Turner, or Shirley MacLaine? Or you can concentrate on more mundane things, like lazing on the gentle beach or at the pool; tooling around in a pedalboat or kayak; taking a scuba-diving lesson or going windsurfing; working out at the Manualua Bay Club, a seaside super-spa that includes six nightlighted tennis courts, sauna, weight room, and aerobics classes. If you have an eye for beauty, take a stroll inside and outside the hotel, and bring your camera. Inside, note the immense multicolored-glass chandeliers, the teakwood parquet flooring from Thailand, the Polynesian-inspired circular rug masterpieces. Outside, wander through the acres of beautiful gardens, with their bamboo groves, waterfalls, rare plantings. There's even a lagoon stocked with fish, giant turtles, penguins, and dancing dolphins who will entertain with the hula.

Where to stay? You have your choice of 369 spacious guest rooms, all with elegantly tasteful appointments, including a large seating area, a lanai in many of the rooms, quiet air conditioning, color television, and knockout his-and-her bathrooms with two separate bath vanities, hair dryer, makeup mirrors, a full minibar, and small refrigerator. The price range depends on whether you face the mountains ($210 to $265 for a double) or the lagoon or ocean ($310 to $430). Magnificent suites run from $685 to $2,060 a day. There is no charge for children of any age sharing their parents' room, and there are daily activity programs for them during the high seasons and at holiday times. An extra person is charged $35. Rates are subject to change.

This, however, is not the place to be alone. You should be here with someone you love—the better for enjoying the romantic nights on the seaside Hala Terrace, where Danny Kalekini presents one of the last authentic Hawaiian shows on the island; for enjoying the lavish Sunday-night buffet; for candlelight dining à deux in the *Travel/Holiday* award–winning Maile Restaurant; or for having afternoon tea or a light meal at the gracious, open-air Plumeria Café; or just for the sheer beauty of being in a place that combines the charm of the old and the excitement of the new Hawaii. AE, CB, DC, DISC, JCB, MC, V. Parking: $5 per night.

   Hawaii's newest world-class hostelry is the **Hawaii Prince Ho-**

tel, whose two rose-colored glass-and-stone towers rise 32 stories at the gateway to Waikiki. The architecturally striking contemporary structure, built at a cost of $150 million, turns its back on Ala Moana Boulevard and faces instead the Ala Wai Marina and the sea, thus deriving its address from the smaller road: 100 Holomoana St., Honolulu, HI 96815 (tel. 808/965-1111; fax 808/946-0811; reservations toll free 800/321-6284).

White-uniformed doormen, a huge, high-ceilinged lobby with geometric, custom-made carpeting, and Italian marble walls highlighted with English slate suggest not just luxury but splendor. Tea, British- or Japanese-style, is served every afternoon. Escalators lead from the lobby to the restaurants, one of them Japanese. On the fifth-floor deck, a pool, a poolside grill, and steeped terraces offer guests swimming, sunning, sunset-watching, entertainment, and refreshments with spectacular views out to sea.

The Hawaii Prince contains 521 rooms, including 57 suites, each with a waterfront view. The Diamond Head Tower offers rooms with two double beds; the Ala Moana Tower has suites and king-sized beds. Other rooms have either twin double beds or kings and are done in warm tones of sand and sunset, cool ocean blues, and greens. They have separate shower and tub in a large, compartmentalized bathroom, color TV, VCR, safe, refrigerator with complimentary fruit juices, and lovely furnishings. There are no lanais, but floor-to-ceiling windows open to the marina and ocean views. Oceanfront rooms, depending on the floor and the view, go from $180 to $320. Oceanfront Suites are $400 to $2,500. A third person is charged $30; children 17 or younger are registered free, with parents using existing bedding.

The Prince Court is the hotel's fine dining showcase, up two escalator flights and with breathtaking nautical views. Breathtaking, too, is the contemporary Pacific cuisine, combining the best of Eastern and Western culinary methods, with the freshest local produce and products available. Breakfast runs about $7; lunch varies from $7.50 to $8.50 light, $13 to $15 more substantial; and dinners are priced from $15 on up, with each bite at every meal a gustatory adventure.

If there is a drawback to the Hawaii Prince, it's that Waikiki Beach is a 10-minute walk away. But shuttle buses take you there and to the Ala Moana Shopping Center every 15 minutes. Service is exemplary throughout the hotel. As you walk in, for example, you are greeted with a flower lei and escorted to your room, where fresh flowers and a basket of fruit await you—symbols of the tender loving care one can expect at the Hawaii Prince.

The elegance of old Hawaii has been born again in the brilliant new interpretation of the classic Hawaiian seaside hotel, the **Halekulani,** 2199 Kalia Rd., Honolulu, HI 96815 (tel. 808/923-2311; fax 808/926-8004; reservations toll free 800/367-2343). The 456-room resort, right on the beach at Waikiki, is a reincarnation of the famed hotel that dates from the 1930s; one of the original buildings has been incorporated into the new design—five interconnecting buildings of stepped heights surrounding courtyards and gardens overlooking the ocean. Understated elegance might be the words to describe the style of this new "House Befit-

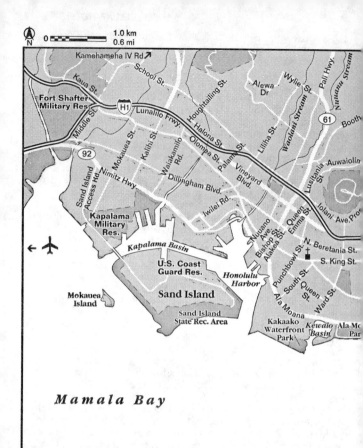

Colony Surf   **5**
Colony Surf East   **4**
Kahala Hilton   **2**
New Otani Kaimana Beach Hotel   **3**
Turtle Bay Hilton and Country Club   **1**
Waikiki accommodations   **6**

ting Heaven." Arriving guests are escorted directly to their rooms, where registration is completed in privacy and a porter offers to unpack the luggage. Guests like this kind of pampering so much that for several years, the Halekulani has been selected as "Hawaii's Best

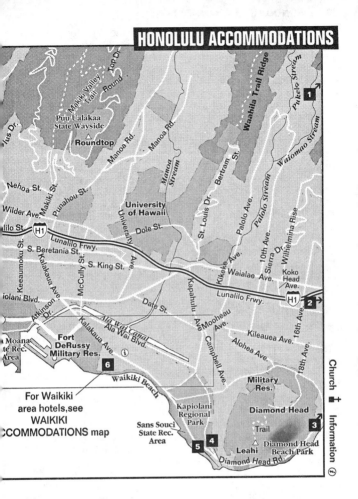

For Waikiki
area hotels, see
WAIKIKI
CCOMMODATIONS map

Church ✝ Information ⓘ

Hotel" by the readers of *Aloha Magazine*. Guest rooms, most of which face the ocean, are very large and have separate sitting areas, no fewer than three telephones (one at bedside, another in the bath, a third at a full-size business desk), cable color TV (operated by re-

mote control and housed discreetly in an armoire), plus a small refrigerator stocked with bottled water and ice. Rooms are done in
tones of beige, white, and gray, with blue flecks in the wool carpets;
only silks, cottons, and wools are used. The tile lanais, with their
chaises longues, tables, and chairs, are large and comfortable, many
with views of the ocean beach and the magnificent pool, its huge
cattleya orchid design made of a million imported South African
tiles sparkling at its base. The orchid and pool have become the symbol of the new Halekulani.

Dining facilities are as superb as one would expect, from the
greenhouselike Orchids, to the elegant French restaurant La Mer
(dinnertime here is a three-hour haute cuisine experience, one seating per evening only, about $75 to $95 per person), to the famous
House Without a Key, rebuilt oceanside under a century-old kiawe
tree, surely one of the most romantic spots in the world for sunset
cocktails and entertainment (breakfast, light lunch, and dinner are
also available here).

The Halekulani recalls the graciousness of living in the Hawaii
of old, in a new and distinctive setting. Its rates are a little higher
than they used to be back in the 1930s: single or double $220 to
$380, depending on location and view. An extra person is charged
$35. Knockout suites run from $525 to $3,000 per night. There is
no charge for children under 14 sharing their parents' room. AE,
CB, DC, DISC, JCB, MC, V.

As much a landmark on the Waikiki skyline as Diamond Head
is the pink stucco Moorish-style hotel called the **Royal Hawaiian,**
2259 Kalakaua Ave., Honolulu, HI 96815 (tel. 808/923-7311; fax
808/924-7098; reservations toll free 800/325-3535). Standing
on the site of King Kalanikapule's home by the sea of a century and
half ago, it was Hawaii's original luxury hotel and has been the subject of newspaper and magazine stories, and the scene and site of
scores of television shows and movies, since it opened back in 1927.
Now under the Sheraton banner and with all its rooms, suites, and
public areas recently redecorated and refurbished, the Royal Hawaiian wears its regal heritage like a proud mantle. You can't help
saying, "They don't build hotels like this anymore."

Surrounded by acres of lush tropical gardens (note the splendid monkeypod tree) and fronting on a handsome stretch of
beachfront, the hotel exudes that unmistakable aura of regality—in
the black terrazzo marble of its lobby floors; the coral-toned, hand-
loomed rugs; the high-ceilinged splendor everywhere. Its famed
Monarch Room is one of the best places in the islands for top-name
entertainment, usually the Brothers Cazimero.

Single or double rooms go from $210 (garden view) on up to
$315 (ocean view). And all are beautiful, immense, and in the old
style. Views are superb, and service is immediate and gracious. As
you would expect, suites are splendid, priced from $380 up. You
can stay either in the older, original six-story hotel building or in the
new 17-story Tower wing, where all rooms overlook the pool and
the Pacific. Guests at the Royal can use the food, beverage, and shopping facilities of the four other Sheraton resorts in Waikiki—the
Sheraton Moana Surfrider, Sheraton-Waikiki, and the Princess
Kaiulani—as well as the Sheraton Resort and Country Club in

Makaha, and charge them to their bill. AE, MC, V. Valet parking $10 per day; self-park at Sheraton Waikiki, $5.

To use the word "hotel" to describe the **Hilton Hawaiian Village,** 2005 Kalia Rd., Honolulu, HI 96815 (tel. 808/949-4321; fax 808/947-7898; reservations toll free 800-HILTONS), is really an understatement. With some 2,523 rooms and suites, 20 acres of lush tropical greenery, three swimming pools, a secluded lagoons, its own U.S. post office, a supper-club theater, international stars Don Ho and Charo in attendance, acres of upscale shops, and more than a dozen places for wining, dining, and catching the celebrities, it's a wonderful world of its own. Henry J. Kaiser built it, Hilton bought it, and the visitors love it. Now, with a vast, $100 million architectural renewal completed, it's greater and grander than ever —truly "A Return to Paradise."

If you're a guest here, you may not find it necessary to leave the Village during your entire stay. You can surf, take catamaran cruises and submarine dives, or just plain swim at what many consider one of the finest stretches of beach in Waikiki, with acres of white sand even at high tide. During the day there are free activities for kids age 3 to 12, walking tours for adults, and lei making, hula, and ukulele lessons for everyone. Come nightfall, you can have your drinks under the stars in the beachfront Tropics Bar, dine on splendid Cantonese cuisine in the *Travel/Holiday* award–winning Golden Dragon, or enjoy superb Continental fare in romantic Bali-by-the-Sea, also a *Travel/Holiday* award winner. Then you might go off to catch salsa fun with international singing star Charo at the Tropics Surf Club Showroom. Or you might choose to go over to the Hilton Dome to see illusionist John Hirokawa or the famous Don Ho show, or have a nightcap at the Paradise Lounge or Tapa Bar— among other possibilities. You could spend your entire vacation shopping if you had a mind to: There are some 100 shops, designer boutiques, and services here, plus a variety of exciting shops in the Rainbow Bazaar.

There is also a wide choice of accommodations, which range from simply lovely to simply breathtaking. Rooms in the Rainbow Tower, the Tapa Tower, and the Diamond Head Tower are all of good size, beautifully furnished, and offer views that range from court and garden to yacht harbor and ocean, at rates that range from $175 to $275 per night single or double; specialty rooms and penthouse suites are available for more. Thirty-four rooms are equipped for the handicapped. An extra person in the room is $25; quoted rates are for single or double occupancy. There is no charge for children, regardless of age, staying in the same room with their parents.

Located within the Hilton Hawaiian Village, the Ali'i Tower, a concierge tower offering 348 ultra-deluxe guest rooms and suites on the ocean, is literally an elegant hotel within a hotel. Guests receive the royal treatment the name implies; they are greeted upon arrival in the lobby and registered in their rooms; enjoy their own health club, swimming pool, ocean-view bar, and the attentions of multilingual concierge staff; and have daily newspapers delivered to their rooms, among many other niceties. Each guest room, furnished in a romantic "old Hawaii" style and done in soft tones of blues and seafoam greens, has a fully stocked refreshment center, in-

A Historical Restoration

Perhaps the most significant historical restoration in Hawaii since that of Iolani Palace, the $50-million restoration of the venerable Moana Hotel has been completed after almost two years of work; the result is a world-class hotel that recalls the charms of turn-of-the-century Waikiki and combines them with every modern comfort and luxury. Built in 1901, the 793-room **Sheraton Moana Surfrider Hotel,** as it is now called, 2365 Kalakaua Ave., Honolulu, HI 96815 (tel. 808/922-3111; fax 808/923-0308; reservations toll free 800/325-3535), was for generations the classic South Seas hostelry on the beach at Waikiki. The restoration has preserved the colonial architecture of the handsome white building, restoring its original porte-cochère and the Kalakaua Avenue verandas, so popular in the early years of the century. Guest rooms combine the best of old-world traditions with modern convenience. New additions include air conditioning, a colonial reproduction armoire fitted with color TV, bar, and refrigerator, and a luxurious bathroom equipped with such amenities as hair dryer, lighted makeup mirrors, and plush bathrobes. Outdoors, the Banyan Court, original home of the famed "Hawaii Calls" radio show, is one of the nicest areas on Waikiki Beach, with a freshwater pool and recreation deck, the restored Beach Bar, and a poolside snack bar. The Beachside Café here, overlooking the ocean, is great for casual dining, as is Captain's Galley, also at ocean's edge in a tropical garden setting. The Banyan Veranda is the setting for light breakfasts, luncheon and Sunday brunch, high tea, and afternoon cocktails. The Moana's fine dining restaurant, the Ship's Tavern, features steak and seafood in an atmosphere that recalls the elegance of turn-of-the-century ocean-liner dining salons.

Guests have access to a wide variety of services, ranging from a supervised children's program in the summer months for children 5 to 12 to a "Golden Guests" program for those 55 and older, which includes hotel room upgrades, discounts at visitor attractions, special tours, and activities with seniors from Hawaii community groups. Classes in lei making, origami, hula, coconut-palm weaving, Hawaiian quilting, croquet, aerobics, and water aerobics are held regularly.

Rates at the Sheraton Moana Surfrider, single or double, are $185 for city view, $255 for partial ocean view rooms in the hotel's historic section, the Banyan Wing; $270 for oceanfront rooms in the Diamond Wing; $285 oceanfront in the Tower Wing. Suites, all oceanfront, begin at $500 per night. Rates subject to change. Children sharing a room with their parents stay free when no additional bedding is needed. Charge for a third person, $35; rollaway $25. AE, CB, DC, MC, V. Parking: $10 per night.

room coffee service, no fewer than three phones (one of which is PC compatible), and even a mini-TV on the bathroom vanity. Ali'i Tower rates run from $215 to $335; one- and two-bedroom suites are available for more. AE, CB, DISC, ER, JCB, MC, V. Valet parking $12 per day; self-parking $9.

The **Hyatt Regency Waikiki**, 2424 Kalakaua Ave., Honolulu, HI 96815 (tel. 808/923-1234; fax 808/923-7839; reservations toll free 800/228-9000), is a $100 million caravansary by the sea that ranks as one of the great showplace hotels of the country. Occupying an entire city block, the 1,234-room hotel accomplishes the seemingly impossible: creating an oasis of calm and tranquility and lush tropical beauty in the midst of the most bustling, heavily trafficked area in town. All the public areas have been placed around a huge, lushly landscaped atrium, or Great Hall, above which the guest rooms rise in twin 40-story towers that afford maximum views of ocean and mountains, and maximum amounts of privacy and peace. The Great Hall, one of the most beautiful spots in Honolulu, replete with tumbling waterfalls, fountains, cascades of greenery, flowers, and plantings everywhere, magnificent sculptures, and dotted with art, antiques, and intimate conversation areas, is, quite naturally, one of the most popular shopping (see Chapter VII), restaurant, and promenade areas in town.

The guest rooms have also been designed with an eye to the utmost in both comfort and glamour. Among the largest in town (425 square feet), each has a lanai with outdoor furniture, a sofa, huge closets, wall-to-wall carpeting, TV, air conditioning, and either twin beds, doubles, or double doubles. Cheerful color schemes and quality artwork everywhere create a harmonious feeling. City-view rooms are $170, mountain-view $200, ocean-view $235, oceanfront $260. The ocean-view Parlour Suites, which have a sleeping room plus a spacious living room, rent for $475 to $1,400. The Regency Club offers rooms at $260 and at $275 with a mountain view, $315 with an ocean view, and $345 oceanfront. And the incredible two-bedroom Presidential Suites—veritable mansions in the sky, complete with living room, library, and no fewer than six lanais—are $1,500 to $2,000 per night. (Rates subject to change.) AE, CB, DC, DISC, JCB, MC, V. Valet parking $10, self-parking $8.

The beach is directly across the street, but guests can also swim and sun at home at the third-floor pool and enjoy drinks at the Elegant Dive poolside. Regency Club guests enjoy rooftop sundecks with a cool-water Jacuzzi. All told, the hotel has six restaurants and six cocktail lounges including the Terrace Grille, an indoor-outdoor restaurant overlooking the ocean; Musashi, a stunning Japanese restaurant; and Harry's Bar, tucked into a corner of the open-air atrium, with the mood of a European sidewalk café. Bagwells 2424, the ultimate in Continental dining; Spats, a Roaring '20s speakeasy; Spats Dance Club, a high-energy disco; the Colony, a steak house; and Trappers, a fashionable club with stylish entertainment, deserve detailed reviews in themselves.

A self-contained resort community that provides enough glamorous diversion for weeks of Hawaiian living is the **Ilikai**, 1777 Ala Moana Blvd., Honolulu, HI 96815 (tel. 808/949-3811 or toll free 800/367-8434 in U.S. mainland and Canada; fax 947-0892). The Ilikai has been one of Waikiki's best hotels for over 25 years; with the recent completion of a $50 million renovation, it's better than ever. Inside this unique island-within-an-island you can choose from more than 800 of Waikiki's largest luxury accommodations housed in two buildings overlooking both the Ala Wai Yacht Harbor and Ala Moana Beach Park, with its acres of green lawns shaded by huge monkeypods, banyans, and coconut palms. Your vacation here can be as lazy or as lively as you wish: There's sunning and swimming in two pools or the nearby blue lagoon; for the more adventurous, there's sailing, surfing, or scuba diving in the waters beyond. One of the rare hotels in Waikiki with tennis facilities, the Ilikai has five courts. There's also a fitness center. You can shop until you run out of traveler's checks, eat your way through a variety of fun restaurants, watch top island entertainment under the stars, and stay in some of the nicest hotel rooms in town.

Rooms at the Ilikai are extraordinarily spacious—those in the Ilikai Tower, for example, are 600 square feet or larger. Many have full electric kitchens, all have honor bars, individually controlled air conditioning, color TV/pay movies, wall-mounted hair dryers, in-room safes, phones, and large lanais overlooking the ocean and the mountains. All rooms have either a king or two twin beds, and most have queen sofa beds. Rates go from $170 to $250 single or double, depending on the floor and the view; suites are $275 to $575. At the Yacht Harbor Tower, rooms have king, double double, or twin beds, air conditioning, phones, color TV/pay movies, wall-mounted hair dryers, honor bar, coffeemaker, and in-room safes; most rooms have lanais. Rates here go from $120 to $160 single or double; suites are $275 to $1,200. AE, CB, DC, DISC, JCB, MC, V. Parking: $7 per day.

Much of the Ilikai's excitement is in its restaurants and nightclubs. Its casual restaurant, Vanda Court Cafe, looks out over the Ala Wai Yacht Harbor. You can dine outdoors under the shade of palm trees and umbrella tables. When night falls, everything goes into high gear, for sunset signals the start of the hotel's traditional torchlighting ceremony. Then you must choose between the Comedy Club and the Top of the I, for entertainment, dancing, and gazing at the lights of Honolulu blinking 30 stories below.

If what you crave is elegant living, glorious views of the ocean, and plenty of room to stretch out, then the **Colony Surf**, 2895 Kalakaua Ave., Honolulu, HI 96815 (tel. 808/923-5751; fax 808/922-8433; reservations toll free 800/252-7873 U.S., 800/423-7781 Canada, 0014 800/125-333 Australia), is an excellent choice. It's located in the quieter Diamond Head section of town, across from Kapiolani Park, directly on one of the best swimming beaches in Waikiki. And the size of the rooms is matched by the splendor of the vistas—would you believe a 25-foot windowed panorama of ocean in many of the rooms? There are two buildings: the Colony Surf, whose elegant one-bedroom suites have fully equipped kitchen, two double beds, color TV, every nicety, and cost from $175 (single or double occupancy) on the limited-view lower floors, all the way up to $325 for direct ocean frontage; and the Colony Surf East, whose studio suites go from $125 to $180, single or double, depending on the view. Although they are smaller than the immense suites in the hotel building, they are luxuriously appointed, with kitchenette, air conditioning, two double-size beds, plenty of closet space, and large bath vanities. You can't go

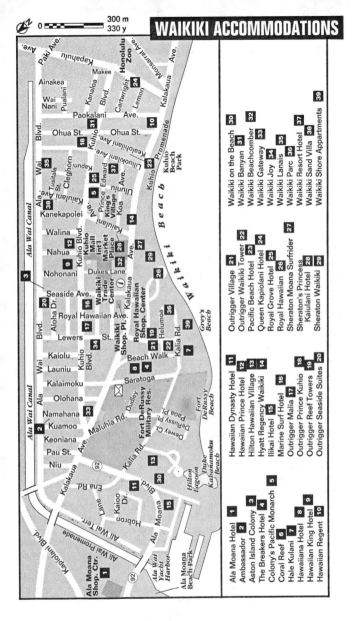

WAIKIKI ACCOMMODATIONS

0 — 300 m
330 y

Map labels (streets and landmarks):

Paki Ave. · Kapahulu Ave. · Ainakea · Makee · Kanaloa · Kanaloa Blvd. · Cartwright · Lemon · Honolulu Zoo · Monsarrat Ave. · Kalakaua Ave.

Wai Nani · Pualani · Paokalani Ave. · Ohua St. · Ohua St. · Kealohilani Ave. · Liliuokalani Ave. · Kuhio Ave. · Kuhio Promenade · Kuhio Beach Park

Ala Wai Blvd. · Cleghorn · Tusitala St. · Kapuni · Kaiulani Ave. · Prince Edward · Uluniu Ave. · Uluniu · King's Village · Koa · Kaiulani Ave.

Ala Wai Canal · Kanekapolei · Walina · Nahua · Nohonani · Kuhio Blvd. · Kuhio Mall · Int'l Market Place · Dukes Lane · Kalakaua Ave.

Seaside Ave. · Aloha Dr. · Royal Hawaiian Ave. · Lewers · Kaiolu · Launiu · Kalaimoku · Olohana · Namahana · Kuamoo · Keoniana · Pau St. · Niu

Waikiki Trade Center · Royal Hawaiian Shop. Center · Helumoa · Kalia Rd. · Grey's Beach

Waikiki Shop. Pl. · Beach Walk · Saratoga · Fort DeRussy Military Res. · Dudley · Dewey Ct. · DeRussy Pl. · Paoa Pl. · Fort DeRussy Beach

Kalakaua Blvd. · Ala Moana · Ena Rd. · Hobron · Kaioo Dr. · Lane · Ala Wai Promenade · Ali Wai Promenade · Kapiolani Blvd.

Ala Moana Shop. Ctr. · Ala Wai Yacht Harbor · Ala Moana Beach Park · Hilton Lagoon · Duke Kahanamoku Beach · Kahanamoku Beach · Hilton Lagoon

Waikiki Beach

Accommodation index:

1	Ala Moana Hotel
2	Ambassador
3	Aston Island Colony
4	The Breakers Hotel
5	Colony's Pacific Monarch
6	Coral Reef
7	Hale Kulani
8	Hawaiiana Hotel
9	Hawaiian King Hotel
10	Hawaiian Regent
11	Hawaiian Dynasty Hotel
12	Hawaiian Prince Hotel
13	Hilton Hawaiian Village
14	Hyatt Regency Waikiki
15	Ilikai Hotel
16	Marine Surf Hotel
17	Outrigger Malia
18	Outrigger Prince Kuhio
19	Outrigger Reef Towers
20	Outrigger Seaside Suites
21	Outrigger Village
22	Outrigger Waikiki Tower
23	Pacific Beach Hotel
24	Queen Kapiolani Hotel
25	Royal Grove Hotel
26	Royal Hawaiian
27	Sheraton Moana Surfrider
28	Sheraton's Princess Kaiulani Hotel
29	Sheraton Waikiki
30	Waikiki on the Beach
31	Waikiki Banyan
32	Waikiki Beachcomber
33	Waikiki Gateway
34	Waikiki Joy
35	Waikiki Lanais
36	Waikiki Parc
37	Waikiki Resort Hotel
38	Waikiki Sand Villa
39	Waikiki Shore Appartments

wrong in either building. There's an extraordinary two-bedroom penthouse suite at $1,500.

The Colony Surf is also the home of the enjoyable Bobby McGee's restaurant and disco, and of the famed Michel's, which we'll describe later in the chapter on restaurants. Elegant and expensive haute cuisine is served here at dinnertime, but breakfast and lunch are both reasonably priced, and the mood and views are superlative. The Colony Surf is a *kamaaina* hangout, a spot where the knowledgeable locals go just to get away from it all. It's that kind of place. AE, DC, MC, V. Complimentary valet parking.

---

3. Deluxe Hotels: Beginning Around $135

Although it's in the midst of the Waikiki madness, at 2552 Kalakaua Ave., Honolulu, HI 96815 (tel. 808/922-6611 or toll free 800/367-5370; fax 921-5255), there's an air of retreat about the **Hawaiian Regent Hotel.** It's wrapped around a cool, lush inner courtyard and the architectural details are striking. The third-floor swimming pool and sitting area, with glorious views of recently widened Waikiki Beach just across the street, is a stunner. The good looks continue in the rooms, which are large and exquisitely furnished in teak and rattan, with divided baths and vanitorium and tub-shower combinations. Breathtaking views of sea, mountains, or Diamond Head are enjoyed from spacious and private lanais. There are TV, radio, air conditioning, direct-dial phone—the works. Prices begin at $140 double for mountain-view rooms, and go to $250 for oceanfront corner deluxe rooms. It's $20 for an extra person in the room. One-bedroom suites are $425; two-bedroom suites, $475; there is no charge for children under 18 sharing a room with their parents. You can eat at the attractive Summery Restaurant or dine on fine Continental cuisine in the award-winning Secret. Have a drink at the Library, a contemporary bar, or a coffee and croissant at the Café Regent, a Parisian-style café set in the gardens of the hotel courtyard. For beef and seafoods, it's the Tiffany Steak House, on the third floor; for Japanese dining, the Regent Hatsuhana. The Lobby Bar hosts Hawaiian entertainment nightly in the center of all the hotel activity in the main lobby. The Ocean Terrace Bar offers casual lunches and poolside cocktails. And for tennis buffs, there's a court, plus pro instruction available daily from dawn to dusk. AE, CB, DC, DISC, JCB, MC, V. 24-hour parking pass $5.

Blessed with a location directly on the beach, the **Sheraton-Waikiki,** 2255 Kalakaua Ave., Honolulu, HI 96815 (tel. 808/922-4422; fax 808/922-9567; reservations toll free 800/325-3535), is a light, gay, vibrant place where everybody seems to be having a good time. The lobby has a wonderfully open feeling about it, and the breezy summer-house mood extends into all the public rooms and the 1,900 air-conditioned bedrooms as well. The "standard mountain view" rooms here—$185 double—are quite large as hotel rooms go, and the appointments bespeak charm. Flower murals in soft pastel shades dominate the color scheme, bathrooms and closets are roomy (so are the private lanais), and, of course, there's color TV. The ocean-view rooms are dazzlers. Most nearby hotels have a view of the Sheraton, but at the Sheraton your views are of a vast expanse of blue Pacific, the sun dancing on the waves in daytime, the lights from Diamond Head to downtown Honolulu glistening under the night sky. These rooms go for $210 double. Suites start at $310, and some, fit for diplomats and royalty, boast a vast, 20-foot living room with an outdoor lanai, and can easily accommodate four people. The best values here are the $90 doubles in the adjoining Manor Wing, all nicely decorated. There is a $10 surcharge in winter. AE, DC, JCB, MC, V.

You'll probably find you're spending a lot of time right at the hotel, what with all those great little shops in the lobby, that vast expanse of beach at your doorstep, and one of the biggest and sunniest pools in Waikiki on the beachfront. When you're hungry, there's the pretty Ocean Terrace for casual meals, the glamorous Hanohano Room for gourmet dining in a spectacular setting 30 stories up (take the glass elevator just for the view), as well as the Kon Tiki Restaurant, Ciao Italian Restaurant, and Esprit Nightclub for drinks and entertainment. If you decide to leave "home," you can, of course, "play and charge" at the other Sheraton hotels in Waikiki, as well as the Sheraton Makaha Resort with its golf and tennis facilities.

Just when you thought there wasn't room in Waikiki for one more room—let alone an entire hotel—**Waikiki Parc** has gone and done it. They've conjured up some space at 2233 Helemoa Rd., Honolulu, HI 96815 (tel. 808/921-7272; fax 808/923-1336; reservations toll free 800/422-0450), and opened a 298-room, 22-story luxury hotel 100 yards from the beach at Waikiki and directly across from the Halekulani hotel. In fact, this hotel has been dubbed the "Halekulani, Jr.," since it is managed by the same corporation and is similar to its parent hotel in its elegant simplicity, personalized service, and sophisticated style. But the big difference here is in the prices: This one has been designed to combine "luxury with affordability," which means that rooms go from $120 to $215 single or double, depending on whether the view is courtyard, mountain, or ocean, and on what floor it is. (A third person is charged $20, only in rooms with two double beds; there are no rollaways.) Prices may rise by 10%. The rooms, however, are all the same, beautifully done in tones of blue and white, with ceramic tile floors with plush inlaid carpeting, conversation areas, armoires, custom rattan furniture, adjustable white shutter doors on the lanai or view balcony, business desks in most rooms, and either a king-size bed or two single beds. There are two phones in each room, a small refrigerator with a fully stocked honor bar, plus central air conditioning, AM/FM radio, a remote control color cable TV, an in-room safe, and the most modern safety and fire protection systems. Eight rooms are equipped for the handicapped.

Waikiki Parc has two excellent restaurants. Parc Café, with its garden terrace atmosphere, is lovely for breakfast buffets, Sunday brunches, and light lunches. At dinner, it becomes a fine-dining restaurant, featuring Continental cuisine and island specialties, as well as an excellent dinner buffet. Kacho, one of Hawaii's few Kyoto-style restaurants, is a charming small Japanese place for true devotees of sushi and Japanese seafood dishes.

Guests too lazy to hop over to nearby Waikiki Beach for swimming, snorkeling, and surfing on one of the best stretches of beach can swim at the freshwater pool on the eighth-floor recreation deck.

Inquire about honeymoon, car-rental, and other packages which may be offered at the time of your visit. There is also an excellent, money-saving corporate program. AE, CB, DC, DISC, JCB, MC, V. Valet parking $7 per day.

The **Waikiki Joy**, 320 Lewers St., Honolulu, HI 96815 (tel. 808/923-2300; fax 808/377-1290; reservations toll free 800/733-5569), is one hotel that truly deserves its name. It's a hidden jewel, an oasis right in the heart of busy Waikiki. Imagine a hotel that offers not only outstanding personal service but a corporate center for busy executives and a Jacuzzi in every room as well! The Italian-marble–accented open-air lobby and the tropical veranda, with a spacious swimming pool and furnished deck, set the scene for the beautifully decorated guest rooms themselves. Rooms are located either in the hotel tower or in the all-suite tower. The hotel rooms, decorated in soft pastels, have a marble entry, a refrigerator, a safe, quiet air conditioning (the unit is outside), a Bose stereo entertainment system, and a lanai wide enough for one to sit and enjoy the views. Rooms with a king-size bed are $120, with two double beds $135. The suites are even more luxurious, all equipped with Jacuzzis. The Club Suites, with either king-size or double double beds, have a refrigerator and wet bar and go for $145 nightly. Executive King Suites have two double beds and a kitchen with microwave and full refrigerator; they are $175. Executive King Suites, at $215, have all of the above but are set up as a separate living room and bedroom and also go for $215. Rates are often lower at certain periods of the year; honeymoon packages and corporate rates are available. Now, as for that Corporate Suite, which is guaranteed to make life easier for business guests: It offers contracted use of secretarial services, plus facsimile and copy machines, free local phone calls, newspapers, express check-in and -out, and many other services. The Waikiki Joy is literally surrounded by restaurants, but right on the premises is charming Cappuccino's, which features moderately priced meals—salads, pupus, and light foods—every day. There's free continental breakfast at the Tropical Veranda each morning. AE, DC, MC, V. Parking: $10 per day.

If you're not going to the neighbor islands this time but you do want a resort vacation in a glamorous country setting, then you can't do better than to choose the **Turtle Bay Hilton and Country Club**, P.O. Box 187, Kahuku, HI 96731 (tel. 808/293-8811; fax 808/293-9147; reservations toll free 800/HILTONS), a self-contained resort and country club on the island's North Shore, not far from Sunset Beach, and about an hour's drive from Waikiki. Set amidst five miles of white-sand beach and rugged shoreline, this gorgeously landscaped hotel is an ideal place for active sports, with its ocean-view championship golf course, 10–plexipave-court tennis complex, horseback riding, idyllic beach, swimming pools, and facilities for snorkeling, scuba diving, and windsurfing. Guest rooms, located in either the low-rise main building or one of the cottages, are beautifully furnished in Polynesian decor. Each room has a private lanai, tub and shower, color TV, and all the amenities. Single or double rooms with a view of Kahuku Bay are $155; ocean view, ocean-lanai, and oceanfront rooms are $175, $210, and $220; cottages are $295 a day. Suites begin at $510. Add $25 for a third person. There is no charge for children, regardless of age, when they stay in the same room with their parents. You could just about have a vacation here without ever leaving the 808 acres that comprise Turtle Bay—there are shops adjacent to the spacious lobby, craft demonstrations daily, even a branch of Liberty House. The Palm Terrace, a handsome restaurant with a view of the ocean on two sides, serves all meals and overlooks the pool and Turtle Bay; for fine dining overlooking Turtle Bay there's the lovely Cove, featuring Continental and local favorites and an excellent wine list. Asahi Restaurant features Japanese cuisine with sushi bar. AE, CB, DC, DISC, ER, JCB, MC, V.

A striking 37-story, 495-room tower has made the popular **Pacific Beach Hotel,** right across from the beach at 2490 Kalakaua Ave., Honolulu, HI 96815 (tel. 808/922-1233; fax 808/922-8061), more exciting than ever—especially since the tower boasts a fantastic three-story, 250,000-gallon saltwater Oceanarium, from which the lobby and restaurant viewers can observe the marine life of the Hawaiian coral reefs without ever having to take snorkel in hand!

Both glamour and practicality are available at the Pacific Beach: glamour in the good views in all of the 850 rooms, whether they face ocean, mountain, or Diamond Head; and practicality in such conveniences as the kitchenette-bar, color TV, air conditioning, shower-tub combination, and double-double or king-size beds throughout in the large and luxurious rooms. The decor is elegant green and brown, the furniture ultramodern. Rates begin at $115 for a standard single or double and go up to $190 for those rooms in the front of the building that have the ocean just outside and a sunset spectacular such as few hotels can boast of. From May 1 to December 26, rooms are $10 less. An extra person is $20.

The hotel also boasts two professionally designed tennis courts, a pool, and several restaurants and lounges that include, within view of the Oceanarium, the Oceanarium Restaurant (see Chapter IV for details) for light dining, Neptune for continental fare, and Shogun, a Japanese steak and seafood restaurant. AE, CB, DC, DISC, JCB, MC, V. Parking $5 per day.

4. Moderately Priced Hotels: Beginning Around $90

A hotel in Waikiki that still has that old tropical feeling is a rarity these days, so praise be for the **Waikikian on the Beach,** 1811 Ala Moana Blvd., Honolulu, HI 96815 (tel. 808/949-5331; fax 808/946-2843; reservations toll free 800/922-7866). Built in 1956, this 132-room Polynesian-style hotel, with a cave-like lobby and the roof of an ancient spirit house, set in lush tropical gardens that lead to a lagoon fronting on the ocean, still maintains that feeling of the old beachside bungalow hotels. At night, the torches are lit in the garden and strolling musicians wander along the paths to serenade the guests underneath their lanais. On Tuesday nights (5:45 to 6:45), guests are treated to a party with all the fresh pineapple they can eat and all the mai tais they can drink (believe it or not, anybody can come to these parties; you don't have to be a hotel guest—this must be the best-kept secret in Waikiki!). Any day of the week, guests can dine in thatched huts or around the palm-fringed pool at the lovely Tahitian Lanai Restaurant, or have tropical drinks at the Papeete Bar, where a lively local crowd gathers for late-evening sing-alongs. And there's plenty of activity, too, out on the lagoon: windsurfing lessons, water bikes, and just plain wonderful swimming.

Lots of illustrious guests have stayed at the Waikikian on the Beach, among them Prince Charles, who registered here when he played in the British-Hawaii polo matches in 1974. James Michener spent time here when he was writing *Hawaii*, and the Symphony Suite has hosted musical greats like Leonard Bernstein and Arthur Fiedler. Rudy Vallee and Dolores Del Rio were among the early guests.

The hotel has two wings. The older Garden Wing has rooms done in simple island decor, with phone and refrigerator (no TVs here). The newer, seven-story Banyan Wing is more modern, has air conditioning and color TV, and is decorated in brighter colors. These rooms face the mountains or the ocean, but with limited ocean views over the tops of the coconut trees. The average room has one double and one single bed. During the low season, April 1 to December 20, standard rooms are $72 single or double, superior $82, deluxe $99, family suite $115, penthouse $160. From December 22 to March 31, standards are $82, superior $98, deluxe $115, family suite $135, penthouse $180. The family suite takes up to four at this price, the penthouse up to six. Kitchenettes are available on request. The hotel is managed by Aston, 2255 Kuhio Ave., Honolulu, HI 96815-2658. AE, CB, DC, JCB, MC, V. Parking: $3 per night.

Sheraton's Princess Kaiulani Hotel, 2342 Kalakaua Ave., Honolulu, HI 96815-3296 (tel. 808/922-5811; reservations toll free 800/325-3535), preserves the memory of Hawaii's beloved Princess Kaiulani, heir to the throne, who died in 1899 at the age of 24. The hotel is located at Ainahau, near the site of the former royal estate which was her home. It is directly across the road from Sheraton's oceanfront Waikiki hotels—the Royal Hawaiian, the Sheraton Moana Surfrider, and the Sheraton-Waikiki—and in the midst of the busy restaurant/shopping scene of Waikiki. The giant, 1,150-room hotel has been popular with families and tour groups ever since the first of its buildings, the 11-story Princess Wing, opened in 1955 and became Waikiki's first skyscraper. Then followed the Kaiulani Wing in 1960, and the most modern, the 29-story Ainahau Wing, in 1960. The three buildings are connected by graceful open-air lobbies and lovely gardens; out front there's a large pool, waterfall, and terrace. A $6 million renovation has recently upgraded all the public areas, making them regal indeed; original artworks and mementoes of the Princess Kaiulani era can be found throughout the hotel. Dining facilities are plentiful, including the Momoyama for Japanese food prepared at table, the Lotus Moon for Mandarin- and Szechuan-style delicacies, the Pikake Terrace, where a sumptuous breakfast is served every day in a tropical garden atmosphere, and the popular fast-food haven, the Minute Chef. One of Hawaii's best shows, the spectacular Polynesian Revue, is presented nightly in the lavish Ainahau Showroom. Entertainment is also featured nightly from 5:45pm poolside.

As for the guest rooms, the older ones are on the small side with twin beds and limited views; rooms in the newer wings, however, have been redone, and feature new decor and double double beds. Regardless of size, all rooms have color TV with first-run movies, telephone, and most have a private lanai. Many rooms have connecting doorways to accommodate families. Prices vary, depending on the size, view, and location of the rooms. Tourist rooms with no lanais are $105, standard rooms are $130, moderate $150, superior $155, deluxe (Ainahau Wing, ocean view) $170. An additional person in the room is $25; children under 18 free when occupying the same room as their parents and not requiring an extra bed. AE, CB, DC, JCB, MC, V. Guests show a parking pass and pay $1.50 each time they take their car out.

One of the most popular small new hotels on the Waikiki scene, the 250-room **Waikiki Terrace Hotel,** 2045 Kalakaua Ave., Honolulu, HI 96815 (tel. 808/955-6000; fax 808/943-8555; reservations toll free 800/445-8811 from mainland U.S. and Canada), has a lot going for it. The owners took over an old hotel, treated it to a $10.5 million renovation, and created a four-star property at affordable prices. The guest rooms are of good size, handsomely furnished with light woods, Berber carpeting, and splendid marble-and-granite bathrooms with grooming products. Each room has air conditioning, color TV, phone, refrigerator, and a dry bar with an instant hot water dispenser and a complimentary basket of coffees and Japanese and herbal teas. Views from private lanais are of ocean or mountains, sometimes a bit of both; sunrise views are especially lovely. There's a fully equipped pool deck on the second floor, with whirlpool, spa, and fitness center. And there's a wonderful restaurant, the Mezzanine, offering light, contemporary cuisine. From April 1 to December 19, doubles are $89 to $119, suites $275. From December 20 to March 31, doubles are $99 to $129, suites $275. An extra person is $15. Children under 12 free when using existing bedding. AE, CB, DC, DISC, JCB, MC, V. Parking $6 per day.

The Waikiki Terrace is located at the entrance to Waikiki, about a 7-minute walk (through Ft. DeRussy Park) from a splendid stretch of Waikiki Beach.

The Aston **Waikiki Shore Apartments,** 2161 Kalia Rd., Honolulu, HI 96815 (tel. 808/926-4733; reservations, toll free 800/367-2353), offers private apartment living right on the beach at Waikiki. Many of the condo owners have purchased their apartments as investments and make them available year round for short-term rentals.

Studio apartments start at $105 during the regular season and at $90 ($82 on a weekly basis) off-season (April 1 to December 16). One-bedroom apartments start at $130 during the regular season and at $115 ($107 on a weekly basis) off-season; two-bedroom apartments start at $165 regular and $145 ($135 on a weekly basis) off-season. Rates for two-bedroom, two-bath apartments and for two-bedroom, two-bath oceanfront apartments begin at $195 and $235 regular, respectively.

The rooms are spacious. Each apartment has its own private lanai that runs across its entire width, so you have views of both sea and mountains, and of the green, spacious lawns of Fort DeRussy, next door. Each apartment is furnished and decorated differently, of course, but all are attractive, and all have complete kitchen with garbage disposal and laundry facilities, as well as private telephone. Request air conditioning if you desire it; many of the apartments have it, and even in those that do not, cross-ventilation is excellent and there are ceiling and desk fans as well. The beach is one of the loveliest around, and dozens of restaurants and shops are just a few steps from the front door of the cool, inviting lobby. You get the feeling of apartment living here, not a tourist hotel. Parking is available in the basement at $6 per day, but since space is limited, it's best to let them know you'll be renting a car and ask to be put on the waiting list.

Half a block from Kuhio Beach is Korean Air's lovely **Waikiki Resort Hotel,** 2460 Koa Ave., Honolulu, HI 96815 (tel. 808/922-4911; fax 808/922-9468; toll free 800/367-5116 in U.S. mainland). It's recently completed a $4 million renovation and redecorating program, and the results are evident everywhere: in the spacious lobby with its sparkling chandeliers, very cozy for relaxing; in the karaoke bar off the lobby, with its small dance floor and glass mirrors etched with Hawaiian flowers and scenes; in the newly improved pool area on the second floor; and in the charming Camellia restaurant featuring Korean cuisine. The 300 rooms are attractive, too, redecorated with either bluish-gray or pink-mauve color schemes; new carpeting, beds, and furniture; new refrigerators, AM/FM radio alarm clocks, and a 19-inch Samsung TV set hooked up to eight pay channels with a remote control beside the bed. Some 34 rooms have new kitchenettes. All rooms have lanais.

From April 1 to June 30 and from September 1 to December 19, double rooms run from $88 to $105, depending on the height of the floor and the direction in which the rooms face. The higher-priced rooms are on a high floor and face the ocean; the lower-priced ones are below the eighth floor and face the mountains. Rooms with a kitchenette (as opposed to just a refrigerator) all face the ocean and are $120 per day double. Luxurious one- and two-bedroom suites are $270 and $420 respectively. Children under 12 stay for free, provided that additional beds are not required; add $15 a day for any additional adult. From December 21 to March 31 and July 1 to August 31, add $10 to all categories. Inquire about their attractive room-and-car package deal.

It could take an entire book to detail the charms of the **Manoa Valley Inn,** 2001 Vancouver Dr., Honolulu, HI 96822 (tel. 808/947-6019; fax 808/946-6188; reservations toll free 800/634-5115), a three-story gingerbread mansion in Manoa Valley near the University of Hawaii, one of the grand old mansions of Honolulu (it is listed in both the Hawaii and National Registers of Historic Places). Under the guidance of Rick Ralston, president and founder of Crazy Shirts and one of Hawaii's most avid preservationists, it has been authentically restored to the resplendence of the 1920s and now functions as Honolulu's most glamorous bed-and-breakfast inn. Furnished with antiques of the period, each of the seven guest rooms (and the intimate cottage) has its own unique personality; each is named in honor of a well-known person who lived in Hawaii. From the Dole Room on the third floor, furnished with a double bed, on up to the John Guild Suite, with a private sitting room and bath, they all resemble some wonderful movie set. Rooms with shared bath are $95 to $100; those with bath are $100 to $150; suites are $175. Rates subject to change. There are phones in all the rooms and private bathrooms in four of the rooms (the others share facilities). All rates are double occupancy and include a generous continental breakfast complete with island fruits, juices, Kona coffee, and freshly baked goodies; fruit, wine, and cheese are served in the afternoon; and soft drinks, juice, tea, and coffee are available at all times. Sherry and port wine are left out for a nightcap. The game room offers an antique piano and nickelodeon for fun; the living room, a collection of art nouveau boxes and hula dolls. The reading room contains a TV and a VCR. There's also a billiard room, and a lanai with a hypnotic view of Waikiki's city lights. Board games, books, and magazines are everywhere—and a croquet set is available, too. The inn does not cater to children under age 14, but it does cater to the curious traveler and the romantic. AE, CB, DC, MC, V. Free parking.

The **Waikiki Beachcomber** at 2300 Kalakaua Ave., Honolulu, HI 96815 (tel. 808/922-4646; fax 808/923-4889; reservations toll free 800/622-4646 in U.S. mainland, 800/338-6233 in Canada), located as it is between Seaside Avenue and the International Market Place, sits astride the heartland of Waikiki. It's an attractive hotel, across the road from the beach, with smartly Polynesian lobby and dining rooms, plus a pool and terrace looking over the avenue. You can eat at the Beachcomber Restaurant, which features casual dining, fresh fish, island cuisine, and a nightly prime-rib buffet; catch live entertainment every night at the Surfboard Lounge; and have snacks and light meals at the Pool Terrace. There are 500 rooms here, all with color TV, air conditioning, dial-out phone, refrigerator, safe, in-room movies, and a furnished lanai for $105, single or double. At this price you'll have a city view; rooms with partial ocean views (somewhat blocked by the Royal Hawaiian hotel across the street) are $120. Higher up, it's higher up—$135 and $145 for ocean-view and deluxe ocean-view rooms. Suites are $250. Rates go up $10 to $35 during the winter season, December 22 through March 31. Children under 12 free with parents and using existing bedding; an extra person is charged $15. We like these rooms, especially the grass-textured wallpaper with its floral designs and the welcome spaciousness. AE, CB, DC, MC, V.

Walking into the lobby of the regal **Queen Kapiolani Hotel,** 150 Kapahulu Ave., Honolulu, HI 96815 (tel. 808/922-1941; fax 808/533-0472; reservations toll free 800/367-5004), is like walking back in time to the Hawaii of a century ago, when royalty was in full bloom. This towering hotel overlooking Kapiolani Park, less than a block from the beach, is the representation of all the elegance that Queen Kapiolani, the consort of Kalakaua, Hawaii's last reigning king, meant to her people. A bubbling fountain surrounded by tropical plants on the outside of the building leads the way to the lobby, which is worth a visit in itself, lavishly done in green wallpapers and accented by magnificent chandeliers of kerosene lamps, reminiscent of the days of the whalers in Hawaii. The bentwood wicker chairs are stunning replicas of old Hawaii furniture. The Kalakaua Dynasty decor carries over to the rooms, too; they are almost royal chambers in themselves, decked out in gold and royal blues. The door to each room, in fact, has a full-color reproduction of the seal of the state of Hawaii over it. The views, too, are splendid, since the hotel is across the street from Kapiolani Park, and there is no new construction to block the view from here to Diamond Head or the ocean. Besides elegance, the rooms offer such modern creature comforts as air conditioning, a telephone, a color cable television with in-room movies, and in-room safes. Most rooms have lanais, and some have kitchenettes. Dining facilities include the handsome Peacock Room, done in Hawaiian Monarchy style, and the Queen's Garden Lanai, scene of some of the most popular buffet meals in Waikiki. The third-floor swimming pool and sundeck are very popular. During the winter season, from January through April, standard rooms are $92 to $102 single or double; superior rooms are $107 to $115; deluxe rooms, with park or ocean views, are $117 to $122; superior deluxe rooms, with park or ocean view and kitchenette, are $123 to $135. A one-bedroom suite with kitchenette, for four, is $215; a one-bedroom, ocean-view suite with kitchenette, for four, is $350. An extra person is $15. During the rest of the year, prices go down by about $10. The hotel is managed by Hawaiian Pacific Resorts, 1150 S. King St., Honolulu, HI 96814.

For luxury accommodations at not unreasonable prices, the **Outrigger Prince Kuhio Hotel**, 2500 Kuhio Ave., Honolulu, HI 96815 (tel. 808/922-0811; toll free fax 800/456-4329; reservations toll free 800/733-7777 from U.S. and Canada, 0014-800-126-985 from Australia) is the place. Everything about this hotel is a delight, from the gracious doormen to the spacious and beautiful lobby, to the luxuriously appointed guest rooms. There's a Business Center with state-of-the-art equipment, plus the assistance of a full-time secretary. No-smoking and handicapped-accessible rooms are available. Each of the 616 rooms has either a king-size bed or two doubles, air conditioning, color TV, direct-dial phone, a small refrigerator and wet bar, and a bathroom done in Italian marble. Each room has its own private lanai, with either ocean or mountain view; from the latter, you can see wonderful sunsets and, at night, the lights on the hills. The 10th floor is the recreation area, with sundeck, big swimming pool, and Jacuzzi, as well as a snack and cocktail bar. Breakfast, lunch, and dinner are served daily in Trellisses Restaurant, overlooking the hotel gardens. Cocktails and entertainment are featured nightly in Cupid's lobby lounge.

The price of your room includes a car from Dollar Rent-A-Car free for every day of your stay if you request the "Outrigger Free Ride" package when making reservations. Rooms are priced from $100 to $130 regular season (April 1 through December 18), from $115 to $145 the rest of the year (the price goes up as you move from the lowest floors up to the 20s and 30s). Suites are available from $350 to $475. An extra person is charged $15; children under 18 free when sharing existing beds; maximum of four persons in a room. On the top floors, with access by key only, is the splendid Kuhio Club, whose guests receive special niceties, like complimentary breakfast in the morning, free newspapers delivered to their doors, hors d'oeuvres and beverages in the evening, plus the services of charming and helpful concierges. A stay here is a true luxury experience, and the price is not as much as one would expect for this level of service: $150 for mountain-view rooms, $160 for ocean-view rooms during regular season, $165 and $175 the rest of the year. One-bedroom and two-bedroom suites are also available at $350 and up. AE, CB, DC, DISC, JCB, MC, V. Parking: $6 per day.

One of the first high-rise hotels to be built in Waikiki, and still one of the largest (885 rooms), is the **Outrigger Reef Hotel,** right on the beach and in the center of things at 2169 Kalia Rd., Honolulu, HI 96815 (tel. 808/923-3111; toll free fax 800/456-4329; reservations toll free 800/733-7777 from U.S. mainland and Canada, 0014/800/456-4329 from Australia). With a top beachfront location, plenty of activities, warm hospitality, and nicely furnished rooms, the Outrigger Reef is always a popular choice. Now that a $30 million renovation has been completed, it's truly up-to-date. No-smoking and handicapped-accessible rooms are available. There's a business center with state-of-the-art equipment plus the assistance of a full-time secretary. The new entrance, a wide stone esplanade with a flowered porte-cochère, leads to an attractive lobby, and to rooms that are prettier than ever; some we inspected had lovely purple bedspreads with bright floral patterns. They all have a refrigerator, an in-room safe, air conditioning, a color TV, and in-room movies. Cars from Dollar Rent-A-Car are free for every day of your stay if you request the "Outrigger Free Ride" package when making reservations. During the regular season, April 1 through December 18, doubles range from $100 to $190, the higher prices for magnificent oceanfront vistas. The rest of the year, most rooms are $15 more. Suites for up to four people run from $195 to $295. A rooftop garden suite goes for $200 to $395. Children under 18 stay for free when sharing existing beds with parents. The Outrigger Reef boasts one of the largest freshwater swimming pools in Waikiki and provides many water activities—catamaran sailing, canoe rides, and surfboard lessons—on the beach. At poolside is the Chief's Hut Restaurant. The Shorebird Beach Broiler offers casual dining with a view of the ocean. AE, CB, DC, DISC, JCB, MC, V. Parking: $6 per day.

In this era of high-rise Hawaii, it comes as a shock to find a low-slung, two-story hotel cozily nestled into a tropical garden, complete with pools, plantings, and that old-time Hawaiian feeling you weren't sure still existed. That's the kind of pleasant shock you'll get when you walk into the courtyard of the **Hawaiiana Hotel,** 260 Beach Walk, Honolulu, HI 96815 (tel. 808/923-3811; fax 808/926-5728; reservations toll free from U.S. mainland and Canada, 800/367-5122). Located on a side street, half a block from the beach on one side and Kalakaua Avenue on the other, the Hawaiiana is not well known among tourists, since it doesn't go about blowing its own horn; but those who know it treasure it and wouldn't dream of going anywhere else. All the units are attractive, furnished as studio rooms or suites, with tropical rattan furniture, complete electric kitchens, color TV, electronic safes, and air conditioning. There are nine Alii Ultra deluxe rooms. All rooms catch the trade winds. Most have lanais overlooking the gardens or one of the two swimming pools. Singles are $80 to $90, doubles $85 to $95. Alii Ultra studio singles or doubles are $165 to $195; the surcharge for any addition-

A Special Hotel

The **New Otani Kaimana Beach Hotel,** Diamond Head Way, at 2863 Kalakaua Ave., Honolulu, HI 96815 (tel. 808/923-1555; fax 808/922-9404; toll free 800/733-7949 from U.S. mainland and Canada), is the kind of find that its regular guests really don't like to tell everyone about. It's small (125 rooms) and quaintly charming, with a staff that gives attention to the slightest detail of service. Ideally located at the foot of Diamond Head, it is somewhat removed from the hustle and bustle of Waikiki, yet it is close enough for one to enjoy all the activities of the city. Best of all, it's situated on just about our favorite beach area in Waikiki—Sans Souci, which, with its uncrowded sands and gentle surf, is a wonderful place to relax quietly in the sun. After a renovation costing more than $10 million, the hotel is now more attractive than ever. It has been lightened and brightened from top to bottom. The open-air lobby, with its wicker bucket chairs and sofas, looks out on the Hau Tree Lanai, a delightful beachfront restaurant, and a beautiful view of the Pacific. Refurbished rooms, which include luxury suites, are spacious and well appointed, done in tones of gray, terra-cotta, blue, and lavender. All are air-conditioned and with color TV, dining tables for two, vanity rooms, massage showers, hair dryers, and other luxury amenities. The corner rooms have lanais on two sides, offering stunning views. Rooms in the Diamond Head wing have refrigerators and microwave ovens. Since the hotel overlooks Kapiolani Park, guests have easy access to such activities as golf, tennis, kite flying, jogging, and bicycling. Kayaking and snorkeling are available at the beach. The hotel also arranges for visitors to climb to the top of Diamond Head Crater and welcomes them to the Diamond Head Climbers Hui when they've completed their hike.

A variety of accommodations is available. Standard rooms go for $105, single or double. But then you get into the type of view. A room with a view of Diamond Head is $150; one with a view of the ocean and Waikiki is $170. Junior suites, with one bedroom, are $190 and $195, depending on the view. Rates in all categories are $10 higher from December 20 to March 31. For any additional person, the charge is $15. Rates are subject to change. AE, CB, DC, MC, V. Parking: $3 per day.

al person is $8. One-bedroom suites for up to four persons are $135 to $143. All rates are subject to change; discounts are available on stays of two weeks or longer. AE, MC, V. Parking: $6 per day.

But the comfort and charm of the rooms are just the beginning of the story here. The hotel believes in doing extra little things for its guests, like serving them free coffee and pineapple juice out by the pool in the morning; placing a pineapple in their rooms when they arrive; giving the ladies leis on departure; presenting two Hawaiian shows a week (free); and leaving a morning or evening paper at the door. Use of the washing machines and dryers is free. Parking is located at the back of the hotel on nearby Saratoga Road. The Hawaiiana is the kind of place where you get to know your neighbors, and many couples who have met here now plan their vacations together and reunite at the Hawaiiana every year! Mapuana Schneider, the hospitable manager, suggests advance reservations, especially during the busy midsummer and midwinter seasons.

After you've seen the Hawaiiana, it's almost a case of déjà vu when you see **The Breakers,** 250 Beach Walk, Honolulu, HI 96815 (tel. 808/923-3181; fax 808/923-7174; reservations toll free 800/426-0494). The mystery is cleared up when you learn that the same architect designed both. Like its neighbor, it has that low-slung, relaxed, Hawaiian-garden feeling. There are about 66 rooms in the five ranch-style buildings, all of them nicely appointed, with complete electric kitchenettes, modern Asian decor, air conditioning; many have lanais. The studio rooms go for $85 and $92 single, $88 and $94 twin. There are also 15 garden suites that rent at $120 single, $128 twin, $136 triple, and $140 quad. You'll enjoy the large pool, the leis on departure, the beach facilities down the road, and the lovely garden setting. There's a snack shop and bar on the grounds. AE, DC, MC, V. Parking: free.

The cool and peaceful **Waikiki Terrace Hotel,** 2045 Kalakaua Ave., Honolulu, HI 96815 (tel. 808/955-6000; fax 808/943-7555; reservations, toll free 800/445-8811) has a top location near Fort DeRussy and the good beaches in that area. The two-level lobby gives a feeling of coolness, with its terrazzo floors and tasteful furnishings. And you certainly won't go hungry or unentertained here. The Makai Sugar Company Restaurant on the mezzanine floor offers excellent food impeccably served. There's cocktail and sandwich service at the pool. And at night, the Sugar Mill Lounge features entertainment of high quality.

The rooms are quite lovely, all air-conditioned, with color television, telephone, and private lanai. And every room has a fine view of either ocean or mountains, not too common in many Waikiki hotels. Most rooms have two double beds or a king-size one. Rooms go from $89 to $129 single or double; an additional person is $15 extra. Children under 12 free with parents using existing bedding. AE, CB, DC, DISC, JCB, MC, V. Parking: $8 per day.

Thanks to a $30 million renovation, the **Ala Moana Hotel,** 410 Atkinson Dr., Honolulu, HI 96814 (tel. 808/955-4811; fax 808/944-2974; reservations toll free 800/367-6025) is nicer than ever, from its elegant porte-cochère and magnificent lobby to its 1,200 guest rooms and suites. There are eight restaurants and lounges in the building, including the famous rooftop supper club Nicholas Nikolas, and the equally noted Rumours nightclub. The Ginger Terrace serves tropical drinks and sandwiches at the pool and sundeck, and the Plantation Cafe offers affordable family dining.

Rooms are of good size, attractively furnished, and have color TV, pay movie system, AM-FM radio, individually controlled air conditioning, direct-dial phones, refrigerators, and safes. Standard rooms in the Kona Tower are $105 in low season. In the taller Waikiki Tower, they are $130 for mountain view, $150 for ocean view. Waikiki Tower rooms have lanais. In the high season, usually mid-December to April 1, add $10. A third person is charged $15, but there is no charge for children 18 and under in their parents' room.

Rooms on club floors, with extra amenities, run $170; suites are $210 and up, up, up to $1,800. Rates are subject to change.

The hotel is located at the entrance of Waikiki, overlooking the Ala Wai Yacht Harbor, within walking distance of Ala Moana Beach Park and about a 10-minute bus ride to the main action of Waikiki Beach. But all you do is exit the rear, descend a ramp, and you are at Liberty House, the first of 200 shops in the Ala Moana Shopping Center. AE, MC, V.

The attractive **Outrigger Malia,** 2211 Kuhio Ave., Honolulu, HI 96815 (tel. 808/923-7621, 926-0679 reservations; toll free 800/733-7777 from U.S. and Canada; 0014/800/126-985 from Australia; toll free fax 800/456-4329), has a lot going for it—including a rooftop tennis court, a therapeutic spa, and a wonderfully central location. And right off the colorful, breezy lobby is the Wailana Malia, one of the best coffee shops in town, open 24 hours a day. And we haven't even told you about the rooms yet! Each of them, cheerfully decorated with cane furniture, crimson carpeting, and printed bedspreads, has a lanai, air conditioning, and color TV. One entire floor features rooms designed especially for physically handicapped guests, with wide doors to accommodate wheelchairs and grab-bars in the bathrooms. The junior suites consist of a sitting room with two daybeds (or *punees,* as they are called in Hawaii), plus a bedroom. They can accommodate up to four people; rates are $90 for up to four during regular season (April 1 through December 18); the rest of the year, they are $100. Regular rooms contain two double beds and have a small refrigerator. Rates for these rooms are $75 to $80 single or double during regular season, $85 to $90 the rest of the year.

At the 740-room **Aston Island Colony,** 445 Seaside Ave., Honolulu, HI 96815 (tel. 808/923-2345; reservations toll free 800/922-7866), elegance begins in the spacious, airy lobby, with its stylish rattan furniture and big, beautiful tapa banners that hang from the ceiling and sway in the breeze. It continues in the pool and sundeck on the sixth floor, the restaurant off the lobby, and on into the rooms, each of which has a very large lanai; some of the views are breathtaking. The rooms all have phone and color TV. You have your choice here of several accommodations. If you want a refrigerator, take one of the hotel rooms, which have one or two double beds. During the summer season, April 1 to December 20, these are $75 to $86; the rest of the year, they are $96 to $106. Or you can have a studio with full kitchenette for $86 to $96 in summer, $106 to $117 the rest of the year. Then there are one-bedroom suites with full kitchen—there are four of these per floor—that go for $133 to $164 in summer, $161 to $194 in winter, for up to four guests. Island Colony is truly a beautiful place, abounding in *aloha.* AE, DC, JCB, MC, V. Parking: $7.50 per day.

Colony's **Pacific Monarch Hotel and Condominium,** 142 Uluniu Ave., Honolulu, HI 96815 (tel. 808/923-9805; fax 808/924-3220; reservations toll free 800/777-1700), is choicely located just a block from Kuhio Beach, right behind the Hyatt Regency Waikiki. It's a handsome modern skyscraper, and a very convenient Waikiki address. Studios and one-bedroom apartments are large, pleasant, and nicely decorated, with air conditioning, color TV, phone, full bath, all the amenities. Studios, all for one or two people, have wet bar, refrigerator, and hot plate, and rent for $85 a day superior, $95 a day deluxe from April 1 to December 21. The rest of the year, it's $95 and $105. One-bedroom apartments, for one to four people, boast full kitchens and cost $120 a day superior, $130 a day deluxe during the regular season; the rest of the year, they rent for $130 and $140. All rates include daily maid service. An extra person is charged $15 per night; children under 17 free when sharing existing beds with parents. Many of the lanais are quite large and offer views (depending on the floor and angle) of Diamond Head, the ocean, and the lights and sights of Waikiki. Facilities are excellent: a secured building, sky-top pool, sundeck, Jacuzzi, and even a sauna with a picture-window view of Diamond Head! Car and condo packages are often available. Tops for comfort, convenience, and easy living. AE, CB, DC, DISC, JCB, MC, V. Parking: $6 per day.

The **Waikiki Banyan,** 201 Ohua Ave., Honolulu, HI 96815 (tel. 808/922-0555; reservations toll free 800/472-8449 from California, 800/854-8843 from the rest of the U.S. 800/824-8968 from Canada; fax 714/497-4183) is perfect for those who want the at-home comforts of a condominium apartment combined with the attentions of a full hotel—daily maid service, bell service, a 24-hour front desk, and much more. That "much more" includes an enormous sixth-floor recreation deck, complete with pool, tennis court, sauna, barbecue areas, snack bar, and a children's play area—a great choice for families—all within sight of glorious mountain views. The Waikiki Banyan is a huge place, 38 stories high, recently renovated (note the stunning lacquer wall mural in the lobby, hand-carved and hand-painted in Hong Kong), with about 295 rental units. Each of these is a two-room suite, nicely if not elaborately decorated, but very comfortable; each has a large living-dining area, a well-equipped kitchen, a sofa bed in the living room, two twins in the bedroom, air conditioning, color TV, private phone. You're well set up for vacation living here. One-bedroom apartments range from $80 to $107 double. Extra persons are $7 each. AE, MC, V. Parking: $3 per day.

Right at the corner of the Ala Wai and Seaside Avenue is the **Outrigger Seaside Suites Hotel,** 440 Seaside Ave., Honolulu, HI 96815 (tel. 808/922-2382; reservations toll free 800/773-7777 from U.S. and Canada, 0014/800/126-985 from Australia; toll free fax 800/456-4329 from U.S. and Canada). Another member of the ubiquitous Outrigger Hotels chain, this 56-room high-rise offers facilities for very comfortable living. Attractively styled in Polynesian decor, these are all one- and two-bedroom apartments, each boasting two bathrooms; a kitchenette with microwave oven, hot plate, refrigerator, toaster-oven; two or three color TVs per unit; two telephones; and air conditioning. There's plenty of covered parking. No pool, but guests can use the pool facilities of nearby Outrigger hotels. From April 1 through December 18, rates for up to four persons are $110 for a moderate one-bedroom suite with kitchenette; $120 for a deluxe one-bedroom with kitchenette; $150 for a two-bedroom suite with kitchenette that can sleep up to six. The rest of the year, rates for the one-bedrooms are $130 and $140, for the two-bedrooms, $190. Complimentary continental breakfast is served daily. Cars from Dollar Rent-A-Car are free for every day of your stay if you request the "Outrigger Free Ride" package when making reservations. AE, CB, DC, DISC, JCB, MC, V. Parking: $6 per day.

5. Budget Hotels: Under $80 Per Night

There's a friendly feeling about the modest little **Royal Grove Hotel,** 151 Uluniu Ave., Honolulu, HI 96815 (tel. 808/923-7691), where the hospitable Fong family is in charge. Just a block away from Kuhio Beach, the six-story pink hotel has a small pool right on the premises, a grocery shop, health-food store, and Korean restaurant off the lobby, an attentive staff, and some 85 nicely put-together rooms whose prices begin as low as $36 for a single or a double. Studio units go up to $60. Comfortable kitchenette units begin at $40.52, and for $52 and up you can have your choice of kitchenette units with their own lanais. The one-bedroom apartments are good buys, too, from $70 to $85, and it's $10 for an extra person. This is a one-of-a-kind place, and the faithful fans who come back year after year practically consider it a second home. AE, DC, MC, V.

If the graciousness and charm of a small hotel mean a lot to you, then we think you'll be as happy as we were to discover the **Ilima Hotel,** 445 Nohonani St., Honolulu, HI 96815 (tel. 808/923-1877), tucked away on a quiet street near the Ala Wai Canal. Comfort and convenience are the keys here: Every room in this attractive hotel has a modern, fully equipped kitchen, color TV, private lanai, radio, telephone, double long-boy beds, and full tub-shower combination. Sun-worshippers will love the two sundecks atop the 10th floor, as well as the ground-level pool area with its ample sunning space on one side and tree-shaded comfort on the other. Fitness fans will appreciate the exercise room and sauna off the pool area. Business travelers will make good use of the fully equipped conference room. And everyone will welcome the free parking and the free local phone calls.

As for the rooms, they are impeccably clean and attractively furnished in Polynesian style, with rattan furniture and plush carpeting. From April 1 to December 14, the studios, which have two double beds and can easily accommodate four, run from $73 to $99 single, $82 to $113 double. They're all the same, but the rates get progressively higher as you go up and the views get better. It's $8 for each additional grown-up, and $6 for a crib or rollaway. There are also one-bedroom suites, which can accommodate up to three persons, at $121 standard, $141 superior, $154 deluxe (the latter for a king-size, waveless waterbed). Large one-bedroom suites, good for up to four persons, are $152 and $168. Two-bedroom suites for up to four are $172 and $189. The penthouse units can be utilized as one-, two-, or three-bedroom suites, and rent for $124, $245, and $369. From December 15 through March 31, add $12 to all rates.

The Ilima is close to the Ala Wai, so it's slightly removed from the hustle and bustle of Waikiki, but just a few minutes' stroll takes you to where the action is. AE, DC, JCB, MC, V.

The **Hawaiian King Hotel,** 417 Nohonani St., Honolulu, HI

96815 (tel. 808/922-3894; reservations toll free 800/727-1707 in the U.S.), is a five-story condominium apartment building centering around a lovely garden and pool area, the place to chat with fellow guests. And accommodations are definitely superior to many in Waikiki. Each unit, designed with the family in mind, is a handsome, beautifully decorated suite, with large living room, separate bedroom, a full kitchenette (and we mean full, down to the disposal unit in the sink) separated from the living room by a counter, and carpeting in the living room and on the lanai. As further blessings, all the apartments are air-conditioned, and as quiet as they are attractive. Many of the apartments here have been uniquely decorated. New here are corporate suites, spacious renovated one-bedroom apartments that include a washer/dryer, microwave, VCR, answering machine, and typewriter. There's a cocktail lounge, minimart, and laundry at hand. Rates during the low season, April 1 to May 31 and September 1 to December 14, are standard $63 a day, moderate $70 a day, deluxe $75 a day, corporate suite $85 a day; each additional person is $5. During high season, December 15 to March 31 and June 1 to August 31, rates are standard $85 a day, moderate $90 a day, deluxe $95 a day, corporate suite $105 a day; each additional person is $10. For quality, comfort, and charm, an excellent choice.

Most centrally located hotels in Waikiki have more than their share of street noise. **Waikiki Lanais**, 2452 Tusitala St., Honolulu, HI 96815 (tel. 808/923-0994; reservations toll free 800/367-7042), has a half-hidden location on a secluded street that seems to block out street noises and traffic, even though it's only a block away on one side from the Ala Wai Canal and a few short blocks on the other side from the sands of Waikiki. This 23-story condominium hotel, with 120 units available for rental, has plenty of good things going for it: attractive one- and two-bedroom apartments furnished with light woods, director's chairs, nice artwork on the walls, and spacious and thoroughly equipped kitchens. All units are air-conditioned, of good size, have color TV, telephone, and private lanai. The rooftop recreation deck, with its panoramic view of mountains and ocean, is great for parties and cookouts. The sixth-floor recreation deck boasts a small pool, Jacuzzi, sauna, and exercise room. From April 1 to December 19, you can get a one-bedroom apartment for one or two people for $90 a night; a two-bedroom apartment for up to four people is $115. In winter, the rates are $110 and $135. Children under 7 stay free with parents; an extra person is charged $10 daily; minimum stay is three nights. Parking is free for guests, and there is a coin-operated laundry on the premises.

The **Marine Surf**, 364 Seaside Ave. (corner Kuhio), Honolulu, HI 96815 (tel. 808/923-0277; fax 808/926-5915; reservations toll free 800/367-5176), boasts a central location just a block from bustling Kalakaua Avenue. And that's not all it boasts. For $70 single or double, from April 1 to December 21 ($85 the rest of the year) you get a spacious studio apartment, not just a hotel room. This means a fully equipped electric kitchen and a dining area. Give them points, too, for color television, sliding glass doors to a furnished lanai, and two extra-length double beds. The views get better as you go up, and the rates go up accordingly: $75 or $90 for superior rooms, $80 or $95 for deluxe rooms; some penthouse suites available at $120 or $135. No charge for children under 12 unless they require a crib, $12. An extra adult is $12, but there is no space for rollaways. The swimming pool in this 23-story building is on the fourth floor. You'll find a quiet, conservative lobby, but bright, colorful apartments. Inside the building is Matteo's, a longtime favorite for superb Italian food. AE, CB, DC, MC, V. Parking: $3 per day.

It's hard to ask for a more central location in Waikiki than the one enjoyed by the handsome **Coral Reef,** 2299 Kuhio Ave., Honolulu, HI 96815 (tel. 808/922-1262; fax 808/922-5048; reservations toll free 800/922-7866). It's next door to the bustling International Market Place, and the mood here, too, is one of excitement and fun, with shops, restaurants, and a supper club all holding forth on the main floor. Upstairs are some 243 rooms, each of good size and nicely furnished in island style, with private lanai, carpeting, air conditioning, a desk, and a cable TV set in every room. Rooms have either two double beds or one double and one single. Rates are $65 single or double from April 1 to December 19, $85 from December 20 to March 31. The hotel also specializes in moderately priced suites, eminently suitable for large families, at around $95. An extra person is $10. The hotel is managed by Aston Hotels and Resorts, 2255 Kalakaua Ave., Honolulu, HI 96815. Public parking next door.

The **Outrigger Village,** 240 Lewers St., Honolulu, HI 96815 (tel. 808/923-3881; reservations toll free 800/733-7777 from the U.S. and Canada, 0014/800/125-642 from Australia; toll free fax 800/456-4329), enjoys a great location in the midst of all the Waikiki action, and one of the prettiest stretches of Waikiki Beach awaits just across Kalia Road. The enormous lobby boasts several shops and a swimming pool located just behind the reservations desk! The hotel is air-conditioned throughout, and there is a TV set in each of the 439 attractively furnished rooms, most of which have lanais. The decor is modern with a Polynesian flair. Cars from Dollar Rent-A-Car are free for every day of your stay if you request the "Outrigger Free Ride" package when making reservations. During regular season, April 1 to December 18, double rates are $80 to $95; kitchenette rooms are $85 to $90. The kitchenette units have a sink, half-size refrigerator with cupboard and counter space, and hot plates—perfectly adequate for light meals. Add $10 per day for each additional person. Two-room suites with kitchenettes go for around $130. During the rest of the year, standard rooms are $90 to $105; rooms with kitchenettes are $95 to $100; two-room suites are $120 and $130. Outrigger Village also boasts an attractive coffee shop and a cocktail lounge. AE, CB, DC, DISC, JCB, MC, V.

If there is a "heart" of Waikiki, the **Outrigger Reef Tower Hotel** must be it. Located at 227 Lewers St., Honolulu, HI 96815 (tel. 808/924-8844; reservations toll free 800/733-7777 from U.S. and Canada, 0014-800-125-642 from Australia; toll free fax 800/456-4329), half a block from the beach in one direction and half a block from busy Kalakaua Avenue in the other, it is right in the midst of everything, as well as being the home of the Al Harrington Show at the Polynesian Palace. The Islander Coffee Shop and Lewers Street Fish Company offer nourishment, and the Irish Rose Saloon is a jolly gathering spot. Accommodations here lean toward the living-room-by-day, bedroom-by-night feeling; most rooms are equipped with a refrigerator, and some—at higher price levels—also have a kitchenette. A Dollar Rent-A-Car is free for every day of your stay if you request the "Outrigger Free Ride" package when making reservations. From April 1 to December 18, standard rooms are $75, moderate rooms $80, deluxe rooms $85. Don't expect much in the way of views here, since the property is really socked in by big hotels. Be satisfied with a glimpse of the ocean or mountains or the pool of a nearby hotel. Moderate kitchenette units are $85, deluxe $95. Suites with kitchenette for up to four people are $100 to $110. The rest of the year, standard and moderate rooms are $85 and $90; kitchenette units are $95 and $105; studio suites are $110 to $120; and suites with kitchenette are $100 to $120. AE, CB, DC, DISC, JCB, MC, V. Parking: $6 per day.

Another very popular part of this chain is the **Outrigger Waikiki Tower,** 200 Lewers St., Honolulu, HI 96815 (tel. 808/922-6424; reservations toll free 800/733-7777 from the U.S. and Canada, 0014/800/125-642 from Australia; toll free fax 800/456-4329), and very pleasant it is. The back of the attractive open lobby looks onto the pool area it shares with its cousin, the Outrigger Edgewater, and the beach is a very short walk away. Just off the lobby is the attractive and moderately priced Waikiki Broiler Restaurant, which is not just the usual hotel coffee shop. The rooms are smartly decorated in brightly colored floral schemes, bathrooms have full tub and shower, and all rooms have a direct-dial phone, a refrigerator, color TV, in-room safe, and air conditioning. Most rooms have a lanai; corner rooms have two lanais; and to create a suite, two corner rooms can be opened up so that you have three lanais and two TV sets! All corner rooms have a kitchenette (they are the only ones that do). Cars from Dollar Rent-A-Car are free for every day of your stay if you request the "Outrigger Free Ride" package when making reservations. From April 1 to December 18, doubles are $80 to $95; kitchenette rooms are $85 to $100; junior suites (for up to three persons) are $120 to $130. The rest of the year, the rates are $90 to $105 for rooms, $95 to $110 for kitchenette units, $120 for junior suites. An extra person is charged $15. AE, CB, DC, DISC, JCB, MC, V.

With only 185 rooms, the **Waikiki Gateway Hotel,** 2070 Kalakaua Ave., Honolulu, HI 96815 (tel. 808/955-3741; fax 808/955-1313; reservations toll free 800/633-8799 from U.S. mainland and Canada) isn't one of the "big" Waikiki hotels, but it is a small charmer. Gray carpeting in the lobby is echoed in the wall murals and beautifully complemented by the rich-toned cane furniture and the deep red-and-blue color scheme. Each room has a telephone, cable color TV, air conditioning, an under-the-counter refrigerator, an in-room safe, and a beautiful bathroom with full tub and shower. And each room boasts a lanai—some even have two. One of the island's finest restaurants, Nick's Fishmarket, is right in the lobby, proclaimed by a large wall aquarium. And there are laundry facilities on the fourth floor, adjacent to the sundeck and the delicious blue pool backed by a wall of lava rock. The Waikiki Gateway is about a 10-minute walk to the beach, but TheBUS, which stops out front, will get you there promptly. From April 1 to December 20, standard rooms (on the 3rd to 7th floors) are $55; superior rooms (8th to 15th floors) are $70; deluxe rooms with partial ocean view are $80; a junior penthouse suite is $95; and a penthouse suite is $115. The rest of the year, these accommodations go for $80, $85, $90, $105, and $125. An additional person is charged $15. AE, DC, JCB, MC, V. Limited parking at $4 per day.

There's a very comfortable feeling about the **Ambassador Hotel of Waikiki,** 2040 Kuhio Ave., Honolulu, HI 96815 (tel. 808/941-7777; fax 808/922-4579). It's neither too large nor too small, has a good location near the entrance to Waikiki, and the rooms are comfortable and attractive. All are done up in studio style, and they have air conditioning, telephone, and a sliding glass door opening onto a private lanai. The views are bigger and better in certain locations, those with higher price tags. Rates are $72 to $96 single, $80 to $104 double. We especially like the one-bedroom suites, which include full electric kitchen, and the corner suites with their great views of the ocean and Diamond Head. Here the price is $140 to $165 single or double; add $15 for an extra person. You can have breakfast, lunch, or dinner at the Café Ambassador, or drinks at the Embassy Bar, right on the premises. And if you're too lazy to walk to the Pacific, there's a large pool and sundeck lanai one floor above the bustle of Waikiki; drinks and snacks are at the ready, too. AE, CB, DC, JCB, MC, V. Parking: $3 per day.

For those who like the feeling of a big and coolly efficient hotel, the 15-story, 204-room **Aloha Surf,** 444 Kanekapolei St., Honolulu, HI 96815 (tel. 808/923-0222; fax 808/924-7160; reservations toll free 800/423-4514), is an excellent choice. The hotel looks out on the Ala Wai Canal and is about a 10-minute walk from the beach. A beauty shop, gift shop, outdoor coffee shop, and pool all adjoin the almost wide-open lobby. Rooms are air-conditioned, and have wall-to-wall carpeting and bright but tasteful color schemes. All rooms have color television and either two twins or two queen-size beds; most have a lanai, and some have a kitchenette. As for the views, which start a few floors above street level, they are of the Koolau Mountains and a tiny bit of ocean. The rates remain stable year round, so don't worry about higher winter rates. Even so, these rates compete well with others in less favorable locations. Standard rooms rent for $75, single or double; moderate rooms with private lanai go for $85; and rooms with kitchenette cost $95. Penthouse units run from $110 to $135. An extra person is $10. AE, DISC, MC, V. Parking: $6 per day.

The **Waikiki Sand Villa** at 2375 Ala Wai Blvd., Honolulu, HI 96815 (tel. 808/922-4744; fax 808/923-2541; reservations toll free 800/247-1403 from the U.S., Puerto Rico, and Virgin Islands), does look like a sandcastle: It's made of sand-colored material and is castle-shaped. The lobby and dining room feature a Hawaiian plantation manor style reminiscent of the 1930s, with ceiling cornices, a pink Chinese slate floor, and tapestry-upholstered couches. Guest rooms all include a refrigerator, color TV, and an in-room safe for valuables. They are of good size and attractively decorated in rattan furniture and printed bedspreads. Rates depend solely on the floor and view, and run $49 single or double for standard accommodations, $59 superior, $69 deluxe. For a triple or quad, add $10 per person. These rates go up $10 to $15 in the winter season. Children under 8 stay free unless they require a rollaway or crib. AE, DC, DISC, JCB, MC, V. Parking: $4 per day.

The **Pagoda Hotel,** 1525 Rycroft St., Honolulu, HI 96814 (tel. 808/941-6611; fax 808/922-8061; reservations toll free 800/367-6060 from the U.S. and Canada), comes complete with a scenic floating restaurant on its premises. The 340-room complex is near the Ala Moana Shopping Center, which means about a 10-minute bus ride or drive to the heart of Waikiki. There are two swimming pools on the grounds. Two buildings face each other across Rycroft Street. One, called the hotel, has 200 newly renovated rooms with refrigerators; these run $75 moderate (floors 1 to 4), $85 deluxe (floors 5 to 12). The other building, called the Pagoda Terrace, has 160 kitchenette units; studios are $70, one-bedroom units for up to four people are $90, and two-bedroom suites for up to four are $105. Add $15 for an extra person in the room.

Closer to Waikiki, across Ala Moana Boulevard from the Ilikai, and equaling it in prime proximity to both the beach and the Ala Moana Shopping Center, is the **Hawaii Dynasty Hotel,** 1830 Ala Moana Blvd., Honolulu, HI 96815 (tel. 808/955-1111; reservations toll free 800/421-6662). Rising 17 stories, this 206-room resort is set well back from traffic noise, and since all rooms are air-conditioned, peace and quiet are doubly assured. There's a large pool and sundeck, a round-the-clock restaurant, and parking available. Rooms are regular size, but the bed sizes are deluxe. When you ask for twins, you get double beds. Closets, too, are big, and a smart vanitorium extends the whole length of the tub-and-shower-equipped bathroom. The rooms, nicely decorated, have color TV with in-room movies, air conditioning, and telephone; most have peeks at the ocean; some feature a lanai.

From April 16 to December 19, standard rooms are $55, deluxe are $60, superior/deluxe are $65, and suites, for up to four persons, are $150. Extra adults pay $12; there is no charge for children under 18 sharing their parents' room. From April 16 to December 19, there is a $15 per-day surcharge. AE, DC, MC, V. Parking: $3.50 per day.

IV

HONOLULU DINING DISCOVERIES

1. ELEGANT & EXPENSIVE: DINNER FROM $40

2. MEDIUM-RANGE MEALS ($20 TO $40)

3. INFORMAL & INEXPENSIVE ($10 TO $20 AND UNDER)

Do tourists spend more time eating than doing anything else? Statistics could never prove it, of course, but it has always seemed to us that dining out is one of the most popular pastimes under the Hawaiian sun. And with good reason: Although Hawaii is not one of the true gourmet capitals of the world, it embraces a wealth of cultural traditions from all over, and dining here can be more fun — and more adventurous — than almost anyplace else. Honolulu itself has perhaps a dozen great restaurants, even a few that are considered world-class, scores of unusual and interesting ones, and many where the food is hearty, well priced, and just what you would expect from a good restaurant back home. Because there are so many restaurants in Honolulu, however, and in so many price categories, some guidance is in order. You're not going to spend every evening dining out with wine and candlelight and nouvelle cuisine; neither are you going to eat all your meals at beachside burger stands or in the coffee shop of your hotel. What we've done here, then, is to track down several dozen of what we consider the best restaurants in town, no matter how much or how little you want to pay or what kind of dining experience you're after. And we've divided these restaurants into three categories. To wit:

1. Elegant and Expensive. Here we'll give you the details on a group of restaurants that are at the top of our list, where the cuisine, the service, the ambience, the view — or any combination thereof — all make for a memorable experience. Expect to pay at least $40, maybe a good deal more, for dinner. A few cocktails before, the proper wine during, and a bit of liqueur after will, of course, add up. Not to mention the tax and the tip. When it's feasible, we'll also tell you how you can enjoy the same glorious surroundings and superb food for a much lower tab—at lunch. At these places, reservations are a must. And when you phone, inquire about dress; although most Honolulu restaurants are eminently casual, a few prefer that men wear jackets and ties. (At some island restaurants, "dress" means pants and shoes.)

2. Medium-Range Meals. The bulk of the restaurants we'll describe cover the range from about $20 to $40 for dinner. Many of these offer excellent table d'hôte dinners for reasonable prices. Here you'll continue to sample some of the international cuisines that have found a home in the islands—Japanese, Chinese, Mexican, Indonesian, Thai, French, Hawaiian, Italian, Continental. And there'll be no shortage of that old Hawaiian favorite, the steak house. (This is the 50th *American* state, remember?)

3. Informal and Inexpensive. Which means exactly what it says. These are casual, come-as-you-are places, a few of them coffeehouses (but in the islands, even the coffeehouses are exotic), where you can expect to get dinner for $10 to $20 or under. Some are open around the clock, in case that hungry feeling should strike at an unexpected hour.

You'll note that under each main category we cover restaurants in Waikiki, in the downtown Honolulu area or beyond, or near the Ala Moana area. With just a few exceptions, all our choices are a short drive, or bus ride, or taxi ride away. (We'll tell you about a few restaurants in Windward Oahu when we take a later tour around the island.)

---

1. Elegant & Expensive: Dinner from $40

Under another name, **The Secret,** the restaurant on the third floor of the Hawaiian Regent Hotel, 2552 Kalakaua Ave., has long held a reputation as one of Honolulu's best. The name-change is only a legality; everything else here is still the same. The decor is extraordinary, the service excellent, and the continental cuisine of a very high order, filled with unexpected touches. You dine beneath open-beam ceilings, magnificent copper chandeliers, and multicolored Camelot banners against a romantic background of rippling fountains flowing over black river rocks, tropical wall plantings, and koa wall mosaics. You certainly have the right to expect the very best cuisine, and the menu of chefs Klaus Saballus and Wolfgang Horndlein lives up to expectations.

We said the touches were unusual, and that they are. Instead of ordinary bread, you are served Indian naan bread, baked in an imported clay charcoal-heated oven. A duck liver pâté is served along with the butter—a whole crock of both. A tray of tiny relishes (miniature baby corn, pickled tomatoes, onions) is yours to nibble on while you study the wine list (the house has an excellent cellar) and order your entrée, priced from $26 to $36.50, à la carte. You could start your meal with the unique iced appetizer buffet, your pick, for $12, of such surprises as blue-point oysters, poached salmon medallions, marinated herring, vinaigrette shrimp, and fresh artichoke

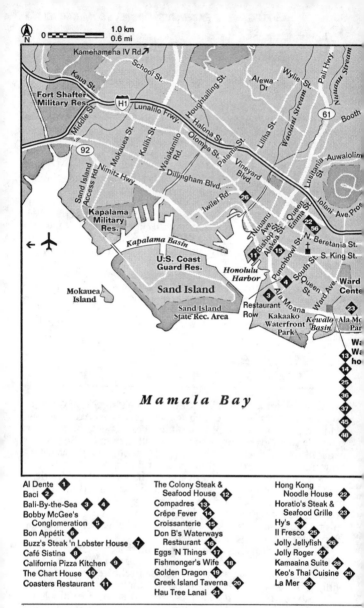

Map legend (restaurant listings):

Al Dente ❶
Baci ❷
Bali-By-the-Sea ❸ ❹
Bobby McGee's Conglomeration ❺
Bon Appétit ❻
Buzz's Steak 'n Lobster House ❼
Café Sistina ❽
California Pizza Kitchen ❾
The Chart House ❿
Coasters Restaurant ⓫

The Colony Steak & Seafood House ⓬
Compadres ⓭
Crêpe Fever ⓮
Croissanterie ⓯
Don B's Waterways Restaurant ⓰
Eggs 'N Things ⓱
Fishmonger's Wife ⓲
Golden Dragon ⓳
Greek Island Taverna ⓴
Hau Tree Lanai ㉑

Hong Kong Noodle House ㉒
Horatio's Steak & Seafood Grille ㉓
Hy's ㉔
Il Fresco ㉕
Jolly Jellyfish ㉖
Jolly Roger ㉗
Kamaaina Suite ㉘
Keo's Thai Cuisine ㉙
La Mer ㉚

hearts. For your main course, choose among the likes of canard à l'orange (gently crisped duck flavored with Burgundy liqueur); scampi provençale; or the splendid seafood casserole. And one person, instead of the usual two, may order the rack of spring lamb provençale, served with mint sauce and such fresh vegetables as

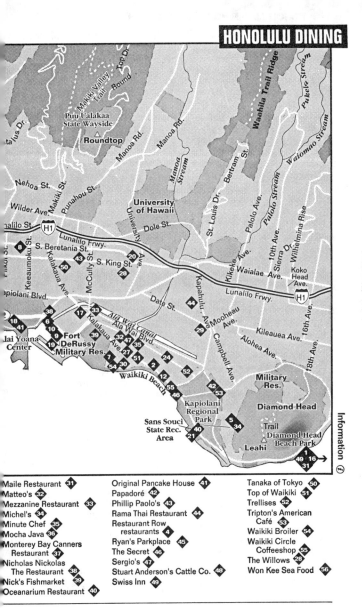

Maile Restaurant ◆31
Matteo's ◆32
Mezzanine Restaurant ◆33
Michel's ◆34
Minute Chef ◆35
Mocha Java ◆36
Monterey Bay Canners
 Restaurant ◆37
Nicholas Nickolas
 The Restaurant ◆38
Nick's Fishmarket ◆39
Oceanarium Restaurant ◆40

Original Pancake House ◆41
Papadoré ◆42
Phillip Paolo's ◆43
Rama Thai Restaurant ◆44
Restaurant Row
 restaurants ◆4
Ryan's Parkplace ◆45
The Secret ◆46
Sergio's ◆47
Stuart Anderson's Cattle Co. ◆48
Swiss Inn ◆49

Tanaka of Tokyo ◆50
Top of Waikiki ◆51
Trellises ◆52
Tripton's American
 Café ◆53
Waikiki Broiler ◆54
Waikiki Circle
 Coffeeshop ◆55
The Willows ◆28
Won Kee Sea Food ◆56

gourmet Belgian endive. Noteworthy specials often include frogs'
legs provençale with garlic butter, fresh onaga, and steak Diane, prepared tableside. For dessert, it's hard to resist the hot Grand
Marnier—or chocolate, lemon, or macadamia—soufflés. But do
save some room for the surprise of the evening, as your waitress

places a frosted dish on your table with white (dry ice) clouds drifting down from it, like a stage setting of a dream. On it are chocolate-covered ice-cream bonbons—courtesy of the house. And, oh yes, while you're feasting, strolling musicians wander from table to table to play your requests.

The Secret is open for dinner from 6:30 to 11pm daily. Reservations are highly recommended: phone 922-6611. Jackets suggested for the men; validated parking.

Hidden away in the far reaches of Waikiki, down steps, around corridors, and behind doors, is a small restaurant to which the gourmets of the world have beaten a path. This is **Michel's,** in the Colony Surf hotel at 2895 Kalakaua Ave. The reason? Michel's chefs, whose culinary artistry is every bit as magical as the view from your table, which can rival anything on the Riviera—you're practically next to the incredibly blue-green Pacific, and you can watch the boats and bathers of the Outrigger Canoe Club as you dine on the fruits of Michel's wizardry. For example, some chefs simply cook snails; at Michel's they're sautéed in burgundy wine and topped with a tantalizing mixture of garlic (ever so slight), parsley, and butter. Some chefs just toss salads; at Michel's, island bibb lettuce is graced with ripe tomatoes, green peppers, hard-cooked eggs, green onions, exotic herbs, and Michel's own French dressing, all gently tossed at your table. Little matter that the snails are $14 the half dozen or the salad $7 per person or that the entrées range from $29 to $50. How can you put a price on ecstasy? We might as well tell you right now that Michel's is not the place to go if you are in a hurry. This is no steam-table operation, and one of the ingredients of the culinary art is time. Many discriminating diners who have been coming to Michel's over the years phone a day ahead for their favorite special dishes. You cannot rush such delights as canard rôti with sauce Bigarade, or chateaubriand for two, or opakapaka simmered in champagne sauce. For dessert, how about strawberries Romanoff, at $6? The very best wines and liquors, *mais certainement.* Check, please.

Inside Information Department: If you can't afford to have dinner at Michel's more than once (or not even once), why, live like the rich at lunchtime. Lunch, served daily except Saturday from 11:30am to 3pm, is also à la carte, with cheese soufflés at $14, salads from $8, omelets and other entrées averaging $12 to $17. Or try the Sunday champagne brunch, served from 11am to 3pm, and a lovely treat. Plus, they open at 7am for delicious breakfasts starting at $8.50. Reservations, of course: phone 923-6552.

Gone are the days when one had to travel all the way to France to experience the finest in French cooking. Now one needs travel only to—Hawaii. **La Mer** at the Halekulani hotel, 2199 Kalia Rd., would surely receive a star or two from Michelin if it were in France instead of Honolulu; indeed, its extraordinary corporate chef, Philippe Padovani, who hails from Lyons, the gastronomic center that has produced many of France's great chefs, has displayed his talent in six Michelin-starred restaurants in the past 19 years. Now he is here and doing something quite wonderful, creating a new kind of French cuisine, one with an island influence. Padovani prefers to let the flavors of juices and herbs highlight the natural flavor of the ingredients—fish from local waters, vegetables and fruits grown on

Sophisticated Dining

If there is one restaurant that bespeaks the sophistication of the new Honolulu, then that restaurant must surely be **The Black Orchid,** anchor and star of Honolulu's upbeat Restaurant Row, 500 Ala Moana Blvd.; you can get there by taxi, bus, or the Waikiki Trolley. An overnight sensation since its opening in 1988, thanks to the skill and celebrity of owners Randy Shock and Pat Bowlen (part owner of the Denver Broncos), the Black Orchid is certainly *the* place for entertainment—be it the top Hawaiian and mainland artists who perform each night, the people to watch, or the truly outstanding gourmet food. The setting is art deco, with black ceilings, etched glass, neon-glow lighting, murals by Tamara of socialites of the 1930s; the place is large, but skillful seating makes it seem intimate; and the tuxedoed waiters are just as nice to the unknown diner as to the big names that like to rendezvous here.

Cuisine is upbeat Californian, with an emphasis on fresh ingredients, deft sauces, and superb island fish fresh from the morning's auction block. The wine list is as good as you would expect. For appetizers ($5.95 to $11.95), you might try the brie and mango quesadilla filled with grapes and herbs, the South Pacific lobster risotto, or the black-and-blue ahi, pan-seared with Cajun spices. Salads, like the seafood pasta salad, are quite special. Entrées ($21.95 to $29.95) change frequently, but are likely to include veal medallions in Armagnac, grilled fresh salmon with guava hollandaise, linguine with tiger prawns in a garlic Chardonnay sauce, rack of lamb with chutney, and grilled breast of chicken in a lemon marinade. Lobster fanciers should not miss "Lobster Sunday," when such entrées as lobster thermidor, lobster with black bean sauce, and live Maine lobster are all served at a reasonable $21.95.

But whatever else you have, save room for one of the desserts, presented on a silver tray and altogether irresistible. Who would dream of passing up the Black Orchid Torte (rum chiffon mousse layered with chocolate truffles and topped with a dark icing) or the fudgelike flourless chocolate cake crowned with champagne zabaglione?

The Black Orchid serves dinner every night, from 6pm on, and a late-night appetizer menu until 3am. Lunch, featuring fresh pasta, hamburgers, sandwiches, and catch of the day, is served weekdays only, from 11am to 2pm, and is very popular with the downtown business crowd. There's entertainment and music to dance by every night. Reservations are essential: Make them at least several days in advance for weekend seating. Phone: 521-1131. AE, CB, DC, DISC, JCB, MC, V.

local farms, imported products from Europe and the mainland. He is a stickler for detail; when fish is smoked, for example, it is smoked for that service only, never for the next day. Trained in pastry baking by the famed Gaston Lenôtre, he creates all his own desserts—and they are in the unforgettable category. Combine this with a setting of subdued elegance—plush carpeting, rich Asian-inspired mural wall coverings, tables set far apart and looking out over the moonlight on the ocean—and a meal at *Travel/Holiday* award-winning La Mer becomes a feast for palate and senses, certainly one of the great dining experiences of Honolulu.

Although there is an à la carte menu, the best plan is to opt for one of the two different five-course, prix-fixe menus at either $75 or $95, which change monthly. As soon as you sit down, you are offered a complimentary glass of French champagne and an appetizer. You may order from a distinguished wine list. A typical meal might begin with crusted hot jellied consommé of duck or a salad of California roasted squab with garlic and spinach leaves; or perhaps a ragoût of Kona crab with fresh pasta. This might be followed by a fish course such as broiled Norwegian salmon with risotto and a Chardonnay sauce or poached onaga with wilted greens and a three caviar sauce; and then a meat course such as roasted rack of veal with sweetbreads and wild mushrooms or marinated loin of lamb in a thyme and garlic sauce. A magnificent assortment of French cheeses —at least 15 of them the night we were there—follows, accompanied by tasty walnut bread. And then, the pièce de résistance—the dessert cart; you're welcome to two or three. Dessert may be the sunburst of strawberries with almond cream and fresh mint; or heavenly crêpes filled with fresh fruits and a Grand Marnier pastry cream with citrus sauce; or lilikoi soufflé and kiwi coulis. Just when you're convinced you couldn't touch another thing, along comes a tray of friandises (tiny cookies and pastries) along with homemade chocolate truffles. *Magnifique!*

La Mer serves dinner nightly from 6 to 10pm; jackets are required for the gentlemen. Sunday brunch is on from 9am to 1pm. Reservations, *mais certainement:* phone 923-2311. AE, CB, DC, JCB, MC, V.

A world-class dining experience can be had at the **Kamaaina Suite,** a restaurant within a restaurant, its host restaurant being the famous Willows (see below), 901 Hausten St. As soon as you mention the Kamaaina Suite at the reception desk, you are escorted through the Willows' Polynesian-style dining rooms to the rear and up a stairway. Then you enter another world. It could be the dining room of a missionary family or a plantation owner. The finery is matched by the impeccable service. Each month there is a different "Discovery of Taste" menu, in which each guest is offered "tasting portions" of a number of superb selections created by the noted chef de cuisine Kusuma Cooray. A native of Sri Lanka and a graduate of Cordon Bleu, Kusuma is a recognized chef and teacher of the Eastern world's distinctive cuisine, with a worldwide reputation.

A recent meal began with freshly baked brioche with Brie, and an appetizer: filet of beef vinaigrette with herbs and island greens. Then came two entrées separated by an intermezzo of minty lemon sorbet. First, Seafood Symphony, a champagne-poached oyster on seaweed, petite salmon paupiette, and crabmeat-spinach timbale; second, roast breast of duckling with honey, red wine vinegar sauce, onion tartlets, and bacon-flavored beet greens. After this, dessert was wheeled over; it's hard not to succumb to such delights as white chocolate mousse with chocolate sauce and fresh berries in fruit coulis, or hazelnut gâteau with fresh berries and crème anglaise. Coffee and tea, of course. The price is fixed at $42.50 per person, without drinks, tax, or tip. But how can you put a dollar value on an experience like this?

The Kamaaina Suite is open for dinner only, starting at 6pm, with the latest reservations at 8:30pm. Reservations are a must: phone 946-4808. Closed Sunday. AE, CB, DC, DISC, JCB, MC, V.

Far from the madding crowds of Waikiki, **Papadoré**, 3058 Monseratt Ave., is reminiscent of elegant fine-dining houses in Paris or Florence. Cool turquoise walls, chairs upholstered in rich champagne-colored brocade, mirrored ceilings, and lavish flower arrangements provide the background; fresh flowers and candles adorn the tables. Among the tempting list of appetizers, hot and cold, my favorites are the fresh salmon marinated in dill and the crab ravioli in shellfish sauce. Seafood is the specialty here, and there is much to choose from: a classic bouillabaisse, pink snapper grilled with tomato and basil, lobster tails roasted with baby vegetables, live Maine lobster, fresh fish filet prepared in a delicate saffron sauce, and salmon with caviar. Or one might have venison with mushrooms in a red wine sauce, roast lamb with herbed pasta, or veal sweetbreads with asparagus. Entrées go from $15 to $38. Desserts are also amazing: We love the chocolate soufflé, the crème brûlée, and the strawberry puff pastry. Dining here is a not-to-be-missed experience.

Papadoré serves dinner only, from 5:30 to 10:30pm. The bar is open from 5pm to 10:30pm, and there's flute and guitar music here Friday, Saturday, and Sunday, from 5:30 to 10pm. Reservations: 732-9561.

For over 21 years, **Nick's Fishmarket,** tucked way behind a door in the Waikiki Gateway Hotel, 2070 Kalakaua Ave., has been one of Honolulu's premier restaurants. The winner of many *Travel/Holiday* awards, it's recently been cited by *Honolulu* magazine as "One of the Top 20 Restaurants in Honolulu" and by *United Airlines Magazines* as "One of the Top 75 Restaurants in the United States." And no wonder. Co-owners Randy Schock and Patrick Bowlen (who are also in charge at the Black Orchid, see above) attract a fashionable celebrity and sports crowd who make a beeline for reservations when they're in town. Everyone appreciates the super service, the cheerful red carpet, and dark-leather ambience. Executive chef Alex Raidl is acclaimed for his creative presentation of scrupulously fresh and delicious fish, the finest from Hawaiian waters, including mahimahi, ono, opakapaka, ahi, opah, auku, ulua, and red snapper. Local ingredients like papayas, avocados, and Maui onions accentuate the special sauces. Mainland catches like sole, trout, catfish, salmon, and sea scallops are also featured.

It's fun to begin with a few drinks at the animated bar and move on to your table for the main event. You can have a complete dinner for $27.95 that includes Fishmarket chowder or Nick's special salad with creamy spinach dressing, vegetable and beverage, with entrées such as fresh island ono, catfish, Pacific sea scallops, or U.S. prime top sirloin. Or go à la carte with great appetizers like blackened sashimi, escargots bourguignonne, mozzarella marinara, soups, chowders, or hot pasta appetizers; prices go from $6.95 to $12.95. Main course specialties, ranging from $17.95 to $35 (more for Maine lobster, flown in from New England every day), include chicken oregano, broiled veal chop with wild mushrooms, filet mignon with sauce béarnaise, and roast rack of lamb, in addition to the many fresh fish and seafood choices. Nick's also offers some wonderful desserts, presented for selection on a silver tray; favorites include a chocolate mousse cake, coconut cream cake, and the house dessert, Vanbana's Pie—ice cream, bananas, and hot caramel sauce! There's live entertainment in the lounge from 9:30pm, perfect for after-dinner dancing. If you're lucky, you may catch some vacationing performers who just might get up and do a turn or two. Stevie Wonder, Dolly Parton, Dionne Warwick, and the Beach Boys have all been known to do so. Nick's Fishmarket serves dinner only, from 5:30 to 11pm (till midnight weekends), seven days a week; naturally, reservations are a must: phone 955-6333. AE, CB, DC, DISC, JCB, MC, V.

Despite its name, **Bali-By-The-Sea** at the Hilton Hawaiian Village does not have Balinese food. What it does have is a romantic, open-air setting overlooking the ocean, in a room that could be in the Mediterranean, done in whites, pinks, and greens, with beautiful watercolors gracing the white walls, handsome Chinese plates and vases on display, bleached-wood furniture, every chair an armchair, and orchids abounding. Everything about this place—from the complimentary valet parking to the excellent wine list to the deft service—suggests an evening of gracious, romantic, and exemplary dining. And that's just what you'll experience here. Sit down, study the menu, and if you want an incredible soufflé for dessert—chocolate, vanilla, or Grand Marnier—place your order now. Among the appetizers, $6 to $15.75, you could have fresh foie gras of duck, sautéed with apple; seafood in puff pastry with a light saffron sauce; Pacific smoked salmon and smoked ahi. Among the soups, the bisque of shrimp and lobster is outstanding, as is the salad of Manoa lettuce with avocado, papaya, and shrimps in a champagne dressing. As for your main course ($27 to $63), choice is difficult: local friends advise that the Kauai Channel opakapaka with fresh basil sauce is the best opakapaka in Hawaii; but also superb is the roast duck Lawrence, with papaya purée and macadamia-nut liqueur, and the tenderloin of beef with a black peppercorn sauce. If you love game, then you'll love the medallions of venison, with pears, cranberry, and poivrade sauce. And now for dessert: the pastry chef creates new marvels each day, but we'll vote for the house's signature dessert, the Bali Hai: three different local fruit sorbets served on a thin bed of fresh raspberry purée with a sprig of mint. Perfection!

The Bali serves dinner only, every day from 6 to 10pm. Reservations, of course: phone 949-4321. AE, CB, DC, DISC, JCB, MC, V.

Certainly one of the most beautiful restaurants in Hawaii, **Nicholas Nickolas The Restaurant,** 410 Atkinson Dr., occupies the top floor of the Ala Moana Hotel, the tallest building in the state of Hawaii. The view, as one can well imagine, is spectacular, as is the restaurant. The interior has been designed so that every table has a view of the city: the tables and booths are placed around the perimeter; the bar, kitchen, and dance floor are in the middle. Circling the outside wall are tables; against the inner wall, a few steps up, are booths—so private that the occupants control their own lighting!

Dinner and late suppers only are served here. The appetizers are special; they include blackened sashimi, filet bits teriyaki, crêpes Madagascar, to name just a few. An inspired lobster bisque and a spicy gazpacho represent the soup department. Complete dinners are priced $27.95 to $29.95; they include a choice of Nick's classic salad, clam chowder, vegetable, starch and beverage, plus entrées such as swordfish Stavros, fresh fish of the day, boneless breast of chicken Greek-style, fresh vegetable pasta, and seafood brochette. On the à la carte menu (most entrées $19.95 to $26.95) you could have salmon, scallops, veal picatta, lamb chops, or porterhouse steak; all steaks and fish are broiled over kiawe wood. Wonderful salads and the "famous" hash-brown potatoes, grilled and topped with sour cream, chives, and bacon bits, are good extras.

Dinner is served from 5:30 to 11:30pm daily. Dance music is provided by varied entertainers, usually from 9:30pm until 2 or 3am. The Late Night Menu—in effect from 11:30pm—offers some of the dinner appetizers and side dishes: Reservations are a must: phone 955-4466. AE, CB, DC, JCB, MC, V.

In a hotel with the unlikely name of Waikiki Park Heights is a famous steak house called **Hy's,** with the unlikely—for Honolulu —decor of the British Victorian era. Located at 2440 Kuhio, Canadian-based Hy's (you may recognize it from Toronto, Winnipeg, Calgary, or Vancouver) looks like somebody's elegant living room—bookshelves, family portraits, upholstered chairs, turn-of-the-century chandeliers, and mahogany-like walls. Here steak is king: prime meat, charcoal-broiled and served on wooden planks with potatoes of your choice done to your specifications. New York strip is $22.95 to $30.95; filet mignon is $24.75 to $27.95, depending on the size of the portion. All entrées come with soup or salad and delicious hot, fresh garlic-cheese toast. Yes, you can also get rack of lamb or several fish entrées (from $23.95 up), but we wouldn't miss Hy's masterful steaks.

Appetizers (from $5.50) are wide-ranging, including lox, linguine with a delicious clam sauce, and escargot, and for dessert there's a variety of gourmet cheesecakes as well as flaming desserts made tableside. There is, of course, a large wine list in the British tradition. Valet parking. Dinner only, seven days a week, 6 to 11pm, closing a bit earlier on Sunday. For reservations, phone 922-5555.

For one of the ultimate dining experiences in Honolulu, don't miss the **Maile Restaurant** at the Kahala Hilton hotel. The Maile keeps on winning *Travel/Holiday* awards and it's easy to see why. From the moment you walk down the winding staircase to the restaurant, set against a lava wall covered with orchids, you'll know you're in a special, rarefied atmosphere. Although the room is large, the feeling is an intimate one; you dine by candlelight, amid a background of sparkling fountains, beautiful flowers, and truly gracious island hospitality. But the true marvels come from the kitchen. The chef has taken classic dishes from around the world, given them his own island variations, and come up with magnificent results. Dinner is $58 complete, including your selection of appetizer, soup, main course, dessert, and coffee or tea. Possibilities include shrimps and escargots with cèpes mushrooms in a garlic-herb butter, or seared rare ahi (tuna) and a shoyu-mustard sauce among the appetizers; a consommé of beef hidden under a "cage" of pastry or a lobster bisque with champagne cognac among the soups; such main courses as the famous roast duckling Waialae, served with Grand Marnier–orange sauce, or the Hawaiian Trio of opakapaka, mahimahi, and onago, each with its own delicate sauce. Dessert selections include a frozen chocolate soufflé with Bailey's Irish cream and raspberries, or wondrous hot soufflés, like the gingerbread soufflé with prune-Armagnac ice cream and fresh strawberry compote. The "Chef's Inspiration" menu changes weekly and offers complete dinners for $50. On the à la carte menu, entrées run from $30 to $44.

Maile serves dinner only, from 6:30 to 9pm Sunday through Friday, from 6 to 9pm Saturday. Jackets required for the gentlemen Monday through Saturday; optional on Sunday. Reservations are a must: phone 734-2211. AE, CB, DC, DISC, JCB, MC, V.

For a good sampling of the Kahala cuisine at a much lower price, you might try the Hala Terrace, the hotel's seaside restaurant, on a Sunday night for the $30 Royal Hala seafood buffet. It's probably the most lavish buffet table in town, and here you'll get a chance to try such island delicacies as lomi-lomi salmon, limu (seaweed), sashimi, and octopus, as well as more familiar fare, like prime rib, mahimahi, and beef Stroganoff. The Hala Terrace also serves a fabulous Sunday brunch, 11:30am to 2pm, $25 adults, $16.50 children 10 and under.

2. Medium-Range Meals ($20 to $40)

We've got quite a selection here, divided into categories depending on type of cuisine.

AMERICAN—MOSTLY STEAK AND SEAFOOD

Upstairs at Ward Warehouse, with its unobstructed view of Kewalo Basin and those beautiful Hawaiian sunsets, **Horatio's Steak and Seafood Grill** is a longtime favorite with local residents. For the past three years, it's been selected by the readers of *Honolulu* magazine as one of the city's top 20 restaurants. It's pleasantly light and airy, decorated in a modern nautical theme. The bar is a comfortable meeting place, and you might want to start here to sample such pupus as nachos, deep-fried calamari, or kalbi ribs to go along with your drinks. Dinner entrées, accompanied by either soup or salad and baked potatoes or rice, run from about $10.95 to $19.95, and include favorites like kiawe-grilled teriyaki, mahimahi, snapper in ginger-and-lime butter, and the very popular slow-cooked prime rib. Seafood, which comes from Alaska, the Pacific Northwest, and Hawaii, can be steamed, baked, or kiawe grilled. Lunch prices, from $5.95 to $9.95, are reasonable, and there's a lot of variety: homemade deep-dish quiche, spinach and romaine salads, clams in butter-wine sauce are a few possibilities. The crème brûlée and Blums Toffee Coffee Pie are divinely decadent desserts. And there are more desserts where these came from. From 9 to 12pm Wednesday through Saturday, John Basebase entertains. Horatio's is extremely popular, but you can walk in with or without a reservation (tel. 521-5002), since only half of the dining room is held for reservations.

Lunch is served from 11am to 5pm, Monday through Saturday; dinner, from 5 to 10pm, Sunday through Thursday, until 10:30pm Friday and Saturday. AE, MC, V.

Rudyard Kipling would have felt right at home at **The Colony Steak and Seafood House** in the Hyatt Regency Waikiki, 2424 Kalakaua Ave. It's a bit of the British Colonial past in India come to life, with its rattan furniture, palm trees, revolving ceiling fans, gazebo-like tables in the center of the room, and the brilliant use of live greenery creating a warm ambience. Choose your meat: It could be New York teriyaki, New York strip, prime rib, or veal chops, $23.50 to $34. Then proceed to the glorious salad bar, included in the price of your entrée, while your meat selection is being cooked to your order. Dishes like fresh opakapaka, lobster, and shrimp are also available, as well as a few side dishes like the luscious sourdough bread, jumbo mushroom caps broiled in herb butter, or crisp Maui onion rings. The room is open nightly from 6 to 10pm, and the lovely adjoining cocktail lounge, in a harmonizing decor, serves from 6 to 11pm. You'll catch a sophisticated performer, perhaps even ukulele virtuoso Herb Ohta, as we were lucky enough to do on our last visit. Reservations important: 923-1234. AE, DC, JCB, MC, V.

The Chart House, 1765 Ala Moana Blvd., has everything a seafood house in Honolulu should have: a glamorous nautical setting overlooking the boats of the Ala Wai Yacht Harbor, a festive air, warm and friendly service, a menu that offers the freshest of fish and seafood—and all at prices that are refreshingly realistic. No wonder it's been popular for over 20 years! A winding staircase leads up to a multitiered room, enlivened with a stained-glass mural and an aquarium: every table has a waterfront view. Prepare yourself for a wonderful evening. Start with some drinks, select a wine, perhaps order one of the appetizers like oysters Rockefeller or Maryland softshell crabs, then decide on your main course. It could be one of the several fresh catches of the day ($17.95 to $20.95); we recently sampled their opakapaka, flavorfully steamed Chinese style with cilantro and ginger. Or it might be one of the live lobsters, crabs, and prawns; the house specialty is Hawaiian spiny and slipper lobster, market priced, and so delicate they're kept swimming in the tank until you place your order. Shellfish specialties include an excellent bouillabaisse, baked stuffed shrimp, and seafood linguine ($16.95 to $21.95). And there's teriyaki chicken, prime rib, and filet mignon from the grill ($10.95 to $21.95). All dinners are served with a choice of tossed green salad or a cup of hearty chowder, plus new potatoes or pasta or rice; plus squaw bread and a vegetable, so there's really no need to order anything more. But you'll probably find the dessert tray hard to overlook, as we always do; chocolate macadamia nut cream pie and Chart House mud pie (triple layers of chocolate, Kona coffee, and macadamia nut ice cream with fudge and whipped cream on an Oreo cookie crust) are the main temptations.

The Chart House does dinner only, daily from 5:30 to 10:30pm (11pm on weekends). The lounge is open from 4pm to 2am. Reservations advised: 941-6669. AE, CB, DC, DISC, MC, V.

Call a meal at **Bobby McGee's Conglomeration,** in the Colony Surf hotel at 2895 Kalakaua Ave., an experience, a happening. The eight dining rooms are illuminated just enough so you can barely make out the incredible conglomeration of antiques and oddities that fill up every inch of unused space. The costumed waiters (we were once served by Dudly Do Right and by Dracula) keep up an amusing line of banter that can turn the meal into a comedy routine if you'll play along. But the food is also good, and so decently priced that the place is always packed with locals and visitors alike; you sometimes have to wait a day or so just to get a reservation.

Bobby McGee's specialties include their famous deep-fried zucchini and fresh fried potato skins on the appetizer list ($3.95 to $8.95), and for entrées, fresh catch of the day sautéed in a macadamia meunière or other sauce, plus an excellent prime rib of beef, for $12.95 to $16.95. The menu offers a wide variety of items, beginning at $8.95 for lasagna and going up to $23.95 for combination steak and seafood dishes. Along with the entrée come Bobby McGee's extras; all the salad you can eat served from an old-fashioned bathtub, or a fresh spinach salad with hot bacon dressing. (Soup and salad alone are $8.95.) Your meal also includes cooked vegetables or potato, and "special" bread (be sure to ask for it). After all that, and what with keeping up the repartee with the waiters, you probably won't have energy for dessert; if you do, try the brownie monster or the triple-layer carrot cake. After dinner, the waiter will ask you to tell your favorite joke (be prepared), and then offer to seat you in the disco part of the operation.

The goofy goings-on go on from 5:30 to 10 Sunday, till 10:30 (Monday through Thursday), and 11pm Friday and Saturday. Disco in the lounge is open nightly from 7pm until 2am. Valet parking. Be sure to make your reservations early: phone 922-1282.

One of the famous old-timers of Honolulu is **The Willows,** 901 Hausten St. The Willows was converted from a private estate into a restaurant over 50 years ago and has since enjoyed an enormous following. It's such a beautiful spot, situated on a pond filled with Japanese carp and surrounded by gorgeous trees and flowers, that it's practically a must, especially if you're not going to visit the neighbor islands, where this kind of unspoiled atmosphere is much more prevalent. After being owned for many years by the McGuire-Perry family (whose good friend Arthur Godfrey made its name famous), the Willows was taken over by Randy Lee, formerly of the Halekulani hotel; and his menu is full of delightful island treats. Lunch is gracious and relaxed, with a variety of salads, sandwiches, pastas, and wok and curry dishes, from about $6.95 to $14.95. In the evening, the Sundowner Dinner Specials, served from 5 to 6pm, are an excellent buy, with an entrée, salad, and beverage for $10.95. On the regular dinner menu, where à la carte entrées range from about $9.50 to $24.95, you can dine on the likes of seafood provençale, garlic steak, their famous chicken, vegetable or shrimp curries, rack of lamb, and a lavish Traditional Poi Supper (the latter repeated on "Poi" Thursdays, from 11am on, with impromptu entertainment hosted by Auntie Irmgaard Aluli; cost is $13). Whenever you dine, though, be sure to save room for dessert. Traditionalists should not miss the legendary sky-high coconut cream pie; but there are also a dreamy chocolate haupia cake, Black Forest crêpes, and strawberries Romanoff. While you're enjoying the natural beauty and the good food (the Willows is one of *Travel/Holiday*'s six recommended restaurants in Hawaii and the only one in a garden setting), strolling musicians will serenade you with old Hawaiian songs.

The Willows serves dinner daily from 5 to 9pm, lunch Monday through Saturday from 11:30am to 1:30pm, and on Sunday there's a splendid garden buffet brunch from 10am to 1pm offering a vast array of delicacies at $16.95 per person.

Reservations are always recommended, especially if you want to sit on the lanai. Phone 946-4808. AE, CB, DC, MC, V.

Tripton's American Café, on the second floor of the shopping complex at 449 Kapahulu Ave., is the latest venture of the people who formerly operated the Beamreach Restaurant in Princeville on Kauai. It's a cool, attractive place with uncluttered, veyr modern decor. The menu here is not one of those that goes on for pages and pages and features a bit of everything, but what Tripton's does, it does expertly. Appetizers ($6.50 to $9.50) include a quite marvelous Cajun shrimp cocktail, salmon mousse, sashimi, a beautiful cheese platter garnished with fresh fruits, and our favorite—caviar pie. All entrées are served with a dinner salad, Tripton's own honey-rye-molasses bread, a choice of pasta or rice or baked potato, and vegetable. They do steaks, roast prime rib, and seafood superbly; seafood selections include lobster tail, steak and lobster combination, shrimp scampi, and fresh catch of the day, broiled or sautéed with capers and accompanied by a fresh dill mustard. Also offered are tempting chicken dishes and homemade pasta. Complete dinners run from $13.75 to $22, a bit higher for the lobster. There are several *keiki* dinners as well, from $6.75 to $12.75. And don't forget to consult "Susie's Dessert Board" for daily selections of homemade pies, mousses, and crisps.

Tripton's American Café is open from 5:30 to 10pm every day. Reservations advised, especially on weekends. Phone: 737-3819. AE, DC, MC.

Honolulu is home to two restaurants in the deservedly famous **Stuart Anderson's Cattle Co.** chain—one on the second level of Ward Warehouse, the other in Pearl City. The Ward Centre establishment, the one we're best acquainted with, does a thriving business with island residents and visitors alike. It's a softly lit, woody, laid-back kind of place; the specialty is beef grilled over a hardwood fire. All dinners are served with either homemade soup of the day or salad, a choice of baked potato or french fries or rice, and freshly baked whole wheat bread. Prime rib of beef is one of the star attractions at Stuart Anderson's—either by itself, or in combination with chicken, shrimp, grilled giant prawns, Alaska king crab legs, or lobster. The prime rib is a hefty serving; it's been slow-roasted and is accompanied by freshly made horseradish sauce. The boneless breast of chicken can be had barbecued, teriyaki, or grilled —and all of these are available as separate dinners as well, without the prime rib. The shrimp is broiled; the crab legs are served with a savory lemon and butter sauce. Top sirloin steak, another winner here, may be ordered in the same combinations as the prime rib; filet mignon and New York–cut steaks are also available. Dinners are priced from $8.95 to $23.95. After dinner, relax over some New York–style cheesecake or mud pie and contemplate the view of the ocean outside the wall-size windows—bustling Kewalo Basin, with its pleasure and fishing boats is just across the street, the beautiful blue Pacific beyond. The same food, with the addition of some sandwiches, is served at lunch; entrée prices are a few dollars less. There's Karaoke music at night.

Stuart Anderson's is open daily, serving lunch from 11am to 4pm, dinner from 4 to 10pm, until 10:30pm Friday and Saturday, 9:30pm Sunday. Reservations are advised. Phone: 523-9692. AE, DC, DISC, MC, V.

It's no wonder that **Top of Waikiki,** on the 21st floor of the Waikiki Business Plaza at 2270 Kalakaua Ave., has long been a favorite with visitors and residents alike. As it slowly revolves, it affords one of the most spectacular views in the islands: a 360° panorama of Waikiki Beach and its surfers, Diamond Head, downtown Honolulu, and the Koolau Mountains. The restaurant is like a gigantic wedding cake, the innermost tier a cocktail lounge, the succeeding layers lined with tables and diners who sometimes find themselves torn between photographing the view and attending to the very good food. Nighttime is the time for romantic candlelight dining with a view of the stars and the lights winking over the city. You feast on appetizers like escargots bourguignonne, on entrées like veal Cordon Bleu, fresh catch of the day, seafood curry, roast duckling à la cantonese, and specialties from the charbroiler, in a range of about $20 to $25. The house dessert specialty is mud pie—chocolate ice cream, Oreo cookies, and nuts. Lunch is quite reasonable—you can get good sandwiches, salads, and entrées like grilled filet of mahimahi, boneless barbecued chicken with Oriental sauce and shrimp, served with garden vegetables and rice or fries, plus dessert, for between $3 and $9. The iced tea, served with a spear of pineapple, is the perfect touch to go with your dessert of pie or coconut parfait.

Top of Waikiki serves dinner daily from 5 to 10:30pm (cocktails till midnight); lunch Monday to Saturday from 11am to 2pm. Reservations advised for dinner. Phone: 923-3877. AE, DC, JCB, MC, V.

Take the escalator to the second floor of the Ward Centre, just Diamond Head of the Ward Warehouse shopping center on Ala Moana Boulevard, and enter the **Monterey Bay Canners Restaurant.** You'll feel as if you are back at the turn of the century, stepping into a Barbary Coast saloon. Ceiling fans, brass-ringed curtains, and hanging plants subdue the sounds of this big, busy restaurant, which offers fresh seafood and fish at refreshing prices. A large blackboard announces the fish catch of the day; the day we dined there, it was tropical fish, ono, wahoo, and opakapaka (pink snapper). These specials run about $15 to $18 and include San Francisco sourdough rolls and New England or Manhattan clam chowder or salad.

Most other entrées such as fish, steaks, and pastas, run from $11.45 to $20.95. The oyster bar has such delicacies as sashimi, mushrooms stuffed with crabmeat, steamed clams, and the like, from $6 to $8. Desserts include a frozen chocolate mousse and a pleasant watermelon sherbet.

Monterey Bay (tel. 536-6197) serves dinner only, Sunday to Thursday from 4 to 11pm, Friday and Saturday to midnight. There's entertainment nightly from 9pm to 1:30am. There's another Monterey Bay Canners (tel. 922-5761) at the Outrigger Waikiki Hotel, 2335 Kalakaua Ave. Reservations are not essential.

Sophisticated contemporary American cuisine in a casually elegant indoor-outdoor setting—these are the ingredients that have made the **Mezzanine Restaurant,** in the Waikiki Terrace Hotel, 2045 Kalakaua Ave., a big hit since its opening last year. Center of attention is the kiawe woodburning oven and grill, which turns out fabulous breads and pizzas; every night the chef dreams up a new pie. Pasta platters ($9.95 to $14.95) are imaginative; salads ($5.95 to $7.95), such as Caesar, spinach, chicken Oriental, etc., are big enough to share; and Northshore prawns and roast chicken ($14.95 and $18.95) are succulent done on the kiawe wood broiler. Every night there's a big list of new and tantalizing specials, so you might want to eat here more than once during your stay. And desserts are different every day, too. At this writing, only breakfast and dinner were being served, from 6:30 to 10am and 6 to 9:30pm daily; if you're lucky, lunch will be added to the menu by the time of your visit. Reservations recommended. AE, CB, DC, JCB, MC, V.

Dolly Parton's highly touted Dockside Plantation Restaurant came and went speedily at this location, but it looks as if **Don B's Waterways Restaurant,** at the Hawaii Kai Shopping Center, 377 Keahole St., is here to stay. Located on the marina, with tiki torches and a white picket fence on the outside, Don B's is also extremely pretty within, with its black velvet booths, white furniture, rattan chairs, pictures of Hawaiian flowers on the walls, and greenery all about. In such a setting, it's very pleasant to relax and enjoy a sophisticated menu. Appetizers range from $2.50 to $4.95; main courses $14.95 to $20.95. Begin, perhaps, with a flavorful liver pâté, fresh shucked oysters on the half-shell, New England clam chowder, or the antipasto platter for two. Favorites among the entrées include roast baby rack of lamb with garlic, rosemary, and a light Burgundy sauce, osso bucco Milanese, fettuccine Alfredo, roast prime rib, and even a comforting old-fashioned meatloaf. At lunch, salads such as the Ceasar or the niçoise are popular, and entrées, $7.50 to $10.95, include fresh pastas of the day and island chicken breast on sourdough roll with roasted peppers and jack cheese. The lounge, open daily from 2:30 until 11pm, features "snacks": oysters on the half shell, grilled fish sandwich, shrimp scampi, burgers. While you're munching, you can listen to live entertainment every Friday and Saturday from 5 to 9pm.

Don B's Waterways Restaurant serves lunch Monday to Friday from 11am to 2pm, dinner nightly from 5:30 to 10pm. Reservations recommended on Friday and Saturday nights: phone 395-2930. AE, DC, MC, V.

Once it was Haiku Gardens, a beloved old restaurant in Kaneohe, on Windward Oahu. Now it's **The Chart House,** a new restaurant in one of the oldest, loveliest gardens on the island. Like all Chart Houses, this one is handsome: tiki torches light the walkway from the parking lot, there's a fountain in front of the door, and inside, one can pause for drinks in the reception room, so comfortable with rattan furniture and soft, big cushions in a pastel print. The dining room has been totally redone, with beamed ceilings, chairs with backs shaped like philodendron leaves, a mural of the ocean and the Koolaus, and wonderful views of the lilypods, the mountains, and the flaming torches. And the food lives up to the setting. For a mere $12.75, one could have a veritable feast on the salad bar alone, laden as it is with the freshest of garden greens including a huge Caesar salad, beautiful fruits, vegetables, pasta salads, ambrosia, chickpeas, hearts of palm—even caviar! With it comes New England Clam Chowder and hot "squaw" and sourdough breads. On the regular menu, there are nifty appetizers like poke (an island delicacy of raw fish marinated in soy sauce and red peppers), smoked fish, imported brie, and a special favorite, coconut chrunch shrimp in tempura batter, served with three sauces. Appetizers go from $3.25 to $11.95. Pride of the house is the hand-carved prime rib au jus, with horseradish sauce. There's also a variety of steaks, two chicken selections, and several seafood dishes, including swordfish, scallops, lobster, and the coconut crunchy shrimp. With the entrée ($15.95 to $24.65) comes a choice of the wonderful salad bar or a large bowl of New England clam chowder. Desserts befit the steakhouse atmosphere—cheesecake, chocolate mousse pie, macadamia nut sundae, and mud pie.

The Chart House serves dinner every day from 5 to 10pm. Limited reservations accepted. AE, DISC, MC, V. There's plenty of parking. Phone: 536-6197.

NOUVELLE CONTINENTAL

With the opening of the Hawaii Maritime Center, Honolulu Harbor began an extensive, much-needed, and much-welcomed redevelopment. And right behind the Hawaii Maritime Center, overlooking the waterfront at Kalakau Boathouse, is a new restaurant that sets the glamorous tone for the new life of the harbor. **Coasters Restaurant** at Pier 7, foot of Bishop Street, is the only two-level harborside restaurant in Honolulu, with exciting views from every table. Service can be slow. Each level is protected by canopies and served by a well-stocked bar. While you're busy watching the harbor activities by day or by night, you'll also be kept busy with an excellent Continental menu. Fresh catch of the day and seafood are featured; lobster sautéed with either black bean, papaya and avocado, or garlic butter is tasty, as are the San Francisco–style cioppino, the scampi Capri (stuffed with crabmeat and baked with hollandaise), and the peppered shrimp sautéed with brandy ($18.95 to $24.95). Also well-executed are several pasta dishes, chicken stir-fry, prime ribs, and steak, from $8.95 to $15.95. Appetizers ($6.95 to $9.95) feature steamers, smoked salmon, and escargots in mushroom caps. Lunch offers many of the same dishes at lower prices, plus good burgers, sandwiches, and salads. Desserts are outstanding, especially the banana-split pie: the home-baked chocolate wafer is on the bottom, layered over with vanilla and strawberry ice cream, and topped with a chocolate sauce with macadamia nuts.

Coasters serves lunch Monday to Saturday from 11am to 2:30pm, a brunch-lunch Sunday from 10am to 2pm, and dinner every night from 5 to 10pm. If you come here on a Saturday night, you'll get to see three cruise ships—the *Constitution,* the *Independence,* and the *Monterey*—all departing from nearby piers between 7 and 9pm. Reservations: 524-2233. AE, MC, V.

The sophistication of a fine meal in one of the great European capitals is what awaits you at **Alfred's,** at Century Center, 1750 Kalakaua Ave., corner of Kapiolani Boulevard. The cozy, romantic restaurant is a "celebration" of the Swiss chef/proprietor Alfred

Vollenweider, who serves his gourmet fare in a serene ambience: blue velvetlike armchairs and dropped-parasol chandeliers, pink tablecloths, locally made hurricane lamps, elegant European china, fine wines from a well-stocked cellar. Service is friendly and professional.

With your dinner entrée, priced mostly between $14 and $25, comes freshly prepared soup, a combination of salads—the last time we were there these included cucumbers in sour cream, shrimp-and-apple salad, egg salad, and tomatoes with dill—and fresh vegetables. Fresh island fish is served every day and done remarkably well. Other good choices include veal Cordon Bleu, entrecôte Café de Paris, coquilles St-Jacques, chateaubriand—and many more. Desserts are too good to miss, so ignore the calories and find some room for, perhaps, the soufflé glacé Grand Marnier, strawberries Romanoff, or Black Forest cake. Then again, there's apple strudel and German cheesecake with pineapple to tempt you.

Weekday lunches offer good value: salads, pastas, steak tartare, escargots, fresh fish, and omelets go from $9 to $13, and a daily lunch special for $10 to $15.50 includes soup or salad.

Reservations are advised: phone 955-5353. Lunch is served Monday to Friday from 11am to 2pm; dinner, Tuesday to Saturday from 6 to 10pm. Validated parking. CB, DC, MC, V.

The **Hau Tree Lanai** at the New Otani Kaimana Beach Hotel, 2863 Kalakaua Ave., has long enjoyed one of the best locations in Waikiki—right on Sans Souci Beach at Diamond Head. And the menu is a match for the al fresco setting. Seated under the same hau tree where Robert Louis Stevenson once whiled away the hours, diners can enjoy sunny breakfasts and lunches and watch spectacular sunsets at dinner time. Having breakfast here has long been one of our favorite things to do in Honolulu; they do excellent eggs Benedict, Belgian waffles, and french toast with fresh fruit, and, for those who like to start the day with a serious meal, the Japanese Gourmet Breakfast—grilled fish of the day, miso soup, fresh fruits, pickled vegetables, nori, a raw egg, rice, and green tea—for $13.50. At lunch, we like their salads—papaya chicken, Oriental chicken, sweet potato, and apple-and-crab-stuffed artichoke ($7.95 to $10.95). There are also fitness selections, burgers, sandwiches, and such entrées as Cornish game hen or broiled ahi steak with a tomato chili salsa, from $9.95 to $12.50. At dinner, best values are the complete meals, which feature soup du jour or salad, sautéed fresh vegetables, dessert and beverage, to accompany (for $26.50) such entrées as New York steak or pesto fettuccine, or, for $28.50, fresh fish of the day or broiled lamb chops.

Breakfast at the Hau Tree Lanai is served from 6:30 to 11am; lunch from 11:30am to 2:30pm; and dinner from 5:30 to 10pm. For reservations, phone 923-1555.

One of the first places in Honolulu to serve contemporary Italian food, **Il Fresco,** at 1200 Ala Moana Blvd., in Ward Centre, continues strong after seven years. The restaurant features a kiawe grill and wood-burning oven totally visible to diners (it's fun, in fact, to sit at the bar and watch the items going into the oven) and is done in a modern, almost minimalist decor, with nothing to detract from the splendor of the food. A long list of daily specials (a pizza dish, several pastas, several fish dishes, steak, etc.) complements the regular menu, but you can almost always count on such wonderful items on the appetizer menu ($3.95 to $9.95) as the grilled oysters with ginger-and-shallot butter, and the grilled Japanese eggplant with an extraordinary chili goat cheese. Among the main courses ($9.50 to $23.95), the boneless breast of chicken with chutney and garlic mashed potatoes, and the blackened ahi (yellow-finned tuna) with tomato-basil vinaigrette, are quite special. For desserts, my favorites are the ice cream in praline and the chocolate decadence.

Il Fresco is open for lunch from 11:30am to 2pm Monday through Saturday, and for dinner nightly from 6pm. Reservations advised: phone 523-5191. AE, DC, JCB, MC, V.

CHINESE

For Chinese dining in the Imperial style, there's no grander place in Honolulu than the **Golden Dragon** at the Hilton Hawaiian Village. The setting is pure Asian drama, the vast room decorated with Chinese screens and sculptures, paintings and vases; black laquer chairs surround white linen–clothed tables topped with red-and-gold china; the room fronts the beach and lagoon, with three gazebos for indoor/outdoor seating. Wherever you sit, you're sure to enjoy the cuisine—and if you've been clever enough to phone 24 hours in advance, you may also get to enjoy the Imperial Beggar's Chicken, wrapped in lotus leaves, encased in clay, and baked ($29.50 for two), or the Imperial Peking Duck, with plum sauce and mandarin pancakes ($33.50 for two). Ready without advance notice are tasty dishes such as the crisp lemon chicken, the five-flavored chicken, the superb braised lobster tail with black-bean sauce, and stir-fried baby eggplant. From the smoke oven (you can watch the chefs at work in the Exhibition Smoke Pavilion), you could have baby pork ribs, smoked tender duck, or smoked boneless chicken. Most entrées go from about $9.95 to $14.75, with some below and above. Desserts here put those in other Chinese restaurants to shame. Consider the chocolate ginger mousse cake with swirls of chocolate shavings on the top, or the unforgettable Chinaman's Hat—that's chocolate sponge cake topped with thick layers of raspberry purée and chestnut mousse piled high, with chocolate icing. We'll have them all, please.

At the end of your meal, a "tea lady" visits your table to serve exotic Chinese teas and to tell fortunes. The Golden Dragon serves dinners only, from 6 to 10pm daily. Reservations advised: phone 949-4321, ext. 39.

FRENCH

There's a bit of the Riviera in Waikiki. **Chez Michel,** in a gardenlike setting in Eaton Square, at 444 Hobron Lane in the Ala Moana area, has long been one of Waikiki's best French restaurants. The restaurant is roofed and walled in by lattices hung with tropical plants, furnished with highbacked and comfortably cushioned wicker chairs, and graced with splashing fountains that create a cool, romantic atmosphere. Michel himself may greet you, if he's not on his annual wine-buying trip to Paris. This is a popular lunch rendezvous (Monday to Saturday, 11am to 2pm), so join the members of the business community dining over the likes of poached eggs sardou with artichoke bottoms, osso bucco provençale, or a superb chicken sautéed with mushrooms and artichoke. Everything is à la carte, from about $8.50 to $12.50, but the dishes are well endowed with Michel's gourmet potato and vegetable creations.

At dinner, the French onion soup is a must. Michel's sauces and gravies are exquisite, so that even chicken livers become a dining experience—not to mention the more exotic selections like carré d'agneau jardinière, fresh opakapaka sauté grenobloise, or the memorable côte de veau Normandie. Entrées range from $22 to $32, including fresh vegetables and potatoes. Desserts are quite special: you can choose from chilled orange soufflé, cherries jubilee, or Grand Marnier soufflé. (Remember to order your soufflé when ordering dinner.) Espresso and cappuccino are offered.

Dinner is served daily from 5 to 10:30pm. Reservations are always advised: phone 955-7866. AE, DC, DISC, JCB, MC, V.

Visitors to Honolulu and local residents can only be grateful that Guy Banal, the young chef/owner of **Bon Appétit**, 1778 Ala Moana Blvd., in Discovery Bay, decided to leave his native France a few years ago and try his luck here on these far Pacific shores. For Banal is a true master, and his superb cuisine has already won him a large and enthusiastic following, not to mention a *Travel/Holiday* award. A visit to his charming bistro, so pretty with its mirrors and red banquettes, potted palms and white curtains, is a must for those who are really serious about French food. Banal's style might be called light country nouvelle and classic cuisine with an island flair. Making good use of local produce and specialties, he also leans to bistro fare, and turns out a creditable three-course dinner, which changes every week, from $18.95 to $24.95. And for real budget dining, he offers the Café Express menu, with many entrées like fresh linguine, lobster ravioli, tartare of steak or fresh crab, warm green asparagus custard, and spinach meat ravioli, at $12.95 and $13.95; such dishes as cassoulet, osso buco niçoise, and bouillabaisse go from about $15.95 to $24.95.

On the regular à la carte menu, there are some incredible appetizers: we're always hard pressed to choose between the ethereal scallops and lobster mousse, served warm with cucumbers, fresh herbs and red caviar ($7.95), and the escargots and wild mushrooms in puff pastry ($8.50). The onion soup is richer, thicker, and more delicious than any we've tasted before, made as it is with both Brie and Swiss cheese. Among the entrées, slow-roasted Niihau rack of lamb with Thai curry and the grilled Hawaiian shrimp and scallops with lemongrass garlic butter and sweet chili peppers are commendable choices.

Guy Banal is also a master pastry chef, so try to save some strength for his marvelous homemade desserts: our favorite is the clafoutis, a custard of peaches and black cherries sautéed in caramel and topped with a warm raspberry sauce. *Magnifique!*

Bon Appétit is not only a superb restaurant, it happens to be Honolulu's largest wine and appetizer bar as well, with a choice of 35 French and California wines by the glass. So you can come by anytime after 4:30pm, or after the theater or the evening's entertainment, for a glass of wine and light entrées like cheese or pâté platters, onion soup, pasta, and the like.

Dinner is served every day from 5:30pm on. Reservations are suggested: phone 942-3837. Validated parking. CB, DC, DISC, JCB, MC, V.

GREEK

A touch of Greece—its charm, music, dances, and cuisine—can be enjoyed at the **Greek Island Taverna,** 2570 Beretania St. near University Avenue. One flight up in a small building with its own parking lot, this authentic Greek restaurant features not only souvlaki, moussaka, and other classic Greek dishes, but also better-known items like gyros, or pita cheeseburgers. We passed up the octopus sandwich for a delicious spanakotiropita (spinach, feta cheese, herbs, and spices in pita bread). Sandwiches run from $4.95 to $5.50. Lunch plates of stuffed cabbage, sautéed mahimahi, or marinated chicken Greek style are $6.25 to $7.50. There's Greek beer to accompany your lunch, baklava to top it off. Dinners are a festive occasion: the Greek music becomes dance music, rich blue cloths cover the tables, and a Greek belly dancer adds a bit of spice to the meal. Tasty hot and cold appetizers—taramosalata, marinated baby squid, or saganaki (green Kasseri cheese flambéed in brandy)—are your starters. Then it's on to moussaka, chicken sautéed in wine sauce, stuffed grape leaves, or souvlaki, among a number of entrées all reasonably priced between $9.95 to $13.95. Well recommended is the spring lamb baked in the traditional manner (arni psito, $12.95). A full combination dinner, consisting of a sampling of entrées plus soup, salad, dessert, and coffee, is a favorite choice at $15.95. Seafood dinners run from $14.95 to $17.95.

Greek Island Taverna serves lunch Monday to Friday from 11:30am to 2pm, and dinner nightly from 5:30 to 11pm. Reservations: 943-0052.

ITALIAN

Baci, right in the middle of everything at 2255 Kuhio Ave., offers a sophisticated Italian respite from the Waikiki madness. One flight up, in the Waikiki Trade Center, it's a large restaurant with a decidedly European mood, and is pretty as a picture, with its black-and-white bentwood chairs, white tablecloths, glorious flower arrangements with their giant proteas and other exotics, and a charming bar aglow with hot-pink neon. The menu can satisfy varied tastes, either nouvelle or traditional Italian. You could start your meal, for example, with such typical Italian appetizers as antipasti, or pasta e fagioli, or mussels on the half shell—or opt for the soncino con anitra—that's roast breast of duck with goat cheese, lettuce, and tomato. Appetizers run from $5.50 to $12.75. Among the pasta dishes, you could have the tried-and-true fettuccines, rigatonis, and linguines, or go for the gnocchi di patate al pomodor rosemarino (potato pillows with fresh tomatoes and rosemary), the pappardelle con anitra (a wide, flat pasta with roast breast of duck, prosciutto, herbs, tomatoes, and cheese), or tutti mare (scallops, clam, squid, and shrimp with pappardelle pasta in a red sauce). Most entrées are $12.85 to $24.50. There are a number of seafood dishes including fresh catch of the day, some fine veal entrées including vitello con aragosta (veal sautéed with lobster and mushrooms in a cream sauce), and several varieties of steak. A Baci specialty that we always enjoy is the petti di pollo Paillard—pounded chicken breast with lime and saffron, very light and tasty. For dessert? It's cannoli, spumoni, tortoni, or one of the freshly baked pastries of the day. Baci is not inexpensive, but prices are a few dollars less at lunch.

Baci is open every day from 11am to 11pm. Reservations recommended; phone 924-2533. AE, MC, V.

Sergio's in the Ilima Hotel, 445 Nohonani St., was recently described by a Honolulu acquaintance of ours as "the best-kept secret in Waikiki." They do no advertising; they don't need to. Honolulu residents who enjoy really fine Italian food keep the place busy every day. It's a lovely room, of good size, with low lights, paneled walls, and booths separated by panels and quite private. Wine bottles and casks and many plants create a warm atmosphere. The favorites are such house specialties as the superb saltimbocca alla romana (veal and prosciutto in a light wine sauce); the pollo all' abruzzese (tender pieces of chicken cooked with tomatoes and bell peppers in sauce); and quaglie stufate al brandy (three plump quails served on a bed of risotto with demi-glace sauce and always fresh vegetables); they run from $18 to $25. After all of this superb gourmet fare, one must literally force oneself to manage dessert, but with specialties such as Biancaneve e i sette nani (literal translation: "Snow White and the Seven Dwarfs")—seven fresh strawberries on a bed of lemon sherbet, topped with a shot of Stolichnaya vodka—it is well worth the effort. Espresso, cappuccino, and Irish coffee are there for the asking, $2.50 to $5. Reservations: phone 926-3388.

Sergio serves lunch from 11:30am to 2pm Monday to Saturday, dinner from 5 to 11:30pm nightly. AE, CB, DC, DISC, JCB, MC, V.

Matteo's, 364 Seaside at Kuhio Ave., in the Marine Surf hotel, is a longtime Italian favorite that just keeps winning kudos year after year; it's always among the "Top 20" chosen as overall "favorite restaurants" chosen by the readers of *Honolulu* magazine. It has a romantic and luxurious look, done in lush earth tones, with deep booths, soft lighting; the dining room is artfully divided to give the feeling of intimacy and privacy. Service is gracious and the wine list extensive; it has won the prestigious *Wine Spectator's* award for the past several years. The food is excellent, and need not be expensive: you can have a complete dinner, served with a fresh green salad, pasta, vegetable, and coffee or tea, from $22.95 to $24.95—and that includes such entrées as the classic saltimbocca (veal in marsala, topped with prosciutto and mozzarella), scaloppine of veal, grenadine of beef tenderloin, and mahimahi Veronica (sautéed fish served with lemon sauce and seedless grapes). From the à la carte menu, you can start with a traditional antipasto platter for two at $12.50, proceed to such entrées as chicken romana, eggplant parmigiana, veal rollatini, or braciola (rolled beef with mozzarella, garlic, and basil baked in a marinara sauce); prices range from $12.50 to $26.95. If you favor a pasta dish, try something unusual, like the fettuccine escargot with scampi sauce, $14.95. Whatever you choose, save some room for dessert: The pastry chef turns out marvels each night—perhaps a chocolate marble cheesecake topped with a raspberry sauce, or a strawberry cream tart, or chilled zabaglione. Finish your meal with dark espresso or the special house cappuccino.

East-West Success

You're going to have to make your way to the residential area of Hawaii K'ai to sample the cuisine at Roy's, but the roughly 8-mile drive from Waikiki will be more than worth the effort. **Roy's,** 6600 Kalanianaole Hwy., is the most highly-praised new restaurant in Honolulu. Thirty-six-year-old wunderkind chef/owner Roy Yamaguchi is being hailed for his innovative marrying of Asian and Western cooking styles and ingredients.

Roy's is a two-level restaurant: downstairs there's a piano bar and lounge with outdoor tables for cocktails. But the main action, and the glassed-in display kitchen from which the wondrous dishes emerge, is upstairs. The huge room, done in peach-and-white minimalist decor with striking flower arrangements, has a wraparound window affording uninterrupted views of Maunalua Bay, Diamond Head, and Koko Head. The lighting is indirect, the decor elegant and subdued, the service meticulous. And the show-biz crowd can be a show in itself.

And the food is exquisite. Since Roy is constantly coming up with new inspirations for his contemporary Hawaiian cuisine, there are perhaps 20 specials on the menu every night—and that always includes original appetizers, salads, pastas, pizzas, and many fresh fish entrées, including local spiny lobster. Between these and the menu regulars, you'll get a chance to try many of his signature dishes. Dim sum and appetizers are priced from $4.50 to $5.25; individual pizzas and pastas from $5 to $8.50; main courses, mostly from $14 to $16. Our favorites among the appetizers are the potstickers, stuffed with seafood and served in a fresh basil-curry sauce or a sesame-seed butter sauce, and the crab cakes, with pickled vegetables and a mustard dip. Pizza is different at Roy's: consider the smoked baked salmon and goat cheese pizza or the marinated Chinese chicken pizza with shiitake mushrooms, pickled ginger, and spicy sprouts, for example. As for main courses, I can recommend the succulent rack of Niihau lamb with island mint chutney and a Thai curry–Cabernet sauce, and the mesquite-smoked Peking-style duck with a mango lime sauce and candied pecans. Roy's impressive fish presentations, which change daily ($17.75 to $21), could include fresh lemongrass salmon with a Thai peanut sauce, or fresh island opah with a mustard crust and lemon parsley butter sauce, and fresh seared mahimahi with a cucumber caper dill sauce. Desserts are special, too, and change every night. The wine list is well chosen, and not overly pricey. Roy himself and his wife Janne are usually present, adding to the ambience (Roy in the kitchen, she in the restaurant and art gallery).

Roy's serves dinner from 5:30 to 10pm weekdays, to 11pm weekends. Sunday brunch, 10am to 2pm, is a great time to sample a big list of dim sum and appetizers, breakfast dishes plus a goodly array of salads, pastas, and imaginative entrées. Reservations are a must: for a weekend night, at least several days in advance. Phone: 396-7697. AE, CB, DC, DISC, JCB, MC, V.

Matteo's is open nightly from 6pm to 2am. Reservations: phone 922-5551. AE, CB, DC, DISC, JCB, MC, V.

Sergio Mitrotti is a Renaissance man—a chef, an artist, and an entrepreneur who knows how to put together a terrific restaurant. So successful has his first Honolulu venture, Café Cambio at 1680 Kapiolani Blvd. (tel. 942-0740), become that he's now opened a sister restaurant, **Café Sistina,** at 1314 S. King St., and it, too, excels in sophisticated, contemporary Italian cuisine. The restaurant is smart-looking, with square marble tables and two splendid murals done by Sergio, one of an Italian street scene, the other (in the works at this writing) of a portion of the Sistine Chapel paintings. Italian opera playing in the backgrounds lends a nice touch. The menu features some wonderful antipasti (bruschetta with grilled tomatoes or with chopped clams in a wine garlic sauce, griglia mista, frittata rustica, etc. ($3.75 to $8), hearty salads like the insalata di mare ($9.25), half a dozen veal dishes, and a huge variety of pastas, which run from about $8.75 to $15.25. Some favorites: linguine alla carbonara, penne al radicchio, pollo al limone, rigatoni in caponata, and several unusual seafood pastas like the caviar and chopped clams in a light pink wine sauce or scampi alla vodka.

Café Sistina serves lunch Monday to Friday from 11am to 2pm, dinner Monday to Thursday from 5:30 to 11pm, Friday and Saturday to midnight. Closed Sunday. MC, V. Phone: 526-0071.

Local friends turned us on to **Phillip Paolo's,** a restaurant at 2312 S. Beretania St. that won an instant and enthusiastic *kamaaina* following when it opened a few years back. Now it's one of our favorites, too. You'll be seated in one of the several dining rooms, so pretty with Victorian decor, lace curtains, and fresh flowers. You're in for a very pleasant dining experience here: The waiters are knowledgeable and helpful, the crowd is attractive, the wine is delicious. Pastas and seafood are featured on the small but choice menu, with various specialties every day. Portions are very generous, so you may want to share. Two of you should start with the mixed antipasto at $9.95. For your main course, priced from $11.95 to $29.95 (most under $20), you might want to try the delicious fettuccine al pesto or the frutti di mare (seafood combination). Or, sample one of the kitchen's more unusual specialties, like the fettuccine Dominique (pasta topped with sautéed smoked salmon, tomatoes, onions, mushrooms, and broccoli). The baked trout, stuffed with crabmeat, bacon, and mushrooms in a lemon-butter sauce, is a winner, as are the deep-fried soft-shell crabs and the manicotti made with crabmeat and ricotta. Only fresh herbs are used in all dishes, and all are served with salad and Italian bread. Everything is cooked to order, so have a drink from the bar while you're waiting. For dessert, have gelato or sorbet, or, best of all, cheesecake served with the house's own fresh fruit sauce, $4.50. Finish with some Italian coffee and relax with a sigh of great contentment.

Phillip Paolo's serves dinner, beginning at 5pm. It closes at 9:30pm Sunday and Monday, 10pm Tuesday through Thursday, and 10:30pm Friday and Saturday. It is open Friday for lunch, 11am to 2pm. Reservations advised: phone 946-1163. There's a wonderful new Phillip Paolo's in Kona, on the Big Island.

JAPANESE

There are now two **Tanaka of Tokyo** restaurants in Waikiki, the original on the fourth floor of the Waikiki Shopping Plaza, at the corner of Seaside and Kalakaua avenues, and the newer one, Tanaka of Tokyo East, at King's Village, 131 Kaiulani Ave. Both have charming traditional settings and an excellent steak and seafood menu with portions big enough for hearty Western appetites. You'll be seated at a table for eight, centered around a table-range combo, watching the chef do amusing antics with knives and spatulas as he prepares your meal. Three main dinners to choose from are the chicken teriyaki, the Pacific red salmon, and the Tanaka sirloin ($13.75 to $19.75). There is also shrimp, scallops, filet, lobster, and a lobster and sirloin combination ($16.50 to $33.50). All dinners include grilled shrimp appetizer, Japanese consommé, cold and crisp salad, steamed rice, teppanyaki vegetables, ice cream or sherbet desserts, and green tea. The lunch menu, priced from $6.75 to $11.75, includes many of the same entrées, served with rice, teppanyaki vegetables, and green tea. You could easily believe you're in Tokyo, with the Japanese music in the background, the waitresses in kimonos (actually, they are all local women of Japanese ancestry who speak perfect English and radiate island warmth rather than Japanese formality), the low lights, and the understated Japanese decor.

Both Tanaka of Tokyos served lunch weekdays from 11:30am to 2pm, dinner Monday through Saturday from 5:30 to 10:30pm, Sunday to 10pm. Reservations are recommended: phone 922-4702 at the Waikiki Shopping Plaza, 922-4233 at King's Village. AE, DC, JCB, MC, V.

Note: Tanaka of Tokyo will send one $5 discount coupon, to be applied to the cost of your meal, to anyone living on the Canadian or U.S. mainland who sends a stamped, self-addressed envelope to: Tanaka of Tokyo, Waikiki Shopping Plaza, no. 406, 2250 Kalakaua Ave., Honolulu, HI 96815.

3. Informal & Inexpensive ($10 to $20 and Under)

AMERICAN

The **Fishmonger's Wife,** on the Mauka Walk at Ala Moana Center, is a cozy place with big, comfy club chairs, soft lights, and lots of fish and lobster tanks. One could have a marvelous lunch or dinner here just grazing on the hot and cold appetizers, notably sashimi, smoked salmon, cracked crab, rumaki, shrimp lumpia, or steamed clams, priced from $5.50 to $8.95. Then there's delicious Oriental duck salad, avocado stuffed with chicken, or crab or shrimp Louis to tempt you—plus all sorts of seafood and chicken sandwiches and burgers at $6.75 or under, as well as wonderful chowders and gumbos. Entrées at lunch or dinner—the same menu is in effect all day—start at $9.50 for Mexican Boboli and go all the way up to $23.95 for the filet and Alaskan king crab combo. Some house specialties include wonderful crab cakes, $13.95, and a variety of stir-fried wok specialties, including scallops, prawns, shrimp, and broccoli, Dungeness crab, and lobster, prepared with your choice of black-bean or garlic sauce—we like them both! Heavenly desserts like strawberries with brown sugar and sour cream or saboyan are priced from $3.

The Fishmonger's Wife is open daily from 10:30am to 10pm. Phone: 941-3377.

Among the second-floor row of restaurants at Ward Centre, 1200 Ala Moana, **Ryan's Parkplace** (tel. 523-9132) is a standout. Their draft beers are temperature-controlled and their huge stock of liquors and liqueurs lines a whole wall behind the long bar from floor to ceiling. With that kind of look, would you expect them to be concerned about heart-healthy dining and to offer a variety of low-saturated-fat and low-cholesterol preparations? It just proves that many different appetites can be soothed here, all in an attractive setting: wood and brass, high ceilings, slowly revolving fans, plants everywhere. Service is excellent; tell them you're in a hurry and they'll make sure you finish lunch in 40 minutes. Even the soups are special—fresh broccoli, borscht, Moroccan lentil, among others. The large entrée salads are in the $7.50 to $9.50 range at lunch or dinner; sandwiches and burgers, from about $5.95 to $7.95. Snacks and starters at dinner run between $4.95 and $6.95. Seafood, pasta, and pizza dishes, sirloin steaks, even specialty dishes, run about $7.50 to $11.50 at lunch, $11.50 to $17.95 at dinner. Go see for yourself. Lunch starts at 11am, runs smack into dinner at 5pm, and closing is at 11pm daily. Reservations recommended at dinner: phone 523-9132. AE, MC, V.

One of the prettiest inexpensive restaurants in town is **Trellises,** in the beautiful Outrigger Prince Kuhio Hotel up Diamond Head way at 2500 Kuhio Ave. Artfully decorated with greenery, overlooking a waterfall and gardens, Trellises serves all three meals plus a bevy of evening buffets at $16.95 ($17.95 on Friday). It's an East/West meal on Monday, Italian on Tuesday, prime rib on Wednesday and Saturday, Oriental on Thursday, seafood on Friday, family-style (prime rib, turkey, fish, etc.) on Sunday. A Sunday champagne brunch is fun at $16.95, and there's a daily breakfast buffet at $8.50. On the regular menu, Trellises offers a plentiful array of salads, sandwiches, burgers, and American standbys, plus such island specialties on the dinner menu as Polynesian chicken, Tahitian shrimp, and chicken teriyaki ($13.95 to $15.50).

Trellises serves breakfast from 6am, lunch from 11am, dinner from 5pm (buffets are 5 to 9pm) daily. Reservation recommended: phone 922-0811, ext. 5151. AE, DISC, JCB, MC, V.

A three-story glass-enclosed aquarium alive with fish dominates the **Oceanarium Restaurant** in the Pacific Beach Hotel at 2490 Kalakaua Ave., corner of Liliuokalani. The Oceanarium is on the ground floor, and there are more restaurants and a disco higher up; but this one affords the best view, and an almost-all-day menu (from 6:30am till around 10pm). It's fun to come at fish-feeding times: 9:30am, noon, 1, 5:30, 7, and 8pm.

Dinner here is an especially good bargain, since even à la carte items come with rice or potato, vegetable, rolls, and butter. The complete dinner adds soup or salad, ice cream, and beverage. Prices for entrées range from $14.50 for mahimahi Islander to $28.95 for steak and lobster. We sampled a tasty Gulf shrimp curry: large shrimps fried with bananas and onions, simmered in a curry sauce, and served with all the condiments; and our roast beef was the finest prime rib, served with yummy Yorkshire pudding and separate juice for dipping.

There's a breakfast buffet at $11.95, and lunch entrées, à la carte, run from about $8 to $14. Reservations: phone 922-1233. AE, CB, DC, DISC, JCB, MC, V.

Seafood and continental cuisine at very reasonable prices can be had at the **Jolly Jellyfish,** 1200 College Walk in downtown Honolulu. An enormous oil painting of fish dominates one wall, there are plants all about, and the look is fresh and attractive. And so is the food. Among the main courses at dinner, nothing is more than $13.75, and that's for grilled lobster tail. Other dishes, like chicken au gratin, European-style beef stew, scallops in cream sauce, and sirloin steak, go from $7.50 to $13.75. Tasty pupus ($3.95 to $6.75) include Italian-style squid, grilled mussels with garlic butter, and German potato salad. Lunch features burgers and sandwiches, spaghetti dishes, pizzas, and special lunch plates, from $4.95 to $6.25.

Jolly Jellyfish serves lunch from 11am to 2pm Monday to Friday, dinner from 5 to 10pm Monday to Saturday. Happy hour is 2 to 6pm. Phone: 523-5659. AE, MC, V.

The **Waikiki Broiler** at 200 Lewers St. (tel. 923-8836), in the Waikiki Tower of the Reef Hotel, provides both indoor and outdoor tables for those who don't want to lose one moment of sunshine. Start soaking it up at breakfast time along with a pancake sandwich with bacon and egg, from $2.29 to $5.95. Lunch runs to salads, burgers, and sandwiches ($4.50 to $7.95), and such pasta specialties as chicken fettuccine and chicken primavera ($10.95). Dinner is a good deal, since the price of the entrées—$8.95 to $11.45—includes steamed vegetables, and a choice of starch and sourdough bread; another $1.25 gives you a salad or soup. Good choices include the teriyaki chicken breast, the shrimp dinner, and the smothered Mexican chicken. Breakfast is from 6 to 11am, lunch from 11am to 1:30pm, dinner from 5:30 until 10pm, seven days a week (the dining room is closed between 2 and 5:30pm). From 9 in the evening until about 1:30 in the morning there is usually a group playing Hawaiian and contemporary music—all of which adds to the fun in this neat nautical spot, a big hit with the visiting crowd. AE, MC, V, DC, JCB.

If you love dining with a view of the ocean—and if you love buffet dining, too—make a note of the **Ocean Terrace,** poolside at the Sheraton-Waikiki hotel. The buffet table really shines at night: juicy prime ribs, mahimahi, fried chicken, plus a hot surprise or two. And there are always plenty of salads, vegetables, desserts, and beverages. Price is $21.50. There's a buffet lunch too—roast beef, stews, chop suey, cold cuts, salads, desserts (we counted some 20 choices recently)—and that's $14.95. The breakfast buffet is $12.50, and it's recommended for the big morning eaters; all you want of fruits, cereals, eggs, breakfast meats, pastry, pancakes. Like all of the Sheraton-Waikiki, this is a strikingly alive spot, with brilliant green-and-apricot colors from floor to ceiling. Dinner is from 5:30 to 9:30pm; lunch, from 11:30am to 3pm; breakfast, from 6 to

11:30am. Reservations are important on weekends: phone 922-4422. AE, DC, JCB, MC, V.

Can't choose between steak and lobster? You don't have to. **Buzz's Steak 'n Lobster House,** 225 Saratoga Rd. (tel. 923-6762) in the Reef Lanais Hotel, makes a specialty of both, and it does a terrific job. Enjoy your candlelight dinner surrounded by many antiques, nautical compasses, old maps of the islands, lamps, and plaques. A full-glass outside wall lets you watch the flaming torches as you enjoy drinks and dinner. Buzz's prices are more than reasonable. Come between 5 and 6:30pm for the Early Bird Special, and you can have unlimited salad bar, plus fish and fries, for just $6.95. After that time, prices begin at $9.95 for the fish and fries, or the ground beefsteak, and go up to around $14.95 to $25.95 for the likes of prime rib, New York–cut steak, Alaskan king crab, sautéed shrimp, and many other varieties of fresh fish and seafood. The average dinner is $13.95—and that dinner includes salad bar, a choice of baked potato, french fries, or rice, and generous helpings of French or rye bread. The bar opens at noon, so you can relax on your way back from beach or shopping with specially priced happy hour drinks until 5pm. A limited luncheon menu—soups, sandwiches, and potato salad—is served from noon to 3pm. Dinner is on every day from 5 to 11pm. Free parking is available. AE, DC, MC, V.

Dining at the Kahala Hilton—at the Maile Restaurant or the Hala Terrace—can be expensive, but the posh resort also has a less pricey restaurant, and it's quite pleasant to pay a visit to the hotel, see the lovely grounds, watch the dolphins being fed, and have a light lunch or dinner, or afternoon tea, at the charming **Plumeria Café,** an open-air restaurant with a European ambience. Different specials are featured every month, so you might find pastas in November or squash and pumpkins in December. There's always a pasta dish at $13.50, and such main courses as wonton soup, a flavorful pizza pie, herb-baked chicken, or prime rib of beef, from $8 to $16. Graze on appetizers like assorted dim sum or beef and chicken satay, or try a Hawaiian chicken salad, from about $7 to $8.50. Or indulge in some luscious fresh fruit smoothies and their wonderful specialty coffee drinks. We loved the Brandy Velvet—a combination of brandy, espresso, vanilla ice cream, and chocolate syrup, $5.

The Plumeria Café is open every day from 11:30am to 11:30pm. Phone: 734-2211. AE, CB, DC, DISC, JCB, MC, V.

CHINESE

Yen King, that popular Northern Chinese restaurant in the plush Kahala Mall Shopping Center, just keeps getting better all the time, gaining new fans among *kamaainas* and *malihinis* alike. It's an attractive place, with beige colors highlighting the filigreed teak screen dividers, tile ceiling, and murals. The menu is vast, at both lunch and dinner, but there's no way to go wrong here, as everything is prepared with master-chef expertise. You can choose among some 30 vegetarian entrées from $3.50 to $5.95 (the local vegetarians swear by this place), and about two dozen seafood choices from $7.25 to $12.50, mostly featuring squid, clams, and shrimp in various styles. Of course there are plenty of beef, pork, and fowl dishes (garlic chicken and roast duck are especially good), and a wide variety of Peking-style, as well as Hong Kong–style, dim sum (dumplings and noodles). Hot Mongolian beef is available anytime, but give them a day's notice if you want to try their beggar's chicken baked in clay—quite unusual. Open daily from 11am to 4pm for lunch, 4 to 9:30pm for dinner. AE, MC, V.

Seafood is delicious. Chinese food is delicious. Add the two together and you have a unique specialty restaurant: **Won Kee Sea Food,** a standout among the restaurants in the Cultural Plaza, at 100 North Beretania St. (tel. 524-6877). This is a gourmet seafood place, where specialties like fresh island fish, island prawns, jumbo shrimp, king crab legs, or Maine lobster are prepared artfully: perhaps steamed with ginger-and-soy sauce, braised with ginger-and-garlic sauce, or stir-fried with black-bean sauce. Specialties go from $11.50 to $25 or more, depending on market price, but most of the dishes are very reasonable: dishes like fresh clams with black-bean sauce, sautéed shrimp with vegetables, Eight Treasures tofu, roast duck with plum sauce, and cold ginger chicken run from about $7 to $9. Soup of the day (ours was turnip), rice, and tea are included in the entrée price. We ordered five courses for four people, and the cost of this banquet totaled under $60 before the tip.

Won Kee is open daily for lunch and dinner. Don't expect an ornate place; here you have white tablecloths, simple wood paneling, and Chinese-style wrought-iron fixtures. It's the food that's ornate. Lunch is 11am to 2:30pm; dinner, 5 to 10pm. Reservations: phone 524-6877. MC, V.

Use your noodle when you're downtown; save money and have a tasty meal for under $5 by visiting the **Hong Kong Noodle House.** This small, plain restaurant on the *mauka-Ewa* corner of the Chinese Cultural Center, 100 North Beretania, facing the river, is one of about seven in a row that feature Chinese, Japanese, Korean, and Mongolian cooking. Even those who are not noodle fans could be converted. There are 12 different noodle soups, and any one of these, priced at about $2.80 to $3.90, is a full meal, like fishball noodle soup or roast duck noodle soup. There are almost as many tossed noodle dishes with soup served separately, priced around $3.30 to $4.50; the noodles with shrimp are delicious. Brave souls might want to try the noodles with pigs' feet. A dozen rice soups in the same price bracket include fascinating combos such as preserved eggs with salted pork. Specialties like crispy roast duck, "tender broiled pig's liver" and "tender broiled pig's stomach" are offered in the same under-$4 price range. Open Monday to Saturday, 10am to 2:30pm and 5 to 8pm. Phone: 536-5409. No credit cards.

ITALIAN

We first went to **Salerno,** in the McCully Shopping Center at 1960 Kapiolani Blvd., in self-defense because our friends in Honolulu refused to give us any peace until we tried it; now that we've been there, we return often. It's a very pretty little place with a mirrored bar, comfortable red velvet chairs, bouquets of orchids on the tables, and seascapes decorating the walls. The food is hearty and delicious. And it's inexpensive. Nothing unusual about the menu —there's the usual range of pastas, pizzas, chicken and veal dishes, seafood, the staples of Southern Italian cooking—but what is unusual is that all of the entrées on the menu (an extensive one for such a small place) are offered in small or regular portions, giving one the opportunity to sample more than one dish, or to dine lightly. Prices range from $8.90 to $11.90 for pastas, from about $10.90 to $14.90 for meat, poultry, and seafood entrées in regular portions; smaller portions are $2 to $3 less. House specialties worth knowing about include the stuffed eggplant, the pollo linguine (boneless chicken sautéed with vegetables and topped with either a pesto or tomato sauce), and the deep-fried calamari. For dessert? Heavenly fresh pastries, baked daily (as are the breads) in Salerno's kitchen. The restaurant also features its "Italian grovery"—marinara sauce, meatballs, homemade Italian sausage, and pasta to take away with you; ask your waiter, then order all your favorites.

Salerno Ristorante Italiano serves lunch from 11am to 2:30pm Monday to Saturday, dinner daily from 5 to 10pm. Reservations are a must. Phone: 942-5273. AE, DC, MC, V.

The Niu Valley Shopping Center, which, in its way, is like a little "Restaurant Row," is home to **Al Dente,** 5730 Kalanianaole Hwy. (tel. 373-8855), a charming Italian place done all in white— furniture, walls, tablecloths—with bentwood chairs and stained glass panels on the walls. The food is traditional Italian with some contemporary touches, and smells and tastes wonderful. Favorite appetizers include the roast sweet peppers, the cold cream of tomato and basil soup, and the broiled radicchio with pancetta. Pastas ($10.50 to $12.95) feature several with seafood—spaghettini frutti di mare, linguine with fresh clams, linguine with salmon Dona Louise. Fresh fish of the day is usually around $17.95. Traditional favorites among the meat and poultry dishes, $17.50 to $18.95, include a hearty osso bucco with saffron rice, veal scaloppine or milanese, and duck. Al Dente is open Tuesday to Sunday from 5:30 to 10:30pm, serving dinner only. Reservations are not necessary. AE, MC, V. The Niu Valley Shopping Center is a 15- to 20-minute drive from Waikiki, en route to Hanauma Bay and Hawaii Kai.

MEXICAN

The mood, the food, the drinks, the lights, and the festive feeling all add up to a resounding cheer for **Compadres Mexican Bar and Grill** at Ward Centre, 1200 Ala Moana Blvd. Prices are moderate and the food is expertly prepared—so much so that the readers of *Honolulu* magazine consistently name Compadres among Honolulu's "Top 20" restaurants year after year. Visiting celebrities can often be found enjoying the scene. Among the house specialties, which run from $7.45 to $19.95, favorites include the classic arroz con pollo and chicken mole; the avocado stuffed with crabmeat and topped with green chili and cheeses; the huajolote, marinated and charbroiled turkey breast; and fajitas de camarones, marinated, sliced, and sautéed Gulf shrimp rolled in soft warm tortillas and served up with frijoles and salsa fresca. *Delicioso!* Nifty appetizers, good salads and sandwiches, smoke-oven baby back ribs and chicken, and a large selection of egg dishes and combination plates offer plentiful choices. For dessert, try the cheesecake—voted best in Hawaii—or the fresh fruit chimichanga! Of course there are terrific margaritas, daiquiris, sangría by the glass and pitcher, Mexican and other imported beers, and other potions that mix well with these Tex-Mex treats.

Compadres is open late every day, from 11am on. There's brunch 9am to noon Saturday, Sunday, and holidays. Phone: 523-1307. AE, DC, MC, V.

PIZZA SURPRISE

Honolulu is known for a wide variety of international foods, but nowhere have we seen so many different cuisines represented under one roof as at **California Pizza Kitchen,** with two locations in town, a newer one in Waikiki at Ala Moana Boulevard and Ena Road, across from the Hilton Hawaiian Village (tel. 955-5161) and the older one at Kahala Mall (tel. 737-9446). Don't let the "California" mislead you—we looked in vain for an avocado-and-alfalfa-sprouts pizza—but we did find the following: Peking duck pizza (Peking-style breast of duck, mushrooms, hoisin sauce); Cajun pizza (andouille sausage and peppers in a spicy Cajun sauce); teriyaki pizza (grilled chicken or shrimp marinated in orange teriyaki sauce). Other exotic pizza creations include Thai chicken (with spicy peanut-ginger sauce); goat cheese (with bacon, red onions, and fresh tomatoes); shrimp pesto (with fresh tomatoes, Greek olives, and sun-dried tomatoes). All of the above are made with mozzarella, but there are also cheeseless pizzas, as well as moo shu chicken and buffala mozzarella calzones. Pizzas—all individual size—are priced from $6.50 to $8.95; calzones are $9.50 and $9.95. A variety of pastas, freshly made on the premises—fettuccine, linguine, angel hair, rigatoni, and fusilli—are available as well, accompanied by such unusual go-withs as Thai chicken, ginger black bean sauce, and chicken tequila, for $6.50 to $8.95. And not only are these pizzas and pastas unusual—they are good!

The California Pizza Kitchens are big, stylish places, with both counter and table service. They are open from 11am to 10:30pm Sunday through Thursday, until 11pm Friday and Saturday. AE, CB, MC, V.

NATURAL DINING

Interested in natural food, delicious food, gourmet vegetarian food? Catch **Crêpe Fever!** It's easy to do, because this charming, open restaurant on the street level of Ward Centre, 1200 Ala Moana Blvd., so pretty with its inviting counter, oak tables on red tile floors, and a few tables in the garden outside, offers delicious food at very reasonable cost and caters to the health-conscious. Crêpe entrées, served with brown rice and green salad, include Mexican chicken (it's not vegetarian only), ham melt, lemon spinach, and veggie burger, and are mostly under $7.25; dessert crêpes on the order of strawberries and cream or cheese-and-fruit blintzes run about $4.25 to $5.50. Stuffed croissants are good too, and so are the excellent breakfast specialties—omelets, crêpes, waffles, and french toast, served all day. We also love their Grain & Green Express Bar, which allows you to build a vegetarian meal from a selection of complementary protein combinations that use grains, greens, beans, and seeds, with a variety of international accents; a medium-sized grazer's bowl is $3.50, a huge grazer's plus bowl is $4.80. Right next door, owner Sandee Garcia has opened a delightful espresso bar called **Mocha Java,** which features a full bar menu and a full exotic coffee menu—which means you can finish, or start, your meal with a strawberry smoothie with rum, an espresso milk shake with brandy, Irish coffee, or a fabulous flambéed sundae.

Crêpe Fever is open Monday to Saturday from 8am to 9pm, Sunday to 4pm, serving the same menu all day. Mocha Java is open from 9am to 10pm Monday to Thursday, until 11pm Friday and Saturday, until 4pm Sunday. Phone: 521-9023 for Crêpe Fever, 537-3611 for Mocha Java. MC, V.

SWISS

Swiss food is a rarity in Honolulu, so should you get the urge, say, for authentic Wiener Schnitzel or Bündnerfleisch or cheese fondue, the way to satisfy that urge is to get into your rented car, drive out to the Niu Valley Shopping Center (a 15- to 20-minute drive from Waikiki, en route to Hauanuma Bay), and stop in at an old favorite, the **Swiss Inn,** 5730 Kalanianaole Hwy., recently named by the readers of *Honolulu* magazine as one of the 20 best restaurants in town. Owner-chef Martin Wyss is a dedicated man who personally cooks every order and really cares about his customers' satisfaction. The place is cozy, with scenic pictures and tole ware on the walls, and several gazebos with hanging plants and tables inside. Begin your meal with the above-mentioned Bündnerfleisch (thinly sliced air-dried beef) or some escargots (appetizers run $3.50 to $6.50), then on to one of the dinners, which include soup of the day, salad, vegetable, and beverage, a complete meal at a very comfortable price—from $12.50 to $19. Everything is good, but we especially like the veal medallions Florentine, the émincé de veau Zurich-style, the garlic shrimp and scallops Madagascar—and that Wiener Schnitzel, of course. Cheese fondue, $8.50 per order (minimum of two orders) is ready on the spot, but give them 24 hours notice if you want the beef fondue, also delicious. Light dinners are even more reasonable—$5 to $7 for the likes of bratwurst, vegetarian pastas, and wienerli, European-style frankfurters with Swiss potato salad. Come for Sunday brunch (10:30 to 1am) and enjoy a European-style buffet with salads, cold cuts, hot dishes, and many desserts, for $12.50.

Swiss Inn serves dinner every day except Wednesday through Sunday from 6 to 10pm; cocktails from 5:30pm. Reservations advised, especially on weekends, as this place is always full. Phone: 377-5447. AE, CB, DC, MC, V.

THAI

Be sure to arrive early if you want to have dinner at **Rama Thai Restaurant,** 802 Kapahulu Ave., as this cozy, 11-table spot is very popular; get there by 6:30pm, and you're not likely to have a problem, but later it fills up and then some. The food is delicious and reasonably priced: Most dishes are in the $5 to $7 price range, but serve two or three people easily, and this applies to appetizers, soups, salads, Thai curries, main entrées, and noodle or rice dishes. Vegetarians will be happy here with a complete menu, from spring rolls to soups to entrées like Thai curry mixed with tofu. We started a recent meal here with the classic satay barbecue sticks—your choice of beef, pork, or chicken—to dip in a tangy cucumber-and-peanut sauce, $5.25. Our ginger chicken soup was a winner: The chicken is simmered in coconut milk with parsley, green onions,

At Restaurant Row

Restaurant Row, at 500 Ala Moana Blvd., not far from downtown Honolulu, has just about everything in the way of restaurants, from posh to budget dining. In the latter category, consider first **Rose City Diner** (tel. 524-ROSE), a restaurant and soda fountain in the style of a roadside diner. Most plate dinners range from $6.74 to $8. Lots of fun and games here, more or less nonstop, from 6am daily. Then there's **Studebaker's** (tel. 526-9888), a scene right out of the '50s, whose theme is "bop till you drop." The deafeningly loud music, the neon, the wild-haired disc jockey, and the ebullient young staff who break out into song and dance every hour, make it easy to do so. From 4 to 8pm, an amazing *free buffet*, with four hot entrées, seven salads, brown breads, and veggies with dip, is served along with your drinks. *Note:* No one under 23 is allowed in after 4pm. Dress code.

Marie Callender's at Restaurant Row (tel. 524-7437) is a popular family restaurant in the islands (there's another at Windward Mall, and one in Lahaina on Maui), specializing in wholesome American fare, in attractive settings, and at most reasonable prices. They're known for their chicken pot pie, under $8 with soup or salad. Lunch dishes run about $7 to $9, dinner entrées $9.75 to $16. And don't miss their home-baked pies. **Captain Jack Seafood Restaurant** (tel. 526-0800) is an attractive, nautically decorated place that does excellent crab, lobster, fresh fish, and the like. Try the Sea Otter's Delight at lunch or dinner—that's steamed clams, mussels, shrimp, crab, lobster, corn, and potato served really hot. Dinner entrées run $10.50 to $28.95, lunch $10.50 to $24.95. **Manzo's** (tel. 522-1711) is a stylish Italian trattoria (pastas $5.25 to $10, most house specialties under $10), and **Pizza Pavilion** (tel. 532-1111) is one of those designer pizza houses with both brick oven and skillet pizza, plus an international array of salads—Greek, Russian, Middle Eastern, Japanese, etc., from $6.75 to $7.25.

Sunset Grill at Restaurant Row (tel. 521-4409) is upscale, a casually elegant restaurant and bar featuring grilled, rotisseried, and roasted foods in a sophisticated indoor-outdoor setting. But you can have pastas from $10.95, fabulous baby back ribs for $12.95, and some of the world's best desserts here. And their $7.95 burger, grilled on kiawe logs, topped with onions, peppers, cheese, and potato salad, is judged by many to be Honolulu's best and a meal in itself. Open daily, 11am to 11pm. **Ruth's Chris Steak House** (tel. 599-3860) is considered top of the class by true meat lovers. Plan on spending about $30 to $35 for a meal here. Dinner only, from 5 to 9:30pm daily, to 10pm weekends. Most exciting of all is **The Black Orchid** (see above), where celebrities play (Tom Selleck is often seen here), and everyone can enjoy the sophisticated setting, upbeat mood and food, jazz music, and entertainment every night.

and Thai ginger. There is a choice of six curries, which can be ordered mild, medium, or hot (we recommend mild), and a score of entrées like fried shrimp with assorted vegetables, beef with Thai red-gravy sauce, and cashew-nut chicken. We topped off our meal with cool and sweet Thai apple-banana-coconut; next time it will be the Thai corn-and-tapioca pudding. Lunch offers similar entrées at slightly lower prices.

Rama Thai serves lunch from 11am to 2pm daily, dinner from 5 to 10pm daily. Phone: 735-2789. MC, V.

GOOD AND FAST

The **Minute Chef** in the Sheraton Princess Kaiulani Hotel, at the corner of Kalakaua and Kaiulani, has long enjoyed a reputation as one of the best places in town for quick, inexpensive food; now that it's been transformed into a "fast-food court for the whole family," it's more popular than ever. Breakfast starts at 6am with some incredible bargains, like three slices of french toast for $1.99, or bacon or ham and eggs for $1.99. Lunch and dinner, served from

---

Sawadee!

Thai food and the name "Keo's" are practically synonymous in Honolulu, ever since Keo Sananikone started opening restaurants and serving his marvelous modern interpretations of classic Thai and Southeast Asian cuisine. There are five outposts in the Keo empire, but the one you should go to to catch the stars—Hollywood celebrities like Richard Chamberlain, Shirley MacLaine, Diana Ross, and Michael J. Fox, Jr., have all been seen here—is **Keo's Thai Cuisine** at 625 Kapahulu (tel. 737-8240). The stars shine in the decor, too—tiny lights are strung into the plants in the jungle-garden setting, and there are masses of orchids and ginger everywhere, umbrellas, ceiling fans, carvings, portraits, and statues. And the stars of the cuisine are Keo's succulent dishes, which use no artificial colorings, preservatives, or MSG, and only the freshest ingredients available. Evil Jungle Prince, an original Keo recipe, a green-chili-and-basil-leaves sauté with chicken, shrimp, or vegetables, is a specialty; so, too, are the spring rolls wrapped in rice paper and served with fresh lettuce and mint leaves. Wonderful soups, noodle and rice dishes, tangy curries, and cooling desserts await your pleasure. Let your waiter guide you as to what's spicy, what's very spicy, and what's bearable. Prices are modest: soups are $2.95 to $3.75, most entrées are $7.95 to $12.95. The Kapahulu location is the most fun, but also pleasant are Keo's at Ward Centre, 1200 Ala Moana Blvd. (tel. 533-0533); Keo's at King Street, a Thai Bar and Grill, 1486 S. King St. (tel. 947-9988); Mekong Restaurant, 1295 S. Beretania St. (tel. 523-0014); and Mekong II Restaurant, 1726 S. King St. (tel. 941-6184). If you're inspired to learn to cook Thai, buy Keo's cookbook, *Keo's Thai Cuisine*, available at the restaurants, and shop for Thai food at his store, Asian Grocery, 1319 S. Beretania St., and you're on your way. AE, DC, MC, V.

11am to midnight, feature Oriental stir-fries, deli sandwiches, salads, burgers (basic burger is 99¢), and that wonderful Lappert's ice cream, fresh from Kauai.

If you love omelets, pancakes, waffles, crêpes—in other words, eggs 'n things, then you're going to be thrilled to discover **Eggs 'N Things,** 1911 B Kalakaua Ave., which, since 1974, has been Honolulu's most unique breakfast shop. Unique not only in the quality of the food, but in the fact that it serves breakfast from 11pm, on into the wee hours of the morning and up through 2pm; and then closes its doors until 11 the next night! Tables are neat and trim, the walls are decorated with wood plaques bearing interesting news items. But it's the kitchen range that's the most interesting. From it are served eggs any style, plus any side meats, from Vienna sausage at $5.25 to steak at $7.25—all accompanied by three of the lightest buttermilk pancakes we've tasted.

More than a dozen three-egg omelets are available, also served with three buttermilk pancakes, from plain at $6.25 to a potato, bacon, and cheese creation at $7.75. Crêpes Suzettes come with or without sour cream and with lemon, blueberry, strawberry, or fresh banana fillings, $5.25 to $6.50. Pancakes and waffles might be plain (no sugar), or made with blueberry, coconut, macadamia nut, or even strawberry whipped cream, $3.50 to $6.50. Fish of the day has recently been added to the menu. There are Early Riser (5 to 9am) and Late Riser (1 to 2pm) specials, of three pancakes and two eggs, for just $1.99. Phone: 949-0820. No credit cards.

A coffee shop that is way out of the ordinary is the **Waikiki Circle Coffeeshop** in the Waikiki Circle Hotel. Directly across from Kuhio Beach, this comfortable place with its red carpet on the floor offers a fine sunset view—through the traffic and exhaust fumes, of course! The food is very good and the prices even better: The $8.95 dinner special offers half a pound of U.S. choice New York steak and includes salad and rice or mashed potatoes. Priced from $7.95 to $13.95 are ground beefsteak, teriyaki steak, mahimahi filet, fried chicken, and lamb chops. Lunch is similarly inexpensive, and a special $3.25 breakfast offers two golden buttermilk hotcakes, an egg, and a choice of ham, bacon, or sausage. Banana hotcakes are $2.95. An excellent lunch special was being offered at the time of our last visit: a sandwich with ham, cheese, and turkey salad or tuna salad, plus soup, is $4.95 between 11am and 2pm. Open daily from 6:30am to 2pm for breakfast and lunch, from 5 to 9:30pm for dinner. AE, MC, V.

If you choose to dine at a **Jolly Roger** in Waikiki, you now have your choice of two locations: one is right on Kalahaua Ave. at no. 2244; the second, Jolly Roger East, at 150 Kaiulani Ave. Both seem to be packed most of the time, since the food is always tasty and reasonably priced. On Kalakaua there are a few sidewalk tables and a cooler and quieter mood inside. At Jolly Roger East, there are comfortable booths, a step-down bar, and entertainment nightly at 9. At both you can eat a good dinner for $8.45 to $11.45; perhaps beef liver with sautéed onions or bacon, honey-fried chicken, or breaded veal cutlet. There are also changing daily specials, from about $6.45. Dinners are served with soup or salad, rice or potato, and a dinner roll. There are also plenty of salads, sandwiches, and burgers to choose from. Doors open around 6am, and breakfast, lunch, and dinner are served until midnight, dinner starting at 4pm. AE, DC, JCB, MC, V.

The **Original Pancake House,** 1221 Kapiolani Blvd., near Ala Moana Center, is for lovers of those breakfast delights who would like to eat them morning, noon, or afternoon. It's an offspring of Portland's Original Pancake House, which later spread around the world and has been given a *McCall's* citation and a James Beard Award. More than 20 varieties of pancakes are at the ready, plus five types of waffles and sourdough french toast; the tab is mostly from $4.75 to $5.25. They're known for their German Dutch baby and German apple pancakes, both baked in the oven. Other tempting possibilities might be Swedish pancakes, coconut pancakes, Kijafa cherry crêpes (a Danish treat), and Palestine pancakes (rolled with sour cream and Cointreau). There's a wide variety of oven-baked omelets (potato, Portuguese, ham jubilee, etc.), plus eggs any style, but the star of this show is pancakes—mandarin pancakes, potato pancakes, pecan-and-apple pancakes. Hot sandwiches and daily under-$5 specials are also offered. Open from 6am to 2pm daily. Validated parking. AE, MC, V.

If you're downtown during the day, pop into **Croissanterie** at 222 Merchant St. near Alakea. Croissants are as popular here now as they are on the mainland. The place is casual, and the service is cafeteria style, but, oh, those croissants! Breakfast croissants, served until 11am, have flavorings like cherry and chocolate, fillings like cream cheese with tomato or fresh spinach. From 11am to the 9pm closing, the fillings become more elaborate—perhaps broccoli and cheese sauce, ham or turkey, cheese—and are priced around $4.25. There are several salads, and excellent coffee, which you can have either plain, espresso, or in some elaborate variations. AE, MC, V.

V

WHAT TO SEE & DO
IN HONOLULU

1. HAWAII, FROM STONE AGE TO SPACE AGE

2. HAWAII, THE MELTING POT

3. HAWAII, THE CULTURAL CENTER

Even though there is more than enough to keep you busy in Waikiki, we don't think you should pass up the rest of Honolulu. For this is a city with more than the usual share of diversity and excitement, with a rich cultural past and a stimulating, cosmopolitan present. And how to see it need present no problem at all. If time is short or if you want to get an overall, bird's-eye view before you begin in-depth exploring, simply take one of the excellent commercial sightseeing tours that hit all the major points. Or you can rent a car and drive to all the things you want to see (details on car rentals can be found in Chapter II). But even without benefit of a car or guided tour, you can get around very well indeed. Honolulu is, after all, a major United States metropolis, and it has an excellent public transportation system: the MTL buses, popularly known as TheBUS. For 60¢ a ride, 25¢ for children, plus a little bit of ingenuity and determination, you can get almost anywhere in Honolulu you want to go.

IN DEFENSE OF BUSES

Besides saving you money, riding the buses gives you an added advantage: You go at your own pace, heading where your interests take you, lingering as long as you like in any given spot. On a guided tour, everybody has to see everything. While the ladies in front of you may just adore Iolani Palace, you might be much happier poking through the rickety little streets and alleys of Chinatown. Or you might want to skip all the historical sights and just come up for air once in a while as you peruse the splendors of the Honolulu Academy of Arts or the Bishop Museum. On TheBUS, you're your own person; you decide when and where to go and how long to stay there. For Honolulu is such a varied city, with such a diversity of things to see, that it should be seen at your own pace.

Renting a car, of course, is the easiest way to do the town, but cars and taxis can get to be expensive. However, bus travel is quite congenial. The buses run all over the city, they maintain good schedules, and the drivers are friendly and genuinely helpful. If you need information about TheBUS, phone 531-1611. Visiting senior citizens can get a free temporary bus pass by applying at the MTL office, 811 Middle St. (tel.848-4144). Bring appropriate proof of age (driver's license, birth certificate, passport, or baptismal certificate with seal). Remember that most major thoroughfares in Honolulu are one-way: Most buses going in a Diamond Head direction should be boarded on Kalakaua Avenue; those going toward downtown Honolulu or Ala Moana, on Kuhio Avenue.

More expensive than the bus, but cheaper than a cab, the **Waikiki Trolley** offers another means of transportation. Old-fashioned motorized trolleys that recall turn-of-the-century streetcars travel between the Royal Hawaiian Shopping Center and Dole Cannery Square daily, making stops en route at Ala Moana Center, the Hilton Hawaiian Village, the Ramada Reniassance Ala Moana Hotel, the Honolulu Academy of Arts, Ward Warehouse and Fisherman's Wharf, Ward Centre, the State Capitol and Iolani Palace, the Mission House Museum and the King Kamehameha Statue, Chinatown, the Hawaii Maritime Center, Restaurant Row, and the Hilo Hattie Factory. Cost is $10 per day for adults, $5 for children. Stay on for the entire two-hour narrated trip, or jump on and off whenever you like and continue on another trolley. Not all of the destinations we mention below are on the route. Phone 526-0112 for exact routes and schedules, or check the local tourist papers.

THE ORDER OF THINGS

In the pages ahead, we outline for you the major sights of Honolulu. The first section will trace, in more-or-less chronological order, the sights that will show you what Hawaiian life was and is like, from the Stone Age days of the Polynesian settlers, through the missionary period and the era of Hawaiian royalty, to the Space Age Hawaii of the 1990s. At the end of this section, we'll show you how to take some walking, bus, and boat tours.

In the next section, we'll tell you a little about the ethnic life of the city, about the important ethnic festivals always going on in Honolulu. Should you be lucky enough to catch the yearly Japanese Bon Dances or the Chinese New Year, for example, these could be the highlights of your trip. We'll also take you on a tour of the Hong Kong of Honolulu, the city's engaging Chinese neighborhood.

The last section of this chapter gives you a look at the museums, galleries, concerts, theaters, experimental films, and educational centers that make Honolulu just about the most exciting combination of beach resort and urban metropolis anywhere. Put on a comfortable pair of walking shoes, arm yourself with some good maps, and off you go to savor the excitement of this cosmopolitan city.

1. Hawaii, From Stone Age to Space Age

BISHOP MUSEUM

One of the most important natural and cultural history museums of the Pacific, the Bishop Museum makes the world of the early Polynesian settlers come alive, through such exhibits as outrigger canoes, a model *heiau,* feather cloaks of the *alii,* rare Hawaiian artifacts. There's an exciting collection of primitive art of Polynesia, Micronesia, and Melanesia. A visit here will give you a basis for understanding much of what you will see later throughout the islands. And the Shop Pacifica is laden with attractive items, everything from $3 kukui-nut pendants to a $1,000 Niihau shell necklace. The Bishop Museum is located at 1525 Bernice St. (tel. 847-3511); open daily from 9am to 5pm. Admission is $6.95 for adults, $5.95 for those 6 to 17, active military personnel, and seniors, and includes admission to Kilolani Planetarium (see below).

QUEEN EMMA SUMMER PALACE

"Hanaiakamalama," the country estate of Kamehameha IV and his consort, Queen Emma, has been restored by the Daughters of Hawaii to its mid-19th-century Victorian splendor. The address is 2913 Pali Hwy.; open daily from 9am to 4pm, closed holidays. Guided tours. Admission: $4 for adults, $1 for ages 12 to 18, 50¢ for those under 12.

ROYAL MAUSOLEUM

This is where the *alii* of the Kamehameha and Kalakaua dynasties are buried. The address is 2261 Nuuanu Ave.; open Monday to Friday, 8am to 4:30pm; closed Saturday, Sunday, and most holidays (open March 26, Kuhio Day, and June 11, Kamehameha Day).

PEARL HARBOR

It would be unthinkable to leave Hawaii without making a pilgrimage to the U.S.S. *Arizona* Memorial at Pearl Harbor. This tomb of more than 1,000 American servicemen who died on December 7, 1941, the day bombs fell on Hawaii, is a silent, stark reminder of the continued folly of war. You can drive to Pearl Harbor or simply take TheBUS no. 20 direct from the Waikiki area to the U.S.S. *Arizona* Memorial Visitors Center, administered by the National Park Service. If you prefer to take a commercial shuttle bus rather than TheBUS, phone 926-4747; round trip is $6.

Try to arrive early in the morning at the visitors center to avoid huge crowds. While you're waiting for the U.S. Navy boat to take you out to the U.S.S. *Arizona* itself—you'll be given a number and time of departure—you can busy yourself with the absorbing exhibits at the visitors center and museum. Many of these show the personal mementos of the attack victims, plus photographs, paintings, and historical documents. A 20-minute film precedes your trip to the ship. Children under 45 inches in height will be permitted in the Visitors Center/museum and in the theaters there, but they are not permitted on the U.S. Navy shuttle boats. Children 6 to 12 must be accompanied by adults. Shoes and shirt must be worn; bathing suits are not allowed. Tours operate daily from 8am to 3pm and are free.

MISSION HOUSES MUSEUM
These three 19th-century buildings are still the way they were when the New England missionaries lived in them, full of antique furniture, mementos, clothing of the missionary ladies, and aging trinkets, plus contemporary exhibits documenting the lives of the families who lived and worked here. A fascinating look into the past, it's at 553 S. King St. Open Tuesday to Saturday, 9am to 4pm; Sunday noon to 4pm; closed Monday. Admission (including a guided tour) is $3.50 for adults, $1 for those under 16, free for children 6 years and under. On Saturdays, costumed players from the museum staff portray the missionaries in a program entitled "Honolulu, 1831." The museum staff is occasionally joined by actors from the community who depict other historical characters. A walking tour of historic downtown Honolulu leaves the museum Tuesday through Friday at 9:30am. The $7 fee includes admission. Special events here are of a high quality; check the local papers for information. There's a charming gift shop, full of Hawaiiana. Behind the Misison Houses is a library containing the collections of the Hawaiian Mission Children's Society and the Hawaiian Historical Society. Researchers are welcome. Phone 531-0481.

KAWAIAHAO CHURCH
The church that the king, his subjects, and missionaries built has been, since its dedication in 1841, the "Westminster Abbey of Hawaii." Even if you don't get to Sunday services (10:30am, conducted partially in Hawaiian; free guided tours afterward), take a look around any day from 9am to 4pm. Note the fine portraits of Hawaiian royalty that hang in the church. The address is 957 Punchbowl St., across Kawaiahao Street from the Mission Houses.

IOLANI PALACE
The official residence of Hawaii's last reigning monarchs, Iolani Palace was designed in the European manner for King Kalakaua, "The Merry Monarch." Royalty resided here for 11 years (1882 to 1893) until the monarchy was overthrown. From 1893 to 1968 Iolani Palace was the site of the provisional government, the Republic, Territory, and State of Hawaii. Since 1978 it has been a museum, opened to the public after a $7 million restoration-reconstruction program. Although some areas are unfurnished, the Throne Room, State Dining Room, King's Library, and Privy Council Chamber are complete. Other rooms and areas are partially furnished. A tour of the building is well worth your time to see the intricate woodwork, the highly polished fir floors, the shining banisters and mirrors. Guides fill you in on the furnishings and the history of each room. Tours are conducted by the Friends of Iolani Palace every 15 minutes from 9am to 2:15pm Wednesday through Saturday; they last 45 minutes and cost $4 for adults and $1 for chil-

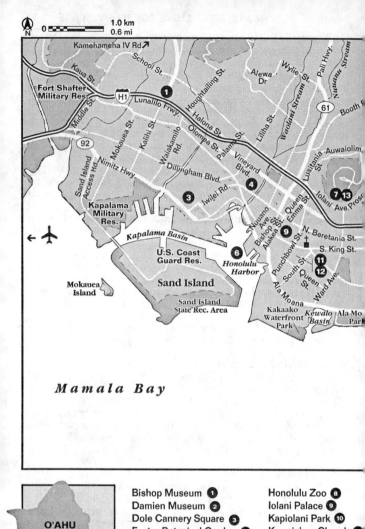

Bishop Museum ①	Honolulu Zoo ⑧
Damien Museum ②	Iolani Palace ⑨
Dole Cannery Square ③	Kapiolani Park ⑩
Foster Botanical Garden ④	Kawaiahao Church ⑪
Gandhi Statue ⑤	Mission Houses
Hawaii Maritime Center ⑥	Museum ⑫
Honolulu Academy	
of Arts ⑦	

dren 5 through 12 (children under 5 are not permitted on tours). Reservations are requested; phone 522-0832.

On the same grounds are the **Archives of Hawaii,** the largest collection of Hawaiiana extant. The location is at King and Likelike Streets; open Monday through Friday from 7:45am to 4:30pm.

Church ✝   Post Office ⌧   Information ⓘ

DOWNTOWN HONOLULU

The high point of a little walk downtown will be the **Aloha Tower,** Hawaii's Empire State Building. Even though it's now dwarfed by the two 21-story AmFac towers and other modern buildings, it's still the symbol of the city, overlooking the harbor and affording spectacular views of the metropolis. It is open 8am to 9pm, seven days a week. A short walk away from the Aloha Tower is the **Hawaii Maritime Center** on Pier 7, a world-class maritime center dedicated to the preservation of Hawaii's rich ocean heritage. An admission fee of $7 for adults, $4 for those 6 to 17, entitles you to visit several attractions. Tour the *Falls of Clyde,* the world's only fully rigged four-masted ship, which plied the waters between Hilo and San Francisco for many years, beginning in 1898. Visit the *Hokule'a,* a replica of a thousand-year-old Polynesian voyaging canoe, which repeats the trip between Tahiti and Hawaii frequently, navigated by the stars and currents, as in ancient times. The $6 million Kalakaua Boathouse is the star of the Hawaii Maritime Center, a state-of-the-art museum that traces the maritime history of Hawaii from its original discovery by Polynesians on voyaging canoes right up to the present. Exhibits, audiovisual displays, and life-size dioramas deal with everything from Captain Cook and the sandalwood trade to the days of the whalers, the luxury ships of the Matson line, tsunamis and weather, sailing and surfing. Kids will love the Widow's Walk for sighting harbor traffic, and the Good Ship Lollipop, a replica of a ship's deck where they can climb into the crow's nest, furl the sails, shoot the water cannon, and steer the ship. There's a snack bar as well as a lovely restaurant, Coasters, for sophisticated lunches or dinners in a setting right out there on the waterfront, overlooking Honolulu Harbor.

The Hawaii Maritime Center is open every day from 9:30am to 5pm. Information: 536-6373.

You can come down to earth now and head for Hawaii's Wall Street, **Merchant Street,** where the major corporate empires of Hawaii, the "Big Five," still have their offices. The architecture of Alexander and Baldwin, Castle and Cook, Theo. H. Davies, among others, is 19th-century elegant. Then you can head toward **Fort Street** and a pleasant shopping mall closed to traffic where you can browse among some of the big downtown department stores.

STATE CAPITOL BUILDING

The first unit and the crowning jewel of the growing Civic Center is undoubtedly one of the grandest capitols in the world. Using Hawaiian materials and motifs, the colors of sand and sea, the building soars upward from expansive pools to an open-air crown suggesting the peak of a volcano. There is a "Welcome, Enter" sign on both the governor's and lieutenant-governor's offices during regular working hours, and they are worth at least peeking into. Outside the building, a huge medallion bears the state seal and motto, *Ua Mau ke ea o ka aina I ka pono* ("The life of the land is perpetuated in righteousness"). Note Marisol's controversial statue of Father Damien out front, as well as the statue of Queen Liliuokalani and the reproduction of the Liberty Bell on the King Street side.

FOSTER BOTANICAL GARDEN

On view are 15 acres of rare tropical plantings from around the world, with beautiful orchid and primitive cycad gardens. The garden dates back to the 1850s, when it was founded on royal lands. A cool interlude, it's at 50 N. Vineyard Blvd. Open daily from 9am to

4pm. Admission is $1, under 13 free with adult. Free guided tours. Phone: 533-3214.

LYON ARBORETUM

Just above Paradise Park, at 3860 Manoa Rd. in lush upper Manoa Valley, this superb arboretum is open to the public from 9am to 3pm Monday through Friday, 9am to noon on Saturday. A free 1½-hour guided tour, held at 1pm on the first Friday and third Wednesday of each month and at 10am on the third Saturday of each month, will tell you all you'll ever need to know about exotic, economic, and tropical plants, as well as the flora of Hawaii. Reservations for these tours are a must: Call 988-7378 between 9am and 3pm weekdays, and inquire, too, about a wide variety of classes, outings, and programs. The Arboretum also maintains a book and gift shop featuring handcrafted notecards, napkins, baskets, pottery, and other unique gifts, as well as a wide selection of books on tropical plants, crafts, Hawaiiana, and culinary arts. Write for schedules or information.

KILOLANI PLANETARIUM

Learn about ancient and modern Hawaiian astronomy in exciting, educational, multimedia star shows held daily. Evening shows on Friday and Saturday also include free observatory telescope viewing, weather permitting. It's part of the Bishop Museum, 1525 Bernice St. (see above). Admission is $2.50, or included with museum admission. Phone 848-4136 for show times and information.

DOLE PINEAPPLE CANNERY & CANNERY SQUARE

Watch those pineapples get into those cans in a $5 walking tour through the world's largest fruit cannery. The tour begins with a film, followed by a walk through the cannery itself, and provides free snacks of fresh pineapple and juice. It ends at Cannery Square, with its shops, restaurants, and exhibits. Also at Cannery Square and very much worthwhile is the **Hawaii Children's Museum of Arts, Culture, Science and Technology,** which provides children with imaginative hands-on experiences in science, arts, technology, and Hawaiian culture. Open Tuesday through Friday from 9am to 1pm and on weekends from 10am to 4pm. Admission is $5 for adults, $3 for children ages 2 to 17. Information: 522-0040.

Cannery Square is open every day from 9am to 5pm, with the last cannery tour beginning at 4pm. You can get here from Waikiki and back via the Pineapple Transit for 50¢; the bus makes frequent pickups from Waikiki hotels. Phone 531-8855 or check local tourist papers for schedules.

NATIONAL MEMORIAL CEMETERY OF THE PACIFIC

Punchbowl Crater, an extinct volcano once named the "Hill of Sacrifice," provides a final resting place for some 26,000 American service personnel who were killed in the Pacific during World War II, the Korean War, and Vietnam. One of the most visited graves here is that of astronaut Ellison Onizuku. Punchbowl is open to the public every day from 8am to 5:30pm, September 30 to March 1, until 6:30pm the rest of the year. Reach it by taking TheBUS no. 2

on Kuhio Avenue heading downtown, getting off a Alapai Street, and transferring to TheBUS no. 15, Pacific Heights.

HISTORY & ARCHITECTURE BUFF'S WALKING TOUR

Begin this morning or afternoon walking excursion at the **Mission Houses Museum,** described above. If you're driving downtown you may, depending on space available, find metered on-street parking. After you've steeped yourself in the atmosphere of the past at the Mission Houses Museum and browsed through the gift shop, walk Ewa on King Street. You will come to historic **Kawaiahao Church,** described above. Continuing in an Ewa direction, you will pass the **War Memorial** in front of the Territorial Office Building. Beyond is the imposing **Statue of King Kamehameha I,** dressed in golden helmet and feathered cape. He stands at the entrace to the **State Judiciary Building, Aliiolani Hale,** built by Kamehameha V for the legislature, courts, and cabinet offices of the king's domain. It was formally opened by King Kalakaua for the legislative session of 1874. Just beyond is the **Post Office,** done in Spanish style with a large courtyard entrace garden.

Cross King Street now, and have a look at **Honolulu Hale— City Hall.** It's the off-white stucco Spanish-looking building on the corner. There is usually an art exhibit in the courtyard. Continuing in a Diamond Head direction (back the other way; we're strolling in an S-shaped route) on the *mauka* side of King, you will pass some very attractive white-trimmed brick buildings that house various city agencies. The thing just beyond them that appears to be numerous sections of cast-off black stovepipe gone mad is really an "art object": *Sky Gate* commissioned by the city and county at a six-figure fee, has caused a bit of artistic controversy in Honolulu. There are often free noontime concerts in its vicinity during the summer, check the newspapers for details.

The tall, gray concrete slab just beyond *Sky Gate* is the **Honolulu Municipal Building** (the rationale behind putting a gigantic structure in the midst of all the low-rises seems to have been making a choice between losing a lot of rolling green lawn or spoiling the view—and the latter won). Diagonally across from it, you will see a monarchy-style building with a terra-cotta roff; that's the **News Building,** home of the *Honolulu Advertiser* and *Star-Bulletin.* Now walk straight through—or around—the Municipal Building, and you'll be on Beretania Street, preparing to walk the third leg of our "S." The soft green building just *mauka* is the main **Board of Water Supply** office complex. Walk Ewa (turn left) on Beretania Street and note the very lovely building across from City Hall. This is **Kalanimoku,** one of the new state buildings. Have a look at the abundant tropical plantings that surround it. Just across Punchbowl from Kalanimoku is the **State Capitol** building, described above, where we end our walk.

GUIDED TOURS

Certainly the easiest way to see the sights of Honolulu and the island of Oahu is to take a guided tour—especially if your time is limited. Of the major tour operators, **Gray Line** (P.O. Box 30046, Honolulu, HI 96820; tel 808/836-1883) is well recommended; basic city tours begin around $23. You can call them, toll free, at

800/367-2420. They also run tours on all the major islands. If you don't mind spending a few dollars more, it's usually more fun to go on one of the smaller tours. **E Noa Tours** (1110 University Ave., Room 306, Honolulu, HI 96826; tel. 808/599-2561), for one, takes you out in a 17-passenger minibus and provides delightful, personalized looks at the island sights. You can't go wrong either way. Travel agents and hotel desks can arrange tours with both companies.

---

2. Hawaii, The Melting Pot

Perhaps the most intriguing thing about Hawaiian life is the fact that everybody here came from somewhere else. First the Polynesians; then, centuries later, the English, the Americans, the Chinese, the Japanese, the Filipinos, the Koreans, the Puerto Ricans, the French, the Irish, and so on, ad infinitum. Since so many of the races intermarried, the result is a colorful mélange, a tapestry of hues and textures unmatched anywhere else. But, fotunately, many of the races have still maintained their own traditions and cultures, and these are particularly evident in their yearly festivals and celebrations. Visitors are warmly welcomed to these events, and we suggest that you take in as many as may be going on when you are in the islands. Some people even plan their vacations around the festival calendar; for them, the Chinese New Year or the celebration of Philippine Independence Day or the Japanese Bon Dances of the summer season are the highlights of their trip. Below is a seasonal caldendar of events to watch for.

Chinese New Year: Help the local people welcome in the Year of the Dragon or the Year of the Horse or the year of the whatever. Chinese New Year is usually at the beginning of February, and for three weeks before and five days after there's the festival. There are cultural shows, banquets at the local Chinese restaurants, the crowning of a Narcissus Queen, parades with lanterns and lions, and dancing in the streets.

Japanese Girls' Day: Look in the windows of the big Japanese department stores at Ala Moana Center and in downtown Honolulu for displays of regally costumed dolls, all in honor of this holiday —March 3—when all Japanese girls receive dolls as presents.

Prince Kuhio Day: March 26 is the day on which the native Hawaiians celebrate the birthday of the "People's Prince," Jonah Kuhio Kalanianaole. Catch the ceremonies at Iolani Palace, at the tomb in the Royal Mausoleum, and at the sites of his home at Kuhio Beach.

Cherry Blossom Festival: Since the Japanese are now Hawaii's largest ethnic group, it seems as if everyone gets in on this spring event. In March or April, for about six weeks, you can see displays of flower arranging, judo, the tea ceremony, parades in the streets, and an "International Revue" straight from Japan.

Wesak Day: April 8, the brithday of Gautama Buddha, is the signal for the islands' Buddhists (mostly Japanese) to gather in Kapiolani Park for a sunrise ceremony. You can join the daylong celebration of music and dance.

Merrie Monarch Festival: The Olympics of hula are held every

April in Hilo, on the Big Island of Hawaii. Participants include outstanding hula halaus (schools) from all over the state. Seats are sold out months in advance, but everyone stays glued to their TVs during the entire week-long event.

Lei Day: May 1 is dear to the Hawaiians. Join the islanders in wearing a lei and be sure to see the Cazimero Brothers' show at night at the Waikiki Shell. In the afternoon there's a lei competition and exhibit.

Japanese Boy's Day: May 5 is the day ancient tradition specifies to decorate the family residence with colorful paper and fabric carp in honor of the eldest boy in the family. On the first Boys' Day after his birth, all of his grandparents and aunts and uncles, etc., would send a carp to be flown in his honor. These days carp are flown for all the family's male offspring, and you'd be surprised how many families of other nationalities also fly the bright fish for their boys.

Kamehameha Day: June 11 is one of the biggest celebrations of the year—a huge parade, luaus, fancy-dress balls, all in honor of the conqueror and uniter of the islands. The statue of Kamehameha in front of Iolani Palace is draped with hundreds of enormous flower leis, and the Mission Houses Museum runs a charming "Fancy Fair" on the grounds, where local craftspeople show their work.

Filipino Festival: Philippine Independence Day and Rizal Day fall in mid-June, and it's then the local Filipino population goes mad with a 17-day, Spanish-accented fiesta including dancing, singing, and big-name show at the Waikiki Shell.

Bon Dances: Watch the papers for the dates of the Bon Odori Dances, which are given throughout the islands in July and August. These ancient religious dances, honoring the spirits of the ancestors who have reached paradise, are probably the most colorful affairs of the summer. The dances are performed outdoors, both by adults and the especially adorable Japanese *keikis* dressed in their native costumes. Visitors can observe or even take a few lessons in Bon dancing (classes are announced in the papers).

Aloha Week: Once a year, from mid-September to mid-October, all the varied racial and ethnic groups get together for one big blow-out, and Aloha Week explodes. Kalahaua Avenue is blocked off, stages are set up along the entire stretch for almost non-stop entertainment, and the whole celebration begins with an enormous parade. The other islands also hold celebrations during different weeks in October—it's a good reason to come to Hawaii in October.

The rest of the big holidays—Thanksgiving, Christmas, New Year's—are observed just as they are back on the mainland. Except that thge faces around the Thanksgiving table gazing at the turkey may be Hawaiian-Chinese and people sing Christmas carols in the sand rather than the snow. That's the fun of Hawaii.

A WALK AROUND CHINATOWN

Whether or not there is anything special going on among the various ethnic groups when you are in Honolulu, you can always have an Oriental adventure of your own. An hour or two spent walking around Chinatown, either by yourself or on a guided tour, is a fascinating experience. A pleasant Chinese gentleman conducts an excellent shopping-and-temple tour sponsored by the Chinese Chamber of Commerce every Tuesday morning at 9:30am from 42 N. King St. The tour costs $4, and there is an optional lunch at $5. Phone 533-3181 for reservations. There is also a tour on Friday from 9:30am to 12:30pm at a cost of $4 per person, sponsored by the Hawaii Heritage Center (phone 521-2749 for reservations). Free two-hour walking tours sponsored by the Chinatown Historical Society are held daily at 10:30am, beginning at the Asia Mall of the Chinese Cultural Plaza, 100 N. Beretania St.

If, however, you dont' have the time for an organized tour or just want to walk about on your own, it's easy enough (although you miss the engaging running commentary that is provided). You should start at the **Cultural Plaza** (in the block bordered by Beretania, Maunakea, Kukui, and River streets). Pause to look at some of the shops, if you like, then continue your walk along Maunakea Street. Here you could poke your head into a bakery and munch on those irresistible Chinese pastries, candies, and buns (don't miss the moon cookies if the Chinese Moon Festival happens to be going on; otherwise, almond or wedding cake will do nicely). Then on to a food market across the street where you can pick up the bladder of an eel or sharks' fin. Or get some bird's-nest soup. It used to take the Chinese cooks days to prepare this, since they had to carefully extricate the feathers from the birds' saliva. Now it's all conveniently packaged, and no traditional nine-course Chinese banquet would be complete without it.

If you've got a cold or tummy-ache, you might stop in at the herbalist's shop next—there are several on Maunakea Street. Lots of *haoles* as well as local people consult the herbalist (who studies for four years, then undergoes an internship and is licensed by the state to practice). He makes a diagnosis by examining your pulse in several different spots, to determine the condition of different organs, then prescribes a concoction to be brewed and sipped; his office is usually behind the pharmacy. The brew may be made out of sea horses and sea dragons, antelope horns, or snakes (they're good for arthritis) and whatnot. Don't say you weren't warned.

There are literally dozens of gift shops in the neighborhood, where you can buy anything from a $1 sandalwood fan (very useful in the hot Hawaiian sun) to a piece of rare jade or an antique Oriental screen. If you're in the market for art, be aware that a number of prominent galleries have opened in Chinatown, which is undergoing something of an artistic reniassance. About a dozen small galleries are centered around Nuuanu Avenue and Smith Street, including Pegge Hopper, Gateway Gallery, Waterfall Gallery, and one showing the works of Ramsay, a pen-and-ink artists who also owns the adjoining Gallery Café. And don't miss **Cindy's Lei Shoppe** at 1034 Maunakea St. Somehow or other, Cindy manages to keep her prices lower than just about any other place in town, her work is beautiful, and the quality of the flowers is the best.

Probably the single most interesting place in Chinatown, and one you should visit whether or not you make the rest of the trip, is the **Kuan Yin Temple** at 170 N. Vineyard St. near the Foster Gardens. It's straight out of Asia, complete to its huge gold-leafed statues of Kuan Yin, the goddess of mercy, and various other gods, burning incense and joss sticks, offerings of fruits and flowers on the altars, and the people rustling about lighting candles. It's an authentic bit of Far Eastern life that should be seen and experienced.

3. Hawaii, The Cultural Center

Too many tourists think there is no entertainment in Hawaii besides hula shows and slack-key music. That's all well and good, but what they dont' realize is that there's plenty going on in the arts-entertainment-culture scene and that they're missing a good bet if they don't join the local people in enjoying it. Most of the shows and events are inexpensive, compared to mainland prices, and the quality is high.

THEATER

It's 5,000 miles from Broadway, but it's pretty good and it's getting better all the time. The top local group is the **Diamond Head Theater** (formerly known as Honolulu Community Theater), housed in the Ruger Theater, just behind Diamond Head. Major Broadway shows are the fare here, and you see them sooner than you'd expect, since the rights are easier to secure 2,500 miles out in the Pacific than on the road-show touring circuit. Sometimes name performers come out to join the local acting company. Check the local papers or phone 734-0274 for specific attractions and prices.

Up at the University of Hawaii at Manoa, serious theater endeavors continue all year long. The **John F. Kennedy Theater** here presents eight major productions a year by its Department of Theater and Dance. Ballet and modern dance productions, too. Information: 948-7655.

Starving Artists Theatre Company, in residence at the Mid-Pacific Institute, near the University of Hawaii, produces a full season of new and avant-garde plays, both local and international. Performances are held at the institute's Kawaihae Building. Information: 942-1942.

Manoa Valley Theatre is another of the top-notch theater groups in town. This nonprofit theater, which bills itself as "Honolulu's off-Broadway playhouse," is an intimate 150-seat theater which produces an annual season of plays and musicals. Established in 1969, MVT has earned a reputation for presenting exciting recent hits from Broadway and off-Broadway. It is located at 2833 E. Manoa Rd. in historic Manoa Avalley, near the University of Hawaii campus. Information: 988-6131.

The nationally acclaimed **Honolulu Theater for Youth** puts on exellent productions for children, but adults enjoy them, too. Most shows are aimed at those aged 6 and up. For information, call 839-9885.

ART

Hawaii's citizens, so attuned to the glories of nature, are also attuned to the glories of art. The islands are producing some tal-

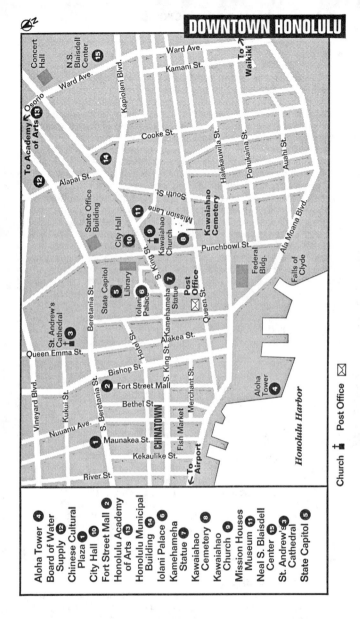

Church ✝ Post Office ⊠

ented young artists, and the local citizenry eagerly seeks out their works at a number of galleries. Art is constantly being commissioned for public buildings, and one of the great prides of the city is the **Honolulu Academy of Arts,** a must-see.

The academy is a supremely graceful building, a model of what

---

A Japanese Adventure

The Japanese neighborhood of downtown Hololulu is all but gone now, its rickety hotels and pool halls and saimin stands torn down for shiny new office buildings. You could visit the wholesale fish market auction early, early in the morning, at Kewalo Basin. But there's an easier way to catch the flavor of the old neighborhood-that-was, and that's to take a trip to **Tamashiro Market,** 802 N. King St. (at the corner of Palama). This is the Kalihi neighborhood, nea the Bishop Museum, and it's easiest to drive here. It's nominally just a fish store, but so unusual that people come from all over Honolulu, and school groups regularly make visits. The place is huge, crowded, pungent with the odors of the wierdest varieties of fresh seafood you can imagine. Like to try octopus? Kona crab? Raw aku? Or sea cucumber? They're all here. There's also a huge table of fresh seaweed, barrels of snails, live clams, live crabs, live lobsters, and live Hawaiian prawns in running water. So fresh is the fish and so excellent the quality that many of the leading restaurants buy here. Besides the fish, there are fascinating local dishes to buy and take out, like Filipino rice cakes made with coconut milk and mochi rice, Puerto Rican pasteles made with pork and bananas, Korean cucumber kimchee, and dozens of types of "poke" (prepeared seafoods, island style). You may need a native to help you pick and choose the dishes, but even if you just look, it's lots of fun. Tamashiro Market is open every day of the week.

---

an art museum should look like. Small galleries look out on serene courtyards through which you can wander after getting your fill of the treasures within. While both island artists and masters of Western art—Picasso, Braque, van Gogh, etc.—are well represented, and the real glory of the museum is in its collections of Oriental scrolls, paintings, tapestries, screens, and sculptures from Korea, China, Japan. Be sure to see the awe-inspiring statue of Kuan Yin, a 12th-century representation of the Chinese goddess of mercy, which is far more beautiful than the one in the Kuan Yin temple in Honolulu. A sculpture garden contains masterpieces from the academy collection, including some Noguchis and Henry Moores. The academy is located at 900 S. Beretania St. (across Thomas Square

---

Theater Hotline

Now it's easy to find out what's going on in Honolulu's busy theater scene. Phone 988-3255 any time of day or night and you'll reach the theater hotline sponsored by the Hawaii State Theatre Council. It provides information on all plays and musicals currently showing on Oahu, including dates, places, and numbers to call for ticket information.

from the Neal S. Blaisdell Center), and is open Tuesday to Saturday from 10am to 4:30pm, and on Sunday from 1 to 5pm; closd Monday. The academy shop is first-rate. TheBUS no.2 going downtown from Waikiki takes you to the academy's front door in about 10 minutes. A delightful lunch is served in the Garden Café. Phone 531-8865 for reservations. Outstanding primitive art of the Polynesian peoples can be viewed here and at the Bishop Museum, which we've discussed above.

Art lovers should also not miss a visit to the **Contemporary Museum** at the Spalding Estate, 2411 Makiki Heights Dr., both for the art and the beauty of its surroundings. A 1920s Honolulu mansion and a breathtaking garden overlooking city and sea house modern galleries and a collection focusing on 40 years of art in Hawaii, as well as on international artists of note. On permanent installation is David Hockney's stage set from the Metropolital Opera production of "L'Enfant et les Sortilèges." There's an appealing gift shop and an upbeat restaurant, The Contemporary Café. Admission $3 ages 15 and over; admission free on Thursday. Open 10am to 4pm daily except Monday, 12 noon to 4pm on Sunday. Information: 526-1322.

There are a number of private galleries that deserve a look-see, like the beautiful **Following Sea** at Kahala Mall Shopping Center, which represents outstanding work by craftspeople from all over the United States. You'll find many beautiful works in wood, fiber, ceramics, glass, jewelry, and more. . . . Other malls also abound with art and art-centered activities. **Images International of Hawaii,** for example, has two locations at Ala Moana Center, one at the Otsuka Gallery and a newly opened one in the Palm Boulevard section of Ala Moana. The gallery is known for sculpture, original paintings, and limited edition mixed media graphics of Southeast Asian art. . . . Ward Centre, 1200 Ala Moana Blvd., boasts two galleries: another branch of Images International and **Art à la Carte;** at adjoiing Ward Warehouse, **Artist Guild** showcases works by leading craftspeople and fine artists; and different local artists are available each day at **Art Cove,** to chat with viewers and discuss their work. . . . Moving downtown, note **Robyn Buntin,** who has three galleries in one at 900A Maunakaea St. One is devoted to Chinese and Japanese antiques; the second to 20th-century Hawaiian, mainland, and Oriental paintings and limited edition prints; the third to estate jewelry. Other Chinatown galleries worthy of note are **Pegge Hopper** at 1164 Nuuanu Ave., **Bakkus** at 929 Nuuanu Ave., and **Ramsay** at 1128 Smith St.

MUSIC

There's more to Hawaiian music than the unkulele and the old island songs. Much more, for Hawaii is a music-minded community. The local people flock to the concerts of the great orchestras and soloists who play engagements here en route to the Far East (or vice versa), and they take great pride in their own splendid **Honolulu Symphony Orchestra.** Since it plays over 100 concerts a year throughout the island chain, including summer concerts under the stars at the Waikiki Shell, you will probably get a chance to hear it.

If you're in Honolulu in February or March, you may get to see the yearly **Opera Festival** at Neilo S. Blaisdell Concert Hall. World-renowned opera stars sing with local choruses, under the auspices of the Hawaii Opera Theater.

DANCE

Hawaii's unique contribution to the art of the dance is, of course, the hula, and it is much more than just an entertainment for tourists. At one time it was a dance of spiritual significance. As you travel through the islands you will become aware of the importance the natives placed on the dance of Laka, the goddess of hula and the sister of the volcano goddess, Pele. You can still see the remains of a *heiau* on the Na Pali Cliffs of Kauai, to which devotees from all over Hawaii—men (who were the original hula dancers) as well as women—came to be trained in the *meles,* chants, and dances sacred to Laka.

Seeing the Hula danced in Hawaii is always pleasant, if not always completely authentic. You should plan to see the **Kodak Hula Show,** which is a good, solid presentation of Hawaiian dance and which, besides, costs only $2.50 for adults, free for children. The hour-long show is presented at 10am Tuesday, Wednesday, Thursday, and Friday in Kapiolani Park. . . . You can watch songs and dances of Polynesia, free or for the cost of a drink, at the poolside terrace of the Sheraton Princess Kaiulani Hotel, every evening between 5:30 and 9. . . . Dancers and musicians from the Polynesian Cultural Center perform on the Village Green of the Hilton Hawaiian Village every Tuesday from 3 to 6pm. . . . Practically a Honolulu institution, the Young People's Hula Show is presented every Sunday morning at 9:30 at the Ala Moana Shopping Center. The adorable performers start at the age of about 5. When school's out, there are also shows on Tuesday and Thursday at 2pm. Check the tourist papers for exact times of all shows, as they change frequently.

If you have a yen to learn the dance yourself, that can usually be arranged. Perhaps your own hotel will be giving hula classes, and there are often series of classes given by the city's Department of Parks and Recreation. Check the local papers for exact dates. There's usually a small admission charge.

But if you haven't got time for concentrated learning, at least observe the hula dancer carefully. You're supposed to keep your eyes on the hands, which tell the story, but you might be distracted by the wind-blown grass skirts (actually made of ti leaves), the flashing slit-bamboo rods used to beat out a tattoo, the featured gourds (*uliuli*) that sound like maracas, the clatter of koa-wood sticks against each other, or the click of smooth stones (*iliili*). And remember, if you see any really violent hula dancing, it's probably Tahitian, definitely not Hawaiian. For the Hawaiian hula is smooth as the trade winds, graceful as the swaying palms.

MOVIES

The latest Hollywood movies and the top films by international directors both draw big crowds in Honolulu. You can see them at various theaters in Waikiki and elsewhere in Honolulu, but you can also catch a Japanese, a Chinese, or maybe even a Filipino or Korean movie—and you probably can't do *that* back home. The entertainment pages of the Honolulu newspapers will provide the data.

Experimental filmmaking is on the rise in Honolulu, especially at the University of Hawaii, and small, informal film screenings are announced periodically.

THE UNIVERSITY OF HAWAII

Pride of Hawaii's nine-campus public system of higher education, the University of Hawaii at Manoa, is well worth your visit—not only for a theatrical presentation or a concert to an experimental film or a presentation of Asian folk dancing, but to see the campus itself.

Located in the lush, tropical Manoa Valley, with the mountains as a backdrop, the campus is just a short drive or bus ride from Waikiki, where a number of university students live. Originally a small, land-grant agricultural college, the university has grown the way everything in Hawaii has since statehood. It's now become an important center of higher leaning for some 21,000 students, many from far beyond the islands. The campus itself is a flower garden, art is prevalent everywhere, and the buildings are beautiful.

There are no guided tours of the university, but visitors are welcome to explore the campus. Maps and directions for self-guided tours are available at the University Relations Office (Hawaii Hall, Room 2). If you're an art enthusiast, be sure to see Jean Charlot's two-story mural of the history of the island in Bachman Hall and Juliette May Fraser's *Makahiki Ho'okupu* in Hamilton Library. There are other important murals by island artists at Bilger and Keller halls and in the Music Building: Good changing art exhibitions are on view at the Campus Center and the gallery in the Art Building; there are occasional exhibits at Burns Hall. For nature-lovers, rare varieites of tropical plants and trees are everywhere. But for us, the most intersting sights of the university are the students, especially the ones in native garb who are studying at the East-West Center. This important institute accepts graduate students from both East (Asia and the Pacific Islands) and West (the mainland), trains them in each other's cultures, and then sends them on fieldwork to those areas. Free tours of the East-West Center leave from Thomas Jefferson Hall every Wednesday at 1:30pm.

VI

HONOLULU NIGHTS

1. THE NAME ENTERTAINERS
2. HAWAIIAN & POLYNESIAN REVUES
3. FOR ROMANCE
4. THE DISCO & ROCK SCENE

We have heard it rumored that there really are visitors to Honolulu who have dinner early, watch TV in their hotel rooms, and go to bed at 10pm. But we strongly suspect these are only rumors. For the streets of Waikiki are thronged at night, the bars and clubs are jammed to the gills, and there's so much to do once the lights go on over the city that it seems a shame to waste time resting (you can always do that during the daytime on the beach). On a night out in Honolulu you might catch anyone from Danny Kaleikini to Don Ho. You could see a hula show or a Tahitian revue, hear some "Hawaiian mod" sounds, drink beer with the kids at the university while the stereo rocks the tables, look in on the disco scene, or sit at a quiet oceanside garden with someone you love and watch the sun set over the Pacific. You may spend a few dollars, or you may have to go all out and blow the budget for the big-time shows. Happily, though, the cost of nightlife is much cheaper here than, say, in New York or Las Vegas. And there's plenty of it.

1. The Name Entertainers

Note: Because nightclub entertainers have a way of moving around a bit, it's always wise to check the local tourist papers and phone ahead to get details on prices before going to a show. Be sure to check the papers for coupons and discount deals. On a recent off-month, we found $40 shows being advertised for as low as $20.

The **Danny Kaleikini** show is practically an institution in Hawaii, as much a part of the scene as Diamond Head or Waikiki Beach. Danny is the star attraction up at the **Hala Terrace** of the Kahala Hilton Hotel. A one-man show in himself (he sings, dances, and plays drums, ukulele, and nose flute), Danny presides over a talented company of Hawaiian musicians and singers. He exudes charm, warmth, and genuine old-fashioned *aloha*. The Hala Terrace is set against a backdrop of particularly romantic sea and sky, and it's great for those hand-holding evenings. Cost of the dinner show is $55.50. The show only is $9 cover plus a two-drink minimum. For reservations, phone 734-2211.

After (or during) dinner, one of the best spots in town is the elegant **Monarch Room** of the Royal Hawaiian hotel, where the islands' leading entertainers perform. You might catch the Cazimero Brothers and their excellent all-Hawaiian revue. The dinner show is $63; at the same show, you can have a drink and see the performance for $26.50; or take in the 10:30pm cocktail show for $15. (Prices are subject to change.) To make reservations for the Monarch Room, call 923-7311.

It will cost you $41.50 for adults, $28.50 for children, to see **Don Ho,** Hawaii's best-known entertainer, at the **Hilton Dome Showroom** of the Hilton Hawaiian Village hotel. That price, for the 9pm show includes dinner, plus a drink, tax, and gratuities. For cocktails only, the tab is $24 for adults, $16 for children. Don heads up a gala Polynesian extravaganza and has less opportunity for making not-so-subtle innuendos to the adoring grandmothers in the audience than he used to. Don is very, very popular, and some people wouldn't consider their trip to Hawaii complete without seeing him. The phone number for reservations is 949-4321, ext. 25.

International star **Charo** sizzles in the **Tropics Surf Club Showroom** nightly except Sunday. Buffet-dinner show prices are $44.50 for adults and $31 for children; cocktail show is $26.50 for adults, $18.50 for children. Showtime is 8pm. For reservations, call 949-4321, ext. 74000.

Hawaiian-born illusionist **John Hirokawa** entertains in the Hilton Dome Showroom nightly. Dinner show prices are $44.50 for adults and $31 for children. The cocktail show is $25 for adults, $17.50 for kids. A 6:30pm showtime makes this a great family entertainment. For reservations, call 949-4321, ext. 25.

The **Polynesian Palace** of the Outrigger Reef Towers, 227 Lewers St., is the lavish home of one of Hawaii's best-loved entertainers, **Al Harrington,** who used to play Ben Kokua on "Hawaii Five-O." The "South Pacific Man" leads a smartly paced review that is always entertaining. The price—$41 for the Sunday through Friday dinner shows—includes a hot entree buffet dinner, a drink, tax, and tips; for those 8 to 15, it's $23. Lower prices of $28 and $19 prevail for the cocktail shows, and include all tips and taxes. Reservations: 923-9861.

Seven of the most talented performers in Hawaii make up the **Society of Seven,** who have been headliners at the Outrigger Waikiki Main Showroom for many a year. Cost of the dinner show is $47.50 for adults, $37 for children under 12. It's $25 for adults, $18 for students 13 to 20 years old, and $13.50 for children for the cocktail show. Reservations: 922-6408.

Another big favorite with the local folks is **Frank DeLima,** a singing comedian whose outlandish parodies and skits can usually be counted upon to keep the patrons of the **Peacock Room** of the Queen Kapiolani Hotel more or less rolling in the aisles. Cover is $5, and there is a two-drink minimum.

The virtuoso of the ukulele—in his hands it truly sounds like a classical instrument—is **Herb Ohta,** also known as Ohta San. He's currently at the **Colony Lounge** of the Hyatt Regency hotel. No cover, no minimum.

2. Hawaiian & Polynesian Revues

Want to catch a great Polynesian show and a great buffet dinner at the same time? The Princess Kaiulani Hotel's "Polynesian Revue," one of the most professional in the Islands, lets out all the stops. The sensational Tahitian shimmy, the gentle Maori slap dances, the heart-stopping Samoan fire dance, and of course the languid Hawaiian hulas are performed by top artists. They're on twice nightly in the stunning Ainahu showroom, and while you're watching the fireworks on stage you can feast on a bountiful buffet for an all-inclusive tab of $46.50 per person, $19 for children under 12. Cocktails and show only runs $20.50 for adults, $14.50 for children under 12. For reservations, phone 971-5305.

3. For Romance

It's hard to imagine a more romantic spot in Waikiki than the spectacular **Hanohano Room** in the Sheraton-Waikiki hotel. The view is nonstop from Diamond Head to Pearl Harbor, the sunset is unforgettable, and from 8pm on, you can listen to piano music while you're having dinner.

The **House Without a Key,** one of Hawaii's traditional sunset spots, is back at the rebuilt and better-than-ever Halekulani hotel. This open-air waterfront cocktail lounge affords a fabulous view of the sun sinking over the water, and while you're enjoying that spectacle, you'll also enjoy relaxing music by either the Islanders or the Hiram Olsen Trio, plus hulas by Kanoe Miller, a former Miss Hawaii. Hawaiian music from 5 to 8:30pm daily. Loverly.

4. The Disco & Rock Scene

Disco and rock are both big in Honolulu, and while clubs come and clubs go (check the local papers when you're there), you can usually count on a few survivors. To join the local fanatics, you can make the scene at such places as **Spats Dance Club,** at the Hyatt Regency Waikiki, where the crowd really dresses on weekends. $3 cover charge weekdays, $5 weekends. . . . The **Point After** at the Hawaiian Regent Hotel, one of the big singles scenes in town, boasts twin dance floors, European decor, and high-tech video dancing. Cover charge is $10 for those 18 to 20, $5 for those 21 and over. . . . An international clientele makes the scene at the posh **Maharaja Restaurant and Disco,** the first Maharaja Club outside Japan, at the Waikiki Trade Center, 2255 Kuhio Ave. Cover charge Sunday through Thursday is $5; Friday and Saturday, $8. . . . There's a live band and lightshow every night at **Wave Waikiki,**

1877 Kalakaua Ave., Hawaii's biggest and brassiest live rock 'n' roll club. Cover is $5. . . . Have a meal after 4pm any day at **Kar Tunes** (whose name says it all) and you get a free pass that allows you to forgo the $5 cover charge. It's at Discovery Bay, 1778 Ala Moana Blvd. . . . Perhaps the prettiest spot for dancing is the semiprivate club **Annabelle's,** at the top of the Ilikai, 30 stories up, from which you can see the glittering kaleidoscope of the city lights below. You can dance from 5pm to 4 the next morning; the $4 cover charge does not begin until 9pm. During the 5 to 9pm happy hour, it's big-band sounds (drinks, $1.75); after 9pm, the music is Top 40, accented with big-screen video clips of popular performers. Women admitted free on Wednesdays. . . . At **Studebaker's,** in Restaurant Row, 500 Ala Moana, the action is "bop till you drop" seven nights a week. From 4 to 8pm they have a terrific free buffet. Cover charge is $1, plus one drink.

Entertainment at Sea

Combining a show with a sail and a view of Waikiki's fabled skyline is such a good idea that there is no end of dinner cruises to tempt the visitor. Among the best and most innovative are those offered aboard the splendid four-masted, square-sailed *Rella Mae*, flagship of the Windjammer Cruise Line. Both two-hour sunset and twilight cruises are offered, with a choice at the latter of seeing either a Polynesian Revue or the Comedy Club at Sea. The Comedy Club, whose home base is the Top of the I at the Ilikai Hotel, features both local and mainland stand-up comics and gets rave reviews from the local press. It's $45 for the dinner show, $35 for the cocktail show. Reservations: 922-1200.

The most inexpensive of such cruises is the No Booze Cruise sponsored by the Hawaii Baptist Resort ministries every Monday, Wednesday, and Friday night aboard the *Holo Holo Kai*, anchored a Kewalo Basin. On Monday and Friday, only appetizers are served, and the donation suggested is $15; on Wednesday, there's a full dinner and a $20 donation. The two-hour cruise, with "Christian music" and hula, leaves at 5:15pm. Reservations: 944-8033.

A HONOLULU SHOPPING BONANZA

Ask anyone who's been there: Honolulu is a great place to shop. In fact, if you walk along Kalakaua Avenue any afternoon or evening, it's sometimes seems that the tourists are doing nothing else. For even though there's no favorable exchange rate here or duty-free shopping, and prices are just about what you'd expect to pay back home, there are so many good buys and so many interesting things that everybody gets caught up in the shopping fever. New shopping complexes have blossomed all over Honolulu, with scads of temptations right in or very near Waikiki. Indulge and enjoy yourself—it can't be helped.

Spend an hour or two in the shops that line Kalakaua Avenue, in the Ala Moana Shopping Center, at the Royal Hawaiian Shopping Center, and you'll have a pretty good idea of the things that everybody wants to bring back from the islands. Clothing is undoubtedly the most popular item—island resort wear in bright, bold Hawaiian prints, the colors of the sun and the tropical landscape, T-shirts with island sayings and designs. And then there are fragrant, flowery perfumes, the carved tikis (figures of the Hawaiian gods), calabashes, carved woods, tapas (bark cloth printed with primitive religious symbols), dolls with grass skirts, ukuleles, shell necklaces, and other fanciful island jewelry. And the food—macadamia nuts, Hawaiian jams, coconut syrup, Kona coffee—not to mention the pineapples and coconuts that you'll want to have or send back home. All these are typical of the islands and they are on sale everywhere.

1. Souvenirs

You will, of course, have to buy dozens of souvenirs—small, inexpensive gifts for a few dollars, to bring to all the relatives and neighbors back home. We've found the best prices for these items—key chains, letter-openers, money clips, and the like, all decorated with some Hawaiian symbol or figure, as well as Hawaiian perfumes—are at the **ABC** discount stores, which are found everywhere in Waikiki (there's a large one at the corner of Kuhio and Kanekapolei). Other good places where you can pick up scads of these items are the **Woolworth's** on Kalakaua Avenue and at Ala Moana Shopping Center, **Long's Drugstore** in Ala Moana, and the Hawaiian gift shop at **Sears** in Ala Moana.

2. Clothing

Could you possibly come back from Hawaii without at least *one* muumuu or aloha shirt or bathing suit? Unthinkable! Let us first, however, tell the ladies a little bit about the Hawaiian fashion scene. Since every kind of contemporary fashion idea has hit Hawaii, it's a great place to shop for sophisticated resort wear, with many of the stores carrying lovely clothes by California designers. But after all, this is Hawaii, and we still think the most beautiful Hawaiian dresses are the graceful full-length muumuus that Hawaiian women have been wearing for over a century. You'll find them perfect for evening, and for daytime there are many lovely "shorty muus" as well as versions of the Chinese cheongsam. Men, of course, will want aloha shirts—boldly printed and cut fuller than men's ordinary sport shirts, since they are designed to be worn outside the trousers. You can find Hawaiian clothing just about anywhere, but we'll give you a few hints on our own special favorites, where we feel the quality is the best for the money.

Liberty House, one of Hawaii's biggest and nicest department stores, can always be relied upon for top resort fashions. There are branches on Kalakaua, at Ala Moana, and elsewhere around town. **Andrade** is another good name to remember, with perhaps 10 branches in Waikiki, including the Royal Hawaiian Shopping Cen-

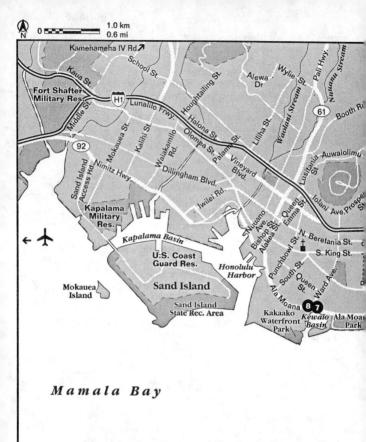

O'AHU

Honolulu ★

Waikiki

ter, the Sheraton Waikiki Hotel, and King's Village. **McInerny's** at Royal Hawaiian Shopping Center and Kahala Mall, is excellent. **Carol & Mary's** at the Royal Hawaiian Hotel and Kahala Mall handles the better Polynesian lines and a large selection of beautiful sportswear from mainland designers as well. **Mamo Howell** at Ward

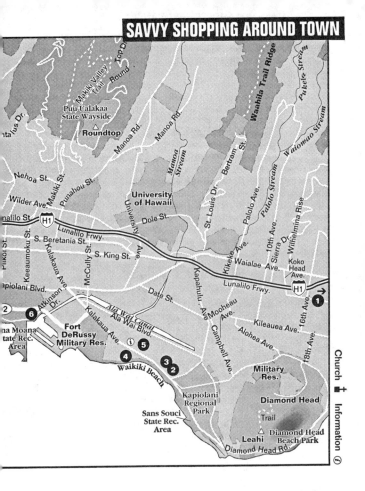

Warehouse uses Hawaiian quilt designs on her stunning muumuus; they can be seen on some of the best-dressed women in Honolulu. There's no beating the distinctive prints in men's shirts at **Reyn's,** with many branches, including Ala Moana Center. **J.C. Penney's** at Ala Moana and elsewhere does a terrific job in medium-priced fashions. **Sears** at Ala Moana has one of the best-priced Hawaiian-wear sections anywhere, and prices are also quite low at **Holiday Mart,** a discount department store near Ala Moana Center, at 801 Kaheka St.

3. Antique Aloha Shirts

You can buy a good aloha shirt anywhere for around $30 to $50 or even less. So why should anyone want to spend up to $1,000 for one? Many people do, since vintage rayon shirts from the 1930s and 1940s have become hot collectors items. **Bailey's Antique & Thrift Shop,** 758 Kapahulu, is the place celebrities and collectors go for their $100-to-$1,000 finds; but if you have only $5, $10, or $20 to spend, they have plenty for you, too. Great browsing here (tel. 734-7628).

4. King's Village

As much fun to browse through as to shop at, King's Village, at the corner of Koa and Kaiulani Avenues, recaptures the flavor of Hawaii's 19th-century monarchy period with its cobblestoned streets and classic architecture. You'll sense the European feeling as soon as you pass through the gate. There's a changing-of-the-guard ceremony nightly at 6:15. The tiny shops might suggest Victorian London at first glance, but their wares are definitely international, with a smattering of Polynesia. Shop and poke around as much as you like; we'll simply point out a few of our favorites en route.

The **Fossil Shop** is full of fascinations, like sharks' teeth pendants, minerals, crystals, shells, fossils, jewelry. Many low-priced items here. . . . **Liberty House** has a good selection of resort togs,

---

Designer Finds

Where do Hawaii's best-dressed women—socialites, celebrities, and others of that ilk—send their designer duds when they've gotten just a wee bit bored with them? In all likelihood, to an extraordinary consignment shop called **The Ultimate You,** at 1112 Auahi St., just opposite Ward Centre. Here's where fashion-conscious Honoluluans pick them up for something like 50% to 90% off their original prices—and so can you. Owner Kelsey Sears also discounts brand-new merchandise, much of it from European designers. The stock changes here constantly, but you might find $600 designer skirts for $90, or a $100 dress for anywhere from $10 to $50, perhaps a $3,000 alligator handbag for $500 or less. Always worth a look (tel. 523-3888). Open Monday to Saturday 10am to 6pm.

and unbiquitous **Crazy Shirts** has a large store here. . . . Prices on T-shirts, dresses, and costume jewelry are always low at **Harriet's Ready Made and Fabrics,** one of the few stores in Waikiki where you can buy fabrics by the yard. . . . The **Royal Peddler** has scads of gift items, with very large selections of brass and nautical items. . . . All kinds of candles in whimsical shapes are available at **Candle Odyssey.** . . . Women's and children's clothing and accessories from the Philippines are shown at **Casa Tesoro.** . . . and sports car accessories are nifty at **Euro Motor Emporium.**

In keeping with the British atmosphere of King's Village, there's an English pub: the **Rose and Crown** is perfect for a glass of ale, a meal or snack, a sing-along at the piano, or even a game of darts. You can have Thai food at **Bangkok Orchid,** Japanese treats at **Tanaka of Tokyo** and **Odoriki.**

5. Atrium Shops at Hyatt Regency Waikiki

The exquisite Hyatt Regency Waikiki, that skyscraper hotel on Kalakaua Avenue across from Kuhio Beach, houses a beautiful shopping complex, glistening with fountains, waterfalls, superb metal sculptures, massive plantings—and all in a stunning Hawaiian monarchy setting. Three tiers of shops are reached by staircase or escalator. Many of the names here are designer—Gucci, Paris Shop, Bugatti—but others are in a more competitive price range. **Cotton Cargo** believes you can't improve on nature, and shows a delightful collection of women's clothing in 100% cotton, with styles ranging from traditional to avant-garde. . . . **Bebe Sports** carries trendy clothing for men and women, featuring fashions by, among others, Jeff Hamilton, North Beach Leather, and Torras of Spain. . . . Popular chains **Benneton, Espirit,** and **Crazy Shirts** all have outposts here. . . . **Folli Follie** is the place for high fashion gold and sterling-silver jewelry. . . . If you need a new pair of shoes, or an extra piece of luggage to take home on the plane, check out the selections at **Cal-Oahu.** . . . **Islander Thongs** is another good place for footwear. . . . **The Royal Peddler** specializes in brass and nautical gifts.

In between shopping chores, catch some of the free events that go on all day—classes in Hawaiian quilt making, lei making, hula dancing, historical walks around Waikiki, and more. Check the local tourist papers to find out about free programs of Hawaiian entertainment and fashion shows that are often held in the Great Hall. The Atrium is ideal for after-dinner walking and browsing and obligingly stays open from 9am until 11pm.

6. Waikiki Shopping Plaza

One expects to find open-air, palm-tree-lined shopping plazas in Waikiki, with booths selling grass skirts and coconuts; what one does not expect is a completely enclosed, several-storied building sporting expensive European, mainland, and Japanese goods, with the Japanese influence growing steadily (many of the shops do not provide English translations). Yet that is basically what you'll find at the **Waikiki Shopping Plaza** at 2250 Kalakaua Ave., corner of Seaside.

Some of the outstanding shops here include European fashion favorites like **Courrèges, Bally of Switzerland,** and **Hunting World;** Oriental outposts like **Yokohama Okadaya** for Japanese folk crafts, with many handmade objects. **Ala Baba Imports,** a major source for eelskin products, has a huge store here, offering handbags, wallets, belts, billfolds, and the like, at wholesale prices. **Leather from the Sea** and **Eelskin Elegance** are also worth checking out. . . . **Art Forum** is a prestigious gallery here. . . . Our favorite clothing shops here are **Villa Roma** and **Chocolates for Breakfast,** both designer's boutiques. **Advantage Hawaii** is an enormous, two-level store with good prices on everything from souvenirs to food to resort wear and much more. Waikiki's only bookstore—**Waldenbooks**—is here, too.

You can use the elevators here, but it's more fun to ride the escalators all the way to the top, admiring the million-dollar waterfall five stories high with dancing waters and changing colors. **Lau Yee Chai,** one of Honolulu's top Chinese restaurants, is here, and on the lower level, a bevy of exotic fast-food establishments.

7. Royal Hawaiian Shopping Center

One of the newer shopping centers in town, this is also one of the biggest and most grandiose: $40 million and 6½ acres of the most valuable real estate in Hawaii went into its making. Located on Kalakaua Avenue, fronting the entrance to the Royal Hawaiian and Sheraton-Waikiki hotels, it is three city blocks full of island shops and restaurants set in a tasteful and still-growing tropical environment. Its courtyard is filled with Hawaiian plants and trailing vines, and new shrubbery, plantings, and palm trees are being added all the time. More than 140 shops and restaurants can provide hours of amusement.

There's so much to see here that you should wander around as fancy leads you. We'll point out a few of our favorites, just to get you started. If price is no object, join the crowds of Japanese and other international visitors who wait in line to get into designer shops like **Louis Vuitton, Lancel,** and **Chanel.** Boutiques bearing such European fashion names as Giorgio Armani, Ferragamo, Hermès, Izod, Burberry, and the like, are all part of the **McInerny Galleria** on the first and second floors. But another McInerny shop here features a "Sale Studio," where prices are marked way down. And at **Swimsuit Warehouse,** all bikinis are just $23.95, all one-piece suits $26.95—so the price range among shops here is enormous. One of our favorite places is the **Little Hawaiian Craft Shop,** where everything is handmade in Hawaii. Rare Niihau shell necklaces, authentic kukui nuts, feather hatbands, and the like are among the traditional handcrafts of old Hawaii to be found here. Prices are modest, beginning at $1 or less, and the people couldn't be nicer. . . . The **Hawaiian Wood Shed,** next door, specializing in replicas of Hawaiian artifacts as well as collectors' items, is run by the same management. . . . Using only silk, cotton, and other natural fabrics, dying them in the subtlest and softest of colors, designer Marlo Shima creates women's clothing of great beauty. Dresses, long and short, plus sportswear, are all on the second level at **Marlo's Boutique.** . . . **Aki International** has lovely gifts that start at low prices. . . . You'll want all the butter-soft leather items in **Raku Leather:** attaché cases, backgammon sets, and beautiful bags.

Eating can be great fun at the Royal Hawaiian Shopping Center. **Beijing Garden** features fresh seafood, Oriental-style. It's inexpensive to eat all the spaghetti you want and then some at **Spaghetti! Spaghetti!** Moderately priced Japanese meals are offered at **Daruma,** while **Naniwa-ya** has an old-fashioned Japanese inn setting for popular Japanese food plus a Teppan Steak House. And at the **Bavarian Beer Garden,** there's *wunderbar* music to eat, drink, and dance to. Free entertainments, lectures, and demonstrations go on all the time; check the local papers for details. The Royal Hawaiian Shopping Center is open from 9am to 10pm Monday through Saturday, until 9pm on Sunday.

---

8. Ala Moana Shopping Center

Ala Moana is a shopping center for those who hate shopping centers. It's 50 acres of island architecture at its best, laced with pools and gardens, plantings and sculptures, fountains and wide shady malls. In between are the shops—and what shops! An international array from East and West, as dazzling a selection of goods as can be found anywhere, in as wide a price range as possible, and a fascinating barometer of how far the 50th state has come into the modern world of merchandising.

All the big Hawaiian names are here: **Sears** has an attractive store with very well-priced selections in souvenirs and resort wear, as does **J. C. Penney.** . . . You'll find excellent merchandise throughout at **Liberty House**'s flagship store. . . . **Reyn's** is tops for men's wear. . . . Join the throngs of local citizens who flock to the Japanese department stores like **Shirokiya.** . . . **Hopaco Stationers** has all sorts of tasteful gifts, Hawaiian specialties, and stationery. . . . At the **Hale Kukui Candle Shop** you'll find tiki gods and pineapples to burn.

The **Sharper Image** is the catalog store to end all catalog stores. You can actually try all those amazing gadgets—exercise machines and electronic massage tables—as well as say hello to a robot or experience the latest in biofeedback equipment. A must! . . . You'll find something at the **Slipper Shop** to soothe your feet, something to read at **Honolulu Bookstore,** something to wear at **Laura Ashley** or at **Tahiti Imports.** . . . **Paniolo Trading Company** is the place for cowboy togs, **Alexia** for women's clothing in natural fabrics from Greece, **Prides of New Zealand** for sheepskin rugs and woolen sweaters. . . . **Elephant Walk** is a must for gifts, **The Compleat Kitchen and More** for household items. . . . Fashion choices include branches of the popular **Benneton** for Italian sportswear, **Défense d'Afficher** for French casual wear, **Banana Republic** for that safari look. . . . There's plenty of health foods at **Vim and Vigor,** plenty of chocolates at **La Maison de Chocolat,** and plenty of everything edible at the gigantic **Foodland Supermarket,** an international food fair under one roof.

Californians lonely for Rodeo Drive now have Palm Boulevard here at Ala Moana. Designed for an affluent crowd, the new area features such shops as **Chanel, Gucci, Jaeger, Adrienne Vittadini, Polo/Ralph Lauren,** and others of that ilk.

As for restaurants, Ala Moana is the answer to a hungry person's prayer: At the **Makai Market,** Hawaii's largest food court, you can sample a variety of international foods—American, Chinese, Filipino, Hawaiian, Italian, Japanese, Korean, Mexican, Thai, and more. Longtime favorites here: **Lyn's Delicatessen** for kosher-style deli sandwiches and special buys on steak dinners, and **Patti's Chinese Kitchen,** where hungry throngs line up for filling, fantastic plate lunches. **Shirokiya** offers serve-yourself Japanese food, and both **Liberty House** and **J. C. Penney** have pleasant restaurants. Stylish **Fishmonger's Wife** has sophisticated cuisine and a great grazing menu.

To reach Ala Moana from Waikiki, take either TheBUS no. 8 or no. 19 from Kalakaua Avenue; it's about a 10-minute ride. The center is open 9:30am to 9pm Monday to Saturday; Sunday hours are 10am to 5pm. There are acres of parking.

9. Ward Warehouse

A shopping center with class and charisma is the Ward Warehouse, 15 minutes from Waikiki at 1050 Ala Moana Blvd., across from Fisherman's Wharf. The artistic level here is surprisingly high, both in the buildings, reminiscent of the dockside warehouses of early Hawaii, and in the shops and boutiques (this is one shopping center equally popular with sophisticated Honolulu residents as with visitors).

Many shops have to do with fine and decorative arts. **Nohea Gallery** is a stunner: Many local and Asian artists show glass, hardwoods, sculpture, jewelry, paintings, prints, and much more. Prices vary, beginning modestly. . . . Posters, prints, original photographs, all at small prices, can be found at **Frame Shack** and **Art Board.** . . . The art of neon comes alive at **Neon Leon:** You're invited to custom-design your own logos, names, frames, or whatever, in this new art medium.

The artistic impulse at Ward Warehouse also translates into clothing at shops like **Pomegranates in the Sun,** which features the work of local artists and designers inspired by the Hawaiian atmosphere. Many items are one-of-a-kind. Highly artful, too, is the clothing at shops like **Blue Ginger Designs,** with its delicate hand-blocked batik fabrics; **Kinnari,** where beautiful long muumuus are handcrafted by a lovely lady from Thailand, and **Mamo Howell,** where striking muumuus, long and short, are based on designs derived from Hawaiian quilt patterns.

You can find toys and educational material for children at **Child's Play,** maternity and baby clothes at **In Bloom.** Fit yourself to a pair of comfy sandals at **Birkenstock Footprints,** go wild with the kitchen gadgets at **Executive Chef,** a gourmet kitchen shop, or with whimsical bath and travel accessories at **Bath and Butler.**

Buy some coffee or tea (Hawaiian teas include up-country Maui blends like Makawao mint) and a big coffee mug at **The Coffee Works.** You can have a cup of coffee, a pastry, or a light meal while you're at it.

Ward Warehouse has many highly enjoyable restaurants, like the **Old Spaghetti Factory,** laden with outrageous Victorian antiques and serving meals at low prices; **Stuart Anderson's Cattle Company,** famous for their well-priced prime ribs and chicken dinners; and **Orson's,** which serves terrific local fish and seafood. Fabulous Japanese buffet meals can be enjoyed at lunch and dinnertime at **Restaurant Benkel.**

Shopping hours at Ward Warehouse are 10am to 9pm Monday to Friday, to 5pm on Saturday, and 11am to 4pm on Sunday. Any no. 8 bus from Waikiki (except those marked "Waikiki Beach and Hotels") will get you there.

10. Ward Centre

Not far from Ward Warehouse, Ward Centre, 1200 Ala Moana Blvd., is island shopping with elegance. Offering the best in women's fashions are places like **Susan Marie** (so elegant with its white grand piano up front); **Lady Judith,** which shows wonderfully romantic fashions for women and girls by designers like Gunne Sax, Jessica McClintock, and Lanz; and **Style Me Petite,** with high style for the smaller woman. . . . **MayeeLok's** free-flowing, very expensive, very feminine georgette dresses are coveted by Honolulu's most chic businesswomen. . . . It's fun to pop into **Sedona,** "Your New Age Resource," explore the crystals, jewelry, and other New Age goodies, maybe get a psychic reading, available every day after noon. . . . Fragrances, potpourris, lacy handkerchiefs, and the like abound at **Peony Arts.** . . . **Art à la Carte** and **La Galerie de Paris** both have excellent collections. . . . Wonderful breads and divine pastries emerge from the ovens at **Mary Catherines** . . . we dare you to resist! . . . Gourmet food items (including the best pastas and cheeses flown in from Europe), plus fine wines and spirits, are offered at **R. Field Wine Co.**

Ward Centre houses some of our favorite Honolulu restaurants, many of which, like Compadres, Il Fresco, Monterey Bay Canners, Crêpe Fever!, Mocha Java, and Ryan's Grill, we've already told you about in Chapter IV. Another winner is the **Yum Yum Tree,** for dining indoors or out on a garden lanai, with reasonably priced food and the best pies in town. Keo's at Ward Centre offers superb Thai food in a graceful indoor/outdoor garden setting. Indeed, Ward Centre has perhaps more terrific restaurants under one roof than any other place in Hawaii!

Operating hours and directions are the same as those for Ward Warehouse, above.

11. Kahala Mall

Islanders love to shop at Kahala Mall, and you very likely will too. It's an indoor, air-conditioned, fully carpeted suburban shopping center, with none of the frenetic pace of Ala Moana. There are many intriguing specialty shops here. It's difficult to know whether to call **Following Sea** a shop or a crafts gallery, but this striking place is such a beautiful visual experience that it should not be missed. You'll see no mass-produced tourist junk here: Everything is one-of-a-kind, created by outstanding American craftspeople, and truly unusual. Jewelry, woodwork, paperweights, stained-glass items, carvings, ceramics, etc., are priced from a little to a lot. . . . **Alion** and **Carol & Mary** are both tops in sophisticated island clothing for women. Alion is decidedly au courant, Carol & Mary more classic. . . . **Something Special** has *very* special T-shirts, as well as toys, imported toiletries, and all manner of enchanting gift items. . . . **Nancy Lang Couture Boutique** is a unique shop, with exclusive imports from Mexico, Greece, and Malaysia, and accessories from the Philippines and the Marshall Islands. They also carry the Malia and Princess Kaiulani muumuus, as well as high-fashion, ready-to-wear clothes from mainland designers. . . . For teens and young career girls, there's trendy **Wildflowers.** . . . Beautiful clothes from Mexico and India, among other places, can be found at **Cotton Cargo.** . . . Lots of neat things from Down Under are available at **Koala Blue,** including women's fashions, koala bears and stuffed kangaroos, and an Aussie Milk Bar, too. . . . **Paradizzio** is a lovely boutique filled with wonderful things for the home, shipped from around the world. . . . There's a branch of **The Compleat Kitchen,** for sophisticated houseware gifts. . . . **Benneton, The Gap,** and **Crazy Shirts,** popular everywhere, also have branches here.

When it's time for a coffee break—or something more substantial—there's **Yum Yum Tree** (known for its fabulous pies and moderately priced meals), **Yen King** for tasty Northern Chinese dishes, and the **California Pizza Kitchen** for an amazing array of wonderful pies. Across the street is a branch of the always enjoyable **Tony Roma's,** for ribs and fun.

To reach Kahala Mall by car, take the Waialae exit from the Lunalilo Freeway East; it's about a 15-minute drive from Waikiki. Most of the shops are open from 10am until 9pm Monday through Friday, and from 10am until 5pm on Saturday and Sunday.

EXPLORING OAHU

1. TRAVEL CHOICES
2. THE MAJOR SIGHTS

The beach was beautiful, the urban sights of Honolulu were exciting, but there's still more, much more, to see before you leave the island of Oahu. For on the other side of the mountains that border Waikiki is a verdant landscape almost as diverse as the city itself. Here are quiet country towns jostling bustling suburbs that feed commuters into the central city; ruins of old religious *heiaus* where sacrifices were made to the ancient gods near the modern meccas of the surfing set; cliffs thrusting skyward along the shores of velvety beaches where children play and campers set up their tents, not far from an enormous concentration of military muscle; acres of pineapple plantations using the most modern agricultural methods, and places where the taro is still cultivated the way it was in the old days. Hotels here are as peaceful as they should be, picnic spots are around every bend, and the restaurants are scenic attractions in themselves. And, of course, there are the sightseeing centers here, some of the most unique and interesting in the state. You'll have to see **Windward Oahu.**

1. Travel Choices

Should your time be short, you might want to pick out just one or two of the important sightseeing attractions windward and make a short, direct trip to them; you can take the tunnels carved through the mountains (the Pali or the Wilson Tunnel) to get you to places like the Polynesian Cultural Center or the Byodo-In Temple in less than an hour. But if you have the time, it is eminently rewarding to head out Diamond Head way and circle the island slowly, basking in the omnipresent natural beauty, stopping en route at the places that interest you the most. You must plan on a full day's trip, and it helps enormously if you have a car. Even without one, however, you can make this trip, thanks to TheBUS no. 55, "Circle Island," which departs from Ala Moana Center at 5 and 35 minutes after the hour, from 6:05am on, every day. It can get you around the island, albeit quite slowly; fare is 60¢, payable each time you board or reboard the bus. You might also take a sightseeing limousine, which is easy and comfortable, but if you're on a group tour, you're not free to stay as long as you want in any one place or jump out of the car for a swim whenever you feel like it. Your own wheels promise the most fun; so get yourself a good road map, take the flat-rate rental, and prepare for the memorable adventure that follows.

2. The Major Sights

We'll begin at Diamond Head Road. Circle around the beautiful residential area here and then get onto Rte. 72, which will lead you past Koko Head to **Hanauma Bay,** a turquoise beach at the bottom of a volcanic crater. Snorkelers rate this as one of the most beautiful spots on the island. Fish are so tame here that they'll eat right out of your hand. Unless you stop here for a swim (or for the day), you'll soon be speeding along a stunningly dramatic coastline where ancient lava cliffs drop down to the surging sea below. But don't speed; slow down to enjoy the beauty. The colors are spectacular, and just ahead is a geyser in the lava called the **Blow Hole.** This is the place to stop the car and lose yourself in the wind and the spray, before you get back to the business of living in the 1990s. Just ahead of you, the island's daring—and expert—body surfers are forgetting their problems in the giant waves of **Sandy Beach,** and a few miles down the road below the lighthouse, at **Makapuu Beach.** You probably won't want to join them, but drive on and join, instead, what will seem like half the island's families at Sea Life Park.

Sea Life Park Hawaii is a great place to take the *keikis,* and also yourself, for it's a thoroughly entertaining enterprise. Marine mammal research goes on here, but what you come for is the fun: You can travel three fathoms down a cavernous ramp and see some 3,000 species of fish swim gracefully by large glass windows in the 300,000-gallon Hawaiian Reef Tank. Comical penguins and darling dolphins perform at the Hawaii Ocean Theatre, and the Whalers Cove show, with its cetacean stars and Hawaiian folklore theme, is always entertaining. The emphasis here is on a truly Hawaiian ocean experience. Brief lectures are held throughout the day. Food and beverages are served at the Galley Restaurant and Spouter Bar. Admission (subject to change) is $14.25 for adults, $9.50 for juniors 7 to 12, and $4.95 for children 4 to 6. Special behind-the-scenes tours are also offered at low prices. Open daily from 9:30am to 5pm, until 10pm Friday when a Hawaiian show is included in the price of admission.

Several special excursion tours are available from Waikiki, including transportation and admission. The phone at the park is 259-7933; in Waikiki, 923-1531.

Back on the highway, the spectacular scenery continues, with beautiful **Bellows Field Beach** (open to the public only on weekends and holidays; other times it's just for the military) coming up on your right. If you want to see **Kailua,** which has some good restaurants and a lovely, peaceful beach, turn right on Rte. 61. If not, turn left on Rte. 61 and then right on Rte. 83. In a few minutes, Rte.

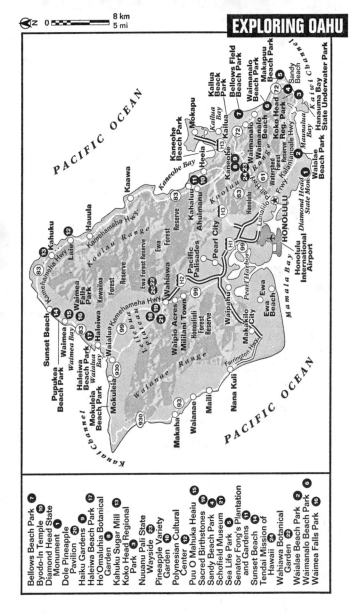

8 km
5 mi

Z
0

PACIFIC OCEAN

Kailua Beach Park
Bellows Field Beach Park
Waimanalo Beach Park
Makapuu Beach Park
Sandy Beach
Koko Head Reg. Park
Hanauma Bay State Underwater Park
Kaiwi Channel
Mokapu
Kailua Bay
Kailua
Kaneohe Beach Park
Kaneohe Bay
Heeia
Kaneohe
Waimanalo
Waialae Beach Park
Diamond Head State Mon.
HONOLULU
Koolau Range
Kahaluu
Ahuimanu
Reserve
Ewa Forest Reserve
Kaawa
Haula
Kamehameha Hwy
Laie
Kahuku
Sunset Beach
Pupukea Beach Park
Waimea
Waimea Bay
Waimea Falls Park
Haleiwa
Haleiwa Beach Park
Mokuleia Beach Park
Mokuleia
Kanai Channel
Pacific Palisades
Pearl City
Wahiawa
Ewa Forest Reserve
Waipio Acres
Mililani Town
Leilehua Plateau
Waialua
Kawailoa
Forest
Reserve
Honolulu International Airport
Pearl Harbor
Honouliuli Forest Reserve
Makakilo City
Ewa
Ewa Beach
Waipahu
Mamala Bay
Waianae Range
Waianae
Maili
Nana Kuli
Makaha
Farrington Hwy
Kanai Channel
PACIFIC OCEAN
Watershed
Kaalaina Range
Kahana
Lunalilo Hwy
Likelike Hwy

Bellows Beach Park ❼
Byodo-In Temple ❿
Diamond Head State Monument ❶
Dole Pineapple Pavilion ⓴
Haiku Gardens ❾
Haleiwa Beach Park ⓱
Ho'Omaluhia Botanical Garden ⓫
Kahuku Sugar Mill ⓭
Koko Head Regional Park ❸
Nuuanu Pali State Wayside ⓬
Pineapple Variety Garden ㉓
Polynesian Cultural Center ⓲
Puu O Mahuka Heiau ⓯
Sacred Birthstones ⓳
Sandy Beach Park ❹
Schofield Museum ㉑
Sea Life Park ❺
Senator Fong's Plantation and Gardens ❽
Sunset Beach ⓮
Tendai Mission of Hawaii ㉔
Wahiawa Botanical Garden ㉒
Waialae Beach Park ❷
Waimanalo Beach Park ❻
Waimea Falls Park ⓰

83 turns left on Likelike Highway, then right again on Kahekili Highway. Drive north on Kahekili for 2 miles, and prepare yourself for one of the most enthralling sights in the islands. No lover of Orientalia will want to miss a visit to **Byodo-In** in the Valley of the Temples, in the verdant Ahuimanu Valley. Byodo-In is a $2.6 mil-

lion replica of the 900-year-old Byodo-In Temple that has been proclaimed a National Treasure by the government of Japan. There is no doubt that this is one of the treasures of Hawaii. It was dedicated on June 7, 1968, almost 100 years to the day from the arrival of the first Japanese immigrants to the islands. The grounds are beautifully landscaped, with the temple sitting in the midst of a Japanese garden planted with plum and pine and bamboo. Before you enter the temple itself, ring the bell for good luck and the blessings of the Buddha. Inside the temple is an immense, imposing golden carving of Amida, the Buddha of the Western Paradise, an important work of sacred art, as are the filigree screens and panels. When you finish gazing at the treasures within, you can buy some fish food to feed the carp in the two-acre reflecting lake. You can also shop for Far Eastern souvenirs, walk through the tranquil gardens, and recharge yourself with the almost palpable serenity of Asia. There is a small admission charge of $2 for adults, $1 for children under 12. (To reach the temple directly from Honolulu, take the Likelike Hwy., turn left at Kahekili Hwy., and you will see the signs for the Valley of the Temples.)

In the mood for a garden tour? Two miles past the Valley of the Temples is **Senator Fong's Plantation and Gardens,** 47-285 Pulama Rd. in Kaneohe. Former U.S. Senator Hiram Fong has opened his magnificent 725-acre estate to the public; visitors are taken on guided tours in open trams. You can have lunch at the visitors center, even take a class in lei making. Plan on an hour or so for this delightful excursion. Admission is $6.50 for adults, $3 for children 5 to 12. Open daily from 10am to 4pm; last tour departs the visitors center at 3pm (tel. 239-6775).

Get back on Hwy. 83 now, and backtrack a couple of miles until you come to Kaneohe Bay and the little village of **Heeia.** Here you may want to drive out to the Heeia Kea pier and board one of the glass-bottom boats to see the coral gardens under the sea. The charge is $7.50 for adults, $3.50 for children under 12, for an hour's trip. (For advance reservations, which are suggested, phone 239-9955 before you leave Honolulu.)

ON THE WAY TO LAIE

The next important destination on your trip is Laie, the site of the Polynesian Cultural Center—you still have a way to go. And what a beautiful way it is, with gardens curving around to the green sea at every turn of the road. On the left are the remnants of the old **Waiahole Poi Factory,** which no longer is in operation. **Chinaman's Hat,** an island that looks just like its name, is the next point to notice on the right, and the ruins of an old sugar mill are on the left. Then, a few miles farther, you'll notice the rock formation called the **Crouching Lion,** which, with a little effort, you could imagine springing at you. But it's not at all menacing; it houses, in fact, a pleasant restaurant where you sit out on the lanai and have lunch. Go along a little farther now, and you'll find yourself at **Pat's at Punaluu,** a marvelously scenic beachside restaurant hidden behind a tall condominium building. Stop here for lunch, or have a picnic and a swim at **Kaaawa Beach Park** or **Swanzy Beach Park,** or stop off to admire the original artworks at the **Punaluu Gallery,** 53-353 Kamehameha Hwy. (Don't spend too long swimming and picnicking, however, if you want to pack all of this trip into one day.)

THE POLYNESIAN CULTURAL CENTER

Laie is a Mormon town. Mormon missionaries have been in Hawaii for over a hundred years, and the state's largest Mormon population makes its home in Laie. Here you can see the beautiful Hawaiian Temple and explore its gardens (enter from Halelaa Boulevard), see the Hawaiian campus of Brigham Young University, and visit the **Polynesian Cultural Center.** Built over 25 years ago to provide work and scholarships for Polynesian students and to revitalize the ancient Polynesian cultures, the Polynesian Cultural Center is one of the top tourist attractions in the Islands.

Seven authentic Polynesian villages have been created at the center—Hawaiian, Tongan, Fijian, Samoan, Maori, Marquesan, and Tahitian—and they are staffed by Polynesians who have been brought here from their respective islands for just this purpose. They demonstrate their crafts, perform their ancient songs and dances, explain their culture to you. Since a visit here means three or four hours (you should arrive no later than 2pm to enjoy it all), you may want to plan accordingly, perhaps saving this as a special trip for another day. Admission to the villages and afternoon highlights is $19.95. Add to this the Gateway Buffet and admission to the spectacular evening production, *This is Polynesia,* and costs will be $38.95 adults, $19.95 children. For $49.95, you get the Luau Package, which also includes the HawaiiMax Theatre presentation, and is considered the best value. Reservations can be made at the center's ticket office on the ground floor of the Royal Hawaiian Shopping Center in Waikiki. Phone 293-3333 or, from the mainland, toll free 800/367-7060.

THE NORTH SHORE

Since you've now covered the major sightseeing points on the Oahu trip, and since it may be getting late, you could drive back to Honolulu through the tunnels and be at your hotel in about an hour. If, however, you're still game for more, and especially for some beautiful scenery, keep going. A few miles ahead, after the road dips inward and then comes back to the shore, you're in surfer's country. This is Oahu's North Shore, and here, along **Sunset Beach** and **Waimea Bay,** where in winter the waves can come thundering in as high as 30 feet, you may see some of the best surfing in the islands. In summer, the water is usually quite gentle here and idyllic for swimming. **Waimea Falls Park,** which is just across the road from Waimea Bay, could be a refreshing stop now; situated in an 1,800-acre lush valley rich in the history of old Hawaii, the park includes one of the world's finest arboretums and botanical gardens, a wildlife preserve and bird sanctuary, miles of hiking trails, and magnificent plants and flowers—many of them rare and endangered (photographers, take note). You can play the ancient sports of old Hawaii—spear throwing, lawn bowling, Hawaiian checkers—at the Hawaiian Games site, and watch the park's resident hula troupe present ancient hulas several times daily. You may also catch the Acapulco-style diving from the cliffs at Waimea Falls. Have a picnic in the meadow, pick up something to eat at one of the snack bars, or have a lovely lunch at the open-air Pikake Pavilion. Twice each month the park opens its gates for free walks to the waterfall and back by the light of the full moon. Incidentally, this is one of the most popular spots for Hawaiian weddings! (For information on planning such an event, write Wedding Department, 59-864 Kamehameha Hwy., Haleiwa, HI 96712.) Admission is $13.95 for adults, $7.50 for juniors ages 7 to 12, and $2.75 for children 4 to 6. Open daily, including holidays, from 10am to 5pm. Phone: 638-8511 or 923-8448.

Should you like to indulge in a bit of *la dolce vita* now, stop at the **Turtle Bay Hilton Hotel and Country Club** (tel. 293-8811), just before you reach Sunset Beach. This luxury caravansary, where the president of the United States and the premier of Japan once met for summit talks, is fun to walk around and explore. You can have a buffet lunch in the attractive Palm Terrace overlooking the pool and ocean, or dinner plus entertainment in one of the two dining rooms. (They have a fabulous Sunday brunch from 9am to 2pm). Or plan your visit for the sunset hour and take yourself to the cocktail lounge overlooking the ocean at the Bay View Lounge in Kahuku, where you can watch the sun slip into the horizon and disappear behind that giant North Shore surf.

You have two more chances for a swim now, at **Pupukea Beach Park** and **Haleiwa Beach Park** on Wailua Bay, before the road will turn inland. (Swimming is safe in summer only.) You cannot completely circle the island of Oahu, since there is no paved road around rugged Kaena Point. You've got to go inland and start out from Honolulu again if you want to see the other coast. Now you pick up Rte. 82, Kamehameha Hwy., make a left, and soon you're in the midst of the largest pineapple plantation in the world, **Leilehua Plateau.** At the top of the road is a stand where you can buy what will undoubtedly be the finest Hawaiian pineapple you've ever tasted. Delicious.

Just before you reach the town of Wahiawa, still in the pineapple fields, look for a sign leading you to **Helemano Plantation,** a center that provides many retarded people with training and vocational opportunities. It has a gift shop, a bakery, and a country store, and serves an inexpensive buffet lunch between 11am and 2pm.

Now you approach **Wahiawa,** an area noted mainly as the home of the U.S. Army's Schofield Barracks. The army has a museum right inside the main gate and you are welcome to visit it. Across from the main gate of Schofield is **Kemoo Farm,** a favorite local restaurant since 1921. The restaurant no longer serves three meals a day, but there is a snack bar for breakfast and lunch, and, best of all, the Kemoo Farm Visitors Center, full of antiques, old photos, and historic memorabilia of the area, some of it for sale. Their famous Happy Cakes are also available. Stopping here is always a charming interlude.

Also in Wahiawa are the **Wahiawa Botanical Gardens,** 1396 California Ave., where you can wander free of charge through four acres of lovely trees, flowers, and shrubs, including a garden of native Hawaiian plants.

Soon Kamehameha Hwy. becomes a four-lane freeway, and you can speed along home. Take Hwy. 99 to the left when it intersects with Kamehameha, or Interstate Hwy. H-2, and proceed onto

Rte. 90, which goes by Pearl Harbor. If it's dinnertime, **Pearl City Tavern** (at the intersection of Kamehameha Hwy. and Pearl City) is a top choice for seafood and/or Japanese cuisine. You'll have fun watching the live-monkey enclosure behind the bar. At Middle Street, cross to the right side of Rte. 92 (Nimitz Hwy.) and it's non-stop past Honolulu Harbor and home to Waikiki.

THE BIG ISLAND: HAWAII

When you live on an island, where do you go for a vacation? To another island, of course. The residents of Honolulu usually take their vacations on what they call the neighbor or outer islands—the Big Island of Hawaii, the Garden Island of Kauai, the Valley Island of Maui, the Friendly Island of Molokai, the Pineapple Island of Lanai. And so should you. Take a vacation-within-a-vacation to one or two or, better yet, all five of the neighbor islands. For while Oahu is the most important place to see in Hawaii, there is a great deal more beyond its shores. Although the outside world is fast catching up with the neighbor islands, they are still much more relaxed than Honolulu. And they offer a panorama of natural wonders un-matched just about anywhere. It's not expensive to visit the islands; interisland plane fares are reasonable, and there are many fly-and-drive packages. As for living expenses, expect about the same mile-age from your travel dollars as you get in Honolulu.

No matter which way you choose to see the neighbor islands, see them you must. The lush mountains and glorious beaches of Ka-uai, the golden languors of Maui, the unspoiled charms of Molokai and Lanai await you. But now, the Big Island of Hawaii beckons.

1. Hawaii: Hotels, Restaurants & Nightlife

On Hawaii the earth is red, the sand is black, and a goddess named Pele still reigns. On Hawaii two jetports boom, the state's second-biggest city grows, and the beautiful people from the main-land arrive to lead *la dolce vita*. The island of Hawaii is a fascinating mix of legend and reality, of old beliefs and new ambitions. It probably contains more variety per square mile than any other part of the 50th state. It encompasses tropical beaches and snow-clad mountains; a very-much-alive volcano that spouts jet fountains of fire into the air quite often; lush, lush vegetation and rainfall, which make the orchids bloom as easily as weeds anywhere else; a cattle ranch as big as they make them in Texas; acres of coffee plantations; some of the best big-game-fishing waters in the world; and a population fiercely devoted to their island and its legendary history. For it was from here that Kamehameha the Great went to conquer and unite the independent island kingdoms around him, and to the federation that resulted he gave the name of his homeland—Hawaii.

Although some people call it the Orchid Island and some call it the Volcano Island, there is just one name that the islanders really use to refer to Hawaii: the Big Island. And big it is—4,038 square miles, almost twice as big as all the other Hawaiian islands combined and about the same size as the state of Connecticut. To really see the Big Island, you should plan on at least three or four days, making your headquarters in either Hilo on the eastern coast or Kona on the western coast. Kona has more in the way of beach, fishing, and resort activity; Hilo is the closest to Volcanoes National Park, which you won't want to miss. A good plan is to spend one night in Hilo, and then move on to Kona.

HILO HOTELS

Several of the major hotels in Hilo have closed in recent years, but those that are left offer good value for the traveler. Don't expect, however, to find gorgeous ocean beaches at these hotels. The shoreline on this side of the island is mostly volcanic rock. Although local kids do swim in Hilo Bay, it is somewhat rocky and swimming is not really good; the hotel pools offer a better answer to the tropical heat.

The traditional site for luxury hotels in Hilo has long been along the shore of Hilo Bay, and it's here that you'll find the fragrant, flowery **Hawaii Naniloa Hotel,** 93 Banyan Dr., Hilo, HI 96720 (tel. 808/969-3333; reservations toll free 800/367-5360), its lobby blending into spacious tropical gardens and overlooking the ocean. A new management and multimillion-dollar renovation have turned it into Hilo's most beautiful hotel. Guests have use of a new health spa, a 50-meter pool, and the golf course at the Naniloa Country Club, just across the way. They can feast on Japanese food at the Nihon Saryo Restaurant, on Chinese dishes at Shokoen, on American-Continental cuisine at the Sandalwood Room overlooking Hilo Bay, dance and listen to music at the Karaeoke Bar, occasionally catch cabaret shows at the Crown Room. And we think you'll like the rooms, especially those from the fourth floor up—the wide-view rooms overlooking Hilo Bay. All of the rooms, from the standard, garden-view at $89, the ocean-view at $109, the ocean-front at $104, single or double ($15 more triple), are attractively decorated in tropical motifs and have full tub-shower combinations, air conditioning, TV, radio, and coffeemaker; most have a private lanai, and there's courtesy ice on every floor. Children under 17 stay free in the same room with their parents. Cribs are free. The elegant suites, some of them with a wraparound lanai big enough to hold your own luau, range from $180 to $574.

The **Hilo Hawaiian Hotel,** 71 Banyan Dr. (tel. 935-9361; fax 808/961-9642; reservations toll free 800/367-5004 in U.S., 800/663-1118 in Canada), is another first-class choice. This beautifully landscaped, eight-story, 285-room hotel overlooks Hilo Bay, and its spacious open lobby with bamboo sofas is one of the most comfortable around. From its lanai terrace and pool you can walk right over to neighboring Coconut Island; in the distance is mighty Mauna Kea. All rooms have recently been refurbished, and are attractively decorated with twin, double, queen- or king-size beds, a table and two chairs, posters of seagulls and figureheads, air conditioning, color TV, separate dressing area, full bath and shower. Lanais are on the smallish side. Standard rooms, at $92 single or double, are on the lower floors; superior rooms, at $104, bring you up in the world somewhat; and deluxe rooms, which are more spacious and overlook Hilo Bay, are $115. Junior Suites are $132; Banyan Suites with kitchenettes go for $230; Ocean Suites, with kitchenettes, are $300 for up to six. Specially designed rooms are available for the handicapped. Rates subject to change. The Queen's

Seeing the Islands in Style
    For a spectacular way to see the neighbor islands, and if money is not a major consideration, book yourself a berth on the S.S. *Independence* or the S.S. *Constitution,* two luxury cruise liners that sail from Honolulu each Saturday, making all-day calls at Hilo and Kona on the Big Island; at Kahului, Maui; and at Nawiliwili, Kauai, before returning to Honolulu one week later. The S.S. *Independence* overnights at Maui, while the S.S. *Constitution* overnights at Kauai. Daily activities, entertainment, accommodations, and food are all first-rate on these "floating" Hawaiian resorts. And you only have to check in and unpack once during your seven-day, four-island visit. Passenger activities include pool games, hula lessons, ukulele instruction, aerobics, and more. Rates range from $1,095 per person, double occupancy, to $3,695. The S.S. *Constitution* also offers three- and four-day cruises combined with four- and three-day land stays, making for a complete seven-day cruise/resort vacation. Cruises also supplement part of the round-trip airfare to Honolulu. Information is available from **American Hawaii Cruises,** 550 Kearny St., San Francisco, CA 94108. The toll-free phone number for reservations is 800/765-7000.

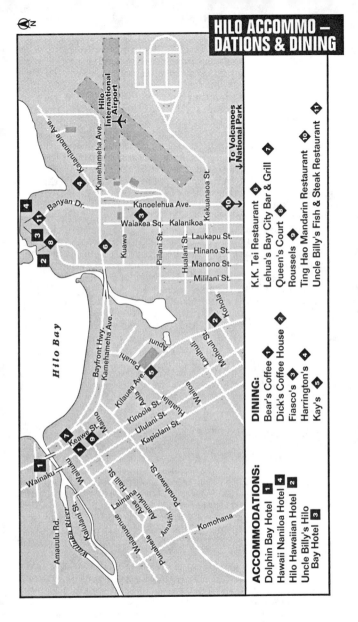

HILO ACCOMMO— DATIONS & DINING

ACCOMMODATIONS:

Dolphin Bay Hotel **1**
Hawaii Naniloa Hotel **4**
Hilo Hawaiian Hotel **2**
Uncle Billy's Hilo
Bay Hotel **3**

DINING:

Bear's Coffee ◆4
Dick's Coffee House ◆2
Fiasco's ◆3
Harrington's ◆4
Kay's ◆5
K.K. Tei Restaurant ◆6
Lehua's Bay City Bar & Grill ◆7
Queen's Court ◆8
Roussels ◆9
Ting Hao Mandarin Restaurant ◆10
Uncle Billy's Fish & Steak Restaurant ◆11

Court Dining Room serves up another marvelous view of Hilo Bay along with good food; and the Menehuneland Cocktail Lounge is a whimsical charmer. AE, DC, DISC, MC, V.

Uncle Billy's Hilo Bay Hotel, on the waterfront at 87 Banyan

Dr., Hilo, HI 96720 (tel. 808/935-0861; fax 808/935-7903; reservations toll free 800/367-5102), has been here for many years, with Uncle Billy Kimi and his large Hawaiian family extending plenty of *aloha*—from the hotel to the restaurant, where you get a free Hawaiian show along with your dinner every night. The 133 rooms are comfortably and nicely appointed in the island style, with private lanai, air conditioning, and view of either a tropical garden or the oceanfront. Room rates are $69, $74, $79, and $89 (oceanfront), single or double, $10 more during the winter high season. Studio suites with kitchenette begin at $79. Room-and-car packages, including continental breakfast, go from $84 to $109 for two. (Rates subject to change.) AE, DC, DISC, MC, V.

Just a few blocks from the heart of town, in an area overlooking the bay, is one of the cutest little places to be found anywhere in the city, the **Dolphin Bay Hotel**, 333 Iliahi St., Hilo, HI 96720 (tel. 808/935-1466). Full kitchens make this place ideal for the budget-conscious, and the hotel is as pretty as it is practical, since the grounds are resplendent with tropical vegetation (which you're welcome to pick and eat). The units are large and very nicely furnished, with big, modern tub-shower combinations; you couldn't ask for a cozier setting. A breeze from the bay provides natural air conditioning, and the price is certainly right—$36 for a single, $46 for a double in the four studio units. The superior studios, a bit larger and fitted out with queen/twin beds, cost $46 for one, $57 for two. There are also one-bedroom units at $67 and a two-bedroom giant at $77; an extra person in any of the accommodations is charged $8. No pools or fancy restaurants here, just comfortable living in a place where you'll feel really at home, plus plenty of good suggestions for sightseeing excursions. Write to John Alexander, the delightful manager, way ahead of time.

HILO RESTAURANTS

A big favorite ever since it opened its doors at 135 Kalanianaole St., overlooking the Ice Pond at Reed's Bay, **Harrington's** combines sophistication, relaxed elegance, scenic views, and terrific food. Call to make a reservation (961-4966), since this place is always busy. Once seated out in the open-air dining room, you can enjoy delicious appetizers ($2.75 to $6.95) such as oysters on the half shell or fresh steamed clams along with your libations. Main courses, which are served with rolls, a choice of salads, and a starch, always include the fresh catch of the day and lobster, market-priced. Prawns, scallops, calamari meunière, prime rib, Slavic steak, and chicken teriyaki, priced from $12 to $18 and up, are featured on the small menu, and certain items are available in combination (your waiter will explain). If you haven't made a reservation, don't fret; you can probably be seated in the lounge area and served from the appetizer and side-dish menu, enjoying the scene at a small price.

Harrington's serves dinner only, nightly from 5:30pm. There's another Harrington's in West Hawaii, at Kawaiahe Center on the Kohala Coast, offering the same menu, an open-air dining room overlooking the harbor, and beautiful sunset views; dinner only, from 5:30pm (tel. 882-7997). MC, V.

Believe it or not, *mes amis*, there's a little bit of New Orleans right here in old Hilo Town. **Roussels**, 60 Keawe St., serves authentic French Creole cuisine in a setting of Southern charm: potted palms, white curtains at the windows, bentwood chairs, white tablecloths, sparkling wooden floors. Bert Roussel and brothers Spencer and Andrew Olivier from New Orleans know their gumbo and their shrimp rémoulade and their blackened fish, to be sure; their menu is authentic and delicious. You'll want to sample the hearty gumbo, thick with bits of shrimp, crab, oyster, and okra ($3.95 for a cup, $14.85 as an entrée), then proceed to such main dishes as shrimp Creole (in tomato sauce), shrimp étouffée (a Louisiana classic, with brown seafood sauce), or trout meunière amandine (with slivered almonds and brown-butter sauce). If you still like yesterday's culinary craze, blackened fish, this is the place to have it: Chef Paul Prudhomme's Louisiana style of blackening the outside, keeping the inside moist and tender, is well carried out here, applied to the local catch of the day, and market-priced. Appetizers run $3.85 to $6.45; entrées from $12.25 to $20.95. A select assortment of French and California wines is available by the bottle and glass.

Call Roussels an experience in elegant dining. The food is exemplary, lights are romantic. It has recently received a *Travel/Holiday* award. Roussels serves dinner from 5 to 10pm every day. The lounge opens at 4:30pm. Reservations advised: phone 935-5111. AE, CB, DC, MC, V.

One of the most popular new restaurants to open in Hilo in many a moon has been **Lehua's Bay City Bar and Grill,** 11 Waianuenue Ave. (tel. 935-8055) in the downtown area. It's become a hangout for a sophisticated crowd who appreciate its friendly atmosphere and its light and imaginative food, a marriage of East and West with an island flair. Everything is made from scratch, using the freshest of ingredients, and many entrées are either marinated or charbroiled, so one can eat well here without worrying unduly about calories. Favorite dinner entrées, priced from $7 to $20, include charbroiled chicken, mixed grill, catch of the day, barbecue ribs, sautéed fresh vegetables, and spinach lasagne. Among the appetizers ($2 to $7), try not to miss the summer rolls —charbroiled chicken wrapped in lettuce and mint leaves, in the Thai style. Similar entrées, plus soup-and-sandwich specials, burgers, and salads, are popular at lunch. Desserts are wonderful: try the chocolate banana cake. Lehua's has lots of plants, mobiles; a big bar up front and a stage and dance floor, too, with dancing nightly from 9pm; on Friday and Saturday nights, it's the place to be for Hawaiian entertainment, which usually continues until late, late.

Lehua's is open Monday to Saturday, serving lunch from 11am to 5pm, dinner from 5 to 10pm. Reserve if you have a party of six or more. MC, V.

An elegant setting for a well-priced meal, the **Queen's Court** of the Hilo Hawaiian Hotel, 71 Banyan Dr. (tel. 935-9361), affords a splendid view of Hilo Bay. Handsomely done in tones of teal and mauve from carpeting to booths to drapes, the restaurant is entered via an etched-glass door picturing Iolani Palace; portraits of Hawaiian royalty, framed in koa wood, carry out the monarchy theme. The meals we enjoy the most here are the buffets: on Fridays, it's a seafood buffet; Saturdays, a Foods of Asia buffet; Sunday, a Hawaiian buffet; each is priced at $19.95. There's also a Sunday champagne brunch at $15.95. The regular menu, featuring Spanish, Italian, and American cuisine, is also good. Dinner appetizers ($2.25 to $14), include antipasto and sashimi, escargots, and sautéed shrimp; there's a lovely fresh fish soup with saffron, a tangy gazpacho, and a variety of salads and pastas. Complete dinners, served with soup of the day, salad, and beverages, are priced at $9.95 to $22.95. The paella valenciana is hearty and delicious, as is the rack of lamb, the veal roll (slices of veal rolled with scampi and cheese in a lemon butter sauce), the chicken cacciatore, and the fresh catch of the day. Chocolate mousse and cakes and pastries of the day round out the menu. Lunch is well priced, with sandwiches, salads, similar pastas, and entrées going from $4.75 to $15. And the Sunday champagne brunch is a fun treat at $14.95. Open daily.

The family that runs the **K. K. Tei Restaurant,** 1500 Kamehameha Ave., between Hilo and the airport (tel. 961-3791), has been serving fine Japanese food for well over 30 years now. The setting is attractive, and dinners, which average about $9 to $15, include sukiyaki, yosenabe (a succulent soup of chicken, seafood, vegetables, and fish), and shrimp tempura (K. K. Tei's specialty). Each dinner comes Japanese-style, with all the extras—miso soup, pickled cold vegetables, sashimi, rice, and hot Japanese tea. No matter what you choose, it's a bargain, and lunch is even more inexpensive, with complete Japanese lunches served in lacquer trays from about $5 to $11.

If there are at least six of you, reserve ahead for one of the teahouse rooms in the rear of the restaurant; they afford a view of a beautiful Japanese garden, complete with graveled walkways, and a spouting pool teeming with lilies and orchids, beautifully lit up at night.

Despite its name, a meal at **Fiasco's,** 200 Kanoelehua Ave., at Waiakea Square, will be anything but, for this is an attractive, lively place, with something on its menu for just about everybody. Local people swear by their salad bar lunch; the table is filled with fabulous fruits and vegetables, and it's just $5.95, along with a choice of soup. Favorite entrées at both lunch and dinner, include stir-fry chicken, herb chicken, country-fried steak, and several good pastas; almost everything is priced from $5.25 to under $10. On the appetizer list, batter-fried chicken drumettes with hot BBQ sauce are very popular, as is the baked Brie with fresh fruit and hot sourdough bread. For dessert, how about a chocolate macadamia nut mousse? Thursday, Friday, and Saturday nights, there's disco at the upstairs dance club.

Fiasco's is open daily from 11:30am to either 10 or 11pm. Reservations recommended on weekends: phone 935-7666. AE, MC, V.

Want some more budget ideas? That's easy. **Ting Hao Mandarin** Restaurant, in the Puainako Town Center (tel. 959-6288), close to the Prince Kuhio Shopping Plaza, enjoys the services of a gourmet chef and the plaudits of its customers for exquisite Chinese cooking, and charges between $5 and $9 for most entrées. Lunch and dinner daily. . . . **Kay's,** 684 Kilauea Ave. (tel. 969-1776), downtown, has just about the best barbecue chicken I've had in Hawaii, low, low, prices, and a lively local atmosphere. Open every day except Monday for breakfast, lunch and dinner. . . . **Dick's Coffee House,** in the Hilo Shopping Center (tel. 935-2769), is a perennial favorite with the local people. Main courses on the à la carte dinner menu, served with soup or salad plus starch, run mostly from $4 to $7, and include New York–cut steak, ham omelet, grilled fish filet, and pork cutlet. Cozy booths, a cocktail lounge, and fine food for the money. Open for all three meals. . . . Dessert heaven might be a good way to describe **Bears' Coffee** (tel. 935-0708), which adjoins The Most Irresistible Shop in Hilo at 110 Keawe St. You can relax at cheerful marble-topped tables and indulge yourself in yummie pastries plus a dozen kinds of coffee and espresso drinks, as well as salads, cold soups, deli and vegetarian sandwiches, and hearty breakfast items. It's Hilo's most popular deli-espresso café and always draws a smart crowd. Open 7am to 5pm weekdays, 8am to 4pm Saturday.

HILO AFTER DARK

A good hula show is the one put on each night at **Uncle Billy's Fish & Steak Restaurant** in the Hilo Bay Hotel at 6pm. The entertainment is in casual island style, and dinners go from about $9.95 to $14.95. Sandwiches are available for light eaters. No cover, no minimum. . . . Monday through Friday from 4 to 8pm is the time to head over to the Hilo Hawaiian Hotels **Menehuneland Lounge** to catch an authentic hula show presented by Alberta and Alvin Kalina, who have their own hula halau. No cover, no minimum, and some of the best prices in town for beer and house wine. Every night from 8pm to closing, Menehuneland Lounge presents contemporary music, with the Bill Brown Trio Sunday through Thursday and the Bobo Brown Trio Friday and Saturday. . . . **Fiasco's** becomes a dance club on Thursday, Friday, and Saturday evenings, from 8:30pm to 2am. Monday is comedy night. Haven't tried **karaoke** yet? These sing-alongs in both American and Japanese are very popular; there's one every night at K. K. Tei's Lounge.

GETTING TO KONA

You'll want to rent a car to get from Hilo to Kona or vice versa, so you might keep the following car-rental agencies in mind. Besides the big companies like **Alamo, Dollar, Hertz, Avis, National,** and **Budget** in Hilo, you'll find smaller outfits like **Thrifty** (tel. 935-1936) and **Sunshine of Hawaii Rent-A-Car Systems** (tel. 935-1108). At most companies standard-shift Datsuns and Toyotas may rent for as little as $23 a day, flat rate, during the off-season. Automatic-shift and larger cars will of course cost more. If you're flying into Kona first and will rent your car there, you can choose from **Alamo** (tel. 329-8896), **Hertz** (tel. 329-3566), **Avis** (tel. 329-1745), **Thrifty** (tel. 329-1730), **Sunshine** (tel. 329-2926), and others at Keahole Airport. Note that there is usually a ferrying charge—$40 Hilo to Kona, $45 Kona to Hilo—if you drop off the car at other than its home base; and since you're most likely driving from Hilo to Kona or vice versa, that will usually be the case. You could take a county bus cross island for $6, but then you miss the sights in between.

KOHALA COAST RESORTS

Make no mistake about it: The Kohala Coast is now the number-one upscale resort destination in the state. A combination of magnificent scenery, the best sandy beaches on the Big Island, and the willingness of investors to pour in millions upon millions to turn ancient lava flows into tropical oases has created a glorious playground for those who can afford the best.

Among certain members of the jet set the words "Mauna Kea" and "Hawaii" have become practically synonymous, ever since Laurance Rockefeller created the fabulous **Mauna Kea Beach Hotel** on the Kohala Coast some years ago, at 1 Mauna Kea Dr., Kohala Coast, HI 96743-9706 (tel. 808/882-7222; reservations toll free 800/882-6060). Presiding over a domain of some thousands of acres of cool ranchlands and gentle beachside, the hotel offers vacationers the best of many worlds: the bountiful slopes of Mauna Kea for hunting; deep-sea fishing in nearby Kona, where the world records are set; golf on an 18-hole championship course designed by Robert Trent Jones, Sr.; tennis at the 13-acre Tennis Park featuring 11 oceanside courts (Mauna Kea is rated as one of the 50 greatest tennis resorts in America by *Tennis* magazine); water sports, swimming, and the sun-worshipper's life on a glorious crescent of beach (where the snorkeling is out of this world). The grounds and buildings are models of landscaping and architecture, with priceless treasures of art from the Far East and the South Pacific vying with the natural splendors of trees and flowers. The rooms are spacious, with every modern convenience, Hawaiian and Polynesian decor, and graceful lanais open to the view everywhere. All of the resort's restaurants are exemplary, and all have tempting new menus—from the exotic Batik Room with its Ceylonese-inspired setting and a menu featuring traditional Mauna Kea dishes, Indian curries, and unique island delicacies, to The Pavilion, with contemporary cuisine and many choices from the kiawe wood broiler, to The Garden, a room celebrating the regional culinary specialties of the Big Island, to The Teppan Yaki, featuring dishes with a taste of Asia in an al fresco setting. Harmonious and serene are probably the best words for Mauna Kea; it is still the standard by which other Hawaii resorts are judged.

And now, oh yes, the prices. For European plan, single or double, mountain-view rooms range from $250 to $290 (the latter for rooms on the higher floors); ocean-view rooms are $370 to $420; and a beachfront room, on a low floor, is $360. For modified American plan, add $65 per person per day. For a third person, a rollaway is $25. Children under 5 free. Golf, tennis, scuba, and honeymoon packages are often available. There are many free activities for children. And whether or not you're staying here, it's fun to stop by for the famous buffet lunch, $21.50.

One of the newest and grandest of the grand hotels along this Kohala Coast is the **Hyatt Regency Waikoloa,** 1 Waikoloa Beach Drive, Kohala Coast, HI 96743 (tel. 808/885-1234; fax 808/885-2715; reservations toll free 800/233-1234), a $360 million "fantasy resort" that promises its lucky guests an extraordinary respite from the everyday world. Completely self-contained, the resort is located on 62 acres of ocean shoreline and features a network of canals stretching from one end of the property to the other, with canal boats ferrying guests along lush, scenic waterways; a spectacular array of gardens and a wildlife collection; a huge saltwater lagoon teeming with tropical fish and providing a home for tame dolphins;

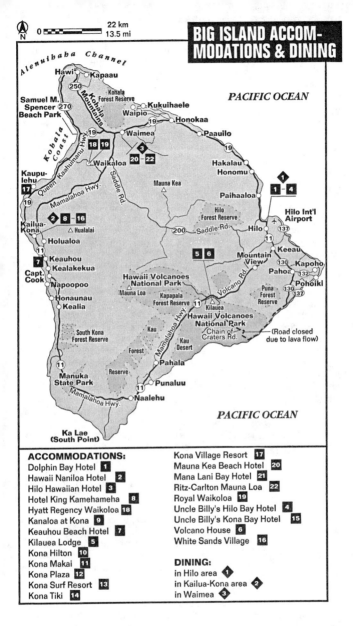

0 22 km
13.5 mi

Alenuihaha Channel

PACIFIC OCEAN

Hawi Kapaau
250
Kohala Forest Reserve
Kukuihaele
Samuel M. Spencer Beach Park
270
Kohala Mountains
Waipio
Honokaa
19
Honomu
Kohala Coast
19
Waimea
Paauilo
19
18 19
3
20 – 22
Waikoloa
Hakalau
Honomu
1
Kaupulehu
17
19
Queen Kaahumanu Hwy.
Paihaaloa
1 – 4
Mamalahoa Hwy.
Mauna Kea △
Hilo Forest Reserve
Hilo Int'l Airport
Kailua-Kona
2 8 – 16
△ Hualalai
Saddle Rd.
200
Saddle Rd.
137
Hilo
11
Holualoa
Keeaau
Keauhou
Kealakekua
7
Mountain View
Keeaau
130
Kapoho
132
Capt. Cook
5 6
Volcano Rd.
Pahoa
Pohoiki
Napoopoo
Hawaii Volcanoes National Park
Mauna Loa
Puna Forest Reserve
130
137
Honaunau
Kealia
Kapapala Forest Reserve
11
Kilauea
South Kona Forest Reserve
Hawaii Volcanoes National Park
Chain of Craters Rd.
(Road closed due to lava flow)
Kau
Kau Desert
Forest
Pahala
Manuka State Park
11
Reserve
Mamalahoa Hwy.
11
Punaluu
Naalehu
Ka Lae (South Point)

PACIFIC OCEAN

ACCOMMODATIONS:

Dolphin Bay Hotel **1**
Hawaii Naniloa Hotel **2**
Hilo Hawaiian Hotel **3**
Hotel King Kamehameha **8**
Hyatt Regency Waikoloa **18**
Kanaloa at Kona **9**
Keauhou Beach Hotel **7**
Kilauea Lodge **5**
Kona Hilton **10**
Kona Makai **11**
Kona Plaza **12**
Kona Surf Resort **13**
Kona Tiki **14**

Kona Village Resort **17**
Mauna Kea Beach Hotel **20**
Mana Lani Bay Hotel **21**
Ritz-Carlton Mauna Loa **22**
Royal Waikoloa **19**
Uncle Billy's Hilo Bay Hotel **4**
Uncle Billy's Kona Bay Hotel **15**
Volcano House **6**
White Sands Village **16**

DINING:
in Hilo area ◆1
in Kailua-Kona area ◆2
in Waimea ◆3

two space-age, tubular trams; enormous swimming pools with slides, waterfalls, grottoes (one of these has a long "riverpool" with current to carry guests along the stream); and a nearly mile-long museum walkway filled with treasures of Asian and Pacific art—just as a start. Then there are the sporting facilities, including a $16 million championship golf course; eight tennis courts in a garden setting and an exhibition court; and a fully equipped Anara health spa. There are over 1,241 beautifully appointed guest rooms in three low-rise buildings, each of which has its own ambience; 75% of the rooms have ocean views. Exclusive Regency Club rooms offer VIP service, complimentary breakfast, late-afternoon hors d'oeuvres, special room amenities, and the ministrations of a concierge. Seven restaurants serve continental, Italian, and Japanese cuisines, as well as seafood and broiler specialties; and there is a variety of lounges, plus a discotheque and a luau area for nightly dinner shows.

Rates, subject to change, are based on single/double occupancy. Garden View rooms are $235; Golf/Mountain rooms, $265; Ocean rooms, $305; Deluxe Ocean rooms, $335; Regency Club Mountain rooms, $370; Regency Club Ocean rooms, $395. No charge for children ages 16 and under using existing bed space; for each extra person over age 16, add $35 per night ($45 for Regency Club). AE, CB, DC, DISC, ER, JCB, MC, V.

The **Royal Waikoloa,** HCR-2, P.O. Box 5000, Kohala Coast, HI 96743-5000 (tel. 808/885-6789; reservations toll free 800/537-9800 from mainland U.S.), was the first major hotel of the planned Waikoloa Development, and it's a stunner. Located in an area once sacred to the Hawaiian *alii,* it abounds in Hawaiian history, from the royal fishponds adjacent to the magnificent lagoon to the most extensive petroglyph fields in Hawaii. The arrow-straight King's Pathway, once reserved only for the feet of royalty, now passes two 18-hole championship golf courses on the mountain side of the hotel. Six tennis courts, a freshwater swimming pool, nearby horseback riding, and most important of all, one of the most perfect white-sand beaches on the island, the half-mile crescent of Anaehoomalu, make this the kind of resort vacation paradise that tempts one to forget all about the world outside.

At the Royal Waikoloa, the boundaries between outside and inside are softened: open-air terraces extending over the surrounding pond make a gentle transition to the indoors. The 540 guest rooms in the six-story building and the 20 lagoon cabanas in their own two-story building are all attractive, decorated in island tones and motifs and each with its own lanai. All rooms have color TV, in-room movies, AM-FM radio with alarm clock, air conditioning, and refrigerator; 65% of them have ocean views. Rooms are all the same, with prices varying according to view and floor. During the summer season, standard, superior, deluxe, and oceanfront rooms are $110, $138, $165, and $215 ($10 for a third person). Lovely cabanas overlooking the lagoon are $250. During the winter, rates are $155, $175, $205, and $245; cabanas are $275. Rates subject to change. AE, DC, DISC, JCB, MC, V.

Dining facilities are as extensive and lovely as you would expect, from the hotel's main dinner showroom, the Royal Terrace, which offers live entertainment every night, to the more intimate Tiare Room for fine dining, to the open-air Garden Room, circled by a stream, offering lunch and dinner. And for sunset viewing—sunsets are spectacular all along the Kohala Coast—the airy Petroglyph Bar, with its open terraces, is just about perfect.

The **Mauna Lani Bay Hotel and Bungalows,** P.O. Box 4000, Kohala Coast, HI 96743 (tel. 808/885-6622; fax 808/885-4556; reservations toll free 800/367-2323 in U.S. mainland, 800/992-7987 in Hawaii), the "Emerald of Kohala," is by far one of the most beautiful resorts in these or any other islands. Built at a cost of about $80 million, this green oasis among the lava flats is an architectural stunner, a sportsman's paradise, and a world-class destination for those who demand—and can afford—the top of the line. A three-time winner of the prestigious AAA Five Diamond Award, it was rated the no. 1 resort in the United States and the no. 2 resort in the world by "Lifestyles of the Rich and Famous" in 1990. The six-story, 354-room hotel is set amid acres of gardens, plantings, ancient royal fishponds, and crystal lagoons: On one side is one of the more scenic golf courses on earth and a 10-court tennis garden, with pro facilities at both; on the other side is a perfect beach, its waves gentled by an offshore reef, and on the sand, deeply relaxing blue-covered cabanas by the palm trees. Blue tile walkways lead to the Grand Atrium, where waterfalls tumble beside the stairways, fish swim in the ponds, the air is fragrant with tropical perfumes. Once you've checked in with the knowledgeable conceirge (and been served juice from a silver tray while doing so), a glass elevator takes you to your room. It is spacious, of course, high-ceilinged, with every comfort (including a refrigerator and a television set hidden away in an armoire), and its lanai probably overlooks the ocean or beach—92% of the rooms do (others overlook the slopes of Mauna Kea). Guests can choose from among six restaurants and four bars, including the signature restaurant, Le Soleil, for contemporary French dining; the stunning oceanfront al fresco restaurant CanoeHouse for Pacific Rim cuisine (see below) right at the hotel and, at the surrounding Mauna Lani Resort, The Gallery, which has won numerous awards for its chef and menu, among the most imaginative in the islands (see below). There is no end to activities: one needs only enough time to stay here. A sampling of possibilities includes, in addition to golfing, tennis, swimming (in either the ocean or the pool surrounded by tropical gardens), daily workouts at the state-of-the-art spa, aquatoning classes in the pool, fishing, hunting, catamaran cruises, sails to secluded beaches, instruction in scuba and snorkeling, glass-bottom boat cruises, morning aerobics classes, jogging, Hawaiian cultural activities—even painting classes by the hotel's artist-in-residence. Children ages 5 to 12 can enjoy Camp Mauna Lani Bay daily during the summer and Christmas and Easter holidays. Mauna Lani's staff are gentle, knowledgeable people who do what they do in the nicest possible way.

For the ultimate experience in luxury resort living, guests may choose one of the five private two-bedroom, three-bath bungalows, each offering the services of a private butler and chef, a limousine on call, private swimming pool, Jacuzzi and spa, and every service that one might desire or imagine. For business summits, the bungalows can be outfitted with all office equipment, including wireless telephone, and specific security needs can be readily met. The bungalows rent for $2,000 to $2,500 a night.

For mere mortals, the rates at the Mauna Lani Bay Hotel, European plan, are $260 garden view, $280 partial ocean view, $350 ocean view, $395 oceanfront, $425 club suites, $700 suites. Ocean villas can be rented for $325 a day or $2,075 a week for a one-bedroom and $295 a day, $2,625 a week for a two-bedroom unit. For modified American plan, add $65 per person per day. Golf, tennis, honeymoon and family packages are available. (Rates subject to change.)

Ritz-Carlton, a name that has graced top hotels around the world, is now here on the Big Island, with the opening of a resort on the same property as the prestigious Mauna Lani Bay Hotel. Nestled on 32 acres of the Kohala Coast, surrounded by waterfalls and lush, tropical foliage, the **Ritz-Carlton Mauna Lani**, 1 North Kaniku Dr., Kohala Coast, HI 96743 (tel. 808/885-200; fax 808/885-8886; reservations toll free 800/241-3333), is as grand as its name suggests, yet beautifully suited to the landscape. It's easy to understand why this land, known in the Hawaiian Islands as Kalahuipua'a, has long been considered a mystical and spiritual place, its ancient history evidenced by a treasure trove of archeological sites, early Hawaiian footpaths, lava formations, and royal fishponds. Against this background, guests of the Ritz-Carlton can enjoy a white sand beach and a protected ocean lagoon for swimming, snorkeling, scuba, sailing, and fishing, a 10,000-square-foot swimming pool, 11 tennis courts, an 18-hole golf course, a fitness center, beauty salon, and shopping arcade. And of course, the ministrations of a concierge, and a multilingual staff ever at the ready to meet or anticipate any needs.

The 452 rooms are large and luxuriously appointed, with marble bathrooms, double vanities, and separate showers. Twice-a-day maid service, two phone lines, and complimentary in-room safes are just a few of the amenities the Ritz-Carlton provides. The club floor features deluxe guest rooms and suites, an exclusive lounge with complimentary refreshments served throughout the day, and a complete concierge staff. Rates go from $250 to $395 double; $425 double on the Ritz-Carlton Club floor; $500 to $2,500 suites. An extra person is $35 ($65 on the club floor). Rates subject to change. AE, DC, JCB, MC, V.

The Dining Room is the resort's showcase restaurant, featuring creative haute cuisine made with fresh, local Big Island produce, game, and fish. For a more informal atmosphere, The Grill Restaurant and Lounge offers steaks and seafood in a clublike atmosphere, with piano music from 6pm. The Cafe Restaurant and Lounge has just about everything, from authentic Asian specialties to fitness cuisine and an enjoyable children's menu, in an informal setting.

CLOSE TO KONA

There's a lot of talk about old Hawaii in the 50th state, but few ever get to really experience it—except those lucky enough to stay at **Kona Village Resort**, P.O. Box 1299, Kaupulehu-Kona, HI 96745 (tel. 808/325-5555; fax 808/325-5124; reservations toll free 800/367-5290), an enchanting old Hawaiian village that has been reborn a century and a half after a lava flow destroyed almost everything around it. The small area that was spared is the village of Kaupulehu, an idyllic 82-acre oasis in a 12,000-acre lava desert, the most purely get-away-from-it-all resort/retreat in the islands. At Kona Village, which is only 15 miles from the bright tourist world of Kailua-Kona and 5 miles from Keahole Airport, there are no lobbies, no elevators, no sidewalks, no cars, clocks, radios, televisions, or room phones to remind you that you are living in the world of the 1990s. Instead, there are 125 *hales*—thatched huts—built in the styles of Polynesia, Micronesia, and Melanesia; these luxuriously "primitive" cottages, with beautiful interior accoutrements (king-size or extra-long twin beds, dressing rooms, refrigerators, baths), stand on stilts facing ocean, beach, lagoon, or garden. They are not inexpensive: Rates range from $375 to $615 a night for two people, depending on location. But they do include three meals; breakfast and dinner are served in the impressive Hale Moana, a New Hebrides longhouse, and lunch is buffet-style in a garden setting. Weekly luaus, international cuisine nights, and paniolo steak fries provide variety. And there is entertainment every night.

Also included is a wealth of activities: tennis, Sunfish sailboats, snorkeling, fishing, guided historical walks to nearby petroglyph fields. You can also swim in a lava-lined freshwater (from an underground ocean spring) pool. Also available are charters for scuba diving, deep-sea fishing, and catamaran sails, as well as tennis lessons. Kona Village will even make all the arrangements for a Hawaiian wedding at sunset, in conjunction with their four-night honeymoon plan.

But the best thing about Kona Village is the feeling of seclusion, of retreat. Walking beside the almost mystically peaceful fishponds (protected long ago by King Kamehameha I), listening to the songs of birds, swimming on a secluded beach, one begins to feel what Hawaii must have been like long before the modern age. AE, CB, DC, MC, V.

RESTAURANTS IN WAIMEA & KOHALA

The picturesque little cowboy town of Waimea is rapidly being transformed into one of the Big Island's most sophisticated shopping and dining centers. One of the main reasons for this is **Merriman's Restaurant,** at Opelo Plaza on Route 19. It's a pretty place, art deco in mood, with lots of plants and flowers, original paintings, flickering candlelight. And the young owner, Peter Merriman, is considered to be one of the outstanding chefs of Hawaii—so much so, in fact, that people are willing to travel good distances to come here, knowing that they will dine regally on the freshest and finest local products, prepared with imagination, verve, and an unfailing sense of rightness. Some chefs put odd ingredients together, and they taste—well, odd. Merriman knows how to mix and match the unusual and make it wonderful. At dinner, for example, Puna goat cheese baked in a phyllo dough with orange sauce makes an excellent start, as does New England–style fish chowder with breadfruit, or a spinach salad with hot balsamic vinaigrette and pipikaula, or Ceasar salad with sashimi (starters run $3.75 to $6.75). Among the main courses, all accompanied by a fresh vegetable, a starch, and a Waimea green salad, the fresh local fish, done in a variety of presentations—grilled with spicy coconut sauce, steamed with Chinese black-bean sauce, sautéed with lemon and capers, or baked in a phyllo dough with a saffron dill sauce, is always wonderful. Wok-charred ahi (a signature dish), a zesty paella, a Mexican-style seafood stew with Big Island avocados, lamb curry with tropical chutney, and fresh roast pork with pineapple, are other delicious possibilities. Entrées run from $14.50 to $22.50; fish is market-priced. Chocolate mousse is everybody's favorite dessert. Lunch is excellent, too, and modestly priced: sandwiches, salads, and entrées from the grill run between $4.50 and $6.75.

Merriman's serves dinner nightly from 5:30 to 9pm, lunch weekdays only, 11:30am to 1pm. Reservations advised for dinner: phone 885-6822.

In the cool upcountry area, just at the entrance to Waimea, lies the former home of Laurance Rockefeller, which has been converted into **Hartwell's Restaurant** at Hale Kea, Kawaihae Rd., Waimea. Choose your setting: the garden room with huge windows overlooking the spectacular coastline, the intimate library, the authentic paniolo (cowboy) room, or the old-fashioned (circa 1897) living room. The lunch menu (entrées average $8) features ranch ribs, teriyaki chicken sandwich, Asian chicken salad, and a stew of the day. For dinner you might choose grilled mushrooms or blackened prawns as an appetizer ($3.95 to $6.95) to compliment a main course (averaging $22) of grilled lamb, seafood medley, duckling, steaks or ribs. On Sunday afternoon there is jazz on the back lawn. Service is down-home friendly, so plan to spend time enjoying the atmosphere. T-shirts and shorts are acceptable attire at lunch, but after the sun sets get into the full spirit of this millionaire's former home and come decked out. Don't leave without touring the gardens and unique shops surrounding the restaurant. Open daily 10am to 9pm. Reservations advised: phone 885-6095.

In the time of King Kamehameha, the area now known as the Mauna Lani Resort was a Hawaiian fishing village. The canoe was vital to its sustenance—and it is the canoe that has been chosen as the theme for Mauna Lani's newest and closest-to-the-ocean restaurant, **The CanoeHouse.** Everything about this place calls for celebration—in fact, people from all over the Big Island like to come here to celebrate special occasions—but we wouldn't miss the chance to come here simply to celebrate the great beauty of the place, the spectacular al fresco setting, or the excitement of its sophisticated Pacific Rim cuisine. The mood is casual, and one can dine in the main dining room, which overlooks the ocean (floodlit at night), our favorite, or on the terrace, patio, or gazebo, which adjoins an outdoor dance floor. A koa fishing canoe hanging dramatically from the ceiling and a wall of petroglyph designs sets the mood, but the decor is basically simple to let you concentrate on the view—and on the food. Chef Alan Wong, who was born in Japan, raised in Hawaii, and has worked at such restaurants as The Greenbrier and Lutèce on the mainland, has put together a menu full of taste surprises from the countries of the Pacific Basin. The menu is so tempting, in fact, that it's hard to make choices. Among the appetizers ($6 to $14.50), for example, you might have wok-fried sesame shrimp on crispy noodles with lilikoi glaze, or curried chicken lumpia with coconut ginger cream and green papaya salad. For your main course, there are such creations as mesquite-smoked five-spice duck with jicama mango relish, or poha barbecued rack of lamb with warm breadfruit salad, or bamboo-steamed mahimahi and Chinese cabbage with a ginger-scallion salsa ($25 to $32). On no account should you miss dessert. Only one is offered, and true dessert lovers will think they've died and gone to heaven. It's a huge tray of regional specialty desserts that include banana lumpia, ginger crème brûlée, pomelo cheesecake, macadamia fudge cake, and tropical fruit sorbet. And not just nibbles, but healthy portions of each. After this and your coffee, you'll probably agree that any meal at the CanoeHouse is very good cause for celebration.

The CanoeHouse serves every day from 11am to 10pm (salads and sandwiches are available for lighter meals), and there's music and dancing every night. Reservations advised: phone 885-6622. AE, MC, V.

Muted lighting, candles, and exotic Hawaiian flowers make **The Gallery** at Mauna Lani Bay Resort a romantic rendezvous. The art deco restaurant overlooking the resort's tennis courts is a haven for fans of local island cuisine. The Gallery offers one of the most creative mixes of Hawaii's indigenous food. Award-winning Chef Ann Southerland has created such extraordinary starters ($7 to $12) as the shrimp-phyllo appetizer in a lemon beurre blanc, or the Cajun pasta with shrimp and scallops, or the lobster tarragon. Among the main courses ($18 to $28), we recommend the wok-charred ahi with its fruit-and-scallion salsa, Brazilian chicken, and the lilikoi shrimp, sautéed with passion-fruit butter and cilantro. Desserts are worth saving your strength for, especially the double chocolate cake. Since this is part of the Mauna Lani Resort, dress is "casually elegant." Definitely make reservations (phone 885-7777) and ask if "Chef Ann" is cooking that night. (If she's not, book another night.) Dinner is served every night from 6 to 9:30pm. AE, DC, JCB, MC, V.

HOTELS IN KONA

Built high up on lava beds that meet the sea at Keauhou Bay, a few miles out of the town of Kailua-Kona, the **Kona Surf Resort and Country Club,** 78-128 Ehukai St., Kailua-Kona, HI 96740 (tel. 808/322-3411; reservations toll free 800/367-8011 from U.S. mainland, 800/524-7200 from Oahu; fax 800/322-3245), enjoys a spectacular site. The $180 million, 530-unit hotel is spread out on some 14½ acres bursting with tropical vegetation (there are 30,000 plants on the property). Magnificent artworks from the Pacific Basin are casually interspersed among the public areas and walkways. There are two pools, one saltwater (the ocean is rough for swimming here), lighted tennis courts, and a golf course that seems to hang over the water. Add to this frequent shuttles into Kailua for shopping and to White Sands Beach for ocean swimming; shell-collecting trips; lessons in lei-making, hula dancing, coconut-palm weaving, you name it. And when you need to relax from all this activity, there's the Puka Bar for cozy drinks, Pele's Court with its handsome mural for casual dining at breakfast, lunch, and dinner; and the handsome S.S. *James Makee* for fine dining on Hawaiian regional cuisine (dinner only). Weekends only there's disco at the Poi Pounder Room. And every Tuesday and Friday there's a spectacular *free* Polynesian show from 5:30 to 7pm; even if you're not staying at the hotel, come by for this one.

Rooms, attractively decorated, all have private lanais, coffeemakers, refrigerators, and, of course, air conditioning, phones, and color television. There are coin-operated washers and dryers on each floor. During the summer season, April 1 to December 23, standard rooms are $125, garden view $145, ocean view $160, oceanfront $195. Suites go from $415 to $540 and are particularly elegant. During the winter season, December 24 to March 31, rates are $125, $155, $170, $205, and $425 to $550 for suites. AE, CB, DISC, MC, V.

Another winner in the Keauhou Bay area is the gracious **Keauhou Beach Hotel,** 78-6740 Alii Dr., Kailua-Kona, HI 96740 (tel. 808/322-3441; reservations, toll free 800/367-6025 from U.S. mainland; fax 808/944-2974), a 318-room, calmly beautiful resort only 6 miles away from the busy center of town, yet relaxing enough to be a world apart. And that it is, sprawling out on grounds that are rich in both natural beauty and Hawaiian history. It is almost a living Hawaiian museum, with two *heiaus,* a reconstructed grass shack, an ancient fishpond or "sacred pool," and petroglyphs carved on a flat lava reef that runs straight out from the hotel, reminding guests of the olden days when this area, from which Kamehameha the Great launched his armies, was a favorite retreat of Hawaiian royalty. An exact replica of King Kalakaua's summer home, Ka Hale Kahakai o'Kalakaua, has been reconstructed on its original site, complete with koa floors and exact reproductions of his furniture.

Nature has been generous here too: The hotel has its own private swimming beach (rare for Kona) adjoining Kahuluu Beach Park, and even a volcanic tidal pool facing the sunning beach where one can watch the creatures of the deep swim in. There's a 27-hole championship golf course three minutes away, six tennis courts and a pro shop (lessons are available using the most modern facilities), and a beautiful freshwater swimming pool overlooking the ocean. And when you're hungry, there's the open-air Kuakini Terrace, very popular for its Chinese buffets (Monday through Thursday, $12.95) and seafood (Friday, Saturday, and Sunday, $19.95). Sunday brunch, $16.95, is one of the most popular in west Hawaii. Hawaiian music, with some of the best of the old-time entertainers, is featured every night at the Makai Bar.

But let's not forget the rooms here. They are spacious and handsome, with every facility for comfort, including a small refrigerator, a spacious bath and dressing area, cable color TV and pay movie service, direct-dial phones, and air conditioning, of course. All rooms have lanais, and many overlook the ocean. Rates, single or double, begin at $85 for garden view, and go up to $95 for partial ocean view, $110 for ocean view, $125 for deluxe ocean view. A third person is charged $12 more. Suites go from $210 to $370. (Rates subject to change.) AE, DC, MC, V.

Our favorite condominium resort in the Keauhou area is **Kanaloa at Kona,** 78-261 Manukai St., Kailua-Kona, HI 96740 (tel. 808/322-2272; fax 808/322-3818; reservations toll free 800/367-6046), an 18-acre complex of 37 low-rise, wood-shingled buildings situated on a gentle rise overlooking ocean and bay on one side, fairways on the other. It's perfect heaven for golfers (the 27-hole championship Kona Country Club Golf Course borders the resort), tennis players (two lighted courts), snorkelers and surfers, and anyone who wants to enjoy the sporting or lazy life in a setting of pure island beauty. The surf is too rough here for casual swimming, but there are three freshwater pools, one reserved only

800-777-1700

for grown-ups. One-, two-, and three-bedroom ocean and fairway villas are superbly furnished, have koa-wood cabinetry, fully equipped kitchen (microwave oven, washer and dryer), phone, color TV, large lanai with its own wet bar. Oceanfront suites even have their own private Jacuzzi! There is daily maid service. The Terrace Restaurant is pleasant, and there are more restaurants, and shops, too, at the Keauhou Shopping Village two blocks up the road. Rates are quite affordable for two couples or a large family. From April 1 to December 19, one-bedroom, two-bath fairway villas are $145 for up to four people; ocean villas are $175. Two-bedroom, two-bath fairway villas for up to six people are $170; ocean villas are $205. Three-bedroom, two-bath fairway villas for up to eight people are $200; ocean villas are $225. The rest of the year, each unit is $10 to $30 more. AE, CB, DC, MC, V.

One of the nicest ways we know to live the lazy Kona life is at the self-contained **Kona Hilton Beach and Tennis Resort,** P.O. Box 1179, Kailua-Kona, HI 96740 (tel. 808/329-3111; fax 808/329-9532; reservations toll free 800/HILTONS), nestled on 12 acres of oceanfront just half a mile from the center of Kailua-Kona village. The three buildings containing some 445 guest rooms make the most of the natural setting here, and wherever you look there are stunning vistas of mountains and sea. You can dine or have a drink or watch the sunset and nightly entertainment in the surfside restaurant and cocktail lounge; you can swim in a split-level circular pool close enough to the beach to hear the breakers crashing on a lava cliff below. And you can also swim at a sandy lagoon beach, unusual for Kona, where the waves can be rough. Children can swim at the half-moon-shaped shallow area of the pool reserved for them. And tennis players have four championship courts and a pro shop at their disposal.

The rooms are as handsome and spacious as you would expect, with dark-wood paneling and tropical colors setting the mood. Under-the-counter refrigerator, separate dressing areas for him and her, air conditioning, coffeemaker, and color TV are standard. A sliding panel leads to your landscaped lanai from which you can view either the garden, mountain, or sea; the view pretty much determines the price tag. From April 1 to December 19, singles or doubles go for $109 standard, $130 with garden or mountain view, $160 deluxe ocean view, $185 deluxe oceanfront, $200 corner king. The rest of the year, the rates are $10 more. A third person is $25, but your child of any age stays free in your room. (Rates are subject to change.) Although there are no rooms with built-in conveniences for the disabled, the hotel will accommodate with necessary changes on request. The entire property is wheelchair-accessible. As for dining, the Hele Mai provides continental fare in an oceanfront setting, and the Lanai Coffee Shop offers all three meals in an open-air, open-to-the-sea setting. There's entertainment nightly in the Windjammer Lounge. AE, DC, DISC, JCB, MC, V.

Right in the village of Kailua-Kona, the **Hotel King Kameha-meha,** 75-5660 Palani Rd., Kailua-Kona, HI 96740 (tel. 808/329-2911; fax 808/329-4602; reservations toll free 800/227-4700) combines the best of Hawaii past and present. Adjacent to the hotel is the royal Kamakahonu ground, where King Kamehameha ruled until his death in 1819; out on the peninsula is the restored Ahuena

Heiau, or sacred temple. Two six-story twin towers with 453 air-conditioned guest rooms—all of which have color TV, radio, refrigerator, and their own lanai—are separated by a shopping mall laced with museum displays. The rooms are richly decorated in pastels, peaches, mauves, and teals, as is the spacious lobby, accented by three-dimensional koa-wood walls, Polynesian murals, and Hawaiian artifacts. Modern conveniences include four tennis courts (two of championship caliber), two saunas, good dining rooms like Moby Dick's for seafood and the Kona Veranda Coffeeshop. On Sunday, from 9am to 1pm, Moby Dick's is the scene of an excellent $17.95 buffet brunch. Not the least of the charms of the Hotel King Kamehameha is the fact that, in addition to its pool and engaging poolside bar, it has its own sandy beach, the only one right in the heart of town. Three nights a week, the Kona Beach luau is held here. Several mornings a week, guests gather in the mall with local *kupunas* for craft demonstrations, singing, and playing the ukulele, or the Hula Experience; frequent historical and ethnobotanical tours are also held.

Single or double rooms at the Hotel King Kamehameha go from $99 standard to $125 superior, to $150 deluxe, to $165 deluxe oceanfront. A third person is charged $15 extra. One-, two-, and three-bedroom suites run from $275 to $485. Children 17 and under free sharing the same room as their parents and using existing bedding. AE, DC, DISC, MC, V.

There's a special feeling at a family-run hotel, and that's what you get when you stay at **Uncle Billy's Kona Bay Hotel** on Alii Drive (tel. 808/329-1393; fax 808/935-7903; reservations toll free 800/367-5102), the local outpost of Uncle Billy's Hilo Bay Hotel. Right in the center of town, within walking distance of all the shopping-dining-fishing excitement, this is a crescent-shaped, 145-room low-rise, overlooking pools, restaurants, and gardens, with the emphasis on comfortable living at a reasonable price. Rooms are of good size, nicely decorated, with full bathroom, ample lanai, air conditioning, refrigerator, TV; and some have a small kitchenette as well. Families are made to feel right at home here. Rates go from $72 to $94 single or double. Studio suites with kitchen are $84. Add $10 to rates for high season, December 15 to April 1. An extra person is charged $10; children under 12 are free. Room, car, and continental breakfast packages for two go from $87 to $109. All rates are subject to change. Banana Bay Buffet provides breakfast and dinner at reasonable prices. Reservations are handled at the central office in Hilo: 87 Banyan Dr., Hilo, HI 96720.

Down the coast, just outside of town and past the Kona Hilton, is a neat little budget find. The **Kona Tiki Hotel,** P.O. Box 1567, Kailua-Kona, HI 96740 (tel. 808/329-1425), seems sleepy enough when you pull off the highway into the parking lot, but once you're up in your room the action begins. This place intrudes upon King Neptune's territory, and he lets you know about it with a nonstop display of rainbow water that crashes against the (thank goodness) sturdy seawall surrounding the hotel. Free breakfast (coffee with doughnuts) is available in the lobby every morning. A freshwater pool competes with the ocean for attention. The rooms are modest but comfortable, with carpeted floors and a queen and twin bed in each room, small but adequate bathroom, and sliding doors that lead to a private lanai from which the sunset is spectacular. Every room has a refrigerator. Standard rooms are $50 for a single or double, and rooms with mini-kitchenette are $55, with additional persons $5 more. The managers are on duty, it seems, just about always, generous with tips regarding excursions and car trips, restaurants, and island history. There are only 15 units here and they fill up fast, so write for reservations (three-day minimum) in advance. Rates subject to change.

CONDOMINIUM VACATIONS IN KONA

If you'd like to stay in your own apartment in Kona, complete with all the comforts of home, a condominium vacation is the perfect answer. The Kona Coast is liberally sprinkled with these vacation complexes, and all offer apartments with spacious living, sleeping, and eating quarters, full kitchen, and all the amenities. Minimum stays of three days are required; daily maid service is usually not included but is available on request.

To stay right in the heart of town, choose **Kona Plaza,** 75-5719 Alii Dr., Kailua-Kona, HI 96740 (tel. 808/329-1132), a quiet, clean 75-unit complex tucked behind the Kona Plaza Shopping Arcade on Alii Drive. Apartments are fully carpeted, and have a large lanai, full electric kitchen (washer-dryer, dishwasher, etc.), cable TV, and pleasant furnishings. There are ocean views from the second through fourth floors along the Alii Drive side. A lovely and spacious sundeck looks out over Alii Drive and the ocean, affording guests a place to gather for potluck or picnic meals. There are also a pool and a light recreation area. Rates vary, but one-bedroom apartments might start at $60 for two; two-bedroom, 1¾-bath apartments at $85; weekly rates from $300 to $500. There is a three-night minimum. Century 21 is the realtor handling most of these apartments: Their phone is 808/329-9566 or toll free 800/255-8052.

If you prefer a location a bit out of town, overlooking the waterfront, **Kona Makai,** 75-6025 Alii Dr., Kailua-Kona, HI 96740 (tel. 808/329-1511; fax 808/329-5480), is a good choice. This sprawling, 102-unit complex has an oceanside swimming pool and Jacuzzi, two tennis courts, and handsomely decorated and spacious modern apartments. Kitchens have everything, including washer-dryer, eat-in bar, and coffeemaker. One-bedroom apartments run $80 for garden view, $90 for ocean view; two-bedroom apartments are $115 garden view, $125 ocean view, and $135 oceanfront. From April 1 to December 14, every seventh day is free. Several realtors handle apartments here, but one with a large number of units is Kona Vacation Resorts, P.O. Box 1070, Kailua-Kona, HI 96745; toll-free reservations 800/533-5351 in the U.S. AE, MC, V.

The thing we like best about **White Sands Village,** 77-6469 Alii Drive, is that it's just across the road from Magic Sands Beach, one of the few swimming beaches in the area. It's a large condo complex, with many recreational facilities, including a pool, sauna, Jacuzzi, tennis courts, and barbecue area; covered parking available. Every unit is a two-bedroom suite and is air-conditioned; they are all individually owned, so furnishings and appointments vary. Rates run from $100 to $125 daily. From April 1 to December 15, they are $600 to $750 weekly; the rest of the year, they are $700 to $875 weekly. As is usual with complexes of this type, several realtors handle apartments here; one with a good number of units is Jean Metz of Triad Management Realtors, North Kona Shopping Center, 75-5629-P Kuakini Hwy., KailuaKona, HI 96740; tel. 808/329-6402. Triad also handles many other vacation rentals—approximately 125 condominiums and houses—so see what they have to offer. AE, MC, V.

RESTAURANTS IN KONA

Huggo's, beautifully situated on the waterfront not far from the Kona Hilton, is a longtime Kona favorite; from your al fresco dining perch, you can watch the sun set into Kailua Bay. And the food is as good as the view, with lots of fresh seafood and fish dishes, plus a good choice of meat and chicken entrées as well. Entrées like shrimp scampi, mahimahi, prime rib, and teriyaki steak are priced from $12 to $18.95; Hawaiian lobster is a bit more. There are several fresh fish selections daily. With all entrées, you can help yourself to all you want at the salad bar. Sashimi is a favorite among the appetizers; side dishes like zucchini fritters are temptations. As for desserts, the mud pie à la mode is memorable, and we dream about Pele's Dream—that's blueberries and strawberries marinated in Grand Marnier, over vanilla ice cream! The wine list is well selected and extensive, and several wines are served by the glass; the bar scene is always lively. Lunch is always jammed, because it's then that you can get tostadas, quesadilla grande, or prime rib melt sandwiches, and terrific burgers on a sesame bun, all from about $5.25 to $7.

Huggo's serves lunch weekdays between 11:30am and 2:30pm, late lunch (chicken burgers, fresh catch burgers, Huggo's classic burgers, and jumbo hot dogs) from 2:30 to 5:30pm, dinner from 5:30 to 10:30pm. Complimentary pupus are served during the happy hour, 4 to 6pm daily. Tuesday through Saturday from 8pm to 12:30am there's entertainment, at the piano bar. For reservations, phone 329-1493.

The setting of the **Kona Inn,** 75-5744 Alii Drive, can only be described as idyllic: Tall wicker chairs and beautifully inlaid koa tables overlook the Pacific, and palm trees sway in the ocean breezes at this popular lanai restaurant. There's a big singles scene up at the bar. In this storybook setting you dine on superbly fresh and beautifully prepared seafood and steak. Start your meal with an oyster shooter or sashimi or deep-fried oysters, or maybe a bowl of their hearty clam chowder, either New England or Manhattan style. Dinner entrées, served with potato or rice, green vegetables, and warm bread, include stir-fry chicken and chicken parmesan, a succulent roast prime rib of beef, stir-fried shrimp, seafood pastas, and top sirloin, all from $13.95 to $17.95. There's a marvelous seafood combination of shrimps, jumbo scallops, and fish, market-priced. The local fish of the day is outstanding; it should be, what with all that big game fishing off the Kona Coast! It's best broiled in lemon butter. Lunch is moderately priced, with everything from a $3.25 hot dog to a $9.95 steak sandwich available; we like their pasta and chicken salad, chef's salad, and fresh fruit salad, too. On no account should you miss their mud pie for dessert at either meal; the taste of chocolate cookie crust, coffee ice cream, and chocolate syrup will live in my memory. Children's menus are reasonably priced. Service is professional and not cloying, as it can often be in the islands. Open everyday from 11:30am til midnight; dinner from 5 to 10pm. Reservations: phone 329-4455. AE, MC, V.

The Terrace at Kanaloa at Kona Condominium, 78-261 Manukai St. in Keahou (tel. 322-1003), located on a ridge of black lava overlooking the blue Pacific Ocean, offers diners a romantic picture-postcard setting. Surrounded by swaying palms on one side and a swimming pool on the other, the Terrace is a wonderful place to enjoy both a great meal and a beautiful sunset. The dinner menu features steaks, chicken, and fish in a price range that goes from $9.95 to $34; our favorites include Korean-style short ribs marinated in a spicy sauce, the chicken and prawn stir-fry, and the islanders favorite, ono (wahoo), baked in a light phyllo dough and topped with a creamy hollandaise. Appetizers run $4.25 to $10. The Terrace offers burgers, sandwiches, and salads for lunch, and it's also a neat place to start the day, drinking your morning coffee watching the sun rising over Hulalai amidst refreshing ocean breezes. Reservations are generally not needed, but the restaurant can be somewhat crowded when the pool crowd next door gets hungry, so plan ahead.

The Terrace is open daily from 8 to 11am for breakfast, from 11am to 2pm for lunch, and from 5:30 to 9pm for dinner. CB, DC, MC, V.

There's an informal, relaxed feeling about dining at **Quinn's Almost by the Sea,** 75-5655A Palani Rd., next door to the Hotel King Kamehameha. A lively young crowd hangs out in the garden dining lanai, whose two open walls and one of lava rock give an outdoor feeling. Blue canvas director's chairs and laminated wooden tables continue the same mood. Dinner entrées run $10.95 to $18.95, and best bets are the daily fresh fish and such seafood dishes as shrimp continental (sautéed in wine, herbs, mushrooms, and tomatoes). Entrées come with salad, vegetable, and potato or rice. French dip, burger, and roast beef sandwiches are fine at lunch, from about $5.50 to $7.25. Lots of cheer inside at the bar. Local residents consider this place a favorite. Lunch from 11am to 5:30pm, dinner from 5:30pm to 1am, to midnight Sunday. Phone: 329-3822. MC, V.

Anyone who knows **Jameson's by the Sea,** one of the most popular restaurants on the North Shore of Oahu, will be delighted to find another Jameson's here in Kona, also located oceanfront, overlooking Magic Sands Beach, at 77-6452 Alii Dr. You can sit out on the deck overlooking the seawall, watching the waves smash up on the shore, or else indoors in a cheerful setting, with pink-and-green-cushioned chairs, wooden tables, ceiling fans overhead, and that old tropical feeling. It's a perfect setting for dining on fresh seafood direct from Hawaiian waters each day. Among the appetizers, $4.95 to $8.95, we love the tangy salmon pâté, served on Hilo soda crackers, a house specialty; you could also have oysters Rockefeller, steamed clams, or deep-fried calamari. Try the Yokohama soup, a bit different: a hearty fish soup with fresh spinach and cream. Main courses, which are served with steamed vegetables and a choice of starch (we like the garlic linguine), run from $13.95 to $19.95, with fresh fish and lobster tail market-priced; specialties include ocean scallops sautéed in lemon butter with capers, baked stuffed shrimp topped with a rich hollandaise, veal piccata, filet mignon, and a tasty shrimp curry, served with bacon and mango chutney. Homemade chiffon pies are the way to go for dessert. Lunch is very pleasant here; you can have hot sandwiches, burgers, a big vegetarian salad, and Jameson's Louies—that's a green salad with Swiss cheese, special dressing, and either crab, shrimp, or mixed seafood, for $7.95 to $9.95.

Jameson's by the Sea serves lunch from 11am to 5pm Monday to Friday, dinner from 5 to 10pm daily. Reservations recommended: phone 329-3195. AE, DC, MC, V.

Exotic food at down-to-earth prices awaits the adventurous diner at **Sibu Cafe,** in Banyan Court, 75-5695 Alii Drive (tel. 329-1112), which at first looks like a fast-food operation, but is much more. You can sit in the little restaurant itself or out on the courtyard, where Balinese decorations set the mood for the specialties of Indonesia. Be sure to try one of their satays—skewers of marinated meats or vegetables broiled over an open flame, and accompanied by either brown or fried rice and a marinated cucumber-and-onion salad. Balinese chicken, ginger beef, Indian curries, and vegetarian stir-frys are also featured, and nothing costs more than $10.50! Appetizers run $3.50 to $5. Sibu Cafe is open daily from 11:30am to 9pm. No credit cards.

Uncle Billy's Fisherman's Landing, oceanfront at the Kona Shopping Village, was being called a "landmark restaurant of the islands" almost as soon as it opened its doors in 1986. Ever since then, it just keeps winning one "favorite restaurant" award after another. You enter the restaurant via a cobblestoned walkway shaded by ancient banyan trees and move on into a series of indoor-outdoor dining areas, skillfully arranged to create a feeling of privacy as you enjoy the fountains, the pool, the ocean waves rolling up on the beach in front of you. A fishing boat near the entrance displays the fish caught that day in Kona waters: kiawe-broiled, priced daily from $17.95 to $19.95, they are the restaurant's star attraction. But there are also other seafood specialties, Asian and wok dishes, chateaubriand, saltimbocca, filet mignon, and New York steak, all from about $14.95 to $22.95. Entrées include soup or salad and home-baked bread. Appetizers like shrimp scampi or mushrooms stuffed with shrimp, fresh oysters on the half shell, desserts like the sensational lava pie, Irish mousse cake, or fresh lychee sherbet round out a perfect dining experience. There's live entertainment every night. Lunch, priced from about $6 to $8, offers made-to-order sandwiches, broiler items, and salads. And you can always stop at the attractive patio bar for drinks and pupus.

Fisherman's Landing is open every day, from 11am to 2pm for lunch, and from 5 to 10 or 10:30pm for dinner. Reservations are essential, as this one is a sellout (tel. 326-2555). AE, DC, MC, V.

Up on Kuakini Hwy., in Kuakini Plaza South, is a change-of-pace restaurant for Kona: instead of open lanais and a view of the harbor, **La Bourgogne** offers a quaint, cozy, European country atmosphere. Guy Chatelard, one-time chef at the prestigious Mauna Kea Beach Hotel, began his apprenticeship in his native France at the age of 15. Now he and his wife, Jutta, run their own charming little place and serve up traditional French interpretations of seafood, steak, lamb, and veal dishes. The à la carte menu ranges in price from $13.50 to $26. Entrées are served with fresh vegetables of the day and freshly prepared potatoes. Everything is homemade, from the onion soup and lobster bisque to the crème caramel, and very nicely done. There is a good wine list, and cocktails are available. Dinner only, Monday through Saturday, from 6 to 10pm. Closed Sunday. Reservations: 329-6711. AE, DC, DISC, MC, V.

There are three areas to hit when the traveler's checks are running low. The first is Waterfront Row, oceanfront on Alii Drive, which has several fast-food possibilities, such as **Spinnaker's Salad Bar, Flying Fruit Fantasy,** and **Hot Diggety Dog.** The second area to remember is the Kona Coast Shopping Center, near the intersection of Hwys. 11 and 19, which boasts **Betty's Chinese Kitchen** for some of the best manapua (dim sum) in these parts; a branch of the popular **Sizzler's Steak, Salad and Seafood** cafeterias, where everything is very fresh and very well priced; **Bianelli's,** a gourmet pizza parlor with an international array of pies, plus pasta dinners, sandwiches, and salads; and **Kim's Place,** for tasty Korean take-out. The third area is Lanihau Center, just across the road: It has several fast-food outlets like **McGurk's,** for fish and chips with very reasonable daily specials, and a Chinese restaurant the local people like very much, called **Royal Jade Garden.**

KONA AFTER DARK

There's plenty of excitement in the Kona night, and much of the action is centered around the big hotels. At the **Kona Surf Resort & Country Club,** you can see a free show, *Polynesian Paradise,* every Tuesday and Friday from 5:30 to 6:30pm at the Nalu Terrace. . . . They pop the pig into the imu every Sunday, Tuesday, and Thursday at the **Hotel King Kamehameha** (reservations: 329-2911). The tab for this in-town luau is around $44, inclusive. It's worth the 15- to 20-minute drive out to Kaupulehu for the festive $54 luau given every Monday and Friday night at the old-Polynesian-style **Kona Village Resort** (reservations: 325-5555). . . . Disco fans can have a great time at romantic **Eclipse,** on Kuakini Hwy., across from Foodland. Dancing begins at 10pm every night except Monday. . . . The **Keauhou Beach Hotel** is the favored venue for authentic Hawaiian music, with top local artists performing every night. The **Kona Hilton** has a variety of nighttime entertainments, including karaoke at the Windjammer Lounge every Wednesday and Friday from 7:30 to 9:30pm and music in the same lounge on Saturday, Sunday, and Monday. . . . For a change of pace, take to the ocean on **Captain Beans' Royal Canoe** for a sunset cruise. It's open bar, plus all you can eat, music, and entertainment, for $45 per person. Adults only (reservations: 329-2955). . . . For all entertainments, check the papers when you arrive, since times and schedules may change. Children are usually admitted to luaus at half the adult price.

BETWEEN KONA & HILO—ROOM & BOARD

If you're driving the southern route (11) between Hilo and Kona, or vice versa, you'll certainly stop off at Volcanoes National Park, and you may become so enchanted with the area that you'll want to stay there for a few days. Great idea! The mountain air is wonderful here, although it is a sometimes rainy area. The most scenic spot is still the venerable **Volcano House,** situated in an incredibly exciting location atop Kilauea Crater; in the last few years, however, with changes in management, prices have almost doubled; crater-view rooms are $125, noncrater-view rooms are $100 in the main building, $75 in a separate building (Volcano House, Hawaii Volcanoes National Park, HI 96718; tel. 808/967-7321). The nicest rooms in this area, and also some of the best food (dinner and breakfast only), can be found nearby at **Kilauea Lodge,** a mile from Volcanoes National Park, in Volcano Village. Full breakfasts are included in the prices of $85 to $125 single or double for the charmingly decorated guest rooms (Kilauea Lodge, P.O. Box 116, Volcano Village, HI 96785; tel. 808/967-7366). The Volcano area also has a number of bed-and-breakfast accommodations, detailed in my other book, *Hawaii on $70 a Day.*

If you're ready for lunch now, you have several choices. The famous buffet lunch at Volcano House is good, but it attracts crowds of hungry tourists. Local people like the restaurant at the **Volcano Golf and Country Club** for good burgers and daily specials in a stylish atmosphere. In a glorious beachfront setting, the **Punalu'u Black Sands Restaurant** at Punalu'u serves a fabulous luncheon buffet, with over 18 dishes displayed in a native canoe, plus elaborate desserts. In the little town of Naalehu, the southernmost community in the U.S., look for the **Naalehu Fruit Stand,** across the road from the library, a local favorite where you get pizza "sandwiches" on homemade Italian bread, health foods, deli sandwiches, and homemade pies; or have a meal at the **Naalehu Coffeeshop,** admire the owner's garden in back, his collection of bonsai, and the informal "gift shop" filled with island paintings and handcrafts.

2. The Sights & Sounds of the Big Island

If you really want to see the Big Island, you should plan on at least four days. The ideal way would be to spend the first day in the city of Hilo; the second, driving to Volcanoes National Park; the third, taking the Hamakua coast trip across the island, driving through the cowboy country of the Parker Ranch; and the fourth day, exploring the Kona coast and luxuriating in the sun and water. You could also start your trip at Kona and work backward. We'll suppose, though, for the purposes of this discussion, that you're starting out—in your own rented car—from General Lyman Field, the Hilo airport.

THE FIRST DAY—SEEING HILO

We hope you'll start your trip early, since the first sight to see is at its most beautiful when the sun is new and the world is not yet too warm. From the airport, take H-12 (Kamehameha Avenue) all the way around the curve in the bay until you reach Waianuenue Avenue, which you'll follow until you get to Rainbow Drive. Here you'll find the glorious **Rainbow Falls,** so named for the transparent rainbows that appear in the mist from the falls when the morning sun glances through it. Drive on a little farther, up to Peepee Street,

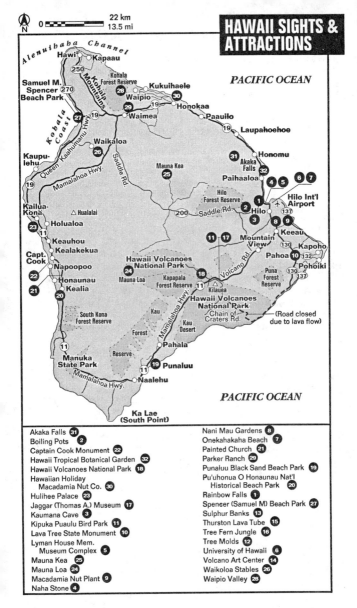

HAWAII SIGHTS & ATTRACTIONS

PACIFIC OCEAN

Alenuihaha Channel

Hawi · Kapaau
250
Samuel M. Kohala 270 · Kukuihaele
Spencer Forest Reserve
Beach Park 28 · Waipio · 30 · Honokaa
27 · 19 · 29 · Waimea · Paauilo
Kohala 19
Coast · 19 · Laupahoehoe
Waikaloa
Kaupu- 26 · Honomu
lehu · Mauna Kea · 31 · Akaka
Queen Kaahumanu Hwy. · 25 · Falls · 32
Mamalahoa Hwy. · Paihaaloa · 4 · 5 · 6 · 7
19 · Hilo · 1 · Hilo Int'l
△ Hualalai · Forest Reserve · 2 · Airport
Kailua- · 200 · Saddle Rd. · Hilo · 137
Kona · 3 · 8 · Keeau
23 · Holualoa · 11 · 17 · Mountain · 130 · Kapoho
11 · Keauhou · View · Pahoa · 10 · Pohoiki
Kealakekua · Hawaii Volcanoes · Volcano Rd. · 130 · 137
Capt. · National Park · 24 · 18 · Puna
Cook · Mauna Loa · Kapapala · △ · Forest
22 · Napoopoo · Forest Reserve · Kilauea · Reserve
21 · Honaunau · Hawaii Volcanoes
20 · Kealia · National Park
South Kona · Kau · Chain of · (Road closed
Forest Reserve · Craters Rd. · due to lava flow)
11 · Kau · Forest
Manuka · Desert
State Park · Reserve · Pahala
Mamalahoa Hwy. · 19 · Punaluu
11 · Naalehu

PACIFIC OCEAN

Ka Lae
(South Point)

Akaka Falls 31 | Nani Mau Gardens 8
Boiling Pots 2 | Onekahakaha Beach 7
Captain Cook Monument 22 | Painted Church 21
Hawaii Tropical Botanical Garden 32 | Parker Ranch 29
Hawaii Volcanoes National Park 18 | Punaluu Black Sand Beach Park 19
Hawaiian Holiday | Pu'uhonua O Honaunau Nat'l
  Macadamia Nut Co. 30 | Historical Beach Park 20
Hulihee Palace 23 | Rainbow Falls 1
Jaggar (Thomas A.) Museum 17 | Spencer (Samuel M) Beach Park 27
Kaumana Cave 3 | Sulphur Banks 13
Kipuka Puaulu Bird Park 11 | Thurston Lava Tube 15
Lava Tree State Monument 10 | Tree Fern Jungle 16
Lyman House Mem. | Tree Molds 12
  Museum Complex 5 | University of Hawaii 6
Mauna Kea 25 | Volcano Art Center 14
Mauna Loa 24 | Waikoloa Stables 26
Macadamia Nut Plant 9 | Waipio Valley 28
Naha Stone 4 |

and you'll see the **Boiling Pots,** another scenic vista. Such beauty so close to the city is no surprise, since the city itself is a spot blessed by nature. It curves around a crescent-shaped bay, and always in sight are the two homes of Pele: the larger, extinct volcano, **Mauna Kea,** and the frequently active, only slightly smaller one, **Mauna Loa.**

Turn around now, and make a right on Puu Hina and another right on Kaumana. Follow this a few miles to the site of the **Kaumana Cave,** a lava tube similar to those you will be seeing later along the circular drive in Volcanoes National Park. This one was formed in 1881, when Pele came close to destroying the city of Hilo. The cave extends about a mile in the direction of the city, and a hardy spelunker could traverse the entire length with the help of a flashlight. The less adventurous can admire the lovely fern grotto at the entrance to the tube on the right (the one on the left is dangerous), and continue on.

Swing back the way you came, but make a right at Laimana Street, then left onto Haili Street. Follow it almost until Kapiolani Street, and in the middle of the block you'll find an impressive New England–type white building with green shutters. This old missionary home, built in 1839, is part of the **Lyman House Memorial Museum Complex** and has been restored to look as it did in the mid-19th century. The ground floor contains a parlor and dining room, plus others rooms furnished with authentic antiques. Upstairs are four quaint bedrooms, complete with four-poster beds, marble-topped dressers, and washstands. Adjoining is the modern museum built to house the many artifacts of the seven ethnic groups living in Hawaii: you'll see a full-size grass hut of the early Hawaiians, artifacts from the missionary era, a 300-year-old Taoist shrine of gold leaf on intricate wood carvings, plus exhibits reflecting the culture of the Japanese, Portuguese, Korean, and Filipino settlers. The top-floor galleries contain, among other exhibits, one of the finest mineral collections anywhere, and a world-class seashell exhibition. Admission to both buildings is $3.50 for adults, $2.50 for ages 13 to 18, $1.50 for ages 6 to 12. Hours are from 9am to 5pm. Monday through Saturday, 1 to 4pm Sunday.

After you've finished here, turn left on Kapiolani and make a right back to Waianuenue Avenue. On your left you'll notice the Hilo Branch of the Library of Hawaii. Right out in front is the legendary **Naha Stone,** believed to be a gift of the gods to mortals. It was believed that any man strong enough to lift the stone would be able to unite the islands of the Hawaiian chain. Kamehameha, the island's favorite son, was able to do so, or thus goes the legend. At any rate, he went on to become first a chief, then king, and the rest is history.

Make a right now when you get to the corner of Kinoole and Waianuenue. Before you turn, though, notice the shaded, somber building in front of you. This is one of the buildings of the Hilo campus of the **University of Hawaii,** the second-biggest center of higher education in the islands. You can complete that turn now, take the next available left, get back onto Kamehameha Avenue, and swing out around Hilo Bay.

Continue on past Pauhi Street until you can make a left onto Lihiwai. Just before you reach the intersection of Lihiwai and Banyan Drive, you'll see an HVB marker on the right side of the road pointing to the fish-auction area. If you can manage to get up with the birds tomorrow morning, you can join the local dealers in a colorful 8am auction. Now, however, continue on Lihiwai as you swing in a circle around beautiful **Liliuokalani Park,** where a Japanese Yedo garden has been completely reconstructed. Stone lanterns and bridges accent the lovely setting here on the shore of Hilo Bay. The **Japanese Cultural Center,** a restaurant, art gallery, tea room, and exhibition space, comes up soon. Off to your left is **Coconut Island,** which used to be a popular recreation spot for the people of Hilo until the 1960 tidal wave carried a good portion of the island soil into the ocean.

Now you can continue around the lip of Lihiwai and turn left onto **Banyan Drive,** so named for the small banyan trees (as banyans go) planted along the middle of the highway by famous people in the past half century. Most of the hotels in the city are ranged along here, and the setting is cool and easy. Follow Banyan Drive to its intersection with Kamehameha Avenue and drive left out of town, taking a left shortly to get onto Kalanianaole Avenue.

Now you're approaching one of the best spots for swimming and picnicking in the Hilo area (Hilo is not known for good beaches), an easy drive along Kalanianaole Avenue; it's **Onekahakaha Beach Park.** Here you either swim in the bay or wade in several wading pools—natural, of course—that the ocean constantly refills. Fishing is permitted from the rocks on shore. There are several pavilion areas, rest rooms, firepits for barbecuing, and a tiny but growing children's zoo that exhibits small samples of wildlife. All in all, there's quite a lot to do here. After you've done it, drive back out onto Kalanianaole and turn right to return to the center of Hilo.

Shopping in Hilo

Since many artists, craftspeople, and people of originality and good taste live on the Big Island, shopping in Hilo can be quite interesting. Head downtown, along Kilauea, Kinoole, and Keawe streets, and Kamehameha Avenue, where you'll find many appealing local shops. **The Most Irresistible Shop in Hilo,** at 98 Keawe St., is laden with tasteful cards, T-shirts, kitchenware, as well as beautiful hand-turned pottery, featherwork, patchwork, stained glass, etc. Kids will be enchanted by the toys and dollhouse furniture, and everyone will want to have a drink and a pastry or a light meal at the adorable **Bears' Coffee,** adjacent. In the same Pacific Building that houses this shop are several other places you will want to browse through, including the **Futon Connection,** with such wonderful decorator items as futons, wall fans, hand-carved banana trees from Bali, porcelain, silks, and much more, and the **Picture Frame Shop,** which frames and sells prints and paintings by island artists, specializing in local koa-wood frames. **Basically Books,** 46 Waianuenue Ave., offers many books on Hawaii, including those published by their own Petroglyph Press. They also carry out-of-print Hawaiiana and boast one of the largest and most complete selections of maps and charts in the state.

The local natural-living set hangs out at two places; right in town at **Abundant Life Natural Foods** at 292 Kamehameha Ave., whose selection of locally produced fruits, vegetables, honey, herbs, and foods-to-go is outstanding; and, a few miles out of town, in Keeau, at **Keeau Natural Foods;** check the bulletin boards for listings of various New Age events. Near the Keeau Police Station is

Puna Natural Buds, with the lowest prices on beautiful anthuriums and other tropical flowers to ship back home.

Hilo has a multimillion-dollar shopping center out on Hwy. 11, **Prince Kuhio Shopping Plaza.** Stop in at **Liberty House** or **Sears,** wander through some upscale boutiques like **Imagination Loves Toys,** for educational and creative playthings, or **Once Upon a Time** for stuffed animals, teddy bears, Victorian dolls. An outpost of **The Most Irresistible Shop in Hilo** can also be found here.

A popular older shopping center is **Kaiko'o Mall,** just behind the county and state buildings, a big place where the locals buy everything from clothes to crafts to papayas and soapsuds. **J. C. Penney** and **Book Gallery 2** are good places to know about.

THE SECOND DAY—IN THE WAKE OF PELE

Although volcanology is now an exact physical science, you could never prove it to some of the residents of the Big Island. As far as they are concerned, Pele, the flaming goddess of the volcanoes, is still alive and well, and she lives in Halemaumau Crater in Kilauea. You'll have to see Pele before you leave the Big Island; you may observe her in action, or you may just see what she's been up to. Either way, the sights are unforgettable. If you have some extra time, make a trip out to the Puna region before you go to **Volcanoes National Park;** it's an exciting territory well worth exploring. *Note:* Because of frequent volcanic eruptions, be sure to check local maps before you set out; new lava flows could make some of these directions obsolete overnight.

To begin your drive to the Puna region, take the southern route, H-11, out of Hilo, perhaps stopping 6 miles out of town at the **Mauna Loa Macadamia Nut Corporation** (9am to 5pm daily) for a tour and free tastings. Then continue on your journey, taking H-130 on its rain-forested drive along the sea. At the fork in the road coming up, take H-132 and head toward the coast. You'll pass **Lava Tree Park,** where you could have a hike or a picnic while you observe the work of the molten lava all around. The casts of tree trunks in solidified lava still stand here; the lava burned out the trees inside and went hurtling on. There are also a few tremendous earth faults, which are fenced off. You can look into mini-canyons for a glimpse of the rock layers under the surface. Picnic possibilities in this area also include MacKenzie State Park and Isaac Hale Park. Continue on, passing fertile papaya fields and orchid farms. Just before the intersection with H-137, you'll pass the village of **Kapoho,** buried under tons of lava in a 1960 eruption that added several square miles to the island's geography. You might even notice the lighthouse, standing isolated and strangely inland. A few signs of village life remain, sticking out from under the smothering lava rock.

Now you turn right onto an unearthly stretch of highway that careens wildly along the seashore, giving you an unforgettable picture of what volcanic fury does to the land. Mound upon mound of rolling lava rock spills down to the ocean on your left, and on the right a few cinder cones, some wisping meaningless smoke, play hide and seek with the foilage that has managed to take root in the rich volcanic soil. The plant life reworks the volcanic earth, producing red dirt, which blows across and colors the highway on which you are riding. The road will dip into shady grottoes and emerge

The Gardens of Hilo

You'll want to take time to soak up the beauty of the many gardens of Hilo, and a good place to start is at its most unique: the **Hawaii Tropical Botanical Garden,** a 45-acre nature preserve and sanctuary developed to protect the natural beauty of a tropical rain forest. Bordered by the ocean, the valley is dotted with waterfalls, streams, and an amazing variety of tropical plants, birds, and marine life; shore birds, forest birds, and giant sea turtles inhabit the nature preserve. Trails along the rugged coastline take visitors through a palm jungle and up to a waterfall past flamingos, to spend as long as they like (the average visit is one hour) enjoying, exploring, and—of course—photographing the wonders therein. Over 1,800 species of plants and flowers are identified.

Admission to the garden, a nonprofit foundation, is a tax-deductible $10; free for those under 16 with their parents. No picnic areas, no food sold. Open daily except New Year's Day, Thanksgiving, Christmas, and when the weather is bad; call ahead for a "weather check" and driving directions (it is 7 miles north of Hilo on the 4-mile scenic route at Onomea Bay). Phone 964-5233.

Another eminently worthwhile stop is **Nani Mau Gardens,** 20 acres of the fruits and flowers of many lands, with a special emphasis on those that have figured in the life of the islands. It has the largest orchid garden and the largest bromeliad collection in the state, a world-class palm garden, a lovely rose garden, and also macadamia nut trees, rare Hawaiian medicinal herbs, and acres and acres of fragrant hibiscus, torch ginger, and bird of paradise. Take the tram tour at $3 per person, or rent a golf cart at $8. Open daily from 8am to 5pm, with an admission charge of $5 for adults, $2.50 for children. To reach the gardens, drive about 3½ miles south on Hwy. 11 (the road to the volcano) from the Hilo airport.

into the brilliant sunlight where nothing but black, frozen rock stares back at you from every side.

Hwy. 137 used to intersect Rte. 130 in the idyllic garden community of Kalapana. In May 1990, however, the flows from the Pu'u O'o vent of Kilauea, which has been erupting continuously since 1983, finally reached the sea. In its path of destruction lay nearly 200 homes, a church, local stores, Harry K. Brown Park, the famed black-sand beach at Kaimu, and the Queen's Bath.

Lava now blocks Hwy. 137 4 miles from the Rte. 130 junction, so there is no choice but to retrace your steps. There is a short cut along the route. Turn left at Opihakao Street, which will take you up to Rte. 130. Turn right at 130, passing through the tiny village of Pahoa; then head back to Kee'au for Hwy. 11 to Volcanoes National Park.

If time is short, however, and you decide to skip the shoreline trip completely, simply take Hwy. 11 out of Hilo and stay on the road all the way to the park. (You may want to call before you start out, tel. 967-7311, for news of latest eruptions and viewing conditions; for recorded information on eruptions, tel. 967-7977 at any hour.) Once you've arrived, park headquarters should be your first stop. The rangers on duty there will give you driving maps and information on nature walks, and tell you when the next movie on volcanology will be shown. It is well worth seeing.

To really see and experience the volcano, you should take one of the hikes that start out from behind Volcano House, across the street; the air is deliciously crisp (we hope you've brought a jacket with you), the views eye-filling, and the mountain flowers and trees different from what you've seen on the tropical beaches below. But if time and energy are lacking, you can get the impact of the place simply by taking the circular drive that surrounds the park and leads you alongside every major point of interest. First you'll come to the **Sulfur Banks,** just out of park headquarters territory; farther on are the steam vents where clouds of evaporating rainwater hiss off hot stones underground.

Farther ahead, you can swing to the right on Mauna Loa Road and come upon the **Tree Molds,** similar to the ones you saw earlier at Puna, and **Kipuka Puala Bird Park,** perfect for a nature walk or a picnic. Head back to Crater Rim Drive now, and make a stop at the **Thomas A. Jaggar Museum,** to learn something about the history and development of volcanoes, and to observe the crater from its lookout point. Continue along Crater Rim Road to Halemaumau Overlook itself, the home of Pele, where people will perhaps be making offerings to the fiery goddess. Continue on to **Devastation Trail,** an artificial walkway stretching with spooky certainty through a forest of dead trees and winding around inert cinder cones. This walk takes about 15 minutes; to conserve energy, you might send one member of your party back to the parking lot to bring the car around to the lookout area at the end of the walk.

Back to the beauty of the forest you go now, and in the midst of an indescribably lush tropical setting you'll find the **Thurston Lava Tube.** Like the Kaumana Cave in Hilo, the tube was formed by cooled lava solidifying around a molten core that kept moving and eventually emptied the circular shell. The short path through the tube is clear enough, and you'll emerge into more forest at its end. **Kilauea Iki** and **Waldron Ledge** overlooks comprise the last two stops on the loop.

Since this is a circular drive, you're now back where you started from, and you've seen the major sights of the volcano. Before you leave the area, stop in to see the tasteful collection of arts and crafts, most of it by Big Island artists, at the **Volcano Art Center,** a rustic gallery occupying the original (1877) Volcano House Hotel. Many items here would make excellent gifts.

Where you go from here depends on you. You can continue along the Chain of Craters Road to its end. But because lava from a recent eruption now blocks the eastern boundary of the park (which leads to the Puna district), you eventually have to go back to park headquarters the way you came. From there, you can head back to Hilo, or continue from the volcano for another 96 miles to the Kona coast. The highway is good, but not especially interesting. You can stop at a black-sand beach at **Punaluu,** and in **Kau** you can still see in the cooled lava the footprints of Hawaiian warriors routed from a battle by a sudden outburst of Pele. Our personal preference is to go back to Hilo for the night, starting out the next morning for Kona by way of the varied and beautiful Hamakua Coast.

THE THIRD DAY—FROM HILO TO KONA

The intriguing thing about driving the **Hamakua Coast** is that, in a mere 96 miles, you pass scenery so unusual and so varied that it's difficult to believe it's all part of the same island—from lush sugar plantation fields curving around the base of Mauna Kea on the Hilo coast, through the grassy pastures of the Parker Ranch, into remote mountain regions, posh seaside watering holes, and across barren lava landscapes until you reach the green and gold of the Kona coast. Plan on a full day and savor it all.

Begin your travels on H-19 in Hilo, which continues straight out of the city. After about 5 miles, you will see a blue sign on the right that reads: "Scenic Route, 4 miles long." Take this and you will be driving around picturesque Onomea Bay. If you've not yet seen it, this is a good time to visit **Hawaii Tropical Botanical Garden** (see above), which you reach after 1 mile on the drive. Continuing on, you'll hug the northern shore of the island now, with Mauna Kea on one side, the surging sea on the other. The rich earth yields a bumper crop of sugarcane here. Your next stop should be in the little village of **Honomu,** 10 miles out, where an HVB marker will point the way up a country road to **Akaka Falls,** a glorious waterfall surrounded by an incredibly rich bit of jungle, tamed enough to turn it into an idyllic little park where you might want to spend all day. But get back to the highway and continue on; there's another pretty park at **Laupahoehoe,** down on the shore. Back in 1946 this village bore the brunt of a tidal wave that swept a school and its occupants into the sea. Swimming, as you will notice, is terribly dangerous in the pounding surf near the jutting rocks. A picnic or a look is enough.

In **Honokaa,** 20 miles ahead, you'll find Waipio Valley Lookout, the takeoff point for a 1½-hour Jeep trip into dreamy **Waipio Valley.** (It's best to have made advance reservations by phoning 775-7121. The cost is $25 for adults, $12.50 for children 2 to 12.) Even if you don't have time for that 1½-hour excursion, be sure to stop at the Waipio Valley Lookout for a view of mountains and ocean far below that is one of the glories of the islands.

A Stop at Parker Ranch

Now Hwy. 19 heads inland, and soon you're in cowboy country (they call them *paniolos* here), careening along the highway that borders grasslands reminiscent of Texas. This is **Waimea** (also called **Kamuela**), home of the enormous **Parker Ranch,** one of the largest cattle ranches in the United States under single ownership. Although most of us don't associate Hawaii with ranching, it is a major industry on the Big Island. Parker Ranch was begun in 1847, when King Kamehameha III deeded a two-acre parcel of land to John Palmer Parker, a sailor from Newton, Massachusetts, who had managed to tame some wild cattle for the king. Today, the ranch covers approximately 225,000 acres, and Parker's great-great-great-grandson, Richard Smart, is its owner.

If time is limited, stop in at the Parker Ranch Visitor Center to see a video plus historic exhibits ($5 adults, $3.75 children). Or visit the Historic Homes at Puuopelu, to see Mana, the 1847 home of the ranch founder, and the art collection of the current ranch owner ($7.50 adults, $5 children).

More About Waimea

Waimea is such a pleasant little mountain town that you may want to spend several hours wandering about, having lunch, and perhaps doing a little shopping. Try to work in a meal at the superb **Edelweiss Restaurant,** on Kawaiahe Road, where chef Hans Peter Hager turns out extraordinary continental cuisine in a country-inn atmosphere (no reservations accepted, and about an hour's wait at dinner; arrive before 1:30pm and you'll most likely be seated for lunch). Or visit **Merriman's Restaurant,** at Opelo Plaza, also known for its extraordinary chef (see review, above), for lunch or dinner. If you like this area well enough to stay a bit, there's the **Kamuela Inn,** an old-time favorite newly and nicely remodeled (doubles from $49 to $72, with or without kitchens; tel. 808/885-4243.

Shopping is wonderful in Waimea, and getting better all the time. **Hale Kea,** a restored plantation house of 1897, features charming gift shops in the cottages and guest quarters of the former estate. Be sure to visit **Maya Gallery** for splendid Japanese folk and fine art. Don't miss Parker Square with its super-tasteful boutiques, especially **Gallery of Great Things,** a treasure trove of decorative items for the home and fine art by local and Pacific Islands artists, and **Waimea General Store,** which is just what its name implies, but with many sophisticated craft and gift items and an excellent collection of Hawaiian books.

There's one more stop you might want to make in Waimea, at the **Kamuela Museum.** John Parker's great-great-granddaughter and her husband, Harriet and Albert K. Solomon, Sr., are the founders, owners, and curators of this largest private museum in Hawaii. It's located at the junction of Rtes. 19 and 250, open daily including all holidays from 8am to 4pm, and boasts a collection of ancient and royal Hawaiian artifacts (many of which were originally at Iolani Palace in Honolulu), as well as European and Asian objets d'art. Among the treasures: an ancient Hawaiian 61-pound, hammer-type stone canoebuster, the only one in existence, used by warriors to smash enemy canoes; many ancient temple idols; a royal Hawaiian marble-top teak table once owned by Kamehameha III; and a traveling clock given to Queen Liliuokalani by Queen Victoria of England. Admission is $2.50; children under 12, $1; phone: 885-4724.

Now some of you might want to take a little side trip up into the **Kohala** region of the Big Island. It's an uphill drive along Rte. 25, and it's 22 miles in each direction before you can get back to Kamuela or Kawaihae and continue your cross-island jaunt to Kona. But the scenery is among the most spectacular we've found in the islands. The Pacific drops off into a far-away, misty horizon, and the snow-topped cliffs of Mauna Loa and Mauna Kea provide an alpinelike background to the drive up the slopes of the Kohala Mountains. At the end of the road, and the end of the island, is the little village of **Kapaau,** the birthplace of Kamehameha and the site of the original statue of the warrior chief (you've probably seen its copy in front of Iolani Palace).

Still game for a side trip? This one is a simple 12-mile jaunt to the deepwater port of **Kawaihae,** where you can either have a swim with the local people at **Samuel Spencer Park** or **Hapuna Beach,** considered the best beaches on the island, or watch the jet set at play at the **Mauna Kea Beach Hotel.** Their buffet lunch is sumptuous, and you couldn't ask for a more perfect spot for a swim or a stroll. To reach the hotel, take Rte. H-26 from Kamuela, which will go past the Puukohala Heiau, and then, on the road to Samuel Spencer Park, to the hotel.

As an alternative to the Mauna Kea trip, you might want to drive farther south along Hwy. 19 until you reach the splendid **Royal Waikoloa** at Aneehoomalu Bay; you can swim at its superb beach. Then, visit the archeological sites and explore some of the oldest petroglyphs in Hawaii. Royal Waikoloa's near neighbor, the **Mauna Lani Bay Hotel,** is well worth another stop, just to soak up the beauty of its gardens and grounds and seaside vistas everywhere, perhaps to have an enjoyable lunch at the scenic CanoeHouse (see above for review). **Hyatt Regency Waikoloa** is another fantasy vacation retreat; you may want to have a meal here, or just a look. (See hotel descriptions under "Kohala Coast Resorts," above.)

Now, whether or not you've made any of these side trips, get back on (or continue along) Hwy. 19 or 190 (the latter trip is a bit shorter) and follow the road south to Kona. The landscape turns into a volcanic wasteland now, with HVB markers dating the lava flows before you, and finally you escape the path of Pele into the golden, glowing welcome of the Kona coast.

THE FOURTH DAY—EXPLORING KONA

Let's face it. Getting up enough energy to go sightseeing in Kona is difficult. The sea is so beautiful, the colors of the tropical blossoms so brilliant, and the mood so deliciously lazy, that you may want to spend all your time fishing or golfing or swimming or just plain doing nothing. But we think you'll find it more than worth the effort to spend a few hours sightseeing, since the culmination of your efforts—a visit to the Pu'uhonua o'Honaunau National Historical Park—is certainly one of the highlights of a trip to the Big Island.

Preliminary sightseeing in Kailua-Kona is simple. The main street, Alii Drive, covers the entire length of the village in less than a mile. Situated in the middle of town is the **Mokuaikaua Church,** dating from 1823, and built by the Hawaiians at the request of the missionaries from lava stones and koa wood from the uplands. It is one of the oldest churches in the islands. Across the street is **Hulihee Palace,** the summer home of Hawaiian royalty, now converted into a museum showing furniture and accessories of Hawaiian royalty plus ancient artifacts. It's open daily from 9am to 4pm. Admission is $4 for adults and $1 for children. Just down the street, in the Kona Plaza Shopping Arcade, Ami Gay dispenses tourist information for the **Hawaii Visitors Bureau.** She is truly one of Kona's wonders and deserves a place on any map. Walk around Kona to get the feel of the place and relax in its atmosphere. There's a public beach area in front of the Hotel King Kamehameha, boats and guides for rent at every turn, and you can even take skin-diving lessons if you feel like it. For a fun adventure, try **Kamanu Charters'** (tel. 329-2021). snorkeling cruise that includes everything from transportation, equipment, and the inner tube in which you enter the water, to a glass of passion-fruit juice, for your $40.

Now, to start your serious sightseeing, get into your car and follow Alii Drive until it becomes a two-way street; take the mountain road and get onto Kuakini Hwy., H-11. Now you're in Kona "up *mauka*," an area of small coffee plantations (this is where they grow that rich, wonderful Kona coffee), and if it's fall harvest time you'll see little red beans glistening against the green leaves of the coffee bushes lining the road. There are also small cattle ranches here. Follow the road past the Hongwanji Mission down the slopes of the mountains until you reach the sea at **Kealakekua Bay.** Across the bay, you can see a white monument that was erected to mark the spot where Capt. James Cook was killed by Hawaiian natives in a scuffle in 1779. At the very spot where you park your car, however, you'll see two shrines: one that commemorates the first Christian funeral in the islands (performed by Captain Cook for one of his sailors) and another in honor of Opukahaia, a sailor who became the first Christian convert in the islands (he was instrumental in bringing those New England missionaries here in the first place).

Continue along the shore road now for your major destination —**Pu'uhonua o'Honaunau National Historical Park,** also known as the place of refuge. This ancient, partially restored *pu'uhonua* still has about it the air of sanctuary for which it was built over 400 years ago. In the days when many chiefs ruled in the islands, each district had a spot designed as a refuge to which *kapu*-breakers, war refugees, and defeated warriors could escape; here *kapu*-breakers could be cleansed of their offenses and returned, purified, to their villages. (There is another such place of refuge on the island of Kauai, near Lydgate Park, but the one here is far better preserved.) The *heiau* has been reconstructed, and wooden images (known as *Ki'i* in Hawaiian) stand guard. A great wall surrounds the refuge, and next to it is a little cove, shaded by coconut palms, where the chief could land his canoe. Although you can wander about this place on your own, swimming (but *not* sunbathing) and picnicking and enjoying the peace, you should attend one of the orientation talks given at 10, 10:30, and 11am, and 2:30, 3, and 3:30pm in the amphitheater by the National Park Service. Sometimes "cultural demonstrators" are also on hand; they carve wood and demonstrate weaving and other ancient Hawaiian crafts. The Visitor Center is open daily from 7:30am to 5pm. Admission is $1 for those 16 to 61, or $3 per carload.

On your return to Kealakekua and on up the hill to H-11, take the turnoff to the **Painted Church,** about one mile in, on a bumpy side road. This tiny church was the first of all the similar churches on the island.

Going back home again the way you came, you might want to take time off for a bit of shopping or a bite. In Kealakekua, the **Grass Shack** is an old-time favorite for authentic Hawaiian and South Pacific handcrafts, with many locally made wood carvings. In the town of Captain Cook is the quaint **H. Manago Hotel,** which dates back to 1917, and still offers clean, comfortable, and very reasonable rooms (with a few wonderful Japanese *furo* accommodations) and home-style meals in its famed dining room, around $10 for dinner.

Park the car in the tiny village of Kainaliu and pick up some island fabrics at **Kimura's,** one of the oldest shops in town, and check out the quartz crystals, jewelry, and other New Age wares at **Crystal Star Gallery,** one of the newest. Then cross the street to the **Aloha Theater and Café,** a hangout for transplanted mainlanders; get yourself a snack, a veggie meal, or a luscious pastry, and have it right here in the artistically decorated little café, or better still, on the terraced lanai that runs down to the meadow beyond. Driving back to Kailua town, you'll spot **Teshima's** on the right, a Japanese restaurant for many years, and maybe catch Sen. Dan Inouye there—he always comes in for a meal when he's in Kona.

3. Shopping in Kailua Village

Return now to the sun and fun of Kailua-Kona. It's a great place to shop, so poke in and out of the arcades along Alii Drive. The **Kona Inn Shopping Village,** oceanside, has a huge collection of tasteful shops: A few of our favorites are **Noa Noa,** which offers hand-printed cotton batiks and other exotic clothes and jewelry from Bali and Indonesia; **Maui Divers,** an outstanding source for black, pink, or gold coral jewelry; **Hula Heaven,** for vintage aloha shirts, and **Alleygecko,** with lots of arts and crafts from Bali and a vast array of colorful gifts from just about everywhere. Across Alii Drive, the **Kona Arts & Crafts Gallery** is a must stop for those interested in native Hawaiian crafts, everything from koa carvings to seaweed art to genuine hula instruments. . . . In the Akona Kai Mall, sterling silver charms and other jewelry is very well priced at **Island Silversmiths. . . . Alapaki** at Waterfront Row is known for sophisticated modern interpretations of traditional handcrafts; everything here is made, tastefully, in Hawaii.

X

THE VALLEY ISLAND: MAUI

1. HOTELS OF MAUI
2. DINING IN MAUI
3. THE SIGHTS & SOUNDS OF MAUI

There is a legend in the Valley Island that the great god Maui was powerful enough to stop the sun in its tracks. He lassoed the sun as it was making its way across Haleakala Crater one morning, and held it captive until it promised to slow up its route across the heavens, making the days longer and the skies brighter. The primitive Hawaiians never doubted the truth of this legend, and we are beginning to half-believe it, too. For any force that could have created the island of Maui must have been doing something right. Oahu is 20th-century brilliant; Kauai is green and lush; Hawaii is immense and exciting—but Maui is pure gold. By all means, make a point of seeing it.

Fortunately, the treasures of Maui—its glorious beaches, its swinging little boating-shopping town of Lahaina, its remote jungle valleys, and its mighty giant of a sleeping volcano—are all just 88 miles from Honolulu. You can fly there by jet in about half an hour. Your plane will land you either at the main airport at Kahului in East Maui, or at the smaller airport in West Maui at Kapalua.

Plan to spend a minimum of three days, four or five if you have them, to sample the island's various charms. The Kahului area (on the bay, but no beach) is centrally located for sight-seeing, but hotels here now cater mostly to large tour groups and local business-people; the Kihei-Wailea area, about a 15-minute drive from Wailuku and on the beach, is the major destination in East Maui. Our personal favorite is the Lahaina-Kaanapali-Napili-Kapalua area in West Maui; although it is a 45-minute drive from Kahului, you'll be living at an exciting beach area, and the coastline is so gorgeous that coming home in the afternoon becomes just as much fun as starting out in the morning for a day of sightseeing.

WELCOME TO MAUI

The natives say that *Maui no ka oi* (there's no place better than Maui), and you'll begi to see why as soon as you arrive at Kahului Airport. The large reception lounge, with its contemporary architecture, is open at one end, so the outdoors beckons immediately. A car is a must, since there is very little public transportation. If you haven't already booked with one of the major interisland companies (Dollar, Budget, Alamo, National, etc.,), some local companies with good rates are **Trans-Maui Rent A Car** (tel. 877-5222 or toll free 800/367-5228), **Atlas Rent A Car** (tel. 871-2860 or toll free 800/367-5238 in the U.S., 800/433-5906 in Canada), and **Sunshine of Hawaii** (tel. 871-6222 or toll free 800/367-2977). Best to reserve in advance.

Note: The local airlines and car-rental companies often offer special package deals with hotels on Maui; you might get a room and a car for $50 to $60 a day. Many of these offers can be booked only in Hawaii.

---

1. Hotels of Maui

HOTELS IN KAHULUI

The **Maui Seaside Hotel,** 100 W. Kaahumanu Ave., Kahului, Maui, HI 96732 (tel. 808/877-3311; reservations toll free 800/367-7000), right on the ocean and with a new sandy beach, is a good bet for a stay in central Maui. It now incorporates the old Maui Hukilau Hotel, which is known as its pool wing. (The ocean is fairly rough here, so most guests prefer to use the pool.) A recent renovation has made everything shipshape; large, comfortable rooms all have two double beds, color TV, air conditioning, and refrigerators are offered on request in the higher-priced rooms. From April 1 to December 14, standard garden rooms are $59 single or double; deluxe poolside rooms are $63; superior tower rooms are $73; kitchenette rooms are $83, junior suite $88. During the winter season, it's $10 more per room. Cars can be rented for another $15 per night. The hotel is managed by Sands, Seaside, and Hukilau Hotels, 2222 Kalakaua Ave., Suite 714, Honolulu, HI 96815.

HOTELS IN KIHEI & WAILEA

For centuries, the calm beaches and windswept sands of the Kihei area of Maui were left relatively untouched. Even as tourist development boomed in the rest of Maui, this dry, sunny area just a 15- to 20-minute drive from Kahului was practically undiscovered —one hotel, a few cottages, that was it. But in the last 15 years or so, Kihei has been discovered in a big way, and now, as the islanders say, it's wall-to-wall condominiums. (In the neighboring Wailea-Makena area, more condominiums as well as a batch of luxury resorts have sprung up.) While Kihei lacks the heady excitement of the Lahaina-Kaanapali-Napili area (less in the way of restaurants, nightlife, and shops), it is growing more interesting all the time.

Telephone Area Code
The **telephone area code** for all phones in the state of Hawaii is 808.

And it does offer excellent, safe swimming beaches, acres of peace and quiet, and plenty of apartment hotels that offer space and comfort enough for a long stay. The tourist who wishes to stay in Kihei has literally dozens and dozens of choices that would require a book in themselves to detail. The few mentioned below are among the most attractive, and they are typical of the many in the area. Note that daily maid service is not the rule in the Kihei condominiums (although it is usually available at an extra price), so be sure to check if this factor is important to you.

Each of the two-bedroom apartments at **Kihei Sands,** 115 N. Kihei Rd., Kihei, HI 96753 (tel. 808/879-2624; reservations toll free 800/882-6284 from the U.S.), is actually a tiny little house; one of the bedrooms is on a balcony right above the living room, the other is to the side. These cute, compact little units also have two baths, a fully equipped kitchen, and a private lanai, and they rent for $70 to $90 for four, with each extra person charged $6, from April 16 to November 30. They can comfortably sleep up to six people. There are also pretty one-bedroom apartments (without the upstairs) and these, capable of housing up to four, go for $60 to $75 double, with each extra person charged $6. From December 15 to April 15, prices go up $15 to $20 a day. Although the white-sand beach, directly on Maalaea Bay with its oh-so-calm waters, is perfect for swimming, Kihei Sands also boasts a freshwater pool. The shake roofs give this place a modern Polynesian feeling that is quite charming. Four-day minimum stay in summer, seven-night minimum in winter.

High-rise rather than low-slung, **Kihei Beach Resort,** 36 S. Kihei Rd., Kihei, HI 96753 (tel. 808/879-2744; fax 808/875-0306; reservations toll free 800/367-6034), is a handsomely modern place each of whose apartments faces directly on the beach. The apartments are spacious and comfortable, the living-dining area is carpeted wall to wall, there's central air conditioning plus cooling fans, and the electric kitchen is complete with every convenience, including a microwave oven. From April 16 to December 15, the one-bedroom apartments, big enough to sleep four (sofa bed in the living room, queen or twin beds in the bedroom), go for $85 to $95 for two, $9 per extra person. The two-bedroom units, big enough for six, are $110 to $125 for four, $9 per extra person. Maid service is included in these rates. The rest of the year, the one-bedrooms are $100 to $110, the two-bedrooms are $130 to $145. More pluses for the Kihei Beach: free coffee in the morning; a freshwater pool for swimming; and six miles of Kihei beach for walking or a morning jog. Three-day minimum stay. MC, V.

If you choose to stay at the **Punahoa Beach Apartments,** 2142 Iliili Rd., Kihei, HI 96753 (tel. 808/879-2720), you know that you'll be in good hands. Punahoa is a small place with just 15

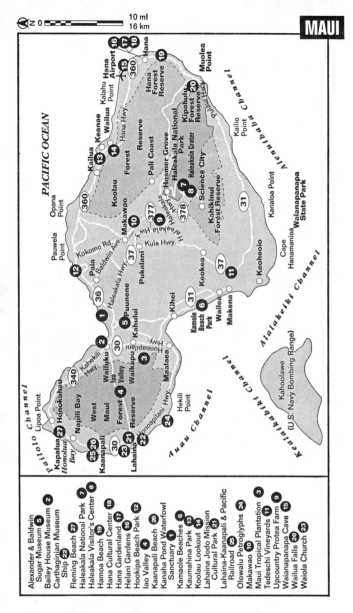

MAUI

Alexander & Baldwin Sugar Museum **2**
Bailey House Museum **5**
Carthaginian Museum Ship **22**
Fleming Beach **27**
Haleakala National Park **7**
Haleakala Visitor's Center **8**
Hamoa Beach **19**
Hana Cultural Center **18**
Hana Gardenland **17**
Helani Gardens **16**
Hookipa Beach Park **12**
Iao Valley **4**
Kaanapali Beach **26**
Kanaha Pond Waterfowl Sanctuary **1**
Kamaole Beaches **6**
Kaumahina Park **13**
Koolau Lookout **14**
Lahaina Jodo Mission **21**
Lahaina-Kaanapali & Pacific Railroad **25**
Olowalu Petroglyphs **24**
Makawao **10**
Maui Tropical Plantation **3**
Tedeschi Vineyards **11**
Upcountry Protea Farm **9**
Waianapanapa Cave **15**
Wailua Falls **20**
Waiola Church **23**

units, all of which have a private lanai, ocean views, a fully equipped kitchen, telephone, and smart, modern furnishings. It's surrounded by gardens, and it's right on the ocean; sandy beaches, with good swimming and surfing, are adjacent; children love it around the rocks because of the fish. The studio apartments rent for $77 daily in winter (December 15 to April 14) and $59 in summer (April 15 to December 14); one-bedroom units are $104 and $78; the one-bedroom penthouses are $106 and $80; and the two-bedroom apartments are $112 and $107. Punahoa gets booked way ahead with repeat visitors in winter, but accommodations are easier to come by in summer. Five-day minimum stay.

About five miles beyond Kihei is Wailea, a 1,500-acre planned resort development that features some of the best weather, best beaches, best scenery, and best resorts in Maui. Wailea's first hotel, and still one of its loveliest, is the **Maui Inter-Continental Resort**, 3700 Wailea Alanui Dr. (P.O. Box 779), HI 96753 (tel. 808/879-1922; fax 808/874-3331; reservations toll free 800/367-2960). The 550-room resort, set on 22 lushly landscaped oceanfront acres, offers just about everything one could want on vacation and then some. The feeling here is of peace, tranquillity, and "old Hawaii"—a nice alternative to the glitz and glitter of some of the newer Hawaii resorts. A newly completed $37 million renovation has made the resort more handsome than ever, with many of the new designs reminiscent of the historic plantation-style buildings of olden times. Guests have the use of two beautiful ocean beaches, three freshwater pools, and a hydrotherapy spa with Jacuzzi. Tennis buffs have three grass courts (the only ones in Hawaii) and 11 all-weather Laykold courts (three of them lit for night play) at nearby Wailea Tennis Club; and the golfers have the 36-hole Wailea Golf Course very close by. Complimentary guest activities range from windsurfing, Hobie Cat clinics and snorkel/scuba classes, to lei making, hula classes, pineapple cutting, supervised children's activities, and more. There's no chance of getting bored eating here, since there is a slew of restaurants, ranging from the elegance of La Perouse, a *Travel/Holiday* award–winning restaurant specializing in seafood, to the relaxed island charm of the oceanfront Lanai Terrace Restaurant, the hotel's "all-day dining room", from which one can often catch sight of whales. The delightful new Hula Moon restaurant at poolside is dedicated to island writer Don Blanding, and is filled with Blanding memorabilia, works of local artisans, and the sounds of Hawaiian music; it also has one of the most lavish salad bars on the island. The hotel is *the* evening entertainment spot in East Maui, with everything from dancing and live entertainment at the Inu Inu Lounge, to Maui's Merriest Luau, one of the best, held three times a week. The Aloha Mele luncheon on Fridays is an island classic, showcasing the talents of two of Maui's most beloved entertainers, "Auntie Emma" Sharpe and Jesse Nakooka.

Guest rooms and suites utilize beautiful island woods, rattan headboards, and color schemes of peach and turquoise. They are large and comfortable, with a king-size bed or two double beds, private lanai, air conditioning, radio, remote-control color TV, and minibar. Rates for single or double occupancy range from $210 and $245 with garden and mountain view, to $285 oceanview, $325 oceanfront, $350 deluxe. Suites begin at $350. Inquire about special room-and-car, golf, tennis, and honeymoon packages.

It's luxury all the way at the **Stouffer Wailea Beach Resort**, 3550 Wailea Alanui Dr., HI 96753 (tel. 808/879-4900; reservations toll free 800/9-WAILEA), one of Maui's premier resorts, a playground for sybarites set in lush tropical gardens sloping to the sea on 15 beachfront acres. A handsome $42 million redesign has more than ever, brought the outdoors inside. From the stunning murals and artwork in the lobby to the outdoor sculptures in the seaside gardens to the glamorous dining spots and beautifully furnished accommodations, there's a high standard of taste and elegance here that makes it easy to see why the Wailea Beach is the only Hawaii resort to receive the AAA Five Diamond Award for 10 consecutive years—not to mention the *Travel/Holiday* award for Raffles, its fine-dining restaurant, for 9. The hotel has just about everything for an active or blissfully lazy vacation, including shuttle service to two 18-hole championship golf courses and the Wailea Tennis Club (dubbed "Wimbledon West" with its 3 grass and 11 Laykold courts, 3 lit for night play); swimming at five sandy beaches or a superb pool; snorkeling off a coral reef; classes in lei making or hula. Camp Wailea offers special activities for children 5 to 12 during Christmas, Easter, and summer holidays. In addition to the prize-winning Raffles (patterned after the famous Raffles Hotel in Singapore, and known for Continental cuisine, seafood, and the most elaborate Sunday champagne brunch in Maui), there's the delightfully casual Palm Court, which features a different buffet nightly; the cute little Maui Onion, a gazebo restaurant poolside; the Sunset Terrace for cocktails with a view; and Lost Horizon, a contemporary nightclub for dancing. Monday and Thursday night luaus are considered among the best on Maui.

The 350 rooms are lovely in an elegantly understated way—quite large, done in a contemporary Hawaiian motif, with bamboo, wicker, or rattan furnishings. All have a private lanai with an ocean, garden, or mountain view; a refrigerator with stocked bar; color TV with in-room movies; individual air conditioning controls; and a direct-dial telephone. Each room has either a king-size or two queen-size beds. The morning wake-up call brings complimentary coffee and the daily paper.

Room rates are $215 double for deluxe on the mountainside; $250 for mountain view; $295 for oceanside; $325 for ocean view; one-bedroom suites $575. Rooms at Mokapu Beach Club, right on the water, are $380. A third and fourth person in a room is $35 each; children 18 or under stay in their parents' room free; an extra room required for a family is 50% less, upon availability. Inquire about their room-and-car, honeymoon, and golf packages. AE, CB, DC, DISC, ER, JCB, MC, V.

Imagine that you're living in the midst of an exquisite flower garden on the oceanside, with the lines between indoors and outdoors so softly diffused that you hardly know where one begins and the other ends, and you'll have some idea of what the **Four Seasons Resort,** 3900 Wailea Alanui Dr., Wailea, Maui, HI 96753 (tel. 808/874-8000; fax 808/874-6449; reservations toll free 800/334-6284 from U.S. and Canada), is like. Approached by a drive lined with royal palms, its entrance marked by classical columns, the eight-story, 380-room resort faces the ocean from its marble lobby via a descending series of gardens and courtyards laced with ponds, pools, waterfalls, fountains, and works of art to one of the best beaches in the islands. This is island innkeeping at its elegant best. Lucky guests have the use of two pools with waterfalls and slides, and a separate children's pool; two on-site tennis courts lighted for night play (and the Wailea Tennis Club is close by); snorkeling, scuba, and sailing equipment and instruction; a health club with exercise equipment and aerobics classes; croquet and bicycles; and much more. The Wailea Golf Club with its two 18-hole championship golf courses is close by. There is a complimentary activities program for children. And dining is exemplary, with Seasons for elegant dining, featuring fresh island seafood; the Pacific Grill for specialty East-West treats (see below); the Cabana Club for light fare and tropical drinks at poolside; and the elegant Lobby Lounge.

Guest rooms and suites are among the largest in the islands, measuring 600 square feet and more; at least 85% of them have ocean views. All have large lanais with teak furnishings and tables for al fresco dining, soft-cushioned rattan and wicker furniture, air conditioning and ceiling fans, TVs with VCRS, and incredibly luxurious bathrooms, each with an 8-foot marble counter with twin vanities, and the shower set apart from the soaking tub. Rates run from $300 for doubles with partial ocean view to $350 for ocean view and $500 for ocean-view executive suites. On the club floor, oceanview rooms are $430, suites $580. One-bedroom suites go from $700 to $2,000, two-bedroom suites from $1,000 to $5,000 per night. A third adult in the room is $50, $100 on the club floor. Children under 18 free when sharing same room as parents. AE, CB, DC, ER, JCB, MC, V.

Wailea Resort's newest addition is one of the grandest resort hotels in the world. Dubbed the "Taj Mahal of the Hyatts," the **Grand Hyatt Wailea Resort & Spa,** 3850 Wailea Alanui Dr., Wailea, Maui, HI 96753 (tel. 808/875-1234; fax 808/874-5143; reservations toll free 800/233-1234), is truly a latter-day pleasure palace, with magnificent Japanese, European, and Hawaiian gardens, artworks by present-day masters, a luxurious spa with state-of-the-art equipment and health programs, a complete facility devoted to child care, a formal pool which becomes a lighted fountain at night, and a wedding chapel which "floats" in the center of a lagoon. In addition to the superb beach which it fronts, the 787-room resort has a 2,000-foot-long river pool with a series of slides, waterfalls, and rapids, which gradually drops swimmers 35 feet. In various swim-in caves, they find a hot, bubbling spring, a sauna, a swim-up bar, and a deep scuba diving pool. At the bottom, swimmers may enter a one-of-a-kind water elevator which lifts them back up to the top again.

The resort's Spa Grande, Hawaii's largest spa, is on a level with top establishments in the United States and Europe, with an expert staff providing consultations on individualized programs of exercise, stress management, diet, and health. Among of the pleasures pampered guests can look forward to are mineral, herbal, milk, fruit, and mud baths, beauty makeovers, shiatsu massage, and even body sonic massage, just for starters. An entire restaurant just outside the spa is devoted to spa cuisine.

Other dining facilities include a Japanese restaurant and gardens featuring giant granite stones from Japan's Mt. Fuji; a dockside seafood restaurant out on the pier surrounded by a saltwater aquarium; the main dining room, 60 feet above sea level, with panoramic views of garden and ocean; two snack bars, and a poolside restaurant.

Guest rooms are set in an eight-story building whose central open-air atrium is filled with tens of thousands of blossoms that are rotated seasonally. Rooms are very large, with spacious lanais, and each has an ocean view. Large marble baths offer separate soaking tub and showers, and every amenity. For those who desire even more luxury and service, the Regency Club offers the finest in VIP attention.

Rates (subject to change) are $350 for ocean-view rooms, $375 for oceanfront, $425 for deluxe oceanfront, and $500 for Regency Club ocean. Suite rates available on request. AE, CB, DC, DISC, JCB, MC, V.

HOTELS IN LAHAINA

Although the major resort areas of Kaanapali and Kapalua are not far away, there's a certain ramshackle charm about staying right in Lahaina. Once the capital of the islands, Lahaina has a history as a whaling port and freewheeling ambience that recalls those lusty days; it is a fun-and-games town from morning through night. Staying in Lahaina is particularly attractive in winter, since it gets more sun and less rain and wind than the Kaanapali and Napili areas farther north.

If you'd like to settle into your own little apartment right in Lahaina, then **Lahaina Roads,** 1403 Front St., Lahaina, HI 96761 (tel. 808/661-3166, or toll free 800/624-8203), could be your place. The five-story elevator building at the Kaanapali end of Front Street sits in a cool and breezy spot right on a good snorkeling beach; you can look down at the ocean—and watch some spectacular sunsets—from your own lanai. A swimming beach is half a mile up the road, but there's a freshwater pool right at home. These are condominium apartments, many of them exquisitely furnished by their absentee owners. They are soundproof, with wall-to-wall carpeting, fully equipped kitchens with washer and dryer, large living rooms with convertible couches, and there are phones for free local calls in your room. One-bedroom apartments go for $75 a day double from April 15 to December 15, $95 the rest of the year (they can accommodate up to four people); two-bedrooms for $105 and $125 double (capable of accommodating up to six); and there are two delightful penthouses (that can house up to six of you) for $150 and $200 for four. Additional persons are $10. Three-day minimum stay. Maid service on request. Covered parking. A free shuttle to downtown Lahaina and Kaanapali is within 3 blocks. MC, V.

Situated right in the heart of Lahaina town, the **Maui Islander,** 660 Wainee St., Lahaina, HI 96761 (tel. 808/667-9766; fax 808/661-3733; or toll free 800/367-5226), is great for anyone who doesn't want to be bothered driving everywhere; it's within a short walking distance of a good swimming beach, the activities of Lahaina Harbor, and all the shops and restaurants and nightlife of Front Street. Set amid 9 acres of tropical grounds, the Maui Islander consists of nine two-story buildings containing 372 units, a combination of hotel rooms, studios, and one-bedroom apartments, all of which offer daily maid service, telephone, and color TV. All except the hotel units (which do have refrigerators) also have a fully equipped kitchen for cooking at home. There's an attractive pool and sunning area, a tennis court lit at night, a hospitable staff, and plenty of activities. The price is $83 for two people in a hotel room, $95 for three in a studio, $107 for four in a one-bedroom. Add $12 to all rates from December 20 to April 14. (Rates are subject to change.) AE, DC, MC, V.

Can you imagine finding a small, quiet, European-style country inn that looks as if it's been standing for years but is really new, just a block from the bustling waterfront and main street of Lahaina? And which, despite its elegance, is very well-priced? All these delicious surprises await at **Plantation Inn,** 174 Lahainaluna Rd., Lahaina, HI 96761 (tel. 808/667-9225; reservations 800/433-6815; fax 808/667-9293), whose owners have come up with some terrific innovations in the art of making guests happy. Each of the 17 rooms is different—most have a queen-size bed and either a daybed or Murphy bed—but all have air conditioning, soundproofing, tiled bath, and are exquisitely decorated with antiques, stained glass, hardwood floors, brass and poster beds, ceiling fans, and floral wallpaper and bedspread. The TV (VCR on request) is tucked away in a graceful armoire; there are silk flower bouquets in every room; wall prints are charming. Guests have the use of a 12-foot-deep tiled pool with spa and sun deck out back, plus a barbecue pit and gazebo for private meetings or dining. Deluxe doubles are $99 to $109; front doubles are $129; a suites (some with cooking facilities) are $159. All rooms include breakfast (worth over $10) at Gerard's, one of Maui's best French restaurants (see below), which occupies the front parlor and veranda of Plantation Inn. Guests also receive a 20% discount on most items on Gerard's dinner menu. The inn books cars as a courtesy to their guests, with rates starting as low as $18 a day or $95 a week for a subcompact. Diving packages are available from Central Pacific Divers (tel. toll free 800/551-6767). The inn provides snorkeling equipment, golf clubs, coolers, beach mats, just about anything you need for a neat and nifty vacation. AE, DISC, MC, V.

Not a commercial resort, not a hotel or typical condo development, **Puumana,** P.O. Box 515, Lahaina, HI 96767 (tel. 808/667-2551; reservations toll free 800/628-6731 from U.S. and Canada) is something quite different under the Maui sun. It is the first planned residential development on the island, a colony of privately owned one- and two-bedroom townhouses, set on 28 acres of tropical gardens right on the beach. The place is secluded, private, and very peaceful; yet it's a short drive from all the shopping and restaurant excitement of downtown Lahaina. Puamana was a private estate in the 1920s, part of a large sugar plantation; the plantation manager's home is now the clubhouse, with a patio overlooking the ocean (the ideal place for sunset watching), a library, card rooms, sauna, and office. There are three swimming pools on the property, an adults-only pool right on the beach, a Laykold tennis court, paddle tennis, and badminton and table tennis, too. The 220 town houses, built back in the 1960s, are all individually furnished, all comfortable, with complete kitchens, sofa beds in the living rooms; they can sleep four to six. During the summer season, April 16 to December 14, one-bedroom units for up to four are $125 with garden view, $150 center garden, $180 oceanfront; in winter, they are $140, $160, and $200. Two-bedroom houses for up to six are $180, $200, and $240 in summer, $210, $250 and $280 in winter. Three-bedroom houses for up to six on the oceanfront are $315 in summer, $350 in winter. Minimum stay is three nights. MC, V.

HOTELS AT KAANAPALI BEACH

Just three miles north of Lahaina is what surely must be one of the great resort areas anywhere in the world—Kaanapali Beach. Stretched out along this fabled strip of white sand, crystal waters, and gentle, rolling surf, with a championship golf course sloping down to the sea and the West Maui mountains offering spectacular vistas in the background, is a small cluster of luxury hotels. We doubt if you could go wrong at any of them, but each offers something a little bit special.

One of the grandest of these resorts is the $80 million **Hyatt Regency Maui,** 200 Nohea Kai Dr., Lahaina, HI 96761 (tel. 808/661-1234; fax 808/667-4498; or toll free 800/228-9000), which opened in 1980. Breathtaking is the word for this 815-room seaside caravansary, which covers 18 acres of prime beachfront and is spangled with eight major waterfalls, Japanese gardens and lagoons, underground grottoes, meandering streams along which swans glide, and an exceptional pool—half an acre of fresh water that roams under waterfalls and bridges, along gardens and lava rocks, and offers swimmers a sensational 154-foot slide. The atrium lobby is dotted with plantings, gardens, and tropical birds—flamingos, parrots, peacocks, even penguins. And throughout the lobby and the adjoining luxury shopping arcade (a kind of Rodeo Drive of the islands) is $2 million worth of original artworks, mostly from the Far East and the South Pacific. Such a setup is, of course, a sightseeing attraction; free art and wildlife tours for the public are held daily at varying times.

But if you are a guest at this hotel, you have a wealth of activities to choose from—Robert Trent Jones's 36-hole golf course right at hand, five all-weather-surface tennis courts, full-service health spa. Classes and clinics go on all day, in sailing, aerobics, weight training, aquarhythmics (water exercises), hula, and coconut weaving, to name just a few. And dining facilities are as splendid as you would imagine. There's the Swan Court (with real swans) for continental and seafood specialties; Lahaina Provision Company, a gardenlike, casual setting for a seafood salad buffet at lunch; at dinner it's a Chocaholic Bar; Spats, an Italian café where the pasta is fine, the decor is early 1920s, and disco rules the night; the Pavillion, for poolside dining; and several bars and lounges, including the "sunken" Grotto pool bar. The Sunset Terrace is the scene of Hyatt's Polynesian Revue, *Drums of the Pacific.*

As for the rooms, they are spacious, artfully decorated in tranquil teal and lavender, and provide every comfort: air conditioning, color TV, private phone, full bathroom, sitting area, tasteful artworks on the walls. They were newly renovated in 1990. Prices vary according to the view, from garden to golf/mountain to oceanfront. Single or twin, they are $220 to $330, up to $360 to $390 for Regency Club. Suites range all the way from $500 for a Golf Suite to over $2,000 for the Presidential digs. Each additional person is charged $25; children under 16 stay free with parents; maximum of four in a room. AE, CB, DC, DISC, JCB, MC, V.

A longtime favorite at Kaanapali is the **Royal Lahaina Resort,**

A Restoration Gem

The **Lahaina Hotel**, a few steps off Front Street at 127 Lahainaluna Rd. (tel. 808/661-0577, toll free 800/669-3444), is a one-of-a-kind treasure. It took two years of intensive work and over $3 million for Rick Ralston (president of Crazy Shirts) to complete the period restoration of an old Lahaina hotel, turning it into a wonderfully romantic, intimate hostelry, the kind travelers to Lahaina enjoyed at the turn of the century. Although the ground-up restoration (all new electric wiring and plumbing) made way for such concessions to period authenticity as private baths in each room, 24-hour telephone service, and air conditioning, the overall result is like being in a living museum. Lobby furniture is over 100 years old; 10 different wallpaper designs, all authenticated from the 1860s to the 1900s, were reproduced; railings and balustrades were brought piece by piece from mansions of the American South. The splendid antiques, most from Ralston's personal collection, furnish the guest rooms as well. There are 10 traditional-sized rooms and three parlor suites, all richly furnished with turn-of-the-century wood, brass, and iron full-size beds, Oriental rugs, leaded-glass lampshades, marble mantle clocks, as well as luxurious decorator fabrics and wall coverings. Fresh flowers fill the room each day; there are yukata robes from Japan hanging in the bathrooms. Continental breakfast is served each morning, to be taken in one's room or in the old-fashioned wicker rocking chairs out on the balconies, which overlook the busy town. No smoking; no television; no children under 15. Room rates go from $110 to $120, parlor suites at $170. Downstairs, David Paul's Lahaina Grill offers superb (and expensive) New American cuisine. AE, MC, V.

2780 Kekaa Dr., Lahaina, HI 96761 (tel. 808/661-3611, or toll free 800/621-2151 from U.S. and Canada, 0014/800/126-985 from Australia; fax 808/661-6150), with 541 rooms, cottages, and suites spread out on 27 acres of beautiful tropical gardens fronting the beach. Recreational facilities are magnificent: you can play at a world-famous tennis facility with 11 courts (including one stadium court), 6 of them lighted at night; golf at two PGA championship courses adjacent to the hotel; swim at any of three pools or in the glorious ocean; or indulge in a multitude of water-sports activities. You can shop at some of the best stores in Maui in two separate shopping arcades, and dine at a bevy of splendid restaurants including **Moby Dick's** for seafood as good as it is in New England; **Chopsticks,** an Oriental grazing restaurant; and the **Royal Ocean Terrace** for all three meals, plus a great Sunday champagne brunch. There's an old-fashioned ice-cream parlor, three cocktail lounges, even a nightly luau. Once you've settled in here, there's little reason to go anywhere else.

Now for the rooms. Even those at the lowest rate are spacious and equipped with color television, air conditioning, phone, refrigerator, and a combination bath and dressing room. During the regular season, April 1 to December 18, rooms go from $120 standard to $195 deluxe oceanfront, and $275 for a deluxe oceanfront cottage with kitchen. From December 19 to March 31, rates range from $150 to $275. The one-, two-, and three-bedroom suites are in the $300-to-$500 range; a third person is $20, which includes a rollaway; no charge for cribs. Request king- or queen-size beds in advance. Rooms for the handicapped are available. Cars from Dollar Rent-A-Car are free for every day of your stay if you request the "Outrigger Maui Free Ride" package when making reservations. AE, CB, DC, DISC, JCB, MC, V. Parking: $3.50 per day.

One of Maui's newer showplaces is the **Westin Maui,** 2365 Kaanapali Pkwy., Lahaina, HI 96761 (tel. 808/667-2525; reservations toll free 800/228-3000; fax 808/661-5764), a $125 million remake of the venerable Maui Surf Hotel. This is indeed one of the ultimate luxury playgrounds of the islands. Situated on 12 acres of glorious sandy beach, great for swimming, snorkeling, windsurfing, the Westin Maui features a spectacular, multilevel aquatic garden: five swimming pools, fed by four waterfalls, connected by a network of super-slides and bridges, with the Beach Bar in the center, so guests can swim right up for a drink. Sports and recreational facilities include a European-style health club, access to Kaanapali's two famed 18-hole, par-72 golf courses, and tennis nearby. Guests enter the hotel through a spectacular lobby cooled by waterfalls and exotic plantings, with swans gliding just a few feet away from the registration desk. Two thousand pieces of art, valued at $2.5 million, grace the public areas and gardens (art tours are held Tuesday and Thursday at 9am, wildlife tours Sunday, Monday, Wednesday, and Friday at 10am, and are free to the public: phone 667-2525 for reservations). Eight restaurants and lounges serve the finest cuisine selections from all over the world. The luxurious Sound of the Falls offers breathtaking views and fine dining. There's Cook's at the Beach, a 250-seat poolside coffee shop, the Villa Terrace, the Villa Restaurant, where guests dine on fresh seafood with a view of ocean, pools, slides, and waterfalls. The 761 guest units, including 28 suites and 37 rooms at the Royal Beach Club, are handsomely decorated, each with a minibar and refrigerator. No-smoking rooms can be requested; so can rooms for the handicapped. Rates, single or double occupancy, are $195 standard, $235 garden view, $250 golf view, $270 partial ocean view, $295 ocean view, $330 deluxe ocean view, and $375 and $395 Royal Beach Club; suites go from $500 to $1,900. Extra persons are charged $25; no charge for children 18 or under sharing their parents' room. (Rates subject to change.)

The Westin Maui believes in thoroughly pampering its guests; there are something like 1,100 people on staff. There's even a concierge at the pools, to cater to one's slightest whim. My only caveat about this place might be that after a week or two of this kind of gilded living, returning to the ordinary world might be just out of the question!

One of the first hotels to be built on the Kaanapali strip, the **Sheraton-Maui,** 2605 Kaanapali Pkwy., Lahaina, HI 96761 (tel. 808/661-0031; reservations toll free 800/325-3535), has been blessed with a spectacular location. It is wrapped around a crater called Black Rock (the ancient cliff from which souls of Hawaiians were said to leap to the spirit world beyond), and its main building winds around the rock in a series of descending, curving parapets that are really the balconies of individual rooms. There's also another wing that is more conventionally high-rise. In both buildings, each room is of good size, has its own private balcony or garden, and tub-shower combination, plus an optional refrigerator on wheels for a modest rental fee. Depending on the view, doubles run from $139 to $260 for rooms in various buildings, the top price being for oceanfront cabanas or "cottages." Ocean-view suites are $400 to $800; a third person in the room costs $25 more; no charge for children under 18. AE, CB, DC, DISC, EURO, JCB, MC, V.

There's a great deal to look at in this hotel. The old lobby with the sky for a roof from which you take the elevators *down* to everything is beautiful, with its pool, fountains, and sculpture; off it is the stylish Discovery Room, for continental dining and nightly entertainment. The Black Rock Terrace at poolside serves breakfast, lunch, and casual evening meals. The beach here is one of the favorites at Kaanapali. Snorkeling buffs love the long reef that goes out from Black Rock, and golfers have the Robert Trent Jones Royal Kaanapali Golf Club next door—so everybody's happy.

Indoors and outdoors merge gracefully at the **Maui Marriott Resort,** 100 Nohea Kai Dr., Lahaina, HI 96761 (tel. 808/228-9290; reservations toll free 800/228-9290 from the U.S., 800/268-8181 from Canada). Since the hotel is built around a courtyard, there's an outdoorsy feeling to the lobby and shopping arcades. The resort, very popular with families, has two pools with whirlpool spa, a game room, an exercise room, tennis courts, golf nearby, and four restaurants, including the airy Moana Terrace, where you can have your meals overlooking the water; and Nikko, a Japanese steak house. Popular Banana Moon is Maui's only video disco, and there's karaoke music at the Lobby Bar. The rooms are furnished very tastefully; much use is made of rattan and dark woods. All have lanais and the usual luxury hotel amenities. Rates are for single or double occupancy; except for suites, all rooms are basically the same (the view and location account for the wide disparity in price). Rooms facing the mountains or golf course are $195; those with partial ocean view are $230; ocean view is $250, and oceanfront—nothing between you and the deep blue sea—is $285. Large suites go from $400 to $1,000, depending on location and type. An extra person in the room is charged $25 a day. Inquire about special room/car packages and other discount and package deals. AE, CB, DC, DISC, MC, V.

A budget hotel on Kaanapali Beach? There's really no such animal, but rates are a bit lower at the **Kaanapali Beach Hotel,** 2525 Kaanapali Pkwy., Lahaina, HI 96761 (tel. 808/661-0011, or toll free 800/733-7777 from U.S. and Canada, 0014/800/126-985 from Australia; fax 808/667-5978). It's a lovely place, right out on the ocean, with an intriguing swimming pool shaped like a whale, acres of trees and flowers, and a full complement of restaurants and drinking spots, including the delightful Tiki Terrace and Tiki Grill as well as the refreshingly inexpensive Kaanapali Koffee Shop, which serves three popular-priced buffet meals a day. This hotel aims to be "the most Hawaiian of the hotels," and there's a real feeling of the old Hawaiian spirit in all of its programs and activities. Each room has its own private lanai, and is large, air-conditioned, and attractively decorated, with the convenience of a refrigerator and color TV. The price for standard rooms is $135. Depending on the views, from courtyard to oceanfront, they then go up from $145 to $175. Deluxe suites go from $180 and $195 for junior suites, to $215 for an oceanfront family suite, to $525 for the Kaanapali Suite Oceanfront. An additional person is $20 per night; rollaway bed $15; children under 17 free when sharing a room with parents and using existing bedding. During special seasons, it's possible to get a free compact deluxe car with the price of your room. AE, CB, DC, DISC, JCB, MC, V.

HOTELS BETWEEN KAANAPALI & KAPALUA

Once you pass the big hotels of the Kaanapali area, you're smack into condominium country. Between Kaanapali and Kapalua, miles and miles of curving coastline are being given over to small apartment hotels that provide every home-away-from-home comfort in an idyllic setting that's nothing like home. Most of these operate much like a hotel. Apartments can be rented on a daily, weekly, or monthly basis; frequent maid and linen service is provided, and the management takes care of all repairs and services. Most do not have restaurants on the premises, but they all have kitchen facilities, and restaurants abound all over the area. *Note:* Since some condominiums do expect you to do your own housework, be sure to inquire about all such details before you send your deposit.

Just about our favorite place here, the **Maui Sands Condominium**, 3559 Lower Honoapiilani Rd., Lahaina, HI 96761 (tel. 808/669-6391; fax 808/669-8790; reservations toll free 800/367-5037), is only a mile from the Kaanapali hotels, and has accommodations as comfortable as any luxury suite at about one-third the price. The 76 one- and two-bedroom suites are set in either a beautiful tropic garden or on the oceanfront. These have an enormous living room with private lanai (great for star-gazing at night), comfortable-size bedrooms, full electric kitchen, tropical ceiling fans, air conditioning, and color TV; a family has plenty of room to really stretch out and relax here. Since each apartment is individually owned, the furnishings are slightly different in each, but all are well appointed and comfortable. Everything has been newly refurbished. The top accommodation, a two-bedroom apartment overlooking the beach, goes for $160 for five persons. In the garden, it's $130; and near the road, $100. One-bedroom apartments for two people are $135 for oceanfront, $95 to $105 for the garden, and $80 for standard. Extra persons are charged $9. There's a swimming pool and sunning area, and a beautiful stretch of oceanfront from which you can view Lanai and Molokai. (Most of the sand has been washed away by storms, but, hopefully, will return.) Laundry facilities are available. Potluck/BYOB parties are held frequently in season. Managers Kay and Adele Kunisawa are exceptional hosts. Inquire about their luxury units on the beach at Papakea, next door. MC, V.

Just a bit farther north in Honokowai is **Hale Ono Loa** (the "House of Good Living"), 3823 Honoapiilani Rd., Honokowai, Lahaina, HI 96761 (tel. 808/669-6362; reservations toll free 800/367-5108). Some 67 condominium apartments in a four-story building are set in a very beautiful garden, with a large pool area in the central courtyard ringed by palm trees. The pool and sundeck—big enough so that guests can play coconut checkers, shuffleboard, or Ping-Pong—is the center of social life here. You can wade out between the coral reefs for swimming and snorkeling, or walk 2½ blocks to a sandy beach. Apartments are individually furnished and decorated and have a very well equipped kitchen and one or two bedrooms. From April 17 to December 17, the one-bedroom units go for $85; those with partial ocean view are $90, those with ocean view $95. Two-bedroom units, all oceanfront, are $180. From December 19 to April 16, the one-bedrooms are $95, $100, and $105, and the two-bedrooms are $220. Weekly rates are available, as well as occasional air/condo/rental-car packages. All apartments are oriented to the trade winds and have a large lanai, which makes sunset watching, whale watching, and just plain relaxing very popular activities here.

Surprisingly enough, really good beaches are not so easy to find along the coastline. Many of the apartment hotels are built on rocky beachfronts, or storms have blown away sandy beaches, so guests do most of their swimming in pools. One place that is, however, blessed with a beautiful, reef-protected crescent beach is **Kahana Sunset** on Kahana Bay, about midway between Kaanapali and Napili (P.O. Box 10219, Lahaina, HI 96761; tel. 808/669-8011; fax 808/669-1488; reservations, toll free 800/669-1488). There are other things to commend this place, too, notably the 79 units that meander down a gentle hillside and are adequately spaced for privacy, comfort, and good ocean views. We especially like the two-bedroom units, which are like little two-story town houses with twin stairways leading to the bedrooms and two baths. Rates go from $135 for the one-bedrooms, up to $165 and $215 for the two-bedroom units. It's $6 for each additional person (maximum of four in the one-bedrooms, six in the two-bedrooms). Inquire about money-saving car/condo packages starting at $150. All the units are handsomely furnished and have a full electric kitchen with all the comforts one might want: dishwasher, garbage disposal, microwave oven, refrigerator and freezer with an automatic icemaker, even one's own washer-dryer. Besides the good beach, there's a 60-foot heated swimming pool, croquet, and barbecue pits down on the beach.

You can also be assured of an excellent swimming beach at a clutch of small hotels coming up now on Napili Bay. Here's where the **Mauian Hotel**, 5441 Honoapiilani Rd., Lahaina, HI 96761 (tel. 808/669-6205; fax 808/669-0129; reservations toll free 800/367-5034), one of the first in this area, is still going strong. Each of its 44 Polynesian-style units is fitted out with a queen-size bed and two twins to accommodate four persons. Rooms boast a fully equipped electric kitchen with microwave oven, private lanai, and plenty of ocean breezes whooshing through. There's a pool for those who can forgo the superb beach, a laundry area, even an island-style minisupermarket next door that makes cooking a breeze. There are golf courses and many good restaurants nearby. From April 15 to December 14, double rates are $87 garden, $95 ocean view, $112 oceanfront. From December 15 to April 14, they are $104, $112, and $129. A third person is $9, a fourth $6; crib,

$10 per day. Maid service every three days; 10% more for daily service. There is a communal TV room, and two public telephones.

Napili Village Suites, 5425 Honoapiilani Rd., Lahaina, HI 96761 (tel. 808/669-6228 or toll free 800/336-2185 from U.S. and Canada), is another popular and well-established place in the lovely Napili area. Each of the 28 units is capable of housing four, with a folding door creating two separate sleeping areas, one with a king-size bed and the other with twins or a queen-size sofa sleeper. An all-electric kitchen, a large lanai, wall-to-wall carpeting, cable TV, radio, and daily maid service make for comfortable living. You have a lovely pool and the beach is just a few steps away, but there are no beachfront accommodations. The minisupermarket, mentioned above, is just behind the pool, and there are also barbecues. Rates begin at $75 in summer, $85 in winter, double or single; $6 for each extra person. MC, V.

A true luxury setup on Napili Bay is **Napili Surf Beach Resort,** Napili Bay, HI 96761 (tel. 808/669-8002 or 669-8003, or toll free 800/541-0638 from the U.S. and Canada), which offers plenty of *aloha* along with beautiful beachfront accommodations. Spaciousness and comfort are the big things here: The studio apartments each contain 500 square feet; the one-bedroom units contains 670 square feet. Each apartment has an all-electric kitchen. All units are soundproof, carpeted, and handsomely furnished. The choice of either the freshwater swimming pool or that blue Pacific is yours. Rates are $95 single and $89 double in the smaller but cozy Puamala garden studios; $105 in the ocean-view studios; and $145 in the one-bedroom apartments on the beachfront. It's $15 for an extra person. Summer specials usually offer lower rates on longer stays. Daily maid service. The managers can usually arrange car rentals and trips at 15% to 20% discounts.

Perched on a hill overlooking Napili Bay, **Napili Point Resort,** 5295 Honoapiilani Hwy., Lahaina, HI 96761 (tel. 808/669-9222; reservations toll free 800/669-6252), is a beautiful hotel in a dramatic setting. Gently sloping lawns, along which the 115 all-suite units are set, lead down to a beach fine for snorkeling; a swimming beach is nearby. There are two freshwater pools oceanside and a picnic area for barbecuing; guests enjoy tennis privileges at a nearby condo. Each of the units is a charming little home, tastefully decorated, some with a dropped living room, white furniture, good art on the walls. Spacious lanais afford ocean views. Each includes an all-electric kitchen with washer-dryer and dishwasher, and each has direct-dial telephone and cable TV. Napili Point is a condo, but it offers hotel services: a resident manager on duty around the clock to provide assistance, and daily maid service. From April 16 to December 21, the rate for a superior one-bedroom suite with ocean view is $129 for up to four persons; oceanfront is $144, deluxe oceanfront is $154. A two-bedroom, two-bath suite with ocean view is $155 for up to six persons; oceanfront is $175, deluxe oceanfront is $185. During the peak winter season, rates go up $30 per unit. Reservations: Write Aston, 22255 Kuhio Ave., Honolulu, HI 96815, or call the number above.

Colony's Napili Shores, 5315 Honoapiilani Hwy., Lahaina, HI 96761 (tel. 808/669-8061; reservations toll free 800/367-6046), is another of these well-managed Colony Resort condominiums. It's a delightful low-rise group of buildings with its own sundries store and two attractive restaurants on the premises: the Gazebo for breakfast and lunch, the Orient Express (with a choice of Thai or Chinese cuisine) for dinner. There's excellent swimming at Napili Bay, plus two freshwater pools (one with Jacuzzi), shuffleboard, putting green, free snorkeling lessons, and once-a-week mai-tai parties. Studio and one-bedroom apartments are all nicely furnished, have fully equipped kitchen, telephone, and color TV. From April 1 to December 20, studios are priced at $125, $135, and $150 for garden, oceanview, and oceanfront, respectively, for up to two people; $12 for an extra person. Winter rates are $140, $150, and $165. The one-bedroom apartments are $145 and $165 for up to four people in summer, $160 and $175 in winter. AE, DC, DISC, ER, JCB, MC, V.

The **Napili Kai Beach Club,** 5900 Honoapiilani Rd., Lahaina, HI 96761 (tel. 808/669-6025, or toll free 800/367-5030), offers luxury-plus accommodations on gorgeous Napili Bay, as well as tennis courts, four swimming pools, and a 20-foot whirlpool, two putting greens, and two very good dining spots: the Sea House and Sea Breeze Terrace restaurants. Three championship Kapalua golf courses are located immediately adjacent to the Napili Kai. Guests here say they never want to leave. Rates begin at $155 for a standard studio for two people, and go to $180, $185 and $195 for oceanfront and deluxe oceanfront. Suites go from $210 to $475. (Rates are subject to change.) The units all have kitchenette, lanai, color TV and radio, and telephone. The ocean swimming is great.

Should you happen to have a generous fairy godmother who will grant you a special wish, ask for a stay at **Kapalua Bay Hotel and Villas,** 1 Bay Dr., Kapalua, HI 96761 (tel. 808/669-5656; fax 808/669-4694; reservations toll free 800/367-8000), near the northwestern tip of the island. Picture a 1,500-acre resort complex, surrounded by ocean and bays, by coconut palms and tall pines, by flowering gardens and gentle landscapes at every turn, combining the ultimate in continental hotel service and elegance with the graceful *aloha* of island living, and you'll get some idea of what Kapalua Bay is all about. "No compromise" is the watchword here. Kapalua Bay provides three sandy ocean beaches for swimming; two freshwater pools; three 18-hole championship golf courses; a "tennis garden" (10 courts surrounded by lush greenery); many dining facilities, including the intimate Plantation Veranda, which has won awards from *Travel/Holiday* magazine for gourmet cuisine, the Pool Terrace for informal food and panoramic views, and the Bay Club, just above the beach, for drinks and dining overlooking a spectacular setting—for starters. The Mayfair Buffet, served on Sunday in the Garden Restaurant, is a memorable treat.

The guest rooms are gracious beauties, tastefully decorated in subdued South Seas style, in warm neutral shades of taupe, rose, and muted terra-cotta. They have twin or king-size beds, his-and-hers vanities, ServiBar, dividers between the bed and sitting areas, floor-to-ceiling shutters leading out to a large lanai, and high ceilings. Rooms are all the same; their location determines their price. Garden-view rooms are $215 to $250; ocean-view rooms are $290 to $340; oceanfront rooms are $400. An extra person is charged $35 more per day. There is no additional charge for children 14 years or younger sharing a room with a parent. Prices are subject to change. MAP available for an extra fee. Discounts are offered on greens fees, golf carts, and tennis.

The Kapalau Bay Hotel and Villas also boasts one of the most tasteful shopping arcades in the island, the Shops at Kapalua, which contains its own little European-style Market Café.

Super-luxurious condominiums, the Villas at Kapalua Bay, are also available, ranging from $275 to $475. Inquire of the hotel. AE, DC, JCB, MC, V.

HIDEOUTS IN HANA

Because of its remoteness, separated as it is from the rest of Maui by the mighty bulk of Haleakala, Hana has remained one of the few places to maintain the spirit of old Hawaii. Since 1946, the **Hotel Hana Maui** (tel. 808/248-8211; reservations toll free 800/321-HANA) has been a retreat for the privileged few, people who can easily afford rates like $300 to $775 double, European plan, about $95 more per person per day for full American Plan. Just in case you're not yet in that category, and still want to spend a little time in Hana, try the comfy little **Aloha Cottages** (P.O. Box 205, Hana, HI 96713; tel. 808/248-8420), where Mr. and Mrs. Nakamura will make you feel right at home. Here $50 to $80 per night gives you a two-bedroom redwood cottage with living room, complete kitchen, and bathroom, very clean and tidy, with a view of either Hana Bay or Kauiki Head. **Hana Bay Vacation Rentals** (P.O. Box 318, Hana, HI 96713; tel. 808/248-7727; reservations toll free 800/657-7970) offers clean, comfy, fully equipped private cabins, cottages, or fully furnished three-bedroom, two-bath homes. Rates vary, according to the season; children are welcome. Manager Stan Collins is at your service. Lovely accommodations in Hana, ranging from a rustic studio inside a banyan tree ($45 per night) to a super solar-powered beach house with annex at $185, are offered by Blair Shurtleff and Tom Nunn of **Hana Plantation Houses,** P.O. Box 489, Hana, Maui, HI 97613 (tel. 808/248-7248; reservations toll free 800/657-8240). Jacuzzis indoors and out, gorgeous locations, and many amenities abound.

---

2. Dining in Maui

RESTAURANTS IN THE KAHULUI-WAILUKU AREA

Excellent Chinese food can be found at **Ming Yuen,** 162 Alamaha St., in the Kahului Light Industrial Park, off Hwy. 380. The local people rave about both the Cantonese and Szechuan specialties here—the former light and delicate, the latter spicy hot at times—and we agree. Favorite dishes like almond duck, lemon chicken, moo shu pork, oysters with ginger scallions, and shrimp with cashew nuts run from about $7 to $8.50. A whole fresh steamed fish is occasionally available, and a special treat. Everybody who's anybody in Maui turns up at Ming Yuen for their Chinese

New Year's banquet—an occasion to remember. Ming Yuen is open daily, serving lunch from 11am to 5pm, dinner from 5 to 9pm. Reservations: phone 871-7787. MC, V.

Wailuku is the place to sample real local food—and **Chums,** 1900 Main St., is an attractive place in which to do so. Here's where you come for dishes like oxtail soup with grated ginger and Chinese parsley, huge noodle lo meins (try their "Super Mein" at $5.25), Hawaiian "plate lunches" ($4.95 to $6.95) with copious servings of meat or fish plus vegetables and macaroni salad, and then a choice of rice or whipped potatoes—all that starch is traditional! Sandwiches, burgers, chilis, salads, round out the menu. Hefty breakfasts are served from 6:30 until 11am, then the regular menu to 10:30pm daily. On Sunday, doors open at 7am. Phone: 244-1000. MC, V.

RESTAURANTS IN KIHEI

Harry Gabel, who is considered one of Maui's best chefs (he was formerly executive chef at the prestigious Four Seasons Resort in Wailea) decided to venture forth on his own a while back, and with his partner Deanne Kost, opened **Gabel's,** at 2439 S. Kihei Rd., upstairs at the Rainbow Lagoon. The result is some of the best dining to be found in Kihei—a menu that uses the freshest of local ingredients in an imaginative way that combines the best of European, American, and island cooking styles. The format of the place, with a large supper club up front and an intimate dining room in back, seems neither fish nor fowl, and is in need of redefinition— But the food needs no improvement. There are wonderful specials each night, like the warm smoked Scottish salmon and roasted shiitake mushrooms with citrus butter among the appetizers, the grilled tomatoes and bitter greens with shoyu vinaigrette among the salads, and the mahimahi in papaya basil butter among the entrées. You can always count on good items on the regular menu, such as fried coconut shrimps with orange horseradish marmalade or steamed clams with tomato, garlic, and basil in beer among the appetizers ($5.50 to $9), or, among the main courses ($16 to $22), a Pacific stew on a bed of angelhair pasta, a hearty veal schnitzel with fresh herb mushroom sauce and spätzle, and stir-fried spicy Szechuan pork with steamed rice. Desserts can only be described as ethereal, so save room for the likes of baked papaya with rum raisin ice cream, or chocolate cheesecake.

Gabel's is open every day from 5pm to 2am, with live entertainment nightly: dancing and easy listening music from 6 to 9pm, plus dancing to Hawaiian contemporary music from 9:30 on. Reservations recommended: phone 879-5600. AE, JCB, MC, V.

If your idea of a good meal is delicious Mexican food and frosty margaritas, a lively atmosphere, and a congenial crowd to enjoy it all with, you've come to the right place. Across from Kamaole Beach Park at Kai Nani Village is **La Familia,** 2511 S. Kihei Rd., a Maui institution for over 16 years. The attractive dining room overlooks the ocean, the sunset, and all of that, but most of the action is right in the dining room, around the bar, and on the outdoor lanai; a lively crowd starts gathering as soon as the 99¢ frosty margaritas become available during the 11:30am to 6pm happy hour. As for the food, served from 11:30am till 10pm, it's great and prices are reasonable: Have some nachos or a Maui Wowie to begin, then plan on spending between $7.95 and $11.95 for specialties like macho burrito, tostada supreme, chili relleno. Combination plates run $10.95. Mud pie and such coffee-liqueur combinations as peppermint Pattie (hot chocolate with peppermint schnapps and whipped cream) are great winders-up. Open daily, cocktails till midnight. Phone: 879-8824.

We've yet to find a Maui resident who doesn't sing the praises of the **Kihei Prime Rib House and Seafood House,** 2511 S. Kihei Rd.; once you've dined there, you'll know why. The rustic, South Seas–style building is decorated with handsome wood carvings and original paintings; its dining room affords splendid views of the sunset over the ocean; and its kitchen is known for superb prime rib, seafood, steaks, and a huge salad bar brimming with fresh, locally grown fruits and vegetables—one of the best in the islands. Prices begin at $8.95 for salad bar alone, and go up to $25.95; a special combination of prime rib and scampi is very popular at $17.95. All entrées include either fettuccine or rice, and home-baked bread, plus your choice of salad bar, Caesar salad, or red snapper chowder. If you like to dine early, make reservations for the popular Early Bird Special, served every night between 5 and 6pm; Polynesian chicken, prime rib dinner, or fresh island fish are $9.95 to $11.95. Dinner only, 5 to 10pm. Prices subject to change. Phone: 879-1954.

Even if you don't get to stay at one of the grand luxury resorts in Wailea, you should definitely plan to have a look at them, and maybe a meal or two. For a perfect lunch in one of the prettiest settings in the area, I'd choose the **Pacific Grill** and the Four Seasons Resort, where you dine in a casual setting with ocean vistas and al fresco patios, with a view to gardens, terraces, fountains, and waterfalls leading to the sea. (You may also get a view of some celebrity guests.) Although the regular lunch menu is attractive—appetizers like baked sweet Maui onion soup with gruyère, or main courses like a chilled lobster club sandwich on sourdough toast, or grilled island fish with wilted spinach salad and mango lime coulis—I heartily recommend the salad buffet. It's a lavish display of changing fresh salads, a homemade soup, and perfectly wonderful grilled chicken breasts. On top of all this, a dessert buffet of luscious sweets is included in the price of $15.50. Regular entrées go from $10.25 to $17.50, appetizers from $4 to $6.75. At every meal, Four Seasons Alternative Cuisine, selections lower in calories, cholesterol, sodium, and fat, are also available.

In the evening, Pacific Grill becomes an East-West specialty restaurant, serving the best of Pacific Basin cuisine. All dishes are meant for sharing, and they are great. Favorites among the starters ($4.75 to $12) are the Vietnamese shrimp soup with spinach and egg flower, and the shrimp and smoked scallop potstickers with chili water soy sauce. Among the main courses ($16 to $25), there's stir-fried spiny lobster in black-bean sauce with tempura soft-shell crab, several wok fries of chicken, shrimp and vegetable combinations, and even a roast suckling pig with Chinese steamed buns.

Pacific Grill is open daily from 6:30am to 10pm. Reservations recommended: phone 874-8000. AE, CB, DC, ER, JCB, MC, V.

The languid, perfumed Hawaii of the 1920s is a part of the visitor's fantasy that is seldom catered to anymore—so it's fun to visit **Hula Moons,** the new restaurant at the Maui Inter-Continental Resort at Wailea, which brings that period to romantic life. Hula Moons is named after a book written by Hawaii's adopted poet, artist, and musician, Don Blanding, and the place is filled with Blanding memorabilia, as well as works by island arisans and the sounds of Hawaiian music. Flickering torches and an ocean view add to the mood of this poolside dining room. The food is pleasant, too. You could actually have a very good salad bar meal for just $9, Or you could go for one of the regular entrées ($22.50 to $30), including fresh seafood specialties like grilled Hawaiian ahi teriyaki or blackned fish of the day, as well as meat entrées like tender marinated lamb chops, paniolo prime ribs, or filet mignon (all from animals raised in local farms). Along with the entrée comes the fabulous salad bar, plus fresh Kula vegetables and a choice of augratin potatoes, citrus pilaf rice, or steak fries. Start with an appetizer like sashimi or escargots, end with a Hawaiian berry cream cake or a white and dark chocolate mousse cake—delightful!

Hula Moons serves dinner only, nightly from 5:30 to 10pm. Reservations recommended: phone 879-1922.

TWO RESTAURANTS UP-COUNTRY

Our favorite up-country Maui restaurant, right in the heart of windsurfing-happy Paia (which makes it an ideal stop to or from Hana or Haleakala), is **Dillon's Hideaway,** 89 Hana Hwy. Dillon's is very cozy, very relaxed, the kind of place where you want to have a long, cool tropical drink and rap with the locals. But don't think that the relaxed attitude extends to the kitchen: Standards are strict; everything is fresh, cooked to order, and delicious. The day starts early for travelers up and about on the road to Hana: eggs Benedict (a special at $5.95 between 7 and 8am), french toast with Kahlúa, delicious frittatas (open-faced vegetarian omelets), homemade quiches, and fresh raspberry pancakes! Most of these goodies are available at lunch, plus a complete fresh fish lunch for $10.95, excellent hamburgers and salads, meatball heros, and more. Ahi burgers are a specialty of the house. Dinners run around $10 to $20 for a complete meal; your main course might be pepper steak, a house pasta, or fresh fish, $15.95. A vegetarian or meat lasagne with soup or salad and French bread can do you nicely too, for $8.95 or $9.95. Burgers are on the dinner menu also. Have the homemade cheesecake for dessert. If you can get up to Paia on a Friday or Saturday night after 9 or on a Sunday afternoon from 3 to 9pm, join the local crowd in a karaoke sing-along; dancing is permitted, and everyone is encouraged to sing. Great fun!

Dillon's is open every day, serving food from 7am to 9:30pm, on karaoke nights until 2am. Phone: 579-9113.

Finding a gourmet restaurant in the middle of nowhere—or, to be more specific, in the middle of a 1,000-acre pineapple plantation in up-country Maui—is not your ordinary kind of experience. But then, there's nothing at all ordinary about the **Haliimaile General Store** at 900 Haliimaile Rd.; ever since it opened a few years ago, it's garnered rave reviews from just about everybody, from local food buffs to visitors who drive many miles for its superlative cuisine, basically American but with international accents. It's easy to schedule a visit into your route if you're driving to either Haleakala or Hana; even if you're not, you should come out here if you're serious about great food. Against a bright and sophisticated background—high ceilings, sparkly blue-green chairs, shelves of pottery and china for decor—sit back and study Bev and Joe Gannon's sophisticated menu. It changes every two weeks, but it always incorporates the freshest locally grown produce, hand-picked herbs, tree-ripened fruits, and seafood fresh from local waters. You might start your dinner with such appetizers ($6 to $10) as a goat-cheese and sun-dried-tomato tart, served with warm red bell pepper coulis; or with Bev's famous crab dip served on a boboli (pizza). Or how about a Brie-and-grape quesadilla? Then proceed to main courses like a Louisiana Creole with chicken and shrimp over Basmati rice; or succulent chicken breasts marinated in tequila lime honey and garlic-grilled; or soused shrimp and scallops, sautéed with wild mushrooms and flambéed with cognac. Entrées run from $13 to $22, with a fresh fish choice every day at market price. The lunch menu is equally imaginative; we usually like to have one of the salads, like the ahi niçoise salad—fresh ahi (tuna) grilled rare, served with tomatoes, snow peas, eggs, and olives and topped with a balsamic vinaigrette—or the delicious Chinese chicken salad. We can also recommend the breast of chicken, bacon, Brie, and grilled onion sandwich, served hot in a sourdough wedge. Vegetable torte and lasagne are house luncheon specialties; nothing is more than $10. Desserts are different every day and always outstanding.

Haliimaile General Store is open Tuesday through Sunday, serving lunch from 11am to 3pm, dinner from 6 to 10pm, and a delightful Sunday brunch from 10am to 3pm. Reservations are a must at dinner: phone 572-2666. MC, V.

RESTAURANTS FROM LAHAINA TO KAPALUA

Don't even think of leaving Maui without a visit to **Avalon,** in the courtyard of Mariner's Alley, 844 Front St., which continues to enthrall diners with its marvelous menu of contemporary Asian cuisine. Recent celebrity diners who have sung its praises include Yoko Ono (she loved the clams in black-bean sauce), artist Peter Max, actors Kathleen Turner and Anthony Quinn. But we ordinary mortals love it too, for there's no telling what kind of wonderful new recipes owner/chef Mark Ellman is likely to come up with. Mark draws on the inspirations of California, Indonesia, Vietnam, Thailand, and Japan, giving everything his personal signature; he uses no MSG, no salt, seasons only with herbs and sauces made to order; you may have your dishes mild, medium, or spicy, as you wish. The place is prettily decorated, with antique Hawaiian shirts on the walls, ceiling fans, flowers, blond bamboo chairs and tables dressed in aloha fabric. Lunch is moderately priced, with sandwiches from the grill at $6.95 and $7.95, and such entrées as char-grilled chicken breast with garlic black-bean sauce or Indonesian chicken stir-fry going from $8.95 to $10.95. There are four vegetarian selections, including a Balinese-style Gado Gado salad, at both lunch and dinner. At dinner, appetizers run from $5.95 to $10.95, main courses from $14 to $26.95. Among the appetizers, Avalon summer rolls, soft-shell crabs in a garlic herb sauce, and the Indonesian satay are especially good. Asian pasta—shrimp, clams, scallops, and fresh island fish in a tomato-and-ginger sauce over linguine—and the Chinese roast duck with plum sauce and steamed buns (Friday and Saturday only) are special favorites. Fish of the day, Asian prawns, and eastern scallops are done in a variety of presentations. There are many daily specials, so choice is difficult. As for dessert, there's no problem: There's only one, the caramel Miranda, a concoction of exotic fresh island fruits, thick, warm caramel sauce, and Häagen-Dazs macadamia-nut-brittle ice cream. Ellman reports that Debbie Fields of Mrs. Fields Cookies gave it a rating of "30" on a scale of 1 to 10, calling it "the best dessert I've ever had!" We agree.

Avalon is open every day, from noon to midnight. Be sure to make reservations for the evening: phone 667-5559. AE, DC, DISC, MC, V.

Another place that's immensely popular in Lahaina is **Kimo's,** at 845 Front St. (tel. 661-4811), overlooking the water, with glorious sunset views. It's exciting rather than peaceful, and packs in the crowds for good fresh fish of the day (the price varies seasonally), top sirloin or teriyaki sirloin, Hawaiian specialties like Polynesian chicken (breast of chicken marinated in a ginger-shoyu sauce and broiled), or kushiyaki (brochettes of marinated chunks of sirloin and chicken breast), from $7.95 to $22.95. Along with your tasty entrée comes a tossed green salad with a good house dressing, steamed herb rice, and a basket of freshly baked carrot muffins and French rolls. Special menus for kids, from $4.50 to $7.95. If you have room for dessert, try the Hula Pie—it's supposedly what the sailors swam to shore for—and Kimo's coffee, served up with a bit of macadamia-nut liqueur.

Kimo's upstairs dining room is open nightly from 5 to 10:30pm, but there's also limited food service downstairs at the bar. Lunch, served from 11:30am to 2:30pm, features local fresh fish, sandwiches, and a terrific fruit salad at $6.50. The bar is known for fabulous house drinks. Reservations: phone 661-4811. AE, MC, V.

Take some of the best French food on Maui, and present it in a charming, European old-world setting, and there you have **Gerard's,** at the Plantation Inn, 174 Lahainaluna Rd. Wicker chairs, rose tablecloths, lace curtains, and gas lights set the mood for exquisite dining, either indoors, out on the patio, or in the garden. Chef Gerard Reversade is an unquestioned master and a visit here is a true experience in gourmet dining. Gerard creates new menus frequently, depending on what's fresh in the market, combining the techniques of the classic French cooking he learned as a child in his native Gascony with island-inspired innovations. Dinner might start with shiitake and oyster mushrooms in a puff pastry shell, or marinated ahi with lime and coconut milk, Tahitian-style (appetizers run about $9.50 to $12.50). Then on to incredible main courses (from about $26 to $36) like grilled rack of lamb with aromatic herbs from Molokai or confit of duck with country-style potatoes, or seafood au gratin in a crayfish butter sauce. Desserts, like the crème anglaise with vanilla sauce or the chocolate decadence cake, or whatever else Gerard has dreamed up for the day, will be inspired. Be sure to have a French champagne or wine with your meal (a glass is only $5), chosen from an excellent list. Gerard will probably stop by your table to make sure everything is perfect. And it will be. Lunch is served only once a week, on Fridays, at $20 for everything from appetizer and entrée to dessert and coffee; the menu changes every week, with three or four choices of appetizer and entrée. A superb Sunday brunch is $24, with Chef Gerard pulling out all the stops. Breakfast daily (including Sunday) is all you can eat for $9.

Gerard's serves breakfast daily 7:30 to 10am, Sunday brunch 11am to 2pm, lunch Fridays 11am to 2pm, and dinner daily 6 to 10pm. Reservations are a must: phone 661-8938. Validated parking.

Climb the stairs or take the elevator to the top of the Wharf Cinema Center at 865 Front St. and treat yourself to a Japanese meal teppanyaki-hibachi–style at the very popular **Benihana of Tokyo.** Just as you would if you were really in Tokyo, take your place at one of the communal tables and, along with the other diners, marvel at the antics of the chef as he wields and juggles his knives with relish, all the while preparing your meal on the center grill. Traditional hibachi dishes ($13.25 to $17.25) include chicken, steak, filet mignon, shrimp, and scallops, all served with Japanese onion soup, salad, a tasty shrimp appetizer, hibachi vegetables, rice, and tea; house specialties ($19.75 to $29.50) include various combinations of steaks and seafood, including lobster tail. Lunch is a quieter time here, and it's then that you can have a festive combination of three hibachi dishes—perhaps calamari, scallops, sesame chicken—for just $13.50. Desserts are simple, drinks excellent.

Benihana of Tokyo is open every day, serving lunch from 11:30 to 2pm, dinner from 5 to 10pm. Reservations advised for dinner: phone 667-2244. CB, DC, JCB, MC, V.

Desserts are legendary at **Longhi's,** 888 Front St., where mango cheesecakes, chocolate-cake pies, strawberry shortcakes, and others have inspired poetry and rapture. Desserts run about $5 and are big and rich enough to share. Just about everything else at Longhi's (new menu daily, depending on what's fresh and in season) is special too, prepared with a gourmet flair. A longtime Lahaina favorite. Dinner will cost about $25 to $30. Phone: 667-2288.

The same people who run Kimo's in Lahaina are also in charge at **Leilani's on the Beach,** overlooking the ocean at Whaler's Village at Kaanapali, another winner. This is a picturesque, multilevel restaurant that makes artful use of wood, plants, tiles—the feeling is tropical all the way. And the food and service are tops all the way. At a recent meal, for example, our expert, witty waiter assured us that he had personally removed the calories from our hula pie and left them in the kitchen. Thus assured, we ate with relish. Everything here is delicious, from meats smoked in the koa-wood ovens or the lava-rock broilers to fresh fish of the day and specialties like scampi and Malaysian shrimp, each $18.95 and excellent. Entrées run around $9.95 to $29.95 for the likes of baby back pork ribs, ginger chicken, teriyaki sirloin, crab, and lobster. All dinners come with San Francisco sourdough bread and Oriental rice, plus green salad with shredded Parmesan and Romano cheeses. You won't go hungry here, but you'll probably want some wonderful desserts like the above-mentioned hula pie (we hope your waiter can remove the calories too) and the chocolate mousse. Have a drink to celebrate the sunset, or just the joy of being in Maui.

The Beachside Grill downstairs is the place for a lighter menu, including appetizers, sandwiches, and Hawaiian local plates, all from about $5.95 to $9.95. Lunch from 11:30am to 4pm, pupus and dinner from 5 to 10:30pm nightly. Phone for reservations: 661-4495.

Overlooking the ocean, and particularly lovely at sunset, **Erik's Seafood Grotto,** on the second floor of the Kahana Villa condominiums a few miles north of Kaanapali Beach, is a most attractive, moderately priced place in the Kahana area. Complete dinners here include soup or green salad with a macadamia-honey-nut dressing, a basket of bread, and fresh boiled potatoes or rice pilaf. What to choose? Perhaps the house specialties of bouillabaisse or cioppino at $18.95 each; or seafood curry, baked stuffed prawns, coquilles St-Jacques, or a wide variety of other seafood specialties, priced from $13.95 to $18.95. Fresh-caught island fish—mahimahi, ono, ahi, ulua, snapper, or Hawaiian salmon—is market-priced. For dessert, we'd go with the fresh strawberries marinated in Grand Marnier, topped by whipped cream, or the Kona coffee ice cream. An Early Bird Special is served from 5 to 6pm at $11.95. Dinner is on from 5 to 10pm daily. The lounge and bar are open at noon. Reservations: phone 669-4806.

About 1 mile before you reach Kapalua, you'll find the Napili Shores Resort and its scenic restaurant, **Orient Express**—part Thai, part Chinese. The food is good and the setting is even better: The restaurant overlooks a Japanese carp pool and a fountain, set in a garden; sparkling beads of light in the ferns are reflected in the wide windows. There is Oriental statuary everywhere. In the midst of this loveliness, you can dine reasonably on Thai, Cantonese, and Szechuan entrées that run mostly about $7.75 to $12.95. Fresh island fish, served in a yellow-bean sauce or sweet-and-sour with fresh ginger, is market-priced. You may want to try the coconut chicken soup, made in a base of coconut milk and seasoned with lemon grass and other spices; and the house special, the chicken wings stuffed with ground pork and chicken, deep-fried, and topped with sweet-and-sour sauce. Honey-lemon duck and garlic shrimp are also quite tasty. Vanilla ice cream, topped with coconut cream and crushed peanuts, is a winner at $2.50. The sweetness of Thai iced tea or coffee goes well with the spiciness of a meal like this (specify whether you want the Thai dishes mild or spicy when you order; they can be hotter than you expect). The Early Bird Special, served between 5:30 and 6:30pm, features a complete five-course dinner for $11.95. Open every day, from 5:30 to 10pm. Take-out is available. Phone: 669-8077.

Perhaps the most beautifully open-to-nature dining room in Maui is the one at the **Bay Club** at the Kapalua Bay Hotel and Villas. While the hotel is, indeed, expensive (see above), and dinner will probably run anywhere from $30 to $50 for food in the finest continental tradition, anyone with a few dollars in the pocket can have lunch here and enjoy the almost breathtaking views of sea and sky. The Bay Club is situated on a rise commanding a spectacular, multi-angled view of the ocean; the feeling is almost of being on board a ship. The atmosphere is serene, with deep, comfortable chairs, wood-and-wicker furnishings, artworks, and flowers everywhere. And lunch is not expensive. A variety of sandwiches like smoked salmon and avocado on sourdough bread; triple-decker Monte

Cristo dipped in egg batter and grilled; and bay shrimp with melted white cheddar cheese on Molokai bread, are priced from $6 to $8. Other menu specialties run from $7 to $13.50. Lunch is ready from 11:30am to 2pm daily. For reservations, phone 669-5656, ext. 39; after 5pm, 669-8008. AE, CB, DC, JCB, MC, V.

The Grill & Bar (tel. 669-5653) at Kapalua has enjoyed an excellent reputation for many years. Located between the Tennis Garden and the Golf Club, it offers fabulous views of the West Maui Mountains and Napili in the distance. The wide glass windows look out over trees, plants—and tennis players. The Grill & Bar is run by the same people who do such a good job at Kimo's and Leilani's on the Beach. The menu features fresh fish and seafood dishes, including Hawaiian lobster and live Maine lobster, as well as poultry and meat selections like tournedos with béarnaise sauce, rack of lamb, and filet mignon. Most entrées run $10.95 to $24.95. There are also some delightful fresh pasta dishes at $17 and $18, a New York steak sandwich at $11.95, and gourmet pizza at $10.95. San Francisco sourdough bread plus oven-roasted new potatoes come with your entrée. For dessert, there's hula pie and chocolate mousse. During the 3-to-5pm happy hour, there are discounts on drinks and pupus. Dinner is served from 5 to 10:30pm, and lunch (burgers, sandwiches, salads, etc.) from 11:30am to 3pm. There's an excellent selection of house liquors and fine California and French wines. AE, MC, V.

In this same lovely Kapalua area, wend your way along a mile-long lane flanked by rows of Norfolk Island pine trees, and you will find yourself in the Hawaii of old. **Pineapple Hill,** one of Maui's finest restaurants, was the plantation home of David Thomas Fleming, a pioneer in establishing pineapples and mangoes on Maui. The old house has been lovingly cared for and is a gracious place for dining, with sunsets that are unforgettable. Complete meals include salad, rolls and butter, and rice or vegetables along with your entrée. One of the house specialties is chicken Pineapple Hill, oven-roasted and served in a pineapple boat. Another favorite is the shrimp Tahitian, jumbo prawns with a special seasoning, broiled in the shell and served with rice. Also good are the Alaskan king crab legs, rack of lamb, roast prime rib, and teriyaki steak. Dinners are priced from $9.95 to $26.95. Some of the vegetables are à la carte, prepared in a variety of interesting ways and served in portions ample enough for two. For dessert, don't miss the Häagen-Dazs hula pie. Cocktails are served from 4:30pm, dinner from 5:30pm until closing (seven days). For reservations, phone 669-6129.

There's a very traditional, "old Hawaii" feeling about the very new **Plantation House Restaurant,** in the Plantation Golf Course Clubhouse, almost as far north as one can go on the paved road that winds up this way. The restaurant sits high on a hill, with its upstairs main dining room affording extraordinary views from different areas of the restaurant—of the mountains, the ocean, the golf course below. A huge, three-sided fireplace dominates the room, and original artwork by local artists graces the walls. The food is called "Kamaaina Cuisine"—meaning friendly, comfortable island food. At lunch, it's fun to have one of the delicious salads, like the free-range chicken salad, the traditional Cobb, or the Oriental (shiitake and oyster mushrooms), from $3.45 to $7.25. Good sandwiches and such entrées as wok-fried vegetables, with chicken or shrimp, and a lime-marinated chicken breast grilled and covered with a spicy papaya salsa, run from $5.95 to $9.95. Dinnertime appetizers, $5.25 to $8.95, are great fun, especially the dragon shrimp or chicken, the Maryland-style crab cakes with a lime-jalapeño mayonnaise, and the brochettes of lamb with warm rosemary balsamic viniagrette served on a bed of cabbage. House specialties among the entrées include fresh local fish (at market price) prepared in a variety of ways; try it en papiotte—stuffed with shiitake mushrooms and limu, sealed in parchment and steamed. Other entrées, $15.95 to $19.95, include fried pork chops smothered with tequila-laced Maui onions and sweet bell peppers; and a wonderful fresh Australian leg of lamb, crusted with fresh rosemary. For a side dish, be sure to have the hand-grated potato pancakes with Maui onions. If calories are no concern, go for the fudge brownie with ice cream and chocolate sauce or the pot de crême au chocolate for dessert; if they are, then the Plantation House sorbet, homemade with fresh pineapple, fresh cream, and Maui's own Tedeschi Maui Blanc, makes a perfect light ending to the meal.

Plantation House Restaurant is open every day, serving breakfast 8 to 11am, lunch 11am to 4pm, dinner 5pm to closing. Reservations advised: phone 669-6299. MC, V.

---

3. The Sights & Sounds of Maui

Millions of years ago the sea bottom between the islands of present-day Hawaii and Oahu erupted with surprising frequency. The results of Pele's work can be seen now as the islands of Molokai, Lanai, Kahoolawe, and Maui. The island of Maui, though, is by far the most glorious result of this constant volcanic action. The western end began as a separate island, with mountains that rise like leavened dough and fold upon each other as they run and spill at golden shores into the pounding surf. The eastern side of the island would have gained renown on its own by virtue of its awesome Haleakala Crater, where the sun rises as it must have on the first day of creation. But as time went on the two volcanic fountains feeding the growing islands caused the two land masses to meet and melt into one single island, creating the Maui that now exists. The ancient Hawaiians believed, though, that their own special god, Maui, pulled up both ends of the island from the sea bottom with his fish hooks. In any case, both versions of paradise are for you to explore and enjoy, driving over modern roads with a minimum of effort. Plan on at least three days to see Maui: the first to explore Kahului, Wailuku, Lahaina, and Kaanapali; the second to see the windswept wonder of Haleakala; the third either for the beach or for an excursion into the lush, tropical rain forest of Hana.

THE FIRST DAY—FROM KAHULUI & WAILUKU TO LAHAINA
Let's suppose you begin your trip at the Kahului Airport. If you follow the signs at the intersection of Hwy. 380 and Hwy. 350 you

will find yourself in about 10 minutes in the sugar-mill town of Puunene, where you can stop off for a visit to the **Alexander & Baldwin Sugar Museum.** A visit here will give you an idea of the importance sugar has played in the life of the island. Exhibits include rare 19th-century artifacts, photo murals, and an authentic scale model of sugar-factory machinery. There's an excellent museum shop. Admission is $2 for adults, $1 for students 6 to 17, free for those under 6. Open Monday to Saturday, 9:30am to 4:30pm (tel. 871-8058).

Or you can proceed from the airport right into Kahului proper, heading west on H-32. Kahului is important to Maui because it has the only deepwater harbor on the island (sugar is shipped from here), and there are several pleasant hotels on the waterfront. If you haven't gotten your muumuu yet, or if your child wants a swimming board, or you're just plain in the mood to shop, you've come to the right place. Both **Kaahumanu Shopping Center** and **Maui Mall** are rewarding.

Kaahumanu is a giant complex, with **Liberty House, Sears, Shirokiya,** and other major island establishments, plus smaller shops like **Maui's Best,** which features such made-on-Maui crafts as jewelry, carvings, clothing, potpourri, and candies, and **The Coffee Store,** chock full of coffee and coffee-making and coffee-drinking accessories. The coffee bar and café area in back is a nice place to have a light snack when you get off the plane. It's fun to explore the Asian items at Shirokiya's, and if you like sushi, get one of their bento lunches to take out. The sushi is tops, and about half the price of what it would cost in a Japanese restaurant. . . . Maui Mall houses huge branches of **Long's Drugs** and **Woolworth's,** good for reasonably priced souvenirs. . . . **Sir Wilfred's Coffee, Tea and Tobacco Shop** also houses **Sir Wilfred's Caffee,** a great spot for espressos and cappuccinos, as well as light meals.

Back in the car, continue to drive to Wailuku along the valley floor on Kaahumanu Avenue; you'll pass both the Maui Pineapple Company (pineapple is important to the island's agriculture) and Maui's Community College, a rapidly growing educational center on the island. **Wailuku,** the civic and business center of Maui, is Kahului's older sister. The streets abound with good and cheap local eateries. If you're into antiques, take some time to shop **Antique Row,** an unpretentious group of shops and galleries on North Market Street. If you're into New Age matters, search out **Miracles Unlimited,** 81 Central Ave., for metaphysical books, crystals, art-to-wear clothing, and the like. Wailuku also has several handsome state and county office buildings, and it's past these that you take Iao Valley Road for a look at the **Bailey House Museum** in the historic missionary home built between 1833 and 1850. Historical displays date from prehistoric times to Hawaii's annexation in 1899. The oil paintings and copper engravings done by Edward Bailey, the instructor at the Wailuku Female Seminary, give a fascinating glimpse of 19th-century Maui. Open 10am to 4:30pm Monday to Saturday; donation of $2 for adults, 50¢ for children.

If you have a few more hours for sightseeing, or if you want a pleasant buffet lunch, backtrack a little to Honoapiilani Highway, make your right, and follow the signs to Waikapu and **Maui Tropical Plantation,** where you can learn all about Hawaiian agriculture on a

40-minute, rather tame Tropical Express train tour ($8 for adults, $3 for children 5 to 12), or visit pavilions and exhibits free. There's a large gift store here with a mailing service, useful for sending gifts back home. The Tropical Nursery also provides good shopping; there's a buffet lunch plus à la carte service, and delicious ice creams, fruit salads, and juices (tel. 244-7643).

Go back to Iao Valley Road now for a drive through magnificent Iao Valley. Watch, on the right, for a mountain that looks uncannily like the profile of John F. Kennedy. Then proceed to **Iao Needle,** a 1,200-foot finger of lava scratching at the sky and draped in green cloaks of luxuriant foliage that are common to this rainy valley. In fact, the clouds are likely to be heavy and brooding here, as if the local spirits were still mourning the slaughter that went on in this valley in 1790, when Kamehameha's men, armed with cannons, devastated the local forces of Kalanikupule. On the way to Iao Needle Lookout, do make a side trip to **Kepaniwai Park,** once the scene of a bloody battle in Hawaiian history, today a gardeny spot where local kids happily play in the swimming and wading pools.

On to Lahaina

Provided you haven't gotten lost in the shopping centers or stood gazing at Iao Needle for too long, this portion of your trip should not take much more than an hour. Now you can continue on to **Lahaina,** 22 miles from Kahului Airport on a road that curves along the western end of the island and allows you to survey some of its glorious beaches. Trace your way out of the valley, back to the outskirts of Wailuku, and take a right onto H-30 out of the city environs through the cane fields to where the road meets the ocean at Maalaea. (If you wanted to make a side trip to **Kihei,** you would have made a left a little while back, onto Rte. 31. There's not much in the way of sightseeing here, but you could have a swim at Kamaole Beach or Kalama Park and do some shopping at one of the new shopping malls.) If it's anytime in February or March, art lovers would be well advised to drive out to one of the major resort hotels in Wailea to see the annual Maui Marine Art Expo, which displays the work of talented local artists, sculptors, and printmakers whose art depicts the ocean environment. It's always a stunner. (Locale varies from year to year; check the local tourist publications.) Now on the road to Lahaina, every turn in the mountain road surprises you with oceanscapes that get more and more wild and spectacular. Continue on, passing a neverending stretch of beach on your left; at some points the high-tide surf splashes right up onto the shoulder of the road. If it's winter, you're very likely to see humpback whales cavorting in the water. Soon you arrive at a busy intersection where Lahainaluna Road crosses the main highway. Turn toward the ocean and you're right in the heart of Lahaina, once the royal capital of Hawaii, the whaling center of the Pacific, and the scene of some of the most colorful—and violent—history of the islands.

Today the Lahaina Restoration Foundation is restoring many of the buildings and relics that remain from the old days when royalty walked the streets and whalers brawled in them. Their office is in the Masters' Reading Room at the corner of Front and Dickenson streets. You can explore **Baldwin House,** on Front Street, home of the devoted missionary Dwight Baldwin, who also doubled as a surgeon and doctor for Maui and its smaller islands. The Baldwin House has been lovingly restored, and a visit—personally guided —will give you a good insight into the incongruous blending of New England and the South Seas that marked the missionary life-style. Admission, which includes a guided tour, is $2 for adults, free for children accompanied by parents.

Another of the foundation's restorations is **Hale Pa'i,** the House of Printing, on the campus of the Lahainaluna School, the oldest school west of the Rockies. It features a replica of the original Ramage Press and a large collection of early printing in the Hawai-ian language. Closed Sunday; free. To reach it, just drive to the top of Lahainaluna Road.

The foundation also sponsors "The World of the Whale" ex-hibit aboard its floating museum, *Carthaginian,* anchored just opposite the Pioneer Inn. The exhibit features a real 19th-century whaleboat discovered in the wilds of northern Alaska, and various multimedia displays on whaling, whales, and the reef life of Hawaii. Open daily; admission is $2 for adults, free for children with their parents.

Across the street from Baldwin House is the **Lahaina Library,** standing in the midst of what was once the taro patch of Kamehame-ha III. Behind this spot are excavations of the foundations of his royal palace; you can view them through glass panes on the ground level. Just behind that you can stand on the edge of the wharf at his-toric **Lahaina Roads** and maybe see a black stone in the ocean, the **Mauola Stone,** which was believed by the old Hawaiians to have sacred healing powers. Anyone who was ill could lie on top of the stone and be washed clean of the malady by the action of the waves. (Don't bother jumping in; it's only a legend.) It's interesting to gaze out across the water at the islands of Molokai, Lanai, and Kahoola-we, and to realize that you're on the precise spot where the whaling ships used to drop anchor over a hundred years ago. This spot is es-pecially memorable at sunset, when half the island's population, it seems, turns out to watch the sun turn the sky to golden fire.

Turn left before you get to the town square and you'll end up at the **Pioneer Inn** (which you've seen in many movies), a hotel hide-away with a long history of attracting beachcombers, movie stars in disguise, and other assorted notables for over half a century. It's a bit rundown now, but the old lazy South Seas nautical flavor is still there, and it's fun to stop for a drink or a bite in its Harpooners' Lanai.

Across the street from the Pioneer Inn is a banyan tree that has been reaching out and monopolizing the town square for many years now. The locals will hotly defend its rank, size-wise, in com-parison with other banyans in the world. It *is* big. The **Court House** faces the ocean behind the tree, and at the end of Wharf Street you'll find the reconstructed remains of an old fort that once stood some-place in the vicinity of the banyan tree. Rebuilding it at the original site would have meant that the tree had to go. Never! The tree re-mained, and the ruins of the fort were relocated.

Just off Front Street, on Prison Street, you'll get a taste of what awaited the whalers in town after the sunset drums were beaten each evening. You see, the whalers were not exactly popular among the kings and missionaries of Lahaina. For too long it was the habit of the native women to swim out to the ships with their own particular brand of *aloha*. When the missionaries decreed the end of such abominations, the sailors replied with riotings and burnings, even shellings of the mission house. So the custom developed that any sailor found ashore after the sunset curfew was immediately clapped into jail, where he might awaken the next morning to find his ship gone. **Hale Paahao,** the old stone jail, is still there.

You should also have a look at an important cultural contribution made to Lahaina by another group, the Japanese. Drive along Front Street and turn left on Ala Moana Street until you come to the Lahaina Jodo Mission. Here an enormous statue of Amida Buddha presides over the **Buddhist Cultural Park,** complete with a temple and a pagoda in the best tradition of Buddhist architecture. The statue was brought here from Kyoto to celebrate the centennial of Japanese immigration to Hawaii. There's an almost palpable serenity to this place, so drink it all in before you get back to the swinging world of present-day Lahaina.

Shopping in Lahaina

Even more fun than seeing the historical sights is seeing the contemporary shops. New boutiques open almost weekly, it seems, and the place is a shopper's mecca on the order of San Francisco's Sausalito. To get an idea, walk along Front Street for a few blocks and you'll find the likes of the **South Seas Trading Post,** with many rare and unusual items from the South Seas and the Far East, plus unusual, low-priced gift items like Hawaiian Christmas tree ornaments for under $5. . . . You can pick up whaling mementos of Lahaina at **The Whaler:** carvings and scrimshaw and ivory, boxes, prints, plus other nautical memorabilia. . . . **Apparels of Pauline** at the Lahaina Marketplace has affordable handmade clothing from such exotic locales as Bali. . . . **Claire, the Ring Lady** shows a smashing collection of loose stones, settings in gold, gold-filled, and silver, plus finished rings. We like the "Maui Diamond," a local quartz.

The **Wharf Cinema Center,** across from the banyan tree in the center of town at 658 Front St., is a nifty little shopping world in itself, with scads of quality boutiques, fast-food and sit-down restaurants, a fountain and stage area for free entertainment, a triplex theater, and a glass elevator that the kids will love riding up and down in. Some of our favorite shops here include the **Maui Mad Hatter** for every type of chapeau, **Earth & Co.** for products and educational materials dedicated to saving endangered species, **Tropical Artware** for handmade works by local artists and craftspeople from around the world, and **Whaler's Bookstore** for a quality selection of books plus coffees and pastries in a European-café setting.

It's fun to browse through **The Cannery** at 1221 Honoapiilani Hwy.; it has branches of favorite island stores like **Sir Wilfred's Coffee, Tea & Tobacco; Reyn's** for tasteful men's casual wear; **Blue Ginger Designs** for clothing made from hand-blocked batik fabrics; and **Super Whale** for great things for the kids. **Maui on My Mind** rates high for wearable crafts and handmade jewelry; its T-shirts have prints by some of Maui's favorite artists. A huge **Safeway Supermarket** here stays open round the clock. **Compadres,** a swinging Mexican restaurant, is here, and so is **Marie Callender's,**

Not to Be Missed!

Much of the adventure of Hawaii—the excitement of flying over a burning volcano, or scuba diving in a coral reef, or hurtling down the slopes of Haleakala on a bicycle—is inaccessible to the average visitor. But all that has been remedied—you can feel you're doing all those things without ever leaving your seat at the **Hawaii Experience Dome Theatre** at 824 Front St., where the extraordinary film, *Hawaii: Islands of the Gods,* is shown. Thanks to state-of-the-art technology, the boundaries between film and viewer disappear; with a screen 60 feet around you and your vision a full 180 degrees, you have the sensation that the floor of the planetariumlike theater gives way under you, and you're off, soaring into space. The spectacular 45-minute film is shown daily, every hour on the hour, between 10am and 5pm. Admission is $5.95. Not to be missed!

known for its wonderful pot pies and a good choice for a family meal.

Maui's newest shopping complex is **Lahaina Center** at 900 Front St. on the Kaanapali side of town, where everything is big—including a huge **Hilo Hattie Fashion Center,** a **Liberty House,** a **Woolworth's**—and an 800-car parking lot! Don't miss the **Madaline Michaels Gallery,** which specializes in three-dimensional media and showcases the work of the outstanding Mexican sculptor Sergio Bustamante. While you're here, you can pop into Lahaina's own **Hard Rock Cafe,** or a brand-new and highly enjoyable restaurant called **Chili's,** with a little bit of something for everybody.

Now you can either drive, take a free trolley, or hop aboard a train for a ride to one of Maui's most upscale shopping complexes, **Whaler's Village** in Kaanapali. The Lahaina trolley provides shuttle service between Banyan Tree Square and the hotels in the Kaanapali Resort, from 9am to 5pm daily (phone 661-8748 for information). The train ride is aboard the **Lahaina-Kaanapali & Pacific Railroad,** a replica of a railroad that carried cane between the villages of Lahaina and Kaanapali from 1890 to 1950. The train clickety-clacks through some perfectly beautiful scenery, the mountains on one side, the sea on the other. (Kids really dig it, especially the ferocious toot of the steam whistle.) Round trip is $10 for adults, $5 for children. (Rates are subject to change.)

Whaler's Village is a "shopping center" that's also a museum, designed to recapture the late 19th-century years when both Lahaina and Kaanapali were major whaling ports. The decor is a combination of New England and Polynesia, and outdoor displays and a small museum document the history and biology of whales and whaling. If you're lucky, you may catch sight of some humpback whales playing offshore; they are regular visitors December through May. The shops here are all attractive. **Ka Honu,** for example, is unique in that it displays handmade Hawaiian Christmas ornaments year round, perfect as gifts to yourself or friends. Other handmade works are also special: bowls of koa and milo wood, Hawaiian dolls of collector quality, needlepoint kits, and beautiful gemstone and jade jewelry. Prices range from $2 to $2,000. . . . **Lahaina Scrimshaw Factory** has one of the largest collections of quality scrimshaw anywhere, much of it done by local artists who create everything from inexpensive gift items and jewelry to collectors' pieces. In addition to whales' teeth, they also work on ivories from nonendangered species, that is, fossilized walrus and mastodon. (Many other outlets include ones on Front Street in Lahaina and at the Marriott Resort at Kaanapali.) . . . **The Sharper Image** has state-of-the-art gadgets to end all gadgets—and you can try some of them out, free.

Sea & Shell is outstanding, for tasteful jewelry, beautiful mirrors, handmade gifts, unusual shells. . . . Check the fascinating antique maps and prints that have made **Lahaina Printsellers** famous. . . . Buy an aloha shirt or a muumuu or some island jewelry at the tasteful branch of **Liberty House**. . . . And end with a daiquiri at the swinging **Rusty Harpoon,** a meal or drink at lovely **Leilani on the Beach,** maybe a Mexican meal at **Chico's Cantina,** or a swim at lovely Kaanapali Beach, just beyond the shops.

On to Kaanapali and Napili

Back in your car, you can drive out of Lahaina in the Napili direction, or you might want to take Lahainaluna Road to its beginning at the **Lahainaluna High School,** walk through the pleasant campus, and see the first printing press on the island. In any case, your path will continue to lead you west as you follow either Front Street or H-36 to the point where the two converge at the site of the **Royal Coconut Grove,** an ancient spot favored by royalty.

Continue on H-36 and you'll pass the incredibly beautiful setting of the **Kaanapali Beach Resorts.** Take a walk around the glamorous **Hyatt Regency Maui,** admiring the gardens and plantings, the colorful birds that abound in the lobby and on the grounds, and the magnificent works of art and sculpture everywhere, especially in the passages between the shops (the shops themselves are noted for their architectural details as well as luxury offerings). Call the hotel (661-1234) to find out when regularly scheduled art and wildlife tours will be held. Pay a visit to the spectacular **Westin Maui,** built by the same developers as the Hyatt and even, if possible, more grand and glorious (phone 667-2525 for times of their art and wildlife tours). You can swim anywhere along Kaanapali; a particularly good beach is the one near the Sheraton Kaanapali, and the snorkeling is excellent around **Black Rock** (watch out, though, for possible sudden, large waves in winter). Several miles farther up the road, almost at the tip of the island, you'll come to the magnificent **Kapalua Bay Resort.** Here we suggest you get out, survey the grounds, maybe have a drink at the Bay Club, and admire the beauty, natural and artificial, all around you. Admire the beauty, too, of **The Shops at Kapalua,** a graceful setting for high-quality boutiques. A visit to **Distant Drum,** for example, brims with the excitement of crafts and artifacts from the cultures that surround the Pacific—perhaps Balinese temple ornaments, New Guinea woodcarvings, rare masks from the South Pacific—collected by owner Candace Shaffer. Much of it is museum quality, but there are inexpensive treasures here, too. **By the Bay** has many gift finds. **Mandalay** is here, with ancient Buddhas, and **Kapalua Kids,** with a young-teen department and lots of handmade-on-Maui fashions. The **Market Café** has gourmet kitchen gadgets, cheese and deli sections, and, behind the swinging half-door, a little café, where a well-deserved cup of cappuccino can bring your shopping labors to a close.

If you've cleverly planned to be here at 10 o'clock on a Thursday morning, you'll be in time to watch one of Maui's best dance shows—free. **Hula Kahiko O Hawaii,** a local hula *halau* (school), performs the ancient dances of Hawaii, with narration and history by Kumo Hula Cliff Ahue. A special treat.

The good road continues just a few miles farther, to Honokohua; from there you'll have to double back the way you came, since the road continuing around the island is much too rugged for anything but a four-wheel-drive vehicle.

THE SECOND DAY—HALEAKALA

Now you're set to visit Maui's Valhalla, **Haleakala,** the home of the great god Maui, and just as the proper home of a god should be, this is an awesome place. To reach it you'll have to drive 1½ hours from Kahului, part of it on a snaky highway high above the clouds. But it's worth whatever effort you have to make to see this sleeping giant, whose crater alone is 7½ miles long, 2½ miles wide. And it makes it even more exciting, as you scale its 10,000 feet, to know that the volcano is sleeping, dormant—not dead or extinct as is Diamond Head (or at least we hope it is). In other words, it *could* erupt in front of you. But don't panic; Pele has not visited here for some 200 years.

You'll want to make this trip on a clear day, so phone 572-7749 to check on weather conditions before you set out. Actually, the best time to see Haleakala is at sunrise; few things on earth can equal the sight, when it seems that the sun has risen only for you. Bring along a warm sweater or windbreaker, since it gets cool up here. And since there are no restaurants or gasoline stations once you pass the lower slopes, be sure to gas up, and you may want to bring a breakfast picnic.

Starting from Kahului, drive east of the city and follow the signs to the junction of H-36 with H-37. Continue on the Kula Road (H-37) and then to H-337, the Upper Kula Road. This is easy driving, but once you turn off to the left, on Rte. 378, you're on Haleakala Crater Road, and it's a winding two-way highway through the clouds. Check in at park headquarters to get maps and a general orientation. Camping, horseback riding, or hiking in the crater, over the same routes that once served as the main avenue of travel between the two ends of the island, is a magnificent experience. The rangers can give you all the details.

If, however, like us, you do most of your hiking in a car, there's still a great deal to see. You can get wonderful views of the crater at both **Leleiwi** and **Kahaluku** lookouts. If you're one of those lucky types who arrive when the sun is strong at your back, the clouds overhead misty, you might get to see your own shadow in the rainbow, a phenomenon known as the **Spectre of the Brocken.** And you may also experience the phenomenon of the double winds. The wind will be blowing right in your face as you view the crater, but then, if you just go back to the road and turn to face the other way, the wind will again be in your face. The effect is caused by the curling of the wind jets as they flow over the lip of the crater.

With or without spooky side effects, the view of Haleakala is awesome. You may also see some of the magnificent silversword plants that bloom in the lava between June and October. As tall as an adult, they blossom once, producing purple-and-golden flowers, and die—leaving their seeds to grow again in the lava rock.

Now hop back into your car again and drive to the **Haleakala Observatory.** Here your gaze encompasses some 30,000 square miles of the Pacific; and below you the crater, its kaleidoscope of colors changing with the sun and the clouds, creates an incredible light show that technology could never approach. Now take the Skyline Drive another half mile to **Red Hill,** the summit of Haleakala and the home of a satellite-tracking station. Stop a while to pay homage to the great god Maui, and down you go, to warmer climes and the golden valleys below. On the way down the slopes, you might stop in for lunch at scenic **Kula Lodge** in Kula. Not far from Kula, on Hwy. 37, you could make a side trip to Hawaii's first—and only— winery, **Tedeschi Vineyards,** which is open for wine tasting and visiting daily between 9:30am and 2pm. A shorter side trip, just a few miles off to the right, is a visit to the little cowboy town of **Makawao,** a growing gallery and boutique center.

THE THIRD DAY—HANA

Whether or not you decide to go to Hana depends on what kind of driver you are. Don't say we didn't warn you. It's rugged driving on a narrow, cliff-hanging road with many blind turns and potholes aplenty (especially on the last stretch, from Hana itself to the Seven Sacred Pools). There are no restaurants or gas stations. The views of dense tropical forests and cascading waterfalls are sensational, though, and if you have the strength for it, well worth the effort. If it's all too much, relax and return to any of the dozen beaches we're sure you've already found.

If you do opt for Hana, head out of Kahului on the same road you took to Haleakala, but continue on Hwy. 36 and stay on it all the way. Coming up soon is **H. A. Baldwin Park,** a favorite picnic camping spot. Farther on you'll pass through **Paia,** a neat little town where you might want to get some picnic fixings at **Pic-Nics** on Baldwin Avenue, or stop to see the imposing Japanese temple, complete with an immense gong. You can also make a little detour here to **Hookipa Beach,** scene of windsurfing championships. Back on the road, it's just you and nature—and a lot of other cars en route to Hana, which has lately been very much "discovered." Pineapple fields drop out of sight after a while as you swing and fly around the inside faces of many valleys, with waterfalls spilling over the mountaintops, rivers running under the roadway, and lush vegetation all around. The white-and-yellow ginger blossoms all along the way are so thick that the air is yellow and perfumed with their scent. (It's illegal to pick them, though, so just admire them from afar.) One is constantly tempted to stop at a particular waterfall and admire its unique beauty, but we suggest that you keep right on until you get to **Keanae** and **Kaumahina State Park,** resplendent with flowers and shrubs. Soon you'll come to **St. Gabriel's Mission** and the "Coral Miracle Church," named thus when an unusual storm in the 1860s tossed coral ashore and provided the villagers with the material to construct their church. **Pua Kaa Park** is another place to stop for a look-see. One more possible side trip before you get into Hana proper is over a bumpy left-turn road that leads the way to the **Waianapanapa Cave,** where poor Popoalea was slain by her jealous husband; the water is said to still run red with her blood every April. At the entrance to Hana, you can visit **Hana Gardenland,** to see the botanical gardens, art gallery, and café. In Hana itself, you'll want to visit the charming little **Hana Cultural Center** right in the middle of town, to see old photographs, quilts, memorabilia from the near and far Hana past. You can swim at **Hamoa Beach,** at **Hana Bay,** or at the black-sand beach at **Waianapanapa State Park.** A must on your list of sights should be the **Hasegawa General Store,** where, it is reported, you can get anything and everything your heart desires (just like at Alice's Restaurant) under one roof. A song was written about the store some years ago, and it has not changed in spite of all the hullaballoo.

Besides such novelties as this, you'll walk in the footsteps of illustrious ghosts in Hana. Captain Cook and his men dropped anchor here. The Hawaiian monarchs made this their vacation territory (they always picked the best places), and the missionaries were only too glad to follow them to enforce their teachings. If you're in a historical mood, you can even see the place where Kaahumanu, the favorite consort of Kamehameha, was born.

The main industry of Hana is the lovely and expensive **Hotel Hana Maui,** where you can treat yourself to an elegant dinner or lunch. There's a good lunchtime buffet at the more casual **Hana Ranch Restaurant.** If you've still got the strength for more of this rugged driving, continue past Hana, about nine miles farther, to the site of the **Seven Sacred Pools.** Here one pool feeds into another and so on, creating an enchanting spot for a swim. And, of course, in true Hana fashion, there are waterfalls all along the way to the pools. Return home the way you came, since the road tapers out beyond this point and becomes just a rugged dirt path, suitable only for four-wheel-drive vehicles. Driving home is a bit easier, since you are on the other side of the road. The view is also extra special from that vantage point. Return time should be about three hours, but do drive carefully. End your day, perhaps, with a terrific dinner at **Dillon's** in Paia, (see "Dining in Maui," above), or at **Mama's Fish House,** for super-fresh fish in an attractive, on-the-beach setting. It's just outside of Paia on Hwy. 36, and open from 11am to 10pm (tel. 579-8488).

XI

THE FRIENDLY
ISLAND: MOLOKAI

1. HOTELS OF MOLOKAI
2. DINING IN MOLOKAI
3. THE SIGHTS & SOUNDS OF MOLOKAI

Have you ever wondered what Hawaii was like before the tidal wave of progress engulfed it? Before the days of high-rises and high prices, of shopping malls and fast-food stands, of freeways and crowds and congestion? If you'd like to visit a more rural, still unspoiled, down-home Hawaii, put Molokai on your itinerary.

Islanders have favored Molokai for years as a getaway retreat. Its thickly forested backcountry makes it perfect for hunting (or for camera safaris). Conditions are ideal for golfing, tennis, riding, wind surfing, big-game fishing, and boating (but not for ocean swimming, since currents, despite the beautiful beaches, are likely to be rough, especially in winter), as well as for just plain getting away from too much civilization.

Molokai has more residents of native Hawaiian ancestry than any other island (with the exception of privately owned Niihau), which is why it's often called the most Hawaiian of the islands. Much of the life-style is still traditional. Fishermen tend to their nets, farmers work in the taro patches, and paniolos (cowboys) ride the ranges—not for the benefit of visitors, but for real. With the phasing out of the pineapple industry, many of the local people are experiencing hard times. Even so, the sophistication of a big city such as Honolulu does not attract them; they like their life-style just the way it is.

You can fly to Molokai in about 20 minutes from Honolulu, 15 minutes from Maui. We love flying the small commuter planes—Air Molokai, Panorama Air, and Aloha Island Air—since they fly low and allow you to see the terrain; but Hawaiian Airlines also runs regular flights daily on 50-seat DH-7 aircraft. The Maui Princess (tel. 808/533-6899) makes daily cruises from Maui to Molokai for about $25 round trip. If time is limited, you can get the feel of Molokai on a one-day trip. For a small island, Molokai is well provided with car-rental service: Budget, Dollar, Tropical, and Avis are all headquartered right at the airport.

---

1. Hotels of Molokai

Choosing a place to stay in Molokai is easy: There are three hotels and five condos—that's it! The most luxurious accommodations can be found at **Colony's Kaluakoi Hotel and Golf Club,** which overlooks Kepuhi Beach, on the western shore of the island. Golfers have the 18-hole Kaluakoi Golf Course; tennis buffs have the four lighted courts and a tennis pro. For those who do not want to risk the ocean, there's a large free-form swimming pool, and for those with food on their mind, the Ohia Lodge and Paniolo Broiler provide excellent food. The rooms, which are in two-story buildings overlooking ocean or golf course, are beautifully appointed (some have high-beamed ceilings) with wood, rattan furnishings, and vibrant Polynesian colors. All rooms have refrigerators. Rates are $90 to $115 double, $125 to $130 studio, $145 to $165 in a suite for four, $225 in a one-bedroom ocean-view cottage for four. Extra person $15; crib $8. Reservations: call toll free at 800/777-1700 (local phone, 808/552-2555). AE, CB, DC, DISC, JCB, MC, V.

The Kaluakoi Hotel and Golf Club is part of the larger Kaluakoi Resort, which also includes three condominium complexes, each beautifully situated and offering many amenities. The newest of these complexes is **Kaluakoi Villas,** consisting of 103 units, all with private lanais affording ocean views. Rates are $105 to $135 for studios; $135 to $165 for suites; $185 for golf/ocean villas. AE, MC, V. Reservations: call toll free 800/525-1470 (local phone 808/552-2727), or write to Kaluakoi Villas, P.O. Box 200, Maunaloa, Molokai, HI 96770. **Paniolo Hale,** containing 77 apartments, also has lovely screened lanais (some of which have hot tubs), a swimming pool, and a paddle tennis court. Rates are $85 to $125 for two; $105 to $145 for one-bedroom apartment for up to four; $125 for a two-bedroom apartment for up to four. Car/condo packages are also available. AE, MC, V. Reservations: call toll free 800/367-2984 from U.S.; from Canada and Hawaii call collect 808/552-2731 or write Paniolo Hale, P.O. Box 190, Maunaloa, Molokai, HI 96770. The most popular choice for families at Kaluakoi is the 55-unit **Ke Nani Kai,** located at the entrance to the resort. It's a charming condominium complex with beautifully furnished spacious apartments, a large swimming pool, and a large dining-barbecue area. Rates are $105 to $115 for a one-bedroom apartment for up to four; $125 to $135 for a two-bedroom apartment for up to six. Crib $8. Inquire about their well-priced golf package. Reservations: call toll free 800/888-2791 (local phone 808/552-2761), or write Ke Nani Kai, P.O. Box 146, Maunaloa, Molokai, HI 96770.

Molokai's two traditional hotels are found close to each other along the oceanfront, just outside the one-street town of Kaunakai, the island's commercial center (such as it is). Both hotels are affiliated with Aston Hotels and Resorts in Honolulu; for reservations phone toll free 800/423-MOLO from the U.S. or 800/663-1118 or 800/268-7688 from Canada. Newly refurbished and redecorated, the **Pau Hana Inn** is the most local and the most laid-back, with about 40 units in small cottages. Rates are $45 to $95 single or double, $90 for a studio with kitchenette, $90 to $125 for a 1-bedroom kitchenette suite. About a mile up the road, **Hotel Molokai** is a gracious inn, with charming rustic bedrooms in three-unit cottages. Rates are $55 to $95 single or double, $110 for oceanfront units, $125 for family units for up to 6. Both hotels have swimming pools (the ocean here is too shallow for swimming), very popular restaurants, and local nightlife on weekends. DC, MC, V.

Molokai Shores, situated between the Pau Hana Inn and the Hotel Molokai, is a three-story, 102-unit oceanfront apartment building with nicely furnished condominium units and a swimming pool. One-bedroom apartments are $80 to $90, 2-bedroom apartments $110 to $120. Reservations: call toll free 800/367-7042 or write to The Hawaiian Island Resorts, P.O. Box 212, Honolulu, HI 96810. DC, MC, V.

On the eastern shore of Molokai, where the swimming is better, there's another condo development, **Wavecrest Resorts,** offering a tennis court, a swimming pool, and one- and two-bedroom apartments. From April 21 to December 19, one-bedrooms are $61 to $81 ($84 to $104 with car), two-bedrooms $81 to $91 ($104 to $114 with car). From December 20 to April 20, one-bedrooms are $66 to $86 ($89 to $99 with car); two-bedrooms $86 to $96 ($109 to $119 with car). AE, MC, V.

---

2. Dining in Molokai

On the western shore of the island, there are really just two restaurants to choose from: the Ohia Lodge of the Kaluakoi Hotel and the down-home Jo Jo's Café in the plantation town of Maunaloa. Dining at the **Ohia Lodge** is a glamorous affair, with music to dance to and views overlooking the water. Steak from local ranches is a specialty; the Pulehu New York Steak is seasoned with cracked peppercorns and Hawaiian rock salt. There is also fresh fish from Pacific waters every night. Pasta-and-seafood dishes, such as prawns and pasta or seafood jamboree, are popular. Appetizers run from $2.95 to $5.75, entrées from $12.95 to $21. Breakfast is served from 6:30 to 10:30am, lunch from noon to 2pm, and dinner from 6 to 9pm. Reservations: phone 552-2555.

Jo Jo's Café (tel. 552-2803) is where the locals hang out. It's cozy, with a big antique bar and a same-all-day menu that includes local plate lunches, as well as Korean ribs, burgers, and saimin. Jo Jo's specialty, however, is fish—frozen or, whenever possible, fresh —and prices are really low: $4.75 to $6.95 for ahi, mahimahi, opakapapa, and other local fish. Closed Wednesday and Sunday; the rest of the week, lunch is from 12 to 2:45pm, dinner from 5 to 7:45pm.

Holo Holo Kai is the dining room at Hotel Molokai (tel. 553-5347) and quite lovely, situated at ocean's edge. It has wonderful breakfasts (papaya pancakes, french toast in a banana egg batter),

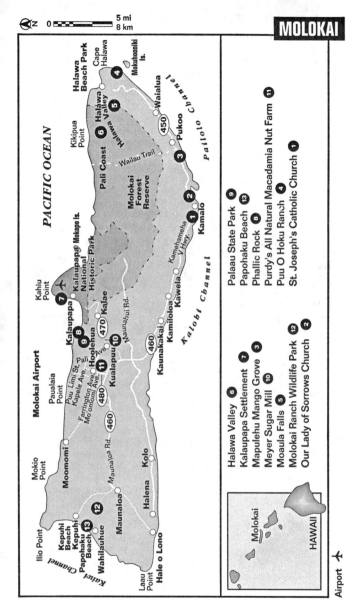

MOLOKAI

5 mi / 8 km

PACIFIC OCEAN

Halawa Beach Park
Cape Halawa
Mokuhooniki Is.
Halawa Valley
Waialua
Pukoo
450
Kikipua Point
Pali Coast
Wailau Trail
Kamalo
Kaunakakai
Kawela
Kamiloloa
Molokai Forest Reserve
Kahiu Point
Kalaupapa Mokapo Is.
Kalaupapa National Historic Park
Kalaupapa
Hoolehua
470
Kalae
Naunahui Rd.
Kualapuu
Puu Limi St.
Kapele Ave.
Pali
Moomomi Ave.
Farrington Ave.
480
460
Molokai Airport
Paualaia Point
Mokio Point
Maunaloa Rd.
Maunaloa
Halena
Kolo
Kepuhi Beach
Kepuhi
Wahilauhue
Papohaku Beach
Ilio Point
Kalohi Channel
Laau Point
Hale o Lono

Pailolo Channel

Kalohi Channel

Halawa Valley **6**	Palaau State Park **9**
Kalaupapa Settlement **7**	Papohaku Beach **13**
Mapulehu Mango Grove **3**	Phallic Rock **8**
Meyer Sugar Mill **10**	Purdy's All Natural Macadamia Nut Farm **11**
Moaula Falls **5**	Puu O Hoku Ranch **4**
Molokai Ranch Wildlife Park **12**	St. Joseph's Catholic Church **1**
Our Lady of Sorrows Church **2**	

Molokai
HAWAII
Airport

pleasant lunches and box lunches, and dinners that feature fresh
catch of the day at around $16.95, including soup and salad bar.
Other entrées begin at $10.95, and there's an Early Bird dinner at
$10.95. Lunch is served from 11am to 2pm, dinner from 5 to
10pm. DC, MC, V.

A hundred-year-old Bengalese banyan tree shelters the outside dining room at the **Pau Hana Inn;** inside is a big rustic dining room with a huge fireplace. The kitchen is known for hearty prime ribs; also popular are honey-dipped chicken, barbecued beef short ribs, and catch of the day, from about $9.75 to $16.95. A salad bar, a vegetable, and starch accompany the entrée. Lunch specials are $4.95, with soup and salad bar at $6.85. Open from 6:30 to 10:30am, 11:30am to 2pm, and 6 to 9pm daily.

Three-block-long Ala Malama is Kaunakaki's main street, and it's good fun to dine there with the locals. Best place is **Mid-Nite Inn** (tel. 553-5302), in business just about forever, serving delicious fresh fried fish dinners for less than $8! Also featured are teriyaki steak breaded, veal cutlet, and fried chicken, from about $3.95 to $7.90. If you're in the mood for Chinese food, walk right in to **Hop Inn** (tel. 553-5465) on Ala Malama. It's a plain-looking place, but the food is good, and the prices couldn't be easier to take: chicken with cashews is $4.75, beef broccoli is $4.95, and a delicious sea-food sizzling plate is all of $7.50. Most regular entrées are $4.25 to $5.50. Open 11am to 9pm daily (except for Sunday dinner). **Kanemitsu Bakery** is famous for its Molokai French bread—up to 1,500 loaves a day. Buy a loaf and then maybe have breakfast or one of the bakery's modestly priced lunch or dinner specials, as well.

3. The Sights & Sounds of Molokai

Molokai does not have a vast string of sightseeing attractions, but there's more than enough to keep you busy for a few days, especially if you have a sense of adventure and appreciate the natural environment. If you like a long drive and maybe a long hike, plan on a day to see beautiful Halawa Valley and Moaula Falls. If you'd like to go on a safari—camera safari, that is—reserve a morning or an afternoon for the Molokai Ranch Wildlife Park. To explore an ancient Hawaiian *heiau* and then adjourn to the beach for a Molokai-style barbecue, take the Molokai Wagon Ride. And to see the most profoundly moving of the sights of Molokai, plan on a day's trip to the isolated peninsula of Kalaupapa, where Father Damien arrived from Belgium in 1873 to bring help and hope to the destitute lepers exiled there.

HALAWA VALLEY

Halawa Valley is one of those places that time seems to have passed by; the scene appears fixed as of the day in 1946 when the area was swept by a tidal wave. Save for a few settlers here and there, the valley is deserted. To reach its junglelike splendor—and the bay, where you can swim (a distance of about 25 miles)—start out early on Kamehameha IV Highway out of Kaunakakai, along Molokai's southeastern coast. Along the way, you may stop to see **St. Joseph's Church** in Kamalo and, farther on, **Our Lady of Sorrows Church,** both built by Father Damien. After driving for 15½ miles, look for a sign to the **Mapulehu Mango Grove,** where 2,000 mango trees bloom. Hidden along this area are sandy beach coves; ask local people for directions. Past Pauwalu, after the 20-mile marker, the road narrows to a one-lane twister, and you climb up through the spread of Puu O Hoku Ranch, whence another narrow road takes you into the valley. Now, if you're feeling really energetic, you can hike for about two hours to the base of towering **Moaula Falls** for an invigorating swim. Finding the trail can be difficult, so you'd better seek local advice before you start out.

MOLOKAI RANCH WILDLIFE PARK

The terrain of the western part of Molokai, near the Kaluakoi Resort, is not unlike that of Tanzania's Serengeti Plain. Some 1,000 African and Asian animals—including giraffes, zebras, greater kudos, wild turkeys, and Axis deer—live and thrive here. They are friendly to visitors, who come every day in 12-passenger vans on camera-safari tours. The giraffes are especially sociable; after the tour, they allow themselves to be petted and fed. The cost of the tour is $25 for adults and $15 for children 12 and under. Reservations: phone 552-2555.

MOLOKAI WAGON RIDE

Take a visit to a 13th-century Hawaiian *heiau,* one of the best-preserved temples in the island, via a 17-passenger, horse-drawn wagon; then cap it with a real down-home, local-style beach party and barbecue, and you will experience two of Molokai's most popular attractions. The cost of the wagon ride is $33 for adults and $16.50 for children 5 through 12 (children under 5 ride for free). Guided horseback rides are also available. For reservations, phone Larry Helm at 567-6773 from 6 to 8am and after 6pm, or at 558-8380 (the wagon-ride site) from 10am to 3pm daily; or write to Molokai Wagon Ride, P.O. Box 56, Hoolehua, Molokai, HI 96729.

MOLOKAI MULE WAGON RIDE

Here's another enjoyable trip. Riding in comfortable custom-built wagons drawn by four mules, visitors are transported through the rolling hills of the Meyer Ranch, all the way to the 2,400-foot-high cliffs overlooking Kalaupapa Settlement, and then back to Kalae Stables (from which the trip begins) by another route. Cost is $30 adults, $15 children under 12. For reservations, phone 567-8088 or, from the mainland, 800/843-5978.

TRIP TO KALAUPAPA SETTLEMENT

Chosen as a leper colony in the mid-19th century for its remoteness, Kalaupapa Peninsula lies at the bottom of an almost vertical, 1,600-foot cliff. In the dismal days when lepers were rounded up and dumped there by boat, the only access was the sea. Today, visitors to the colony, where some 100 former patients still live (the disease has been controlled and is no longer contagious, but the former patients prefer to live out their days in the settlement's sheltered environment), have various ways of getting there; they can fly, they can hike, or they can ride a mule down the steep pali. Once there, you are given a four-hour guided tour; you cannot walk around the settlement on your own. If you wish to fly, contact Damien Molokai Tours at 808/567-7171 (between 7 and 9am and 5 and 8pm). The travel agency will arrange a $42 round-trip flight from upper Molokai; the cost of the ground tour is $22. To hike or to ride a mule down the trail, contact Rare Adventures/Molokai Mule Ride. The cost of the mule ride and tour is $90; the cost of the hike and tour is $30. Write to Rare Adventures, Ltd., P.O. Box 2000, Kualupuu, HI 96857 (tel. 808/567-6088, or toll free 800/843-5978 from the U.S. mainland).

On the ground, Richard Marks, an ex-patient and Kalaupapa advocate who knows more about the place than anybody else (he's the unofficial "Mayor of Kalaupapa") will show you the magnificent vistas, the historical sites, and maybe even his own collection of Kalaupapa memorabilia, including antique bottles and clocks. The tour includes a stop at the Kalaupapa Visitors Center, which has an excellent bookshop. No food is served, so bring your own. Children under 16 are not allowed. The visit to the settlement is not your usual tourist experience; seeing this place is a profound, a moving experience that leaves a lasting imprint on your mind and heart.

KALAUPAPA OVERLOOK

If you don't get to make the trip to Kalaupapa itself, at least make a drive to the Kalaupapa Overlook, just about 10 miles from Kaunakakai on Hwy. 460. Make a right turn on 470 and park at Palaau State Park; it's a short walk to the overlook, where you can see the world's tallest sea cliffs and the peninsula far below. On your way down, two miles below the overlook, visit the **Meyer Sugar Mill,** an authentic restoration of an 1878 mill, whose original machinery is still in operating condition. Open 10am to noon Monday to Saturday and Sunday from 1 to 3pm. The admission price is $2.50 for adults and $1 for seniors and students (tel. 567-6436).

SHOPPING MOLOKAI

The pickings are lean, but what there is is fun. In Kaunakakai, Ala Malama Street has some enjoyable general stores and a good place for souvenirs—**Molokai Fish and Dive.** Out in Maunaloa, not far from the Kaluakoi Resort, artists and craftspeople live and work. Jonathan Socher runs the **Big Wind Kite Factory,** where he and his wife, Daphne, make beautiful kites that are sold all over the islands; he also runs the **Plantation Gallery,** which shows the work of a number of talented craftspeople. It's all very relaxed, very laid-back (stores may close when the surf is especially good or the fish are running), and thoroughly enjoyable.

XII

THE PINEAPPLE ISLAND: LANAI

1. HOTELS & RESTAURANTS OF LANAI
2. THE ACTIVITIES & SIGHTS OF LANAI

As far as the modern world of tourism goes, it's almost as if Lanai had just been born from the sea. For years, the sleepy little island, the second smallest in the Hawaiian chain (13 miles wide and 18 miles long), was known as the world's largest pineapple plantation—and little more. Almost completely owned by Castle & Cook, the parent company of Dole, the island has 15,000 of its 89,000 acres given over to pineapple cultivation. In one way or another, the livelihood of the entire population of some 2,500 people is dependent on the company. Most visitors used to come on business. Tourists would come on one-day boat trips from Maui to swim and snorkel; some came to spend a few days on the island's rugged trails and nearly deserted, pristine beaches. The 10-room Hotel Lanai, built in the 1920s as a kind of clubhouse for Dole executives, was the beginning and end of the hotel scene.

But now things have begun to change. With the opening of the Lodge at Koele in 1990 and of the Manele Bay Hotel in 1991—two luxury resorts owned by Castle & Cook, managed by Rockresorts, and designed to attract affluent, world-class travelers who've already been everywhere else—Lanai has been suddenly catapulted into the world of modern tourism. Its agricultural economy will be largely replaced by one based on tourism, as the pineapple plantations are phased out this year (1992). Local reaction is mixed. Many young people are thrilled at the job opportunities the new resorts will provide; in the past, when they finished school, they either had to go into the pineapple fields or leave the island for work. Other groups fear the changes that the coming of outsiders will inevitably bring; they cherish and would like to keep the simple life-style they've known for so long. But for the traveler, who stands apart from the local debates, the news is very good, indeed. The new resorts make Lanai a glorious place to visit.

GETTING THERE

Getting to Lanai couldn't be easier. **Hawaiian Airlines** (tel. toll free 800/367-5320) provides daily flights from Honolulu and Maui. Both **Aloha Airlines** (tel. 800/367-5250) and **Aloha Islandair** (800/323-3345) provide daily jet, as well as propeller service to Lanai, with flights scheduled to meet mainland connections. Round-trip fare is under $100. You can also get there by boat from Maui. The Maui-Lanai boat shuttle, run by **Expeditions** (tel. 661-3756), charges $25 per person each way ($20 for children 2 to 11) and departs several times a day from Lahaina. The captain is known to stop for whales and dolphins.

CAR RENTALS

If you're staying at the Lodge at Koele or Manele Bay Hotel, you probably won't need to rent a car; an employee of either establishment will pick you up at the airport and take you wherever you want to go, including to the beach and on sightseeing excursions into the backcountry. However, if you want to explore the rugged, remote areas on your own, you are advised to rent a Jeep: only about 30 miles of the island have paved roads. **Lanai City Service,** Lanai City, HI 96763 (tel. 808/565-6780), a Dollar Rent-A-Car franchise, is the place to contact. They also have custom and group tours.

---

1. Hotels & Restaurants of Lanai

THE LUXURY RESORTS

Imagine a splendid English country lodge, graced with Far Eastern art and artifacts and set down on a tropical island in the middle of the Pacific, and you'll have some idea of what the **Lodge at Koele,** P.O. Box 609, Lanai City, HI 96763 (tel. 808/565-7300; fax 808/565-4561; reservations toll free 800/321-4666 or 800/223-7637), is all about. The 102-room Rockresort, secluded among towering Cook Island pines at an elevation of 1,700 feet in Lanai's highlands, is all that superb taste and style, as well as a generous budget (the combined cost of the island's two resorts—the Lodge at Koele and the Manele Bay Hotel—has been estimated at more than $260 million), could make it. It is exquisite in every detail, from the glorious flower arrangements everywhere and the hand-painted "wallpaper" to the high-beamed, 35-foot ceilings, with their heavy timbers, and the massive natural stone fireplaces of the lodge's Great Hall. Adding to the majestic architectural design are the graceful verandas that surround the lodge; from them guests can view the spectacular mountain sunsets. The sleeping rooms are all upstairs, in the two-story building, beautifully appointed; each room boasts a four-poster bed with pineapple finials, decorator furnishings, and window seats and is provided with every comfort. Elegant suites, some of which come with butler service, are also available. Behind the hotel there are formal gardens, groves of pine and eucalyptus, banyan trees, and an orchid greenhouse. The reservoir, framed by banyan trees, is stocked with a variety of fish. Guests can relax in the Music Room or the Library (the only place where TV interrupts the privacy of the retreat), have afternoon English tea or cocktails in the Tea Room, enjoy the swimming pool or the Greg Norman–designed 18-hole championship golf course, or play a gentle game of croquet or lawn bowling or a more active game of tennis. There are also facilities for hunting and horseback riding. And when guests want to enjoy the ocean or a warmer climate, they can simply wend their way down to the shuttle that leaves frequently for the Manele Bay Hotel and picture-perfect Hulopoe Bay.

Dining at the Lodge is somewhat like having dinner in a baronial manor, perhaps in front of a blazing fireplace if the night is cool, with a staff of attendants anticipating your every whim. Those who like a more casual atmosphere can dine on the adjacent lanai, with a view of the hillside gardens. Wherever you sit, you will find the food up to your expectations. The resort makes sure it serves only the best and freshest: it has a 50-acre farm growing organic fruits and vegetables and some 5,000 acres for raising livestock. The menu, a sophisticated California-island mix, begins with wonderful breakfasts: the eggs Benedict are just about the best we've had anywhere, and the scrambled eggs and lomi-lomi salmon on a Jasmine rice cake are a local treat deliciously refined. For lunch (entrées $10.50 to $18), the resort does an excellent job with the pan-fried Kona crab cakes and grilled banana, bathed with a warm citrus vinaigrette. Herbed chicken tenderloins are served on a salad of wheat noodles and broccoli flowers, and ahi is seared and presented on a salad of field greens and vegetables with a cilantro dressing. Dinner really shows off the chef's skill, with such appetizers as steamed seafood gyoza with a caramelized shallot-and-oyster mushroom broth or loin of rabbit with grilled eggplant; a lusty Hawaiian snapper soup with red beans, green banana, and ginger; and unusual entrées like lilikoi-marinated and seared Axis deer with marjoram potato cakes and vegetable pearls and a grilled veal chop with pumpkin and oregano fettuccine (entrées $26 to $34). The pastry chef is a master as well; his pineapple tempura with vanilla ice cream and his chocolate almond meringue with papaya purée are memorable. The wine list is choice, of course.

Prices for accommodations at the Lodge at Koele range from $275 to $350 for guest rooms and from $425 to $900 for suites, some of which enjoy the services of a classically trained butler.

The **Manele Bay Hotel,** P.O. Box 609, Lanai City, HI 96763 (tel. 808/565-7700; fax 808/565-2483; reservations toll-free, 800/321-4666 or 800/223-7637), opened its magnificent doors in the spring of 1991. The site, high above the white sand beaches of Hulopoe Bay, with brilliant red lava cliffs and rock formations providing a dramatic contrast to the Mediterranean-blue waters below, is glorious. The hotel features 250 luxury villas and suites, all with a view of the sea. The two-story buildings reflect a blend of traditional island and Mediterranean architecture, with arcaded loggias and sloping roofs and lush courtyards with gentle waterfalls, fountains, and reflecting ponds. Guests can swim at the pool or at the white-sand beach, which is one of the best snorkeling spots in the islands; they can play tennis or championship golf either at Koele or at the

Jack Nicklaus seaside course, which will open in early 1993; or they can go hunting. In addition, they can stay in shape at the Spa at Manele Bay, which offers customized workouts, personal-fitness training and evaluation, and low-impact exercise classes in a seaside setting. The main dining room features fresh Lanai-grown products and the specialty dining room provides an intimate dining experience featuring Pacific Rim cuisine. The Terrace, with its romantic ocean-view setting, is the place for afternoon tea, evening cocktails, entertainment, and after-dinner dancing. Beautifully appointed guest rooms and suites have private lanais surrounded by lush courtyards with waterfalls and ponds; 75% of the rooms have ocean views.

Rates at the Manele Bay Hotel range from $295 to $405 for guest rooms and from $500 to $1,500 for suites, some with butler service. For those who want to experience the best of both worlds and enjoy mountains *and* seashore, stays can include several days at one resort, several days at the other. Guests can cross-charge between both resorts.

THE BUDGET CHOICE

Hotel Lanai, the 10-room hotel that was Lanai's sole hostelry for years, is still there, and it is a very pleasant, low-keyed, island-style place, overlooking the central square in Lanai City and surrounded by tall pine trees. The rooms are not fancy, but they are clean and comfortable; they do not have a phone or TV. The hotel's porch doubles as a cocktail lounge; its dining room is always good. Dinner entrées include soup and a wonderful salad bar (baby crookneck squashes, Maui onions, locally grown tomatoes, etc.) at $6.50 as well as fish of the day, sea scallops, stir-fried chicken, and New York steak, served with salad bar and a choice of starch, from $13 to $15. Lunch features burgers and sandwiches under $6. Herbs and vegetables are homegrown. (Breakfast 7 to 9:30am, lunch 11:30am to 1pm, dinner 6:30 to 8pm.) The Hotel Lanai is a family-style hotel, with a friendly staff that will help you plan your trips around the island. As of this writing, rates were $55.59 single, $63.22 double, including tax. The hotel is also managed by Rockresorts; changes are expected, so it is quite likely that rates will rise, but probably not drastically. Write to Hotel Lanai, P.O. Box A-119, Lanai, HI 96763 (tel. 808/565-7211; reservations toll free 800/624-8849).

DINING WITH THE LOCALS

There are two other restaurants open to the public, both in Lanai City. They are not gourmet quality, but they are fun. If you want to see where the local people hang out, most of whom are of Filipino origin, visit **Dahang's Bakery Shop.** It has excellent pastries, plus good hot meals, and you'll be hard put to spend more than $5 here. Locals swear that Dahang's burger is the best on the island. **S. T. Property, Inc.,** is your typical greasy spoon—and is very popular with the pineapple field workers. It offers hot dogs, sandwiches, and burgers and plate lunches at very low prices. Call it a sociological experience.

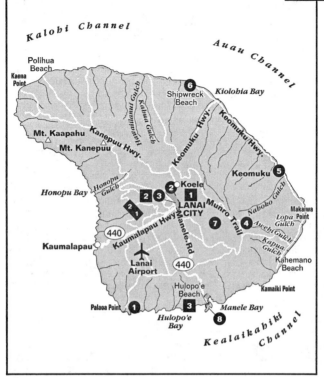

0 ━━━━ 4.8 km
3 mi

Kalobi Channel

Auau Channel

Polihua Beach

Kaena Point

Shipwreck Beach

Kiolohia Bay

Mt. Kaapahu
Mt. Kanepuu

Kanepuu Hwy.

Hauaiwaloa Gulch

Kahua Gulch

Keomuku Hwy.

Keomuku Hwy.

Keomuku

Honopu Bay

Honopu Gulch

Koele

LANAI CITY

Munro Trail

Naboko Gulch

Makaiwa Point
Lopa Gulch

Auehi Gulch

Kaumalapau Hwy.

Manele Rd.

Kapua Gulch

Kahemano Beach

Kaumalapau

Lanai Airport

Hulopo'e Beach

Kamaiki Point

Palaoa Point

Hulopo'e Bay

Manele Bay

Kealaikahiki Channel

Lanai

HAWAII

ACCOMMODATIONS:
Hotel Lanai **2**
Lodge at Koele **1**
Manele Bay Hotel **3**

DINING:
Dahang's Bakery Shop ❶
S.T. Property, Inc. ❷

ATTRACTIONS:
Kaunolu historical village site ❶
Keomoku historical village site ❺
Lanai Ranch Stables ❸
Luahiwa Petroglyph ❼
Munro Trail ❹
Pu'upehe (Sweetheart Rock) ❽
Shipwreck Beach ❻
The Experience at Koele ❷

---

2. The Activities & Sights of Lanai

Most visitors readily find plenty to do in Lanai. Forget shopping, nightlife, commercial luaus, and the kind of entertainment one associates with the busy islands of Oahu, Maui, and Kauai. Here one of the big entertainments is hunting—wild game, including Axis deer, a prized game animal that now outnumbers Lanai's human inhabitants. Mouflon sheep also abound; and there is a plethora of game birds—pheasant, quail, partridge, and wild turkey. Any of the hotels can help you make arrangements for hunting. Some visitors like to play golf; there will soon be two championship courses at the resorts, in addition to the free public Cavendish Golf Course on the outskirts of Lanai City. Others like to play tennis, which they can do either at the resorts themselves or on two courts near the Lanai School. Still others like to fish: Ask the local folks in Lanai City Park where the best places are; they'll probably direct you to Shipwreck Beach. For those who prefer aquatic activities, there are swimming, snorkeling, and scuba diving; the most accessible beaches are at Hulopoe and Manele bays, which are next to each other.

After they've tried any or all of the above, visitors may want to do some sightseeing. Since there are only 30 miles of paved roads on the island, and the remote areas are reachable only in Jeeps via some pretty rugged red-dirt roads, our considered advice is to take one of the excellent tours offered at the Lodge at Koele, usually by Solomon Kahoolahahala. Sol, a gently spoken native Hawaiian, knows more about Lanai than just about anyone else; he is the hotel's Hawaiian culture director. He will fill you in on history, geography, flora and fauna, legends and tales, and local opinion as he drives the van to the Munro Trail, Lanai's highest point (3,370 feet), or to Shipwreck Beach, where the rustling hull of a World War II Liberty ship has been bleaching in the sun for almost 50 years. (Several nights a week at the Lodge, Sol sings the old chants of Lanai, while another artist performs the island's ancient hulas. Let's hope you'll be lucky enough to catch this authentic slice of old Lanai.)

If you like exploring rugged country on your own, and want to get in some hiking, rent a Jeep at one of the car-rental places mentioned above and get detailed instructions before setting out. Popular destinations, in addition to the Munro Trail and Shipwreck Beach, are Palawai Basin, where Walter Murray Gibson tried unsuccessfully to found a Mormon colony in 1854, and the nearby Luahiwa Petroglyphs, considered to be among the best examples of early rock art in the Hawaiian Islands. You might want to observe the busy activity at Kaumalapau Harbor; the port ships pineapples from Lanai and receives the island's food and other supplies from the outside world. At the southwestern tip of the island is Kaunolu, where Kamehameha the Great liked to get away from it all to go fishing with his warriors. You can also see the opening in the rocks 60 feet above the ocean called Kahikili's Leap, from which that chieftain's men sometimes jumped to prove their skill and daring.

LANAI FOR THE DAY

Should your vacation time be limited and you still want to see Lanai, consider taking an one-day excursion aboard the *Trilogy* from Lahaina, Maui. The boat leaves at 6:45am and arrives in Lanai about an hour and a half later. You're given a tour of Lanai City, and you can swim and snorkel (lessons for beginners) at Hulopoe Bay Marine Preserve, enjoy a delicious lunch, and be back to Maui in time for dinner. Cost is $139 for adults, $69.50 for children 3 to 12. Reservations: 808/661-4743, or toll free 800/874-2666. *Note:* It's also possible to take a Trilogy Excursions boat out one day, stay over in Lanai, and sail back to Maui the next day.

XIII

THE GARDEN ISLAND: KAUAI

1. HOTELS IN KAUAI
2. DINING IN KAUAI
3. AFTER DARK IN KAUAI
4. THE SIGHTS & SOUNDS OF KAUAI

Where do Honolulu residents go when they want to get away from it all? To a magic island that any visitor can reach by spending less than 20 minutes on a jet. Only 95 miles northwest of the bustling freeways and crowds of Honolulu is a verdant little island that seems to belong to another time. It exudes a peace and tranquillity that is decidedly not of the 1990s.

And yet, with its comfortable hotels and restaurants and golf courses and nightclubs and shopping centers, you couldn't exactly call Kauai behind the times. The only thing old-fashioned about it is the openheartedness of its people, the lack of pressure, the gentleness that is everywhere.

To our way of thinking, you should have at least four days to spend here, to discover the myriad beauties of this jewellike island. For nature has been good to Kauai, creating craters and canyons (Waimea Canyon is even more spectacular, in some ways, than the Grand Canyon), mountains and rivers, glorious stretches of sparkling sand and graceful, palm-fringed beaches. The oldest of the islands in the Hawaiian chain, Kauai was born from the sea millions of years ago by violent volcanic eruptions occurring far below the ocean floor. Pele, the Hawaiian goddess of volcanoes (who, incidentally, is still revered by more than a few natives), made her first home here before moving on to the other islands; Kauai's volcanoes are now extinct. The centuries have turned the red volcanic earth green and glorious, and abundant rainfall has earned Kauai the title of "The Garden Island." But don't despair; rain falls where it's needed here, and only occasionally on tourists. Mount Waialeale, 5,240 feet high, receives something like 486 inches of rainfall a year, making it the second-wettest spot on earth. Other areas just a few miles away receive fewer than 20 inches. It rains in Kauai, but not enough to spoil your fun.

KAUAI—PAST AND PRESENT

Kauai has always been attractive to visitors. The very first were the Menehunes, who, according to legend, were here long before the Polynesians ever dreamed of leaving the South Seas. No one knows where these two-foot-tall gremlins came from (could they be the descendants of the lost colony of Lemuria? could a flying saucer have deposited them?), but whatever their origins, they accomplished remarkable engineering feats whose remains you can still examine. In about A.D. 750, the first Polynesians arrived, beaching their outrigger canoes on the banks of the Wailua River, on Kauai's north shore. It was along this side of the island that religious temples and villages sprang up. (Interestingly, an international yoga group has chosen this area as its headquarters; seems the vibrations are still special.) You can explore the remnants of these *heiaus* (temples) on the Wailua (sacred) River today. Capt. James Cook, the next notable visitor to the island, was heartily greeted on the southern shore, at Waimea. This deepwater harbor had become a favorite of the *alii* (royalty) who ruled here in pre-Cook days.

Kauai is proud of the fact that it is the only one of the Hawaiian Islands that was not conquered by Kamehameha the Great. The island was ceded to Kamehameha's federation in about 1790, and from then on its importance as a political power declined. The **Koloa** section of the island, though, is notably proud of its own contribution to Hawaiian politics, Prince Jonah Kuhio, Hawaii's first representative to Congress (1902–1922), and the much-beloved "People's Prince." (Kuhio Beach and Kuhio Avenue in Honolulu were, of course, named for him.) Each March 26 his birthday is celebrated with great pomp and pageantry, not only on Kauai but all over the islands.

The modern world is rushing in on Kauai, as it is all over Hawaii, but it is still a haven of peace and beauty. To see it properly, you will have to rent a car, since there is a minimum of public transportation. There are sightseeing limousines and a limited bus service, but the best way to see the island is on your own. Seven or eight car-rental places are lined up in a stall across the road from the airport lobby at Lihue, and many rent inexpensive cars. Better still, make arrangements in advance with one of the major car-rental companies that rent on all the major islands: try **Alamo** (tel. toll free 800/327-9633), **Dollar** (tel. toll free 800/367-7398), **Budget** (tel. toll free 800/527-0700), **Avis** (tel. toll free 800/331-1212), all of which offer good flat rates for both stick shifts and automatics.

---

1. Hotels in Kauai

HOTELS IN LIHUE

To call the **Westin Kauai** at Kauai Lagoons, Kalapaki Beach, Lihue, HI 96766 (tel. 808/245-5050; reservations toll free 800/

228-3000 from the U.S. and Canada), a hotel or even a resort is something of an understatement; it's the megaresort to end all megaresorts, in Hawaii or possibly anywhere else. No expense has been spared in its creation: the $380 million seaside caravansary that replaced the old Kauai Surf encompasses its own 847-room world-class hotel, a private road to the airport (where guests are greeted by hotel staff, whisked to the property in Cadillac stretch limousines, and given chilled towels on silver trays), and 580 acres of botanical gardens and lawns, fronting a half-mile expanse of superb sandy beach (the most swimmable on Kauai) bordered by a promenade of crushed marble and mosaic tile. Kauai Lagoons is a network of artificial lagoons and inland waterways that connects the hotel to such features as a 26,000-square-foot swimming pool (the largest in Hawaii) with its own island, fountains, and waterfalls; a two-acre Palace Court reflecting pond with white marble statuary, reminiscent of Versailles; two golf courses designed by Jack Nicklaus; seven tennis courts and a stadium court with seats for 600 spectators; and a complete European health spa. The waterways also connect to six islands, some of which serve as habitats for exotic wildlife (zebras, gazelles, birds, kangaroos, wallabies), and to Fashion Landing which houses some handsome boutiques. A $2½ million collection of Asian art is everywhere; many of these are reproductions built on a larger-than-original scale to fit in with the incredibly grandiose surroundings. Since no private cars are allowed, guests and visitors are transported by outrigger canoes, mahogany taxi boats, and horse-drawn carriages.

There's a bevy of restaurants and lounges, including Prince Bill's and Inn on the Cliffs for gourmet dining with spectacular sunsets; Cook's at the Beach for indoor and outdoor informal fare; Tempura Garden for Kyoto-style Japanese delicacies in an authentic Japanese garden; a high-energy disco called The Paddling Club; and many lovely cocktail lounges.

As for the guest rooms, there are 847 of them in five towers, a great many of which have ocean views. All have lanais (except those in the Surf Tower) and are beautifully decorated in muted pastel tones. All rooms are fully air-conditioned, have direct-dial telephone, stocked private minibar, in-room safe, immense closets, robes, either a king-size bed or twin double beds, and many amenities. These rooms go for $195 with a courtyard view, $235 garden view, $285 ocean view, $315 beachfront. Rooms in the Royal Beach Club, which feature special amenities, are $350 and $395 per night. There is no charge for children under 18 sharing a room with their parents; a third person in the room is charged $25. There are no-smoking rooms on no-smoking floors, and rooms for guests with disabilities. Exquisitely furnished guest suites (some of them bigger

---

Telephone Area Code

Please note that the **telephone area code** for the state of Hawaii is 808.

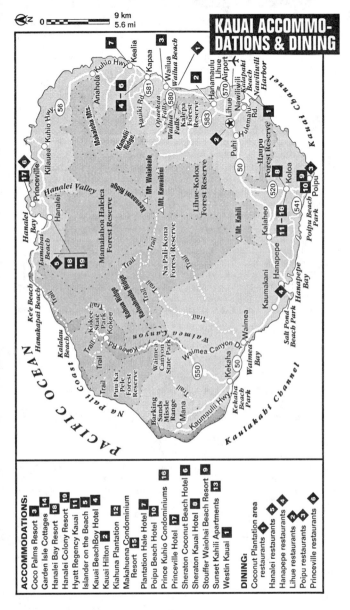

KAUAI ACCOMMODATIONS & DINING

0 ___ 9 km / 5.6 mi

ACCOMMODATIONS:

Coco Palms Resort **3**
Garden Isle Cottages **14**
Hanalei Bay Resort **18**
Hanalei Colony Resort **19**
Hyatt Regency Kauai **11**
Islander on the Beach **5**
Kauai BeachBoy Hotel **4**
Kauai Hilton **2**
Kiahuna Plantation **12**
Makahuena Condominium Resort **15**
Plantation Hale Hotel **7**
Poipu Beach Hotel **10**
Prince Kuhio Condominiums **16**
Princeville Hotel **17**
Sheraton Coconut Beach Hotel **6**
Sheraton Kauai Hotel **8**
Stouffer Waiohai Beach Resort **9**
Sunset Kahili Apartments **13**
Westin Kauai **1**

DINING:

Coconut Plantation area restaurants ◆**4**
Hanalei restaurants ◆**5**
Hanapepe restaurants ◆**4**
Lihue restaurants ◆**2**
Poipu restaurants ◆**3**
Princeville restaurants ◆**6**

plete fort is restored there's not much to detain you here.

Now watch for the sign leading through a quiet valley up to the site of the **Menehune Ditch.** Those busy little gremlins were at it again. Here they built an aqueduct to feed mountain water to the

Hemmeter, the force behind this tour de force (he is also responsible for the Hyatt Regencys in Waikiki and Maui and for the new Westin Maui) hath wrought.

Located on 25 acres at Hanamaulu Beach, the **Kauai Hilton,** 4331 Kauai Beach Dr., Lihue, HI 96766 (tel. 808/245-1955; reservations toll free 800/445-8667), is a beautifully designed and appointed resort. The elegant, inviting lobby, with its sand-colored floors and columns and ocean-hued furniture, overlooks the pool area and the beach beyond. Original paintings of Hawaiian subjects by such renowned island artists as Pegge Hopper and Kenneth Bushnell grace the walls.

Outdoors, there are four tennis courts and three swimming pools, each connected to the others by small waterfalls and cascades; one of the pools is just three feet deep, lovely for little ones. The beach is great for sandcastles and walks, but swimming, alas, is not advised. Handsome suites are furnished in an Asian motif. Bedrooms have either one king-size bed or two double beds, original paintings and upholstery and draperies in a variety of festive color combinations. Rooms are spacious and each has a lanai. Closets abound. Standard doubles $130; superior, $165; deluxe, $180; an extra person is $25. In keeping with Hilton's policy worldwide, there is no charge for children, regardless of age, when they stay in the same room with their parents. Room classifications are based on view. Suites start at $225. All rates are subject to change. There are two restaurants here, Midori, the fine dining room, and the Jacaranda Terrace.

For reservations, you can call the toll-free number above. However, Hilton headquarters in Hawaii advises us that for answers to detailed questions, or to reserve suites, it is always best to contact the individual hotel.

HOTELS IN THE WAILUA-WAIPOULI AREA

It might be said that no hotel in the islands is as Hawaiian as Kauai's **Coco Palms Resort,** P.O. Box 631, Lihue, HI 96766 (tel. 808/822-4921; reservations toll free 800/338-1338 in the U.S.), close to the sea at Wailua Beach and a few miles north of Lihue. Here you can live even more graciously than did the Hawaiian royalty (this was the estate of Queen Deborah Kapule, Kauai's last reigning monarch) who once strolled along the banks of the palm-fringed lagoon around which the main hotel and small thatched-roof cottages are spread. The evening torchlighting ceremony is an authentic moment relived—as the conch shell blows, and one by one, scores of torches are ignited. And then, dining by torchlight in the Lagoon Dining Room, with its ancient firepit, you have the feeling that you are there by invitation of the old Hawaiian *alii.*

There's little chance of getting bored at Coco Palms, even if you hardly ever leave the grounds. You can dine in several glamorous settings: at the Lagoon Dining Room, where there's a Polynesian show; perhaps overlooking the ocean at the Seashell Restaurant, or at the Queen's Pool Broiler and Bar. There are nine tennis courts (three of them clay) and a tennis pro, three swimming pools, (and swimming in the ocean at Wailua Beach just across the road), a jogging path through the palms, pole fishing from the lagoon, a shopping arcade, and the 18-hole Wailua Golf Course nearby. Don't be surprised if you run into a few movie stars or celebrities here—Coco Palms has been hosting them for years—as well as ordinary folks who treasure that special feeling of old Hawaii the hotel has been so careful to preserve.

The 390 guest accommodations at Coco Palms are lovely: done in soft pastels with distinctive furnishings, all offer views of either gardens, lagoons, or ocean, plus an exotic giant clamshell basin, refrigerator, air conditioning, color TV, clock radio, an ironing board, and many exotic touches. Rates do not increase in high season as they do at so many other places: Standard rooms start at $95 per night and moderate rooms at $110 per night. Superior rooms are $130; deluxe rooms, $145. A variety of romantic thatched-roof cottages is available, such as the Queen's Cottages at $155, the King's Cottages at $165, the Prince of Hawaii Cottages at $250, and others, up to the Coconut Palace Suite at $300 for up to four people. (Some of these are more lavish than a movie set. Would you believe clamshell basins and lava-rock bathtubs, some outdoors in secluded little nooks?) No charge for children 18 or younger when occupying existing bedding; an extra person is charged $15. Quite often, the hotel runs a special package deal with a leading car-rental company, making free use of an air-conditioned car available. Inquire. And since Coco Palms is one of Hawaii's most popular wedding spots, wedding and honeymoon packages are also popular. AE, CB, DC, DISC, MC, V.

About a mile past Coco Palms, on the ocean side of the road, is a more moderately priced hotel that is also very pleasant, Colony's new **Kauai BeachBoy Hotel,** 484 Kuhio Hwy., no. 100, Kapaa, Kauai, HI 96746 (tel. 808/822-3441; fax 808/822-0243; reservations toll free 800/777-1700). Colony Hotel Resorts are new managers of the hotel, and they've spruced up its guest rooms and public areas, and made it nicer than ever. There's a branch of Honolulu's terrific Perry's Smorgy Restaurant, which serves three hearty and reasonably priced buffet meals a day. Rooms are nicely decorated, face either the garden or the sea, and each of the 243 units has its own lanai, air conditioning, two double or twin beds, a color TV, a small refrigerator, tile bathroom with stall shower, and a lovely, large dressing room. You can swim in the ocean—the hotel is located on the white-sand beach at Coconut Plantation—or in the almost-Olympic-size swimming pool. Coconut Marketplace, a Hawaiian-style shopping village, is just across the street.

From April 16 to December 20, rates, single or double, are $85 for a standard garden room, $95 for superior partial ocean, and $105 for deluxe ocean; the rest of the year, rates are $105, $115, and $125. Charge for an additional person is $15 daily. Children under 17 free in their parents' room using existing bedding. AE, CB, DC, DISC, MC, V.

Islander on the Beach, Coconut Plantation, Kapaa, HI 96746 (tel. 808/822-7417; reservations, toll free 800/367-7052 in U.S., 800/663-1118 in Canada), is located right on Waipouli Beach, where an off-shore reef creates a secluded spot for swimming and scuba diving. The three-story buildings, grouped around a free-form pool, provide a plantation feeling, and ironwood trees form a protective windbreak against the sea. Entering the lobby, you could easily imagine yourself in a gracious Southern manor house if it were not for the vivid, lighthearted colors and Polynesian art reflecting the spirit of the islands. There's a large poolside area with an outdoor whirlpool spa, a beach activities center, and special programs for children. The large air-conditioned rooms, all refurbished and redecorated, are attractive, with wet bar and refrigerator, color cable TV, phone, and spacious lanai. During the low season, April 1 through December 16, rooms with garden view are $92, ocean view $103, oceanfront $115 for one to three people; a junior suite for five is $130, an oceanfront suite for five is $160. During the high season, December 17 through March 31, the rates are $92, $103, $115, $130, and $160. Rollaways are available at $10 per night, cribs at $15. Rates and seasonal dates subject to change. AE, MC, V.

Sheraton Coconut Beach Hotel, Coconut Plantation, Kapaa, HI 96746 (tel. 808/822-3455; fax 808/822-1830; reservations toll free 800/325-3535), is a spacious, sprawling place. The decorative emphasis throughout is on the arts and artifacts of Polynesia, from the stained-glass Hokule'a (the hotel has chosen the legendary Polynesian canoe as its logo) and the mural *The Floating Island* by noted artist Herbert Kawainui Kane in the lobby, to such meticulous details as authentic tapa designs carved on the doorknobs of each individual room. The setting is a beautiful one, with groves of coconut palms, Norfolk pines, flowers, and tropical vegetation all about. The hotel is set on 10½ acres of Waipouli Beach, fine for snorkeling but a little rough for swimming; guests can use the large waterfront pool or try one of the good swimming beaches nearby. Tennis buffs have the use of three courts and have a tennis pro on hand; they can use the courts all day for a small fee, rent rackets, and have the use of a ball machine.

Dining and entertainment facilities are top-notch. The Voyage Room serves a splendid noontime buffet, plus breakfast and dinner; the poolside stand is popular for foot-long hot dogs with salad served from 11am to 4pm; and the hotel's luau, held every night, is considered one of the best on Kauai. Within walking distance are all the restaurants and shops of the Coconut Marketplace and the Kauai Village Mall.

Rooms at the Sheraton Coconut Beach have all been tastefully decorated with authentic Polynesian touches, and over 70% of them have an ocean view. All have portable refrigerators. Rates for single or double rooms are $125 coconut grove view, $145 garden view, $165 partial ocean view, $185 ocean view, $210 oceanfront, $320 for suites. Third and fourth persons in the room are $25 each, and children under 17 stay free with their parents in existing bedding. (Rates subject to change.) AE, CB, DC, DISC, ER, JCB, MC, V.

If you'd like to settle into this area and have a place with your own kitchen, you can't do better than at the **Plantation Hale Hotel,** Coconut Plantation, Waipouli, HI 96746 (tel. 808/822-4941; reservations toll free 800/733-7777 from U.S. and Canada, 0014/800/125-642 from Australia; toll free fax 800/456-4329), which has three swimming pools and some of the most eye-catching, luxurious rooms we've seen in the islands. The hotel is of the cluster type; there are several two-story buildings grouped around the three pools. Within are 160 air-conditioned units, all exactly the same. Each consists of a living room with sofa bed and a bedroom with two more double beds, all expensively decorated with beige carpeting and beautifully made cane furniture; a dressing room complete with built-ins; a large bathroom with tub and shower; a private lanai; and a full kitchen with a pass-through to a counter in the living room. From April 1 to December 18, rates are $100 for up to four people; the rest of the year, $115. Although it has no restaurant, it is directly adjacent to Coconut Marketplace, with many eating places, and there are other excellent restaurants less than a mile in either direction. Plantation Hale is managed by Outrigger Lodging Services, and is part of Honolulu's Outrigger Hotels chain.

HOTELS IN THE POIPU-KUKUIULA AREA

On the dry and sunny leeward side of Kauai, about 14 miles south of Lihue, is a glorious area that comes as close to the real Hawaii as you can get. Around every bend another little garden curves down toward the sea, and the white, sandy beaches look out on a crashing, spectacular blue-green surf. Swimming is ideal here. If you want to settle down in Kauai, this, in our opinion, is the place to do it. But even if you have just a few days, it's a convenient base for island sight-seeing.

Right on Poipu Beach, surely one of the loveliest in the islands, is the deservedly popular **Sheraton Kauai Hotel,** 2440 Puuholo Rd., Koloa, HI 96756 (tel. 808/742-1661; reservations toll free 800/325-3535), stretching across 20 acres of prime Poipu Beach property. The 456 guest rooms, split between a Garden Wing and Ocean Wing (the latter totally renovated and redecorated), are housed in low-rise, two- to four-story buildings set amid lush tropical gardens and meandering waterways. The Garden Wing has spacious and modern rooms, all with air conditioning, television, radio, telephone refrigerator, and private lanai. The Ocean Wing boasts 224 oceanfront guest rooms, plus suites. Entertainment and dining facilities are quite special. The Drum Lounge, perched alongside the ocean, features live entertainment and dancing every night. There's continental cuisine at the Outrigger Restaurant, kiawe-grilled delicacies at Breakers, and Japanese cuisine at Naniwa.

The Sheraton Kauai is just steps away from an excellent sandy beach, but the hotel also has two freshwater pools and a wading pool for the kids. For the tennis buff, there are three tennis courts lit for night play. Golfers have two championship 18-hole courses and a nine-hole public course within close proximity to the hotel.

Single or double rates begin at $190 garden, $245 luxury lagoon, $260 beachfront, $295 luxury oceanfront. Children under 17 stay free with their parents; an extra adult is $25. Suites begin at $225. Rates subject to change. AE, CB, DC, DISC, ER, JCB, MC, V.

In a location once favored by the *alii* of Hawaii for its sunny climate and splendid swimming beach, the **Stouffer Waiohai Beach Resort** (tel. 808/742-9511; reservations toll free 800/HO-TELS), now carries on the tradition of old Hawaiian hospitality. A century ago, the area housed vacation cottages for wealthy Kauai families; later it became the Waiohai Beach Hotel, and still later, in 1981, a new building emerged from the rubble of the completely razed older hotel. The new complex is modern and handsome in its own way, with lobby, corridors, and three restaurants open to the trade winds, the ocean, and the lush gardens. One of Kauai's premier haute-cuisine restaurants, Tamarind, is here, and so, too, is the Waiohai Terrace, overlooking the restaurant and just perfect for breakfast or sunset dinners; the Sunday brunch here is famous throughout the island. The oversize guest rooms are furnished in rattan with Polynesian-print bedspreads, wet bars, cable TV with in-room movies, refrigerators, and big lanais. Some 426 units offer an incredibly wide range of accommodations, from the standard room with mountain view at $195 double, to the two-bedroom Waiohai Suite at $1,400. Mountainside, garden, oceanside, and beachfront rooms are $195, $225, $275, and $360, respectively. One-bedroom suites begin at $540 a day for two. An additional person is charged $30; children under 18 free when sharing with parents. Rooms are available for handicapped guests. (Rates subject to change.) AE, CB, DC, JCB, MC, V.

The Waiohai has everything one would require of a resort hotel: six Laykold tennis courts close to the water's edge, the championship 18-hole Kiahuna Golf Village designed by Robert Trent Jones, Jr., just across the street, a fitness center, two swimming pools (three, if you count the children's pool), and most important of all, beautiful Poipu Beach.

The older **Poipu Beach Hotel** (tel. 808/742-1681; reservations toll free 800/426-4122), Waiohai's sister resort, has been newly renovated and absorbed into the grander Waiohai as its family wing. It's a low-key and pleasant spot. Dining at the Poipu Beach Cafe is informal and enjoyable. We've always liked the rooms here; they are large and nicely furnished, each with twin beds or a double bed and cable color TV. And every room has a compact little kitchenette as well as a dressing room—all of which make for very easy, very comfortable living. Every room is the same, but standard rooms go for $95, those that have a garden view $125, those with an ocean or pool view go for $140 to $170, single or double; suites from $250. There is a charge of $10 per extra person. There's a pool, of course, with a Jacuzzi, but you can practically fall out of your room onto the beach—it's that close. And it's a favorite snorkeling spot. (Rates subject to change.) AE, CB, DC, DISC, JCB, MC, V.

Although the **Hyatt Regency Kauai,** 1571 Poipu Rd., Koloa, Kauai, HI 96756 (tel. 808/742-1234; fax 808/742-1557; reservations toll free 800/233-1234), is the newest hotel at Poipu Beach, it has a graceful, old-fashioned, very Hawaiian air about it, done as it is in the classic, traditional Hawaiian architectural style reminiscent of the 1920s and 1930s. Bucking the trend toward ever more grandiose fantasy resorts, the low-slung (no higher than a coconut tree), 600-room, $200 million hotel, set along 50 oceanfront acres, is full of quiet charms, from the Hawaiian artifacts everywhere to the extensive gardens, open-air courtyards, and terraces meandering down to the sea. Sensitive to the environment and history of Kauai, it has set up a series of fascinating programs for its guests, ranging from complimentary talks and walks by members of the Kauai Historical Society (archeological tours, dune walks to study plants and sealife of the area, etc.) to extraordinary "Kauai by Design" excursions around the island for extra fees. Although the beach here is beautiful, it can sometimes be rough (it was formerly known as Shipwreck Beach), so water has been brought into the property, with 5 acres of meandering saltwater swimming lagoons featuring islands, plus an "action" pool with waterfalls, slides, water volley-ball, Jacuzzis, and an area for children. The resort has its own riding stables, four tennis courts, a 200-acre, 18-hole golf course designed by Robert Trent Jones, Jr., and a magnificent Anara spa facility which includes a 25-meter lap pool in an open courtyard and mas-sage rooms that overlook a private garden. Kamp Kauai operates every day, offering plenty of projects for kids 3 to 15.

As for dining, there's the elegant Dondero's for Northern Ital-ian cuisine, and the romantic Tidepools (see "Dining in Kauai," below). The Ilima Terrace offers Pacific Rim cuisine in an open-air atmosphere, and Kuhio's provides high energy entertainment and late-night dancing in an art nouveau atmosphere.

As for the guestrooms, 70% of which have ocean views, they are lovely, with plantation-style furnishings and pastel earth tones, white ceiling fans, remote-control cable color TV in a wooden ar-moire, Hawaiian quilt print pillows, white ceiling fans, in-room safes, and lovely bathrooms with double marble sinks. Each room has a separate sitting area.

Garden-view rooms are $175 single or double; golf/mountain view, $250; lagoon, $250; ocean, $300; deluxe ocean, $330; Re-gency Club ocean, $390. Suites range from $425 to $1,800 a night. An extra person in a room is $25 in regular rooms, $45 in Regency Club rooms. Children under 17 may stay free in their parents' rooms. AE, CB, DC, DISC, JCB, MC, V.

Kiahuna Plantation, R.R. 1, Box 73, Koloa, HI 96756 (tel. 808/742-6411; reservations toll free 800/367-7052 from main-land U.S., 800/663-1188 from Canada; fax 808/742-7233), has gained a reputation for itself as one of the ultimate condominium resorts in the islands. Some 333 decorator-furnished one- and two-bedroom beach houses covering 37 acres ramble down to the water (only a few are at the water's edge). The luxurious apartments have space to spare, beautiful appointments, either a king-size bed or two twin beds in the bedrooms and queen-size hideabed sofas in the liv-ing room, and garden or ocean vistas. There's cable TV and daily maid service. Right at hand is the delightful Plantation Gardens Restaurant (see below) for continental dining.

Water sports are superb here, there are 10 championship tennis courts, and an 18-hole championship golf course designed by Rob-ert Trent Jones, Jr.—all of which makes Kiahuna a mecca of sorts for the sporting set. From April 1 through June 30 and September 3 through December 20, one-bedroom apartments, which can sleep four, are $145 to $320. During the rest of the year, they are $152 to $340. Two-bedroom, two-bath apartments, which can house six, are $225 to $375 during the low season, $245 to $390 during the high season. Rollaways are $15 per night, cribs $12. Special vacation packages are available at attractive prices; at certain times of the year, a free car may be included in the price of accommodations. AE, MC, V.

Now here's good news: lovely apartments at reasonable prices. **Sunset Kahili Apartments,** 1763 Pe'e Rd., Koloa, HI 96756 (tel. 808/742-7434; reservations toll free 800/82-POIPU from the U.S. or Canada; fax 808/742-6058), are situated on a bluff, with a fine sandy beach just two blocks away and a swimming pool at home. You have your choice of a one- or two-bedroom apartment.

In either case, you'll have a fully equipped kitchen including a dishwasher and a washer-dryer. Each apartment has beautiful, thick wall-to-wall carpeting, floor-to-ceiling draperies, and a private lanai. One-bedroom apartments for two persons, with garden views are $85; with ocean view, $90. Two-bedroom, two-bath apartments for four persons, with similar views, are $115 and $120. The one-bedrooms can accommodate a family of five; the two-bedrooms, a family of seven; each extra person is charged $6 per day. Minimum stay is three days; rates get progressively lower the longer you stay. Weekly maid service.

Sharon and Robert Flynn, the hospitable owner-managers of **Garden Isle Cottages** in Poipu, R.R. 1, 2666 Puuholo Rd., Koloa, HI 96756 (tel. 808/742-6717 from 9am to noon daily, Hawaiian time), have only a small number of cottages at their disposal; you'll be lucky and happy if you can get one. Their cottages are scattered along the Poipu shore, nestled in tropical gardens, and artistically decorated with batiks, tapas, and some of Bob's own sculptures and paintings. Sea Cliff Cottages consists of four large one-bedroom apartments overlooking a small ocean inlet, renting for $90 to $100 double, as well as two studios at $72 to $80 double and a deluxe one-bedroom at $114 to $123 double or, with two bedrooms and two baths, at $150 to $160. Hale Melia, across from the ocean, has a beautiful one-bedroom apartment at $80 to $90, and there are two studios, one at $49 to $53, another at $54 to $56. Hale Waipahu is a beautiful duplex with a 360-degree view from the highest point overlooking Poipu Beach; it rents for $114 to $150.

Makahuena Condominium Resort, 1661 Pe'e Rd., Koloa, HI 96756 (tel. 808/742-5500; reservations toll free 800/828-0360), is a most attractive three-story condominium apartment complex located high on the cliffs above Poipu Beach in a dramatic, wind-swept setting. The grounds are beautifully landscaped and feature a freshwater swimming pool, a jet spa, tennis court, and a barbecue area. All of the 46 units in the hotel are privately owned, so decor is entirely different in each one; however, every apartment has a lanai, color TV, a fully equipped kitchen with dishwasher, its own washer and dryer; many have ceiling fans. All the apartments that we inspected were simply beautiful. Two-bedroom garden-view apartments go for $120 to $135; two-bedroom ocean-view, $135 to $150; two-bedroom premium oceanfront, $195 to $225; and three-bedroom ocean-view, $165 to $195. A minimum stay of four nights is required; between December 14 and January 15, when the higher rates are in effect, the minimum stay is two weeks. *Note:* Signs around the property warn of the sheer dropoff from the cliffs to the rocky coast below; there is a fence, but parents of very small children might feel more relaxed on lower ground.

THE GOOD LIFE AT PRINCEVILLE

Located on a lush green plateau that extends from the mountains through some 11,000 acres of rolling pastures, river valleys, and undeveloped forest lands down to spectacular white-sand beaches, Princeville at Hanalei is a multimillion-dollar planned resort where the living is easy and the outdoor recreational facilities superb: there's a spectacular Robert Trent Jones, Jr., 45-hole golf course considered one of the top 100 in the world, six outdoor ten-

A Budget Find

Attractive accommodations, budget prices, a warm and hospitable management, and an excellent location all combine to make **Prince Kuhio Condominiums,** c/o Prince Kuhio Rentals, P.O. Box 1060, Koloa, HI 96756 (tel. 808/742-1409; reservations toll free 800/722-1409), very, very popular in this area. Den and Dee Wilson, the charming owner-managers, are on hand to make everyone feel right at home. Apartments are attractively furnished, have full kitchens, and are fully equipped for comfortable living. From April 15 to December 15, studios with twin beds are $59, one-bedroom apartments for four are $69 and $79, and a wonderfully spacious two-bedroom apartment with its own private deck is $95. From December 15 to April 15, the studios are $69, the one-bedroom apartments are $84 and $94, and the penthouse is $125. These are some of the best values in inflationary Kauai. Apartments overlook Prince Kuhio Park and the ocean; studios overlook the courtyard and pool or Prince Kuhio Park. Good swimming beaches are a short, 1-mile drive away, and there's a good snorkeling beach right across the road. Also across the road is the terrific oceanfront Beach House Restaurant. Golf and tennis are available nearby. The Wilsons can arrange car rentals at attractive prices.

nis courts, facilities for swimming, sailing, snorkeling, trapshooting, horseback riding, and more. Accommodations in some 18 different condominiums and area resorts range from medium-priced to deluxe; there are about a dozen restaurants on the premises. Focal point is the extraordinary Princeville Hotel.

Built in a series of three terraces on the face of Pu'upoa Point, the **Princeville Hotel,** P.O. Box 3069, Princeville, HI 96722 (tel. 808/826-9644; reservations toll free 800/325-3535), overlooks Hanalei Valley, green mountains sparkling with waterfalls, and across clear, blue Hanalei Bay to the ocean. While the hotel was special enough before the recently completed multimillion-dollar transformation, it is truly spectacular now, indoors and out. The 23-acre grounds feature a freshwater swimming pool and whirlpool spas, elegant ponds, and access to the calm (in summer) waters of Hanalei Bay, perfect for swimmers, snorkelers, and scuba divers. There is complimentary transportation to the Mirage Princeville golf courses and tennis courts. The feeling at the hotel is that of a special retreat; the decor is elegant, with the lobby opening onto a view of Hanalei Bay and the mountain known as "Bali Hai" in the movie *South Pacific*. The lobby-level cocktail lounge, open to the same beautiful view, has a living room atmosphere with bookshelves and a wood-burning fireplace. The main dining room, overlooking Hanalei Bay, provides all-day dining with indoor and outdoor seating. An Italian restaurant is open nightly for dinner and on Sundays for brunch. There is al fresco dining poolside. Rooms are lovely enough to be in an elegant private home. All are beautifully furnished, with individual air conditioning, remote-control TV, original oil paintings and prints, two telephones with Dataport, oversized desk, custom-designed furnishings. Bathrooms are a study in marble, with artwork, telephone, and many amenities. Rates begin at $240 for a room with garden view, and advance to $295 for golf and pool views, $340 and $375 for ocean view and oceanfront, and go up to $450 for the super-luxurious oceanfront bed–sitting rooms. Suites go from $750 to $2,000. Guest rooms adapated for the disabled are available on request. AE, CB, DC, DISC, ER, JCB, MC, V.

Picture-perfect Hawaii is what we call **Hanalei Bay Resort,** P.O. Box 220, Hanalei, Kauai, HI 96714 (tel. 808/826-6522; fax 808/826-6680; reservations toll free 800/827-4427), a separately owned and managed luxury condominium hotel in the Princeville complex. The setting is a spectacular one, with the lobby and outstanding Bali H'ai Restaurant on the top level, and low-slung buildings winding down 20 acres to the white sands of Hanalei Beach below. Tennis players have 8 courts (three of them lighted), full pro shop, and teaching program; golfers get a discount at the 27-hole Princeville "Makai" course surrounding the property. A multimillion-dollar "beautification program" has resulted in some graceful new additions here, like the center pond in the port-e-cochère, which drops into a waterfall that drops into the new free-form, sandy-bottom swimming pool, with a natural sand "shoreline," and a swim-up bar. There is also good swimming in the ocean, which is, however, a long walk from many of the apartments (a roving jitney provides on-call service around the sometimes steeply sloped complex). Inside the buildings, which are named "Hibiscus," "Bougainvillaea," and the like, to correspond with the flowers growing outside their doors, apartments have been newly remodeled to include antique replicas and handmade Hawaiian quilts, all designed to reflect the feeling of a Hawaiian plantation guesthouse. These are exquisitely furnished studio and one- and two-bedroom apartments, with plentiful space, rattan furniture, beautiful dressing rooms, large baths, complete electric kitchens, and coral fronds and other artful decorations on the wall. Daily maid service. Prices are $105 for mountain-view standard studios, $120 for mountain-view with kitchenette, $135 for waterfall/garden view, $190 ocean view. One-bedroom suites are $215 mountain, $250 ocean. Two-bedroom suites are $330 mountain, $630 ocean. Other suites run from $500 to $1,000. (Rates subject to change.)

If your idea of heaven on a vacation is jumping out of your door and right into the ocean, then **Hanalei Colony Resort,** P.O. Box 206, Hanalei, Kauai, HI 96714 (tel. 808/826-6235; fax 808/826-9893; reservations toll free 800/628-3004) may be the place you've been dreaming about. It's a secluded retreat, just before the end of the road at the Na Pali Cliffs and at the beginning of the hiking trails. Set out on 4½ oceanfront acres, this is a cluster of 47 luxury condominium apartments, each of them individually and handsomely furnished, with views of ocean, bay, and mountains. Each unit has two bedrooms, a living room and dining area, bathroom, fully equipped kitchen, and private lanai. No TVs, no phones in the rooms, nothing to distract you from the beauty of nature all about. There's a pool with Jacuzzi located in the gazebo area. Charo's Restaurant is next door, and the shops and restaurants of nearby Hanalei and Princeville are reached by about a 15-minute drive across winding country roads and narrow one-lane bridges—this really is "the end of the road." For up to four people in a unit, rates are $95 to $115 garden view, $115 to $135 ocean view, $150 to $170 oceanfront; car/condo packages are available at substantial savings, and a car is a must in these parts.

2. Dining in Kauai

RESTAURANTS IN LIHUE

Whether or not you're based in Lihue, you'll undoubtedly come into town and want to spend some time here, so it's fun to try some of the local restaurants that consistently serve up tasty food at very decent prices. Turn onto Kress Street in downtown Lihue and you can't miss the **Lihue Barbecue Inn,** 2982 Kress St., which has been a favorite for nearly half a century; it's homey, it's friendly, and along with the wonderfully low-priced meals come freshly baked bread, soup, homemade desserts, and a beverage. You could bite your nails at dinnertime (no nutritional value in that) choosing from dishes like roast stuffed turkey breasts, island T-bone steak, teriyaki steak and shrimp tempura, teriyaki chicken and shrimp scampi, from about $6.95 to $12.95 (lobster is priced daily, usually at about $21). Luncheon specials, priced around $7 for a complete meal, include a variety of salads such as somen, Chinese chicken, and sandwiches on their homemade bread. Try their exotic drinks; the "chi-chis" are excellent. A great place to hang out with the *kamaainas.* Open every day but Sunday for breakfast, 7:30 to 10:30am; lunch 11:30am to 1:30pm; dinner 4:30 to 8:30pm. Phone: 245-2921.

The Westin Kauai at Kalapaki Beach has a bevy of attractive restaurants, but the one we think is the prettiest and the most fun is the **Inn on the Cliffs,** which is quite far from the hotel proper, way up on the cliffs above Running Waters Beach. Just getting here is an adventure; after you arrive at the hotel, you can take a horse-drawn carriage or a taxi launch boat to reach your destination. The two-story restaurant has a 200-degree view of the ocean and a lovely terraced dining room done in white and ivory, with potted trees, myriad plants, and a very modern and uncluttered feeling. The emphasis here is Pacific Rim cuisine, specializing in seafood. You can begin your dinner with hot appetizers like broiled scallops or sautéed ginger shrimp or with cold island sashimi ($8.50 to $11.50), then move on to wonderful main courses like calamari steak with sweet Maui onion, Alaskan king crab steamed Chinese-style in black-bean sauce or Thai curry lobster. There is always a fresh catch of the day. Dinner entrées run $20 to $38. Spa preparation is available on many items.

Inn on the Cliffs serves dinner only, nightly from 5:30 to 10pm. The upstairs lounge, with its open fireplace, features live entertainment nightly, plus appetizers, desserts, and specialty coffee drinks; it stays open until midnight. Reservations advised: phone 245-5050. Casual attire; jackets not required. AE, CB, DC, DISC, MC, V.

Prince Bill's at the Westin Kauai was named in honor of William Lonalilo, the popular "people's king" who reigned in the 1870s, who enjoyed fine food and drink and was greatly loved by his subjects. Were Prince Bill alive today, he would surely love this restaurant; it's thoroughly enjoyable in every detail. The dining room, situated on top of the Surf Tower of the resort, commands spectacular views of the Pacific Ocean, Nawiliwili Bay, the harbor, and the Haupu mountains across the river. You'll be in heaven if you can get one of the tables overlooking the water, but actually every table in this multitiered room open to the sea enjoys spectacular views. The room is casually elegant, with paintings of old-time hula dancers on the walls, wicker chairs and white tablecloths, flowers on every table. Included with every dinner is the spectacular salad, chilled shrimp, and appetizer bar, which is so generous, and so filled with delicious surprises, that you could be well satisfied on this alone. Along with the likes of Szechuan shrimp salad and Oriental chicken, limu poki, Caesar salad, and marinated pipikaula salad, you could help yourself to a fruit and cheese buffet as well. And that's just for starters. Back at your table, your bread basket is filled with exotic fruit breads—it could be coconut, banana, macadamia nut, or papaya. Now comes the main course—exquisitely prepared double lamb chops, double breast of chicken, filet mignon, roast prime ribs of beef (only Certified Black Angus Beef is used), fresh salmon, fresh catch of the day, seafood brochette, pepper steak with green peppercorn sauce, plus island specialties like Hanalei T-bone (buffalo steak) and Lanai venison. Various "surf and turf" combinations—crab, shrimp, or lobster with steak or chicken—are also featured. Entrées range from $19 to $36. The dessert bar ($4.50 extra) is also a wonder: Help yourself, again, to as much as you want of treats like the double chocolate truffle cake, fresh pastries, homemade pies, and more. Dinner is served nightly from 6 to 9pm; reservations advised; phone 245-5050. Casual attire; jackets not required.

Now, if you're going to be in Kauai on a Sunday, by all means come back for Prince Bill's extraordinary champagne brunch at $21.95 adults, $12.95 children, which is now running neck and neck in popularity with the famed Sunday brunch at the Waiohai Terrace (see "Restaurants in Poipu & Hanapepe," below) in the Poipu area. The chefs pull out all the stops on this one: In addition to the sashimi platters, the fruit platters, the island smoked fish, the eggs Benedict, the many Oriental cold dishes, and the like, there's fresh steamed fish, stir-fried chicken, an omelet station that turns out things like shiitake mushroom and char siu omelet and, at the carving station, a full roast suckling pig, served Chinese style, with Chinese steamed buns and plum sauce. For dessert, what could be more perfect than fresh fruit with chocolate fondue? Stay and feast to your heart's content. The Sunday brunch buffet is on from 9am to 2pm. Early arrival is advised; reservations are taken only for parties of six or more: 245-5050. AE, CB, DC, DISC, MC, V.

J.J.'s Broiler, 3614 Rice St., in Anchor Cove, has been a Kauai tradition for over 20 years. Now in new quarters, this family-owned restaurant is located in a huge warehouselike building with high ceilings, a spacious setting in which to enjoy old favorites. And since it faces the water, overlooking Nawiliwili Bay, it's a perfect spot for lunch if you're spending the day at Kalapaki Beach, or for dinner no matter what you're doing. Specialty of the house is the Jasper's "world-famous Slavonic steak," which really is delicious: It's broiled tenderloin, sliced thin and dipped in a sauce of butter, wine, and garlic; $17.95. Have it alone, or in a variety of combinations— with teriyaki chicken breast, fish of the day, scallop or shrimp kebab, or lobster tail. Other possibilities among the entrées, which run from about $15.95 to $21.95, include filet mignon, teriyaki filet, mahimahi, chicken Oscar, and smoked barbecue pork ribs; along with your entrées come old-fashioned beef vegetable soup, salad bar at your table, baked potato or rice, and hot sourdough rolls. There's football on the TV Monday nights, Jazz and live bands Friday, Saturday, and Sunday. Lunch features excellent charbroiled burgers, a variety of sandwiches (the hot pastrami with melted Swiss cheese on sourdough bread is great), salads, and delicious appetizers, like potato skins, shredded onion strings, nachos, and the freshest of sashimi. Hula pie is the favorite desert.

J.J.'s Broiler is open every day, serving lunch from 11am to 5pm, dinner from 5 to 10pm, and cocktails and pupus in the downstairs lounge from 5pm. Reservations: 246-4422. AE, MC, V.

All-in-the-family department note: A few miles up the road, in Kapaa, the Jasper's son, Jimmy, is in charge at **Jimmy's Grill** (4-1354 Kuhio Hwy.; tel. 822-7000), a lively spot with the atmosphere of an on-going beach party. Reasonably priced chicken, steak, ribs and pasta entrees ($8 to $18) are also excellent. MC, V.

Where do the local people take guests when they want to treat them to something special? To one of the nicest places around Lihue town, the **Hanamaulu Restaurant and Tea House,** 2 miles north of Lihue on Hwy. 56. While the indoor part of the café looks like just another pleasantly ordinary Asian restaurant, the garden is something else again. Individual Japanese tea rooms look out on a beautiful garden with stone toros, bonsai, carp, all in a tranquil and moody setting. The nicest thing about all this is that you don't need a minimum group to get one of these *ozashiki* rooms (but it is a good idea to make reservations), in which you can order anything on the menu, even the $6.50 plate dinners. There's a variety of à la carte Asian dishes starting at about $7. Or treat yourself to a multicourse banquet for about $15 per person. Cocktails are available. The sushi bar turns out delicate morsels of fish and vegetables, plus robatayaki dishes—meat, chicken, and assorted vegetables cooked on a special grill. The food is subtly seasoned—delicious! Take-out available. For reservations, phone 245-2511 or 245-3225. MC, V.

RESTAURANTS IN POIPU & HANAPEPE

Dining at **Tidepools** in the new Hyatt Regency Kauai at Keoneloa Bay is a singular experience, for this is one of those few places where the setting, food, and service are all on an equally high level. We can't think of a more romantic place to spend an evening in Hawaii. The setting is perfection, a series of *hales* (thatched huts) on stilts overlooking saltwater lagoons near the beach; one of the rooms is under a waterfall! It's hard to tell where indoors and outdoors merge. The decor, which makes use of beautiful woods and plentiful floral arrangements, is Polynesian in motif, and the food is extraordinary. You could begin your meal with a marvelous Kula onion soup blended with two cheeses, or perhaps with the grilled sea scallops and asparagus and a saffron sauce. Tidepool Mahi-Mahi, the house's signature dish, raises the humble mahimahi to a work of art: it is served on a wooden plank with a circle of braided pizza dough, topped by vegetables, then baked—superb! Their other signature dish, a mixed seafood grill of lobster, fresh fish, scallops, and shrimp, is also memorable. From the grill, there are marinated lamb chops, porterhouse, veal chops, and prime rib with fresh horseradish. Entrées run from $19 to $25. A delicious nine-grain bread, baked right here, is brought to your table with butter in the shape of a seashell. For dessert, treat yourself to one of the best mud pies on the island. And after your meal, take a walk out on the moonlit grounds—a magical experience from start to finish.

Tidepools serves dinner only, nightly from 5:30 to 10:30pm. Reservations advised: phone 742-1234. AE, DC, DISC, JCB, MC, V.

Dondero's, premier dining room of the Hyatt Regency Kauai, is the kind of restaurant you might expect to find in Rome rather than Hawaii. It's a serene, sophisticated setting for elegant Italian dining, handsomely done in inlaid green marble and ornately-patterned tilework. The food is excellent. You can start with a variety of pastas ($9 to $12 as first courses, $15 to $22 as entrées), then move on to such house specialties ($19 to $26) as the breast of chicken with prosciutto and sage, the osso bucco alla milanese, a lusty cioppino, or the capesanti al cognac, a memorable combination of sautéed scallops, asparagus, and sun-dried tomatoes. Desserts are rich and splendid, especially the zuppa inglese and the tiramisù soaked in rum.

Dondero's serves dinner only, nightly from 6 to 10pm. Reservations advised: phone 742-1234. AE, DC, DISC, JCB, MC, V.

A spot favored by locals as well as tourists, **Plantation Gardens Restaurant** sits majestically in a seven-acre botanical paradise of cacti and rare plants. Part of Kiahuna Plantation (see "Hotels in Kauai," above), the restaurant is a restored 19th-century plantation manager's home, an incomparable setting for dining on gourmet cuisine. You could begin, for example, by having a drink in the Poi Pounder Room (where Hawaiian calabashes and stone tikis are displayed in antique French armoires), or outside in the garden bar. Then on to dinner, perhaps in a Victorian drawing room, or in the main dining room, open on three sides to look out over lily ponds, cactus gardens, palm trees, and the blue Pacific beyond. The international menu features fresh local fish caught daily (market-priced), imported seafoods, plus prime rib and steak. Most meat and seafood entrées run between $13.95 and $17.95, and are accompanied by fresh vegetables and potatoes or rice. Appetizers like crab-stuffed mushrooms are delicious, and so are desserts like Naughty Hula Pie, a macadamia-nut ice-cream pie topped with chocolate sauce and whipped cream. Plantation Gardens serves dinner only, nightly from 5:30 to 10pm; the very popular bar is known for luscious tropical drinks and pupus in a relaxed setting. Reservations: 742-1695. AE, DC, V.

If you can manage to work out your itinerary to do so, you'll be well rewarded by being in Kauai on a Sunday morning. That's when you can join the island people in what is perhaps the most spectacular Sunday champagne brunch in Kauai—at the **Waiohai Terrace** of the Stouffer Waiohai Beach Resort. So famous is this brunch that people gladly wait in line for an hour or more to gain entrance (reservations are taken only for parties of five or more); if you arrive by 9:30am we were told, you'll have your best chance of a short line; most people are seated before 10am. Once admitted, you'll be rewarded by a seat in a graciously decorated, open-to-the-sea room with the beautiful beach right in front of you. You'll also be rewarded with a view of half a dozen buffet tables laden with great delicacies—smoked fish and sashimi, many pastas, shrimp dishes, salads, prime ribs, flavorful pâtés, fresh fruits, hot breads, macadamia-nut pies, strawberry sherbets, special dishes that the chef has dreamed up that day. Omelets will be created at your command. New dishes are brought out frequently, and off you go to the table again—and again—and again. The servers estimate that most people spend about two hours eating here! The cost of this unforgettable repast, which includes champagne, is $25, and it's served between 10am and 2pm. A Hawaiian trio provides background music. AE, CB, DC, DISC, MC, V.

A not-to-be-forgotten dining experiences awaits you at Waiohai's award-winning **Tamarind** restaurant, hailed by a Honolulu critic as one of the top seven restaurants in the state. The setting is of unsurpassed elegance, from the exquisite chandelier to the silken fabrics and brass decorations, the rattan throne chairs and the bouquet of flowers on every table. Service is excellent, and the food, served on fine crystal and china, lives up to its elegant setting.

The menu features Pacific Rim cuisine with a unique Hawaiian touch—such as the ravioli of Pacific lobster with two sauces, and wok-charred sashimi with mustard cream sauce among the appetizers. Entrées include Thai-style sautéed tiger prawns with red curry paste, basil, and coconut milk; medallions of veal with angel-hair pasta; broiled ono with black-bean ginger sauce and stir-fried vegetables, and much more. Entrées à la carte range from $23.50 to $28.75; appetizers and soups go from $4 to $9.75. The dessert cart offers extravagant treats; should you want a soufflé, order it when you choose your main course. There is also a prix-fixe dinner which ranges from $42.50 to $45.50 per person. The Tamarind serves dinner nightly from 6 to 10pm. The Tamarind Lounge is open until midnight, with Kimo Gardner at the grand piano from 7:30 to 11:30pm. Reservations requested: 742-9511. AE, CB, DC, DISC, MC, V.

For those nights when you don't feel like cooking in at the condo or going out to dine at someplace fancy, the **Koloa Broiler,** on Koloa Road, is a great compromise; cook your steak, mahimahi, or other fresh fish, barbecued chicken, marinated beef kebabs, marinated fish kebab, or burgers right there, over the open grill. While everything's sizzling, you help yourself to salad bar and baked beans. And the price is right: $8.95 to $10.95 at dinner or lunch, plus a $4.75 lunch burger, a $6.25 dinner burger. There's a lively bar, a pleasant lanai to sit on, and a good, casual time to be had by all. Open daily from 11am to 10pm. Phone: 742-9122. AE, DC, MC, V.

Visiting Waimea Canyon is a Kauai must, and another Kauai must is stopping at the **Green Garden Restaurant** on Hwy. 50 in Hanapepe for a meal either before or after. Green Garden is a long-time *kamaaina* favorite (it has been run by three generations of the same family for some 40 years), and it manages to serve delicious food at moderate prices in a spirit of real island aloha. The place does look like a garden, full of plants and flowers, done in a bamboo-and-white motif. The menu is a combination of Asian and American dishes, with special kudos for the dinner selections from the kiawe-wood charbroiler, most from $6.75 to $14, a few going up to $23. These include pork chops brushed with butter or teriyaki sauce, "butterflied" rock lobster tail, sumiyaki (charbroiled beef kebab brushed with teriyaki), and steaks. They are served with fruit cup or homemade soup, tossed salad, and coffee or tea. Most complete dinners run $6 to $8, with such main-course choices as shrimp tempura, boneless teriyaki chicken, sweet-and-sour spare ribs, with all the extras. And you could also declare a special holiday and have a nine-course Asian dinner on about a half hour's notice! The Green Garden's homemade pies are a must: Even the strongest will falter at the sight of their coconut-cream or chocolate-cream or their famous macadamia-nut and lilikoi pies.

The Green Garden is open from 7am to 2pm and from 5 to 9pm, but closed Tuesday evenings. Phone: 335-5422.

If fresh fish and seafood are your passion, then, by all means, have dinner at **The House of Seafood** at Poipu Kai Resort, 1941 Poipu Rd., which has been featured in both *Bon Appétit* and *Gourmet* magazines for its outstanding presentations. The outside does look like a little house, front porch and all; the inside is pretty, with ceiling fans and many, many plants. Some 8 to 10 varieties of fresh fish from Hawaiian waters are offered every night, and each one is prepared differently, including one cooked and flambéed at your table. You could start your meal with the likes of oysters Rockefeller or sashimi, proceed to hearty New England clam chowder or a lighter seafood gazpacho (appetizers and soups range from $4.50 to $10). Fresh fish, the specialty of the house, varies according to the catch, and is market-priced. But you could also have a spicy cioppino or shrimp and pasta, bouillabaisse or paella; entrées are accompanied by soup or salad, two fresh vegetables, rice pilaf, and freshly baked rolls; they range in price from $17.50 to $35. *Keiki* menus are available, too. If you want to go all out with dessert, discuss the possibilities of crêpes Tiffany or chocolate soufflé or cherries jubilee when you phone to make your reservations: 742-6433.

House of Seafood serves dinner only, nightly from 5:30 to 9:30pm. AE, CB, DC, MC, V.

RESTAURANTS IN THE PRINCEVILLE-HANALEI AREA

Right in the little town of Hanalei itself, next to the Hanalei Trader shop, is a restaurant on the river called **Hanalei Dolphin**. Tiki poles mark the entrance, and inside, tapa-topped lacquered tables, glass-float lights, a redwood interior with dramatic inlaid windows set the scene for relaxed dining. The food here has always been good, and a local friend swears that the Dolphin's teriyaki ahi (listed on the menu as fresh fish) is the finest to be found in Kauai (she also recommends fish over the steak here). Other favorites, from $14 to

$22 and market price, include Alaskan king crab, haole chicken (boneless breaded breast with parmesan cheese, with a side of sweet-and-sour sauce), two kinds of shrimp (charbroiled or baked in a butter sauce and topped with sour cream), and an excellent New York–cut teriyaki steak. Light dinners, with choices of broccoli casserole, seafood chowder, or salad, are $6 and $9. All entrées are served with family-style salad, steak fries or rice, and hot homemade bread. Home-baked desserts are another plus for the Dolphin (they've got a whopping-good mud pie), as well as solid appetizers like ceviche and yummy stuffed mushrooms. Dinner only, 6 to 10pm, no smoking preferred. Phone: 826-6113. AE, MC, V.

All steak lovers in these parts are unanimous in singing the praises of the steaks at the **Beamreach Restaurant,** in the Pali Ke Kua complex at Princeville. Well, of course you could have some very good fish and seafood dishes here, but why bother, when you can savor the likes of an exceptional steak teriyaki (featured in *Bon Appétit* magazine), an equally tasty chicken teriyaki, a terrific ground sirloin, filet mignon, and more. Prices start at $10.95 for the ground sirloin and go up to about $20.95 for many dishes, to about $35 for lobster. You'll have more than enough to eat, since your entrée comes with a good salad bowl, homemade bread, and a choice of baked potato or rice, but you may want to start with the homemade liver pâté or sashimi among the appetizers to go along with your strawberry daiquiri, the house specialty. Beamreach has an open feeling with its beamed ceilings and attractive nautical decor. Dinner only, from 6pm. Reservations: 826-9131. AE, DC, MC, V.

RESTAURANTS IN THE COCONUT PLANTATION AREA

When a restaurant has been in business for over 20 years, and the crowds keep coming, you know it must be doing something right. So it is with the **Seashell Restaurant,** overlooking a bluff on Wailua Beach, and just across the road from Coco Palms Resort, of which it is a part. You can't miss this place, for its circular, seashell shape is easily seen from Highway 56. Views are glorious, as you are seated right over the beach. The seashell motif is repeated in the scalloped chairs, in the serving bowls of the salad bar, even in the pattern of the carpet. And, as you may have guessed, the specialty is seafood and fresh fish. Entrées, well priced from $14.95 for pasta and seafood up to $23.95 for a seafood platter, and market-priced for fresh fish, include a lusty cioppino (the Hawaiian version of the Italian seafood stew) tasty shrimp scampi, prawns and pasta, grilled breast of chicken Chardonnay, and New York steak. With them comes a generous salad bar or clam chowder, vegetable, sweet rolls, and butter. Potato skins and calamari rings make fun appetizers ($3.95 to $8.95), and there are nifty desserts like the amaretto cheesecake. Ask about special low-cholesterol and low-sodium preparations. *Keiki* menus run $4.95 to $5.95. The Seashell serves dinner by the sea nightly from 5:30 to 10pm, happy hour from 4 to 6pm. Reservations: phone 822-4921. AE, DC, CB, DISC, MC, V.

Across the road at Coco Palms, you could have dinner in the **Lagoon Dining Room.** Make your reservations before 7:30pm so you'll be seated in time for the impressive torchlighting ceremony, done with great authenticity and a true feeling of the olden days.

Pacific Rim Delights

Jean-Marie Josselin is one of the wunderkind chefs of the islands, one of the handful of talented young cooks who are putting Hawaii on the culinary maps of the world. Ever since the opening of his own restaurant, **A Pacific Café**, in Kauai Villae in Kapaa in mid-1990, locals and visitors alike have been gathering to sample his dazzling creations of Pacific Rim cuisine, a unique blend of the freshest locally grown ingredients with the culinary techniques of Europe and Asia. The decor of the restaurant is also a blend, with such Hawaiian native woods as sandalwood, mango, and koa, Hawaiian print cushions on the black lacquer chairs, and Asian art and decor, including an antique sushi bar. Josselin has designed the menus so that guests can create their own meals—perhaps choosing a variety of appetizers instead of a traditional three-course dinner. So, then, consider such "first tastes" as smoked chicken lumpia with a curried lime dip, or steamed Vietnamese spring rolls with a basil-peanut dip. Soup and salad choices might be grilled onaga salad with a tangerine vinaigrette, or Thai-style fish soup with lemon and basil. (Soups and appetizers run from $4.25 to $7.50.) Main courses from the wood-burning grill, rotisserie, and wok ($13.50 to $19.75) include such possibilities as deep-fried Chinese catfish stuffed with ginger, or grilled Australian lamb loin with a tamarind sauce. Desserts change every day; you can be sure they will be wonderful.

Before opening his own place, Jean-Marie Josselin had been executive chef at Coco Palms Resort. Among his many awards are the prestigious National Seafood Challenge and Hawaii Seafood Championship in 1989, as well as culinary recognition from the city of Paris and the Culinary Society of France. Undoubtedly, the list will continue to grow.

Dinner is served nightly except Tuesday from 5:30 to 9:30pm, Sunday brunch from 10:30am to 2pm. Reservations are a must: phone 822-0013.

Although you could order à la carte ($15.75 to $22 to market-price for fresh island fish and Pacific lobster tail), the best bet is to have the Royal Torchlighting Buffet, an elaborate spread with appetizers, salads, creative entrées, and fresh baked desserts. At 8:30, the Larry Rivera Show begins, offering an hour of exciting Hawaiian entertainment. Nominal cover charge; reservations recommended. And on Sundays, between 10am and 2pm, there's a spectacular brunch, with a lavish display of Continental and Polynesian cuisine. Price is around $19. Reservations: 822-4921. AE, CB, DC, DISC, MC, V.

Just north of Coconut Marketplace and its attractive fast-food stands are many restaurants in the little town of **Kapaa**, all catering to the large crowd of visitors and condo dwellers in this part of the island. There are two tried-and-true favorites here on Kuhio Hwy. **Kountry Kitchen** (tel. 822-3511) offers wonderful omelets for breakfast, burgers, sandwiches, reasonably priced entrées for lunch, and excellent dinners, which feature barbecued spareribs, sesame shrimp, fresh local fish, quiche, etc., at prices of about $7 to $14. **Ono-Family Restaurant** (tel. 822-1710) is also known for terrific breakfast omelets (all their jellies and syrups are made fresh daily), very good fish sandwiches and burgers (they serve buffalo burgers, low in cholesterol and fat), plus plate lunches at noontime, and such dinner specialties as fresh ahi buffalo steak; entrées run about $10 to $13. This is a warm, family-run operation, with many return guests each year.

3. After Dark in Kauai

Nightlife in Kauai is where you find it. There's nothing spectacular enough to warrant going from one side of the island to the other, but wherever you are, something will be going on — perhaps Hawaiian entertainment, rock music, or just soft sounds to sip your cocktails by. Most of the big hotels provide Hawaiian shows for their dinner guests. Hawaiian shows here are usually relaxed, informal affairs, much less pretentious than those in Waikiki. Besides, you'll probably recognize the faces of the entertainers: They may be the hotel clerks or busboys or cab drivers you met during the day! In the islands, everybody dances, everybody sings, and surprisingly well. Unless it's a dinner show, a drink or two gets you a ringside seat for the action; unless there is name entertainment, there's usually no cover or minimum charge.

LIHUE
A walk around the glamorous **Westin Kauai** resort will be entertainment in itself, but there's a bevy of nightspots to drop into. Start your evening with the free torchlighting ceremony at Kalapaki Beach, held every evening at dusk. If you're after high-energy disco, then **The Paddling Club,** open every night until the wee hours, is your place; if you want a romantic spot for hand-holding, try the elegant **Colonnade Bar,** perched above the waterfalls of the reflecting pool, where it's easy-listening and popular show tunes every night. If you dine at **Inn on the Cliffs,** you can also listen to jazz and dance to live music. . . . **Gilligan's** is a popular disco venue at the also lovely Kauai Hilton at Hanamaulu. . . . And down by the wharf at Nawiliwili Harbor, **Club Jetty** continues to be the local hangout, as it has been for years, alternating between live band and disco until the wee hours.

COCONUT PLANTATION—WAILUA—WAIPOULI
Lots of nighttime activity out in these parts. There's always entertainment at the **Sheraton Coconut Beach Hotel,** including dance music at Cook's Landing on Thursday, Friday, and Saturday, and a popular luau every night. Admission is $45 for adults, $27.25 for children, includes one-hour bar, buffet dinner, and show. . . . Local youngsters perform in Leilani's Polynesian Revue on Monday, Wednesday, and Friday nights at the **Aston Kauai Resort:** it's $16.50 for the show plus the prime-rib buffet, $10 for the show alone. . . . An exciting show called "The Golden People of Kauai"

provides the entertainment at the luau held at **Smith's Tropical Paradise** Monday through Friday nights at 6pm; price is about $45. . . . Larry Rivera's dinner show, one of the longest-running entertainments in Kauai, continues at the Lagoon Dining Room of the **Coco Palms Hotel,** every night at 8:30pm. Dinner is an $18.95 buffet or à la carte; nominal show charge.

POIPU BEACH

The opening of the Hyatt Regency Kauai has definitely enhanced the night scene in this part of the island. **Seaview Lounge** offers both indoor and outdoor dancing until 11pm nightly. Until 4am, there's high-energy entertainment and disco dancing in the art nouveau atmosphere of **Kuhio's** at the same resort. . . . The Sheraton Kauai is always a popular spot, with entertainment nightly at the **Drum Lounge** overlooking the ocean, and dancing to groups like the Top 40 Seattle Band. Wednesday is the night for the "Legends of Polynesia" show, with all the traditional luau entertainment, including an amazing fire dance. Cost for the dinner and show is $42 adults, $24 children. . . . There's always something going on at the **Poipu Beach Café** of the Poipu Beach Hotel, with dancing and entertainment—including reggae and rock—every night of the week, and a Sunday jam session from 5 to 10pm Sundays.

PRINCEVILLE AND HANALEI

The luaus at **Tahiti Nui** (tel. 826-6277) are so much fun that people call from the mainland to make reservations! They're held Monday, Wednesday, and Friday nights, and cost $35 for adults, $17.50 for children under 11. Tahiti Nui's Auntie Louise Marston and her friendly crew have been at this funky tropical café for over 20 years and know how to make sure everybody has a good time. Dinner—fresh South Pacific catch, stuffed calamari, chicken curry, smoked ribs and steak, from $11 to $17—is on every night. . . . The open air Happy Talk Lounge at the **Bali Hai Restaurant** (tel. 826-6522) has something going on just about every night of the week. On Tuesday, Thursday and Friday from 6 to 9pm it's contemporary Hawaiian music; on Wednesday, Friday, and Sunday from 5:30 to 9pm, jazz takes the spotlight. Sunday afternoon from 3 to 7pm, bring your own instruments for the liveliest jam session on Kauai! . . . Different artists perform every night, during dinner, at Princeville's smart **Lanai Restaurant** (tel. 826-6226). . . . **Hanalei Gourmet,** in the center of Hanalei Town, is a casual spot that attracts a lively crowd. There's usually entertainment Wednesday through Sunday featuring easy-listening and jazz fusion on Saturday, rock and roll on Friday.

---

4. The Sights & Sounds of Kauai

Since you cannot circle entirely around the island of Kauai and see it all in one day, you must plan on at least two full-day sightseeing excursions. The trip to **Waimea Canyon** (the southern and western route) is best made on a clear day; call the weather bureau before you go. If it's foggy, take the eastern and northern trip first.

Both trips are about 40 miles from Lihue each way, and since each offers a full share of gorgeous little beaches as well as awesome natural wonders, you should plan to leave early in the morning, pick up a box lunch in town for a picnic (or check the restaurant selections above), throw your bathing suits and suntan lotions into the backseat, and head off for an adventure.

WESTWARD TO THE CANYON

Get thee to **Lihue,** the center (for all practical purposes) of the island and the site of a delightful shopping complex in the center of town. Nearby, at 3016 Umi St., Suite 207, you will find the offices of the **Hawaii Visitors Bureau,** where you can pick up a variety of information.

Your next stop in Lihue should definitely be the **Kauai Museum,** a two-building complex at 4428 Rice St., housing a splendid collection of Hawaiiana (quilts, calabashes, furniture, artifacts, etc.) as well as the permanent exhibit, "The Story of Kauai," which includes a video showing the highlights of Kauai's scenery. Note the Museum Shop, with many fine Hawaiian and South Pacific items. Open Monday to Friday from 9:30am to 4:30pm. Admission is $3 for adults; children under 18 get in free with an adult.

Now cross Eiwa Street and walk to the site of the new **Civic Center,** whose daring architecture is strikingly modern in this setting. Back in your car now, follow Rice Street until you almost reach its junction with Hwy. 50. To your left is the quaint little **Haleko Drive** and four restored homes once belonging to sugar plantation workers, which now house several restaurants, including cozy little **The Eggbert's,** a favorite breakfast spot.

Now follow Hwy. 51 to **Nawiliwili** (the place where the willow trees grow), Kauai's largest harbor, where the cruise ships pull in. There are two big attractions here: lovely Kalapaki Beach, one of the best in Kauai, and the spectacular Westin Kauai at Kauai Lagoons, which fronts the beach. Since Kalapaki is the town beach, you're welcome to swim here, and swimming is wonderful. Then you may want to take a sightseeing tour—via horse-drawn carriage or water taxi—to see the splendid grounds of the Westin Kauai. Wildlife islands, Fashion Landing, and Artisan's Landing are all intriguing. Now you might want to head for some entertaining shopping at the huge **Kukui Grove Center,** about a mile from the airport on Rte. 50. Check out the wonderful collection of arts and crafts at **Stones Gallery** and perhaps sample some heavenly pastries and coffees at **Rainbow Coffees,** which sits right in the middle of the store. Popular restaurants include **Rosita's Mexican Restaurant** for good food and drinks and the **Kukui Nut Tree Inn** for pleasant and inexpensive family-type meals.

Practically across the road from Kukui Grove Center is **Kilohana Plantation,** a combination historical house–museum (it was the elegant plantation home of the Wilcox family in the 1930s) and shopping bazaar. Wander through charming boutiques and galleries, perhaps take a 20-minute horse-drawn carriage ride ($7) for a guided tour, or explore the extensive grounds with their manicured lawns and gardens. **Gaylord's,** a handsome courtyard restaurant, makes a good stop for lunch.

Poipu

About 14 miles out of Lihue you head into the tranquil **Koloa** region of Kauai, where a recent restoration has created **Old Koloa Town,** with some enjoyable restaurants (see "Dining in Kauai," above) and shops, and a historic site here and there like the old Koloa Hotel built in 1898 for traveling salesmen from Honolulu. After you've browsed a bit, maybe purchased some prints or posters by leading Hawaiian artists at Images International, or picked up some trinkets or treasures at Indo-Pacific Trading Post, and had some ice cream at Lappert's, get back into the car, swing off the main drag onto Hwy. 52, and follow the markers to Poipu Beach. At **Kiahuna Plantation** is a remarkable botanical garden whose Hawaiian name is Pa'u A Laka, the Skirt of Laka, goddess of the hula and sister of the volcano goddess, Pele. It is believed that this site was once the training grounds for her disciples. The place abounds in history as well as horticultural beauty (a cactus garden, an orchid garden, a plumeria plantation), and you are invited to walk through the gardens free; markers identify plants. The gardens are, alas, smaller than they once were, but still beautiful. (If you walk straight through the gardens, you emerge at the Sheraton Kauai Hotel.)

Now you continue on to the glorious **Poipu Beach** region. Although luxury hotels abound along this stretch of crystal and golden sand, the very best beach, the one to which even the hotels send their guests, is the Poipu public pavilion. It's the perfect place for a picnic and a swim.

Continue along the Poipu shore highway and you will come upon the monument, on the right side of the road, commemorating the birthplace of Prince Jonah Kuhio Kalanianaole, who represented Hawaii in the U.S. Congress from 1902 to 1922. Up the road, the **Kukuiulua Small Boat Harbor** is the best place to take in, in one swoop, the grandeur of the south shore of Kauai. Set your sights now for the **Spouting Horn** blowhole on your right, and then drive on down the highway to see it up close. A lava tube under the black rock funnels the force of the waves into a veritable geyser; the effect is spectacular. At Spouting Horn Park, vendors offer some of the best prices anywhere on island-style jewelry. You can probably do much of your gift-shopping here.

Back on Hwy. 50, you'll come to the HVB warrior pointing directly to the lush and lovely valley of **Hanapepe.** It's a fine miniature of some of the grander valleys you'll see on Kauai. If you're hungry, stop for lunch at the **Green Garden.** The **Salt Pond Pavilion** is a good spot for a picnic lunch and a swim; turn toward the ocean on Hwy. 543 outside Hanapepe. Down the other fork of the highway are located the ancient salt ponds where the *Hui Hana Paakai O Hanapepe* still practice the ancient art of salt-making. These drying beds are almost 200 years old.

On you go now, hurtling into the historic town of **Waimea,** where Captain Cook first landed in 1778, looked around him, and claimed the Sandwich Islands for England. You'll first pass a state marker indicating the site of a Russian fort where a member of the Alaska Fur Trading Company, hoping to capture the island for his czar, built—and watched crumble—the walls of his six-pointed fort. Parking facilities have already been built, but until the com-

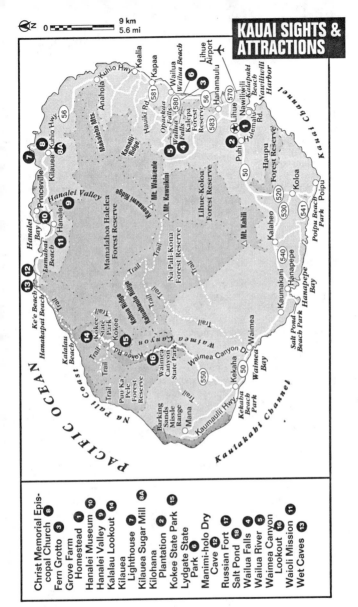

KAUAI SIGHTS & ATTRACTIONS

N 0 — 9 km
         5.6 mi

Lihue Airport

Kauai Channel

PACIFIC OCEAN

Kaulakahi Channel

than nice houses we've seen) run from $400 to $1,500 per night.
AE, CB, DC, ER, JCB, MC, V.

Whether or not you're staying at the Westin Kauai, you must
stop by to have a meal or a drink, stroll along the grounds, or take a
carriage ride or a boat taxi, and see the wonders that Christopher

highlands of the valley. All that remains is an expanse of cutstone bricks, two feet higher than the road and 200 feet long, inscribed with markings whose significance the archeologists can only guess.

To the Canyon

Just outside Waimea, take the Waimea Canyon Road on your right. Don't continue to Kekaha, since most of the beautiful beach here, the area's major charm, has been closed off. Winding and doubling back, the Waimea Canyon Road carries you higher and higher into the cool, crisp **Kokee** region, 3,600 feet above the green seas of Kauai. The scenery is spectacular: on one side stretch sloping mountainsides emptying into the ocean, and on the other drops the magnificent Waimea Valley. You can get different perspectives on the valley from numerous roadside clearings, but we suggest you wait until you reach the **Puu Ka Pele Lookout.** There, below you, is the Grand Canyon of the Pacific, a 10-mile-long, mile-wide gorge, the result of an ancient crust fault that split miles of solid stone into a maze of jagged ridges. A rainbow of colors dances along the peaks, spiraling and cascading down the mountain slopes.

Before you reap the full gift of the canyon at **Kalalau Lookout** farther up, relax for a few minutes at the **Kokee Museum,** right next to the **Kokee Lodge Restaurant.** Just after you pass this point, follow the signs to Kalalau Lookout. Driving the winding road for these last few miles, you will pass the Kokee tracking station, now world famous for its part in the success of the Apollo 11 mission to the moon. It was from this site that a laser beam was flashed to reflectors that Neil Armstrong had set up on the lunar surface.

At the end of the road is a sight that may make you forget the moon and stars and your own petty concerns as you stand at the edge of the world: Suddenly, 4,000 feet below you, past long-abandoned cliffs that once supported ancient villages, the turquoise ocean crashes noiselessly on far-away beaches. White birds glide to and fro on gentle breezes. It is rumored that a wise man once lived here in a cave by the sea; he never came back to civilization again. You may not want to, either; if you must, your drive from Kalalau Lookout to the highway will be about an hour's worth of concentrated driving.

Note: Some people like to drive directly to the canyon, arriving there in the morning, to avoid having one's view obstructed by clouds, which sometimes form in the afternoon. To do so, just run this trip backward, ending in Lihue.

THE NORTHERN AND EASTERN ROUTE

As you start out on your second exploratory tour of Kauai—this time along its eastern and northern shores—you might keep one thing in mind: If there is something spectacular to see, the Menehunes made it. And if they didn't, the gods did. In any case, you will find this end of the island steeped in a mythology that lends an aura of mystery to the breathtaking sights.

Again, plan on a full-day trip, and be sure to take along your bathing suits and perhaps a picnic lunch. Head out of Lihue and past the airport on H-56 until you go through the little village of **Kapaia** just a mile away. Heading down the road, you'll pass the Wailua Golf

Course on your right, just before the entrance to **Lydgate Park,** a beautiful beach area that is open to the public and snuggles right up to the grounds of the Kauai Resort Hotel. The beach is safe and great fun for children; rest rooms and showers are provided. Just up the road from this spot you approach the Wailua River. Turn left before you reach the bridge over the river and drive to the **Wailua Marina,** where you can hop a boat to the magnificent **Fern Grotto,** where ferns form a frame for a cave under a waterfall. A 1½-hour cruise is $10, half-price for children 4 to 12.

Just behind the marina (take the access road on the Lihue side of the bridge), you'll find **Smith's Tropical Paradise,** where you might stop to visit a 22½-acre botanical garden (admission $5 for adults, $2.50 for children). You can also see the gardens here if you come back for their highly praised luau and Polynesian show, about $45 (tel. 822-4654 for information), so for now, make your way back to H-56 and turn left just before the sign for the Coco Palms Hotel. Now you're on **Kuamoo Road,** formerly known as the King's Highway, upon which the corpulent *alii* of old Hawaii were borne by their servants (their feet were too holy to tread common ground). Just up the road is the **Holo-Holo-Ku Heiau,** where human sacrifices were offered up to the gods, and not too long ago. Up a skinny stairway on the right side of the *heiau,* you'll discover an old Japanese graveyard, bespeaking the settlement of Japanese that grew up in this area many years back. Continue on the road to its conclusion at the head of **Opaekaa Falls,** where white birds soar in silence above the steaming, rainbowed waterfalls. Shrimp used to gather at the foot of the falls to spawn, and the tumbling motion that the churning waves put them through suggested the name—Opaekaa, "rolling shrimp." At the top of the falls is **Kamokila Hawaiian Village,** where you can take an informative and entertaining guided tour ($5 adults, $1.50 children) through a tasteful restoration of an ancient settlement. Open Monday through Saturday, 9am to 4pm; tel. 822-1192.

Once you turn around and head back to H-56, you can take the one-way fork off Kuamoo Road that leads, as the signs indicate, to the **Bellstone,** just beyond the place where the king's home and temple were once located. One of the rocks here is supposed to respond with a clear, bell-like tone when you hit it with another rock. We've never figured out which one, but you're welcome to try your luck. The rock was once used to signal news of danger from the sea —possibly in the form of enemy canoes—or to ring out the news of a royal birth.

At the base of Kuamoo Road now, you'll be passing the beautiful grounds of the **Coco Palms Hotel.** If it's lunchtime, stop in for the lovely buffet. This has always been a very special area. Long before the days of tourists, Hawaiian royalty lived here, and the lagoon was a series of fishponds. The old days are recalled each night in torchlight ceremonies at 7:30pm.

You'll certainly want to make a stop at Coconut Marketplace, coming up now on the ocean side of the road, and the temptation will be to stay *too* long here; what with something like 70 shops, about a dozen restaurants or tempting ethnic snackbars, a twin movie theater, and even colored fountains and an irrigation system that the kids can have fun playing with, it may be hard to tear yourself away. You'll recognize a number of places from Honolulu, like **Liberty House, Andrade's,** and **Crazy Shirts.** But don't miss some local favorites like **Waves of One Sea** for international gift items, many from Indonesia, Bali, and the Far East; and **Kahn Gallery** for outstanding arts and crafts by island artists. If you can, come back to the Market Place on a Thursday, Friday, or Saturday around 4pm, when they present free Polynesian shows. Bring the cameras.

Back on the highway, you'll soon notice an HVB marker indicating the **Sleeping Giant** rock formation, and you can pull off to the side of the road to figure this one out. It's our favorite rock formation in the state, since, unlike the others, very little imagination is needed to see that it does indeed resemble a reclining Goliath. He was, in fact, the giant Puni, who befriended the Menehunes. Once, while he slept, enemy canoes threatened the shoreline, and the little men threw boulders onto his stomach to wake him up. He swallowed a few and died in his sleep, but a few stones ricocheted off his belly and destroyed the invaders' canoes.

As you drive through Kapaa, watch for the **Kauai Village Market,** where you might want to make a stop at the **Kauai Village Museum & Gift Shop,** a project of Aloha International dedicated to "Peace Through Aloha." The museum shows free videos, and the gift shop is a good source for books on Hawaiiana, Hawaiian music, and many arts and crafts made in the islands.

Past the little town of **Kealia** you go, and perhaps stop at **Anahola Beach Park** for a picnic. Beyond the beach turn-off point you can get a good view of lovely **Anahola Valley.**

A possible side trip is in Kilauea, to the **Kilauea Point National Wildlife Refuge.** The old Kilauea Lighthouse here is no longer operative, but the view from a high bluff overlooking the sea is spectacular, and it's a great spot for watching unique Pacific sea birds. The U.S. Fish and Wildlife Service is in charge and can provide helpful information at the visitor center and bookstore. Open daily except Saturday, from noon to 4pm.

Another stop in Kilauea might be to see the **Guava Kai Plantation,** where you can see the orchards, the processing plant, the gift shop, and restaurant, and get free samples of guava juice and fruit. Kilauea, by the way, is the "Undisputed Guava Capital of the World." Watch for the sign to the left on Hwy. 56; open daily, 9am to 5pm.

It seems hard to believe that **Kalihiwai Bay,** which you come upon next, was once the scene of savage tidal waves that twice, in 1946 and 1957, destroyed its little village. All is peaceful here now, and the road continues along, winding upward until it affords one of the most splendid views in the island of **Hanalei Valley.** Neatly terraced and squared off for irrigation purposes, with its rice paddies, taro patches, and the Hanalei River far below, it looks remarkably like a bit of the Far East.

Now you might want to take a few minutes out to visit **Princeville at Hanalei,** a luxurious resort complex described in the hotel section (above). Take a drive through the complex, stop in to see the stunning Princeville Hotel and soak up the views. **Chuck's Steak House** here is an old island favorite.

Now proceed to quaint Hanalei Valley itself, where the surfers hang out. You might want to have a look at the 1837 **Waioli Mission**

House, a small historical house–museum (excellent guided tours are offered on Tuesday, Thursday, and Saturday, from 9am to 3pm), perhaps check out the **Chin Young Village Shopping Center,** a rather sterile, if serviceable, replacement for the funky old general store that was here for eons. Next door to the Dolphin Restaurant is **Ola's,** where you can find lovely handcrafted items, plus tasteful toys, books, and clothing for children. The **Old Hanalei School** is an authentic restoration of a 1920s schoolhouse; it now houses some attractive gift shops and a restaurant.

Continuing on, you'll skirt a cliffside road that looks out over the much-photographed **Lumahai Beach.** It's one of the most beautiful in the islands, but just to look at. Rocks and currents make it unsafe for swimming, which may be the reason for its untouched appearance. Don't attempt to thread the path down the mountainside to the beach. There's great swimming coming up ahead.

Now your drive takes you through the enchantingly beautiful Haena region, over narrow one-lane bridges, into country that is truly unlike anything else in the islands. Soon, on the left side of the road, you'll see the **Manini-holo Dry Cave** and, a little bit past that, two wet caves, **Waikapale** and **Waikanaloa.** Both figure in the mythology of Kauai, and sometimes the islanders swim in them. But that's a bit dangerous and besides, you're practically at **Ke'e,** one of the most serene of island beaches. Park where the Na Pali trail begins (devoted hikers claim it is unforgettable). Here, under the towering Na Pali cliffs, once the scene of Hawaiian religious rituals, you can bask in the sun, swim in safe waters, and let the rest of the world go by and not miss it a bit.

Kauai has spectacular regions not accessible by car: You may want to consider hiking the Na Pali Coast, taking a boat expedition (**Na Pali Zodiac** runs some terrific ones; tel. 826-9371) or, best of all, a helicopter flight. For many, swooping down the walls of Waimea Canyon, flying into the mists of Mt. Waialeale, experiencing the wilderness areas and remote beaches of Kauai, constitute an extraordinary, almost mystical experience. All of the helicopter companies are good: Some well-recommended ones are **Menehune Helicopter** (tel. 245-7705), **Jack Harter** (tel. 245-3774), **Papillon Helicopters** (tel. 826-5691), and **Will Squyres Helicopters** (tel. 245-7541). A newer outfit, **Niihau Helicopters** (tel. 335-3500) is the only one with a license to fly over Niihau, "the forbidden island."

APPENDIX

A. THE AMERICAN SYSTEM OF MEASUREMENTS

LENGTH
    1 inch (in.) = 2.54cm
    1 foot (ft.) = 12 in. = 30.48 cm = .305m
    1 yard (yd.) = 3 ft. = .915 m
    1 mile   = 5,280 ft. = 1.609 km

To convert miles to kilometers, multiply the number of miles by 1.61. Also use to convert miles per hour (m.p.h.) to kilometers per hour (kmph).

To convert kilometers to miles, multiply the number of kilometers by .62. Also use to convert kmph to m.p.h.

CAPACITY
    1 fluid ounce (fl.oz.)= .03 liters
    1 pint   = 16 fl. oz. = .47 liters
    1 quart   = 2 pints = .94 liters
    1 gallon (gal.)   = 4 quarts = 3.79 liters =
                          .83 Imperial gal.

To convert U.S. gallons to liters, multiply the number of gallons by 3.79.

To convert liters to U.S. gallons, multiply the number of liters by .26.

To convert U.S. gallons to Imperial gallons, multiply the number of U.S. gallons by .83.

To convert Imperial gallons to U.S. gallons, multiply the number of Imperial gallons by 1.2.

WEIGHT
    1 ounce (oz.) = 28.35g
    1 pound (lb.) = 16 oz. = 453.6 g = .45kg
    1 ton   = 2,000 lb. = 907kg = .91 metric tons

To convert pounds to kilograms, multiply the number of pounds by .45.

To convert kilograms to pounds, multiply the number of kilograms by 2.2.

TEMPERATURE

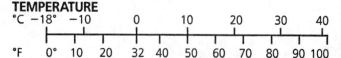

°C −18° −10   0   10   20   30   40

°F   0° 10 20   32 40 50 60 70 80 90 100

To convert degrees Fahrenheit to degrees Celsius, subtract 32 from °F, multiply by 5, then divide by 9 (example: $85°F - 32 × 5/9 = 29.4°C$).

To convert degrees Celsius to degrees Fahrenheit, multiply °C by 9, divide by 5, and add 32 (example: $20°C × 9/5 + 32 = 68°F$).

B. CLOTHING SIZE CONVERSION

The following charts should help foreign visitors choose the correct clothing sizes in the U.S. However, sizes can vary, so the best guide is simply to try things on.

WOMEN'S DRESSES, COATS, AND SKIRTS

American	3	5	7	9	11	12	13	14	15	16	18
Continental	36	38	38	40	40	42	42	44	44	46	48
British	8	10	11	12	13	14	15	16	17	18	20

WOMEN'S BLOUSES AND SWEATERS

American	10	12	14	16	18	20
Continental	38	40	42	44	46	48
British	32	34	36	38	40	42

WOMEN'S STOCKINGS

American	8	8½	9	9½	10	10½
Continental	1	2	3	4	5	6
American	8	8½	9	9½	10	10½

WOMEN'S SHOES

American	5	6	7	8	9	10
Continental	36	37	38	39	40	41
British	3½	4½	5½	6½	7½	8½

MEN'S SUITS

American	34	36	38	40	42	44	46	48
Continental	44	46	48	50	52	54	56	58
British	34	36	38	40	42	44	46	48

MEN'S SHIRTS

American	14½	15	15½	16	16½	17	17½	18
Continental	37	38	39	41	42	43	44	45
British	14½	15	15½	16	16½	17	17½	18

MEN'S SHOES

American	7	8	9	10	11	12	13
Continental	39½	41	42	43	44½	46	47
British	6	7	8	9	10	11	12

MEN'S HATS

American	6⅞	7⅛	7¼	7⅜	7½	7⅝
Continental	55	56	58	59	60	61
British	6¼	6⅞	7⅛	7¼	7⅜	7½

CHILDREN'S CLOTHING

American	3	4	5	6	6X
Continental	98	104	110	116	122
British	18	20	22	24	26

CHILDREN'S SHOES

American	8	9	10	11	12	13	1	2	3
Continental	24	25	27	28	29	30	32	33	34
British	7	8	9	10	11	12	13	1	2

INDEX

GENERAL INFORMATION

SIGHTS & ATTRACTIONS

HAWAII (BIG ISLAND)

HONOLULU

KAUAI

M A U I

M O L O K A I

O A H U

ACCOMMODATIONS

H A W A I I (B I G I S L A N D)

KEY TO ABBREVIATIONS: *B* = Budget; *Co* = Condominiums; *E* = Expensive; *M* = Moderately priced; *VE* = Very Expensive

HONOLULU

KAUAI

FROMMER'S CITY GUIDES

(Pocket-size guides to sightseeing and tourist accommodations and facilities in all price ranges.)

☐ Amsterdam/Holland. $8.95		☐ Minneapolis/St. Paul. $8.95
☐ Athens $8.95		☐ Montréal/Québec City $8.95
☐ Atlanta $8.95		☐ New Orleans $8.95
☐ Atlantic City/Cape May $8.95		☐ New York. $8.95
☐ Barcelona $7.95		☐ Orlando. $8.95
☐ Belgium $7.95		☐ Paris $8.95
☐ Berlin $8.95		☐ Philadelphia. $8.95
☐ Boston $8.95		☐ Rio $8.95
☐ Cancún/Cozumel/Yucatán . . . $8.95		☐ Rome $8.95
☐ Chicago $9.95		☐ Salt Lake City $8.95
☐ Denver/Boulder/Colorado		☐ San Diego $8.95
Springs. $7.95		☐ San Francisco $8.95
☐ Dublin/Ireland $8.95		☐ Santa Fe/Taos/Albuquerque $10.95
☐ Hawaii $8.95		☐ Seattle/Portland. $7.95
☐ Hong Kong $7.95		☐ St. Louis/Kansas City $9.95
☐ Las Vegas $8.95		☐ Sydney $8.95
☐ Lisbon/Madrid/Costa del Sol. . $8.95		☐ Tampa/St. Petersburg $8.95
☐ London. $8.95		☐ Tokyo $8.95
☐ Los Angeles. $8.95		☐ Toronto. $8.95
☐ Mexico City/Acapulco $8.95		☐ Vancouver/Victoria. $7.95
☐ Miami. $8.95		☐ Washington, D.C. $8.95

SPECIAL EDITIONS

☐ Beat the High Cost of Travel . . $6.95		☐ Motorist's Phrase Book (Fr/Ger/Sp). . . . $4.95
☐ Bed & Breakfast—N. America $14.95		☐ Paris Rendez-Vous $10.95
☐ California with Kids $16.95		☐ Swap and Go (Home Exchanging) $10.95
☐ Caribbean Hideaways $14.95		☐ The Candy Apple (NY with Kids) $12.95
☐ Manhattan's Outdoor		☐ Travel Diary and Record Book $5.95
Sculpture. $15.95		

☐ Honeymoon Destinations (US, Mex & Carib) $14.95

☐ Where to Stay USA (From $3 to $30 a night) $13.95

☐ Marilyn Wood's Wonderful Weekends (CT, DE, MA, NH, NJ, NY, PA, RI, VT) $11.95

☐ The New World of Travel (Annual sourcebook by Arthur Frommer for savvy travelers) . . $16.95

GAULT MILLAU

(The only guides that distinguish the truly superlative from the merely overrated.)

☐ The Best of Chicago $15.95		☐ The Best of Los Angeles. $16.95
☐ The Best of France. $16.95		☐ The Best of New England $15.95
☐ The Best of Hawaii $16.95		☐ The Best of New Orleans $16.95
☐ The Best of Hong Kong $16.95		☐ The Best of New York. $16.95
☐ The Best of Italy $16.95		☐ The Best of Paris $16.95
☐ The Best of London. $16.95		☐ The Best of San Francisco $16.95

☐ The Best of Washington, D.C.. . . . . $16.95

ORDER NOW!

In U.S. include $2 shipping UPS for 1st book; $1 ea. add'l book. Outside U.S. $3 and $1, respectively.
Allow four to six weeks for delivery in U.S., longer outside U.S.
Enclosed is my check or money order for $_____

NAME_____

ADDRESS_____

CITY_____ STATE_____ ZIP____

0391